A&S

G. V. Stauf

After Seven Years

Photo by Brown Brothers

RAYMOND MOLEY

Raymond Moley

AFTER SEVEN YEARS

Harper & Brothers Publishers

NEW YORK *and* LONDON

1939

AFTER SEVEN YEARS

Printed in the United States of America

For information address
Harper & Brothers

9-9

FIRST EDITION

H-O

"*If you flatter him, you betray him; if you conceal the truth of those things from him which concern his justice or his honour . . . you are as dangerous a traitor to his state, as he that riseth in arms against him.*"

FRANCIS BACON TO GEORGE VILLIERS

CONTENTS

☆

ILLUSTRATIONS

FOREWORD

The chief value of a foreword is the opportunity it offers for disclaimers. Hence I wish to make clear what this book is not. It does not claim to be a history of the past seven crucial years. It is not a treatise on economics, politics or political philosophy. It is not the biography of any public figure. It is the account of political events as I saw them, of what those events signified as I understood them, and of my opinions of them as I was able to form and express opinions. It is based upon my notes, memoranda, documents, my daily journal and other first-hand material. If, in the broad history of these times, it serves as a footnote, I am content.

This book was not hastily written, nor was its publication decided upon without a full consideration of all the factors involved. It could not have been written and published sooner because, in many cases, judgments had to wait upon the unfolding of time and circumstance. To publish it at some later date would, it seemed to me, lessen its modest value as a commentary upon contemporary problems and decisions. An obligation to give to the public that which belongs to the public rests upon anyone who is privileged to participate in public affairs. This obligation to that inexorable master, the public interest, I have tried to pay with all the candor, fairness, sincerity and authenticity I could summon to my assistance. I do not apologize for frankness. I should feel like apologizing for anything short of it.

With no idea of divesting myself of responsibility for the facts and opinions in this book, I should like to note my indebtedness to a number of friends who have generously given advice and help. Pages and sections telling of events of which they had first-hand knowledge were looked over by Arthur Ballantine, Elliott Thurston, Rex Tugwell, Herbert Bayard Swope, Arthur Dean, Averell Harriman and Vincent Astor. There were many others who must be nameless here who gave assistance unselfishly to the end that the record might be as accurate as possible. To Ernest Lindley and to Ralph Robey I am indebted for a careful reading and intelligent criticism of the entire manuscript. Dorothy Woolf, of the staff of *Newsweek*, assisted in the checking of many facts. Carol Hill, Martin Sommers and Frank Prince made exceedingly helpful suggestions.

Foremost among those to whom I am indebted in the preparation of this book are my two assistants, who have been associated with my work for nine years. Annette Pomeranz Gettinger has given the invaluable contribution of care, accuracy and skill not only in putting together the manuscript, but in her knowledge of the materials essential to it. Celeste Jedel assisted me in maintaining and preserving the records upon which this account rests, and collaborated in the arrangement of material, in the countless decisions of relevance and accuracy and, much more important, in the actual composition of the text. It is the simple truth that the book could not have been written except for her industry, discernment and keen understanding of public problems.

For the faults in this narrative, which are doubtless many, I cheerfully assume the blame.

R. M.

New York
August, 1939.

After Seven Years

CHAPTER I

THE BIRTH OF THE NEW DEAL

THIS is a story that began, in so far as it can be said to have an exact beginning, on a dim January day in 1932. Guernsey Cross, the secretary of the Governor, had darted in and out of the cluttered executive office for perhaps the dozenth time in a half hour. The Governor gave an empty dish on his desk a restless push, looked at me earnestly, and said, "Make no mistake about it. I don't know why anyone would *want* to be President, with things in the shape they are now."

I had provoked that remark by reference to the Governor's presidential candidacy. Familiarity with the curious reticences and evasions of politicians should have prepared me for the answer. But, even so, I could hardly resist a smile. Whatever Roosevelt thought or said, fate, fortune, and the travels of Jim Farley were working in a not very inscrutable way to make him the leading candidate for the Democratic nomination.

Prudence dictated my reply. It may seem a *non sequitur* in type, but it was the retort courteous in the language of politics. I said that I should be delighted to help in any way I could.

Governor Roosevelt nodded approvingly. He would be glad to call on me, he answered.

And so our luncheon talk resolved itself—momentously for me.

It had been a curious conversation that wandered, with apparent casualness, from the immediate occasion for my visit, the work of the Commission on the Administration of Justice, of which I was the Governor's ranking member, to the Seabury investigation, to the case of Sheriff Thomas M. ("wonderful tin box") Farley of Tammany Hall, and on to national politics. Roosevelt had been guarded, indefinite, reserved. It would, of course, have been the grossest impropriety for him to discuss the political implications of the Sheriff Farley case, since he was going to act in a quasi-judicial capacity on the issue of Farley's removal. But Roosevelt did say, ruminatively, that Sheriff Farley was an idol to his people, and he was obviously pleased with my quiet offer of service.

Nothing more had to be said. Both of us realized what a spot the inexorable Seabury had selected for Roosevelt and what might come later should Seabury carry his investigation to a point where the issue of Mayor James J. Walker's removal was put to Roosevelt. On the one side was an angry and already outraged political machine which would control most of New York's ninety-four votes in the national convention. On the other side was the reformer Seabury, most of the New York press, and "good" citizens, an army of them throughout the nation, whose support a presidential candidate would most assuredly need. All this had been understood.

I couldn't help but be pleased with the way things had gone as I rode back to New York on the train that afternoon. Looking out at the river and the hills that were to become so familiar in the months ahead, I could permit myself a bit of speculation on what might come of that visit to Albany. It seemed to me that Roosevelt had intimated, in a way peculiarly his own, that he might let me move in from the outer reaches of his circle pretty close to center. At any rate, I'd probably be called in on the Farley case. There'd been no express commitment, naturally. But then, my earliest associations with Roosevelt had led me not to expect that.

I had first met him on an autumn day in 1928 when Louis Howe, with elaborate offhandedness, took me into Democratic headquarters "just to have you meet 'The Boss.' " Roosevelt, a big, handsome man with the shoulders of a wrestler, was sitting at his desk sorting out letters. He looked up, smiled, and then explained, to my surprise and to Louis' dismay, that my visit wasn't at all unexpected. He wanted to simplify the administration of justice in the state. He wanted to say something about it in his campaign. Louis had suggested that I might "shape out" some ideas he could use—perhaps dig up some vivid examples of cases that had dragged on in the courts.

I was pleased. A memorandum from me was transformed into a speech made in the Bronx a few days later. Apparently Mr. Roosevelt was pleased too.

Ensued, in the next three years, a number of similar assignments and two bigger ones: first, membership on a committee that drafted a plan for a model state parole system and, following that, appointment to a commission to improve the administration of justice in the state.

This last, coming in the summer of 1931, was important. The subject was so close to the Governor's heart that he had fought for over two years to get the state legislature to authorize the commission. My appointment made me his chief adviser in that field.

But it did something more than that. It provided the opening for a demonstration that I could be trusted to handle awkward political situations with a reasonable amount of sense. There was, for instance, an embarrassing misunderstanding between the Governor and the Republican leader of the Senate concerning the organization of the commission. I was told that the Governor was delighted with the maneuverings which dissipated the issue so that he didn't have to meet it head on.

In any case, by the time he'd asked me to visit with him, in January, 1932, he seemed to feel that I could be useful.

It would be idle to pretend that I wasn't excited that afternoon, as the train rattled on toward New York in the gathering darkness. Since October, 1928, I'd believed Roosevelt would be elected President in 1932. I had no political ambitions. But I did want to see and know intimately what went on at the heart of politics, for politics had been the absorbing interest of my life. It had dictated my choice of courses in the small college from which I graduated. The next year, 1907, it led me through a successful campaign for village clerk in my Ohio town—three years, incidentally, before a young New Yorker named Roosevelt was elected state senator and four years before, down the river a bit, another young man named Farley was elected town clerk. It moved me to the inevitable study of law, under difficulties, at night in Cleveland; to the decision to study and teach politics, after a two years' siege of T.B. in New Mexico and Colorado had summarily blasted my law studies; to a brief return to local politics as mayor of an Ohio town when I was able to come back East; to graduate study in politics at Columbia; to a teaching job on the Mark Hanna foundation in Western Reserve University; to the directorship of Americanization activities under Governor Cox during the war; to four years as director of a research foundation in Cleveland; to a return to New York and Columbia—there to build up a department of government in Barnard College (the happiest job I've ever had); to ten years of intensive professional investigation of the seamy sides of criminal-law administration in Ohio, Missouri, Illinois, Virginia, Pennsylvania, California, and New York; to the writing of three books and many articles on the relationship of politics and criminal justice, the preparation of which carried me to twenty states and to Canada; and, finally, to a year with Judge Seabury and his investigations.

I had long since made perhaps the most important decision of my life up to 1932, when, during the war years, I'd declined a place on the slate of the Democratic organization for the legislature of Ohio. That was the decision to retain, in my practice of politics, the status of a private citizen.

In all these diversified years I'd been no professional reformer. I felt deeply that such a role, like that of the professional officeholder, operates as a subtle intellectual opiate on anyone who wants to understand what politics is about. We needed the professional reformer, just as David Harum's dog needed fleas. But I had a horror of the humorlessness, the intentness, and the intolerance of most reformers. Besides, it had seemed to me reform needn't come through reformers alone. It could be organically associated with the normal process of politics. Government failed vastly more often through ignorance than through sin.

The older I'd grown the more I'd come to believe that effective political change was achieved by mutual understanding and consent, not by denunciation and recrimination from without. At ten I was stirred by Bryan—romantically, emotionally. I wept when he was defeated in 1896. But the solid reforms of the practical Tom Johnson during his nine years as mayor of Cleveland suggested the vanity of tears. Johnson's technique was educational. His cosmos wasn't a befuddled miracle play where good men fought with bad. He believed that people, enlightened, would save themselves. I knew him only as a public figure. But he gave my interest in politics point and direction. It was from him and from his brilliant protégé, Newton Baker, under whom I sat briefly as a law student in Cleveland, that I learned something of the evolutionary improvement of political and economic life.

As the thoughtlessness and aimlessness of the 'twenties became more and more apparent, I'd grown convinced that someone must be found who could do on a national scale what Tom Johnson had done in Cleveland. There was no Tom Johnson. But out of the field, by January, 1932, it seemed to me that the buoyant, likable man in Albany was the only hope.

I was, at my age, no longer a creature of impulse. But, as I saw it, in the hours after my first vague approach to an intimate talk with Roosevelt, an opportunity was about to offer itself—an opportunity to satisfy my desire for a wider experience in politics and, at the same time, to help, in a small way, in the realization of old and time-tested concepts of political evolution.

I was on the eve of a great adventure, if I had the wit to go through with it. I could look forward with security to a lifetime of being called in by governors, mayors, special investigators, and citizens' committees to study the local administration of justice. Or I could throw everything I had into the pursuit of my interest in the wider field of politics. And I wanted passionately to do the second.

The account of the opportunity that opened up that January day—and of the education that came of it—is the substance of this story.

2

The thing happened very quickly. In mid-February, 1932, I was helping to draft the definition of policy on the basis of which Tom Farley was removed. In early March I spent some time in Albany working on a speech on judicial reform which the Governor delivered at the New York City Bar Association on the twelfth. By the first week in April I was at work in Albany assisting with the document which came to be known as the "Forgotten Man" speech, and the first meetings of what later was called the "brains trust" had already taken place.

Observe these dates. In early March my sphere of activity still seemed to be limited to questions of law administration. By early April I had entered the promised land of national politics.

How did it happen?

The popular story has it that one night in March Samuel I. Rosenman, Counsel to the Governor, was chatting with the Governor after dinner and took the opportunity to suggest the need for advisers competent to prepare a national program for him. Rosenman is supposed to have argued that "the usual programmers of presidential candidates—business fat cats and political bosses—had been discredited by the Hoover debacle." He's said to have climaxed his remarks with the question, "Why don't you try the universities for a change?" And on the basis of one of Roosevelt's "smiling assents, which may mean anything or nothing," Rosenman is supposed to have invited me in to organize the group that became the "brains trust."[1]

I do not doubt the fact that some such conversation as this may have taken place, although it seems very queer indeed that a man who had been closely associated with Roosevelt for two years should say "Why

[1] See, for example, *Men around the President,* by Joseph Alsop and Robert Kintner. Doubleday, Doran & Company, Inc.; New York, 1939; pp. 19-20.

don't you try the universities for a change?" to a Governor who had habitually consulted with Professors Robert Murray Haig, James Bonbright, Frank A. Pearson, William I. Myers, former Professor Milo R. Maltbie, and, I may add, with me, in constructing his state policies. But I do question the implication that such a conversation was anything more than an incident in a development wholly unrelated to Sam Rosenman's planning or imagination. Sometimes the lady who smacks the champagne bottle against the ship's prow has the illusion that she is causing the ship to slide down the ways.

The process was smooth, unspasmodic, almost inevitable.

First, March was a dreadful month for the Governor. Before leaving Albany the state legislature had dumped on his desk literally scores of bills that had to be studied and analyzed before he could decide whether to sign or veto them. It took hour after hour, day after day, to handle these. At the same time Roosevelt was obliged to direct what had now become an intensive drive for delegates to the national convention. As though this were not enough, he was attempting not only to anticipate the plays of Seabury, who was creating new embarrassments, but to keep an eye on Al Smith, who was fighting him tooth and nail. Finally, he was desperately trying—and failing—to make time to prepare some speeches he was scheduled to deliver in April—speeches critical to his nomination. No one knew better than he that he needed all the help he could get. He spoke of that to me early in March when we were at work on the Bar Association speech, and took occasion to add that, while Sam Rosenman had been of the greatest assistance to him in state business, he did not, in fact, know very much about national affairs.

Second, Rosenman was thoroughly aware of his own limitations and aware of the Governor's awareness of them.

Third, my performance was evidently satisfactory. The Sheriff Farley removal order had lent itself to favorable quotation throughout the country. The speech on judicial reform, delivered before a sophisticated audience of lawyers, had been exceedingly well received. But more than that, I think, the work on those two jobs illustrated a technique no one else then around Roosevelt possessed. It seemed to help crystallize his own ideas and inclinations, reflect them accurately, extend them where necessary, and present them congruously—in brief, to relieve him of a good deal of personal drudgery. As April drew on, and with it the moment for preparing and projecting a national program, what more natural than that he should employ it again? I moved into a vacuum in his scheme of things.

Finally, I was able to achieve almost the impossible—the maintenance of friendly relations with both Louis Howe and Sam Rosenman—and the rivalry of these two men was the single factor that might have disrupted the logical course of events.[2] If either had suspected that I was more than politely friendly with the other, if either had been given the slightest reason to resent any association of mine with Roosevelt at that crucial time, he would not have hesitated for a moment to block me off completely. It was lamentable but true that anyone, regardless of the contribution that he might have been able to make to Franklin Roosevelt, would have found the going hard unless he had appeased both these men.

I had already learned the melancholy fact that such antagonism is likely to imperil the best interests of a common cause, and I was destined to expose myself to some of the bitter corollaries of that fact in the months to come. But at the moment, in March, I was taking no chances.

Louis was then in New York City, working at Roosevelt headquarters on Madison Avenue. The Governor, who was deeply devoted to Louis, was characteristically careless about keeping in touch with Louis as often as Louis' insatiable interest, curiosity, and affection would have dictated. This wizened, gnarled little Nibelung had watched his Siegfried grow to hero's size and now he lived in an agony of apprehension that "someone" (obviously meaning Rosenman) would smash all his well-laid plans. Louis was constantly torn between the *idées fixes* that his preconvention work in New York was indispensable and that, in his absence from Albany, "someone" would "give Franklin bad advice or let his impulses run away with him."

I had a room across the street from Louis', in the offices of the Commission on the Administration of Justice, and I went to see him frequently during February and March, as indeed I had been doing for years. I kept him informed of the developments that were taking place in my relations with Roosevelt—of the trips to Albany, the telephone calls, the correspondence—and I continued to do so thereafter. In some

[2] It seemed that Howe was forever trying to humiliate Rosenman. I remember well Rosenman's blazing fury when, during the campaign, Howe attempted to assign him to a routine job at headquarters which Sam considered menial. Rosenman never overlooked an opportunity to warn me against Howe: again and again he used a phrase of Basil O'Connor's—"Louis'll 'give you the foot' if you don't watch out."

way this seemed to assuage Louis' fears, and it became clear from his conversation that he firmly believed that he had "planted" me in Albany to see that "someone" made no mistakes and to sound the sirens so that he could hurl himself into the breach if anything threatened his "Franklin's" availability. I confess that I did nothing to dislodge this unlovely idea from Louis' head. It comforted him. It minimized his potential opposition to the adoption of the kind of program I hoped to see Roosevelt champion. And it stamped his visa on my passport for the time being, at any rate.

The appeasement of Rosenman was more easily achieved.

Sam had come up from the hurly-burly of New York City's district politics. Sam had been well educated and, by dint of hard work before, during, and after his service in the state legislature, had acquired an admirably detailed knowledge of state business. He was essentially an "inside" worker. Often brusque and tactless, this capable, conscientious man could obviously never look forward to the kind of political career Al Smith or Bob Wagner had shaped out of the same beginnings as his, and he had shrewdly cut his ambition to fit his cloth. Sam's one desire was to be appointed to New York's Supreme Court before Roosevelt left the Governorship.

The fact that he was able to serve Roosevelt as well as he did during the pulling and hauling of Seabury and Tammany, though he knew his ambition could not be realized without the tacit assent of the Tammany leaders, was a tribute to his own devotion to Roosevelt. But Louis was merciless in holding him responsible for the worst blunder made in that process—the Governor's truculent reply to the charges filed against Mayor Walker by Rabbi Stephen Wise and the Reverend John Haynes Holmes.

Sam's very weaknesses smoothed the way. As early as February he had asked me to write to the Governor urging his appointment to a vacancy on the Supreme Court. This friendly gesture I was able to make with a good conscience, for I was certain he would become the fine judge he has since proved to be. Moreover, as I have suggested, the Governor's awareness of his need for assistance on national affairs was evident by early March, and Sam was not the man to stand in the way of the inevitable. Sam also loved Columbia University in a boyish and rather touching way, and the fact that I taught there was a point in my favor.

Finally, when Sam announced one mid-March evening, with the air of one who makes a tremendous discovery, that Roosevelt needed expert, professional advice on national issues and that we ought to get some people together to assist him, he made it easy for me to encourage the notion that he was the originator of this happy idea. To have said that it had occupied my thoughts every waking hour since Roosevelt's pre-Bar-Association-speech remarks to me would have been unkind and stupid.

And so Sam, too, was won—convinced, with the passing of time, that he had plucked me from academic obscurity, washed me, pitted me, and dished me up on a silver platter to the Governor.

The rest followed naturally.

Sam, Basil ("Doc") O'Connor, Roosevelt's law partner, and I made a list of possible topics upon which Roosevelt's campaign might touch. As we jotted them down, I suggested the names of individuals who had expert knowledge about each.

Thus was the "brains trust" born, thus my personal Jordan crossed.

3

All this seems unadulteratedly cold-blooded. It wasn't, actually. Whatever the keenness of my desire to see what went on backstage, I was no tinpot Bacon—cunning, dispassionate, intellectual. If, say, I had been presented with the same opportunity to take part in the Hoover campaign, I could not have availed myself of it. Doubtless this was a great weakness—a weakness that would have made me an abominable lawyer—but I was constitutionally incapable of espousing any cause in which I did not believe. Worse than that, my beliefs, decisions, judgments were not arrived at by an orderly process of thought. They rose up, willy-nilly, out of a sea of feelings, senses, "hunches," to confront, grapple with, and finally take possession of me.

I liked Franklin Roosevelt for the same elemental reasons that millions of other people were soon to like him—for his vibrant aliveness, his warmth, his sympathy, his activism. I had faith in him. The rest did not precede, it followed those bare facts.

Now people who used only their heads could and did tell me that I was utterly mistaken. People who were merely "intellectual" were almost unanimous on the subject of Roosevelt's inadequacy in the spring of 1932: he was a "weakling," they said, an "opportunist," "an amiable gentleman who wants to be President." I must have written a dozen argumentative letters in March and April to nervous friends who ventured the opinion that "This shilly-shallying with Tammany doesn't promise well," or "Your candidate seems to be just any politician on the make," or (from a newspaper editor in a Midwestern city) "Waddya mean—'progressive'? The guy just doesn't seem to have any stuff." Yet it wasn't a question that you could settle with words. It was, in essence, a matter of belief, of faith.

The fullest and far-and-away the frankest description of my feelings about Roosevelt in those days is contained in a letter to my sister, replying to one from her about Roosevelt's ten-minute speech on the Lucky Strike hour, the "Forgotten Man" speech. I think it warrants inclusion here, rough and incomplete though it is, because it is a record of what I felt at the time rather than an attempt to recapture those first sensations. It is dated Tuesday, April 12, 1932, and reads:

> Dear Nell—
>
> Thanks for writing me about the Gov.'s speech last wk. Your reaction is important in getting an idea of how it struck the country—especially since the speech got so much hell from the conservative papers—Republican and Democratic. The Governor is quite indifferent to these attacks—in fact, rather likes them because they show that he is being taken seriously—and he realizes that the alienation of some standpatters is necessary if the campaign is to seem to the rank and file . . . something other than the usual campaign futilitarianism.
>
> You ask what he is like and that isn't easy to answer because I haven't had the chance to confirm a lot of fleeting impressions. One thing is sure—that the idea people get from his charming manner—that he is soft or flabby in disposition and character—is far from true. When he wants something a lot he can be formidable—when crossed he is hard, stubborn, resourceful, relentless. I used to think on the basis of casual observation that his amiability was "lord-of-the-manor"—"good-to-the-peasants"—stuff. It isn't that at all. He seems quite naturally warm and friendly—less because he genuinely likes many of the people to whom he is pleasant (although he does like a lot of people of all sorts and varieties) than because he just enjoys the pleasant and engaging role, as a charming woman does. And being a born politician he measures such qualities in himself by the effect they produce on others. He is wholly conscious of his ability to send callers away happy and glowing and in agreement with him and his ideas. And he particularly enjoys sending people away who have completely forgotten (under his spell) the thing they came to say or ask. On the whole, his cordiality and his interest in people is, to all appearances, unfeigned.
>
> The stories about his illness and its effect upon him are the bunk. Nobody in public life since T. R. has been so robust, so buoyantly and blatantly healthy as this fellow. He is full of animal spirits and keeps himself and the people around him in a rare good humor with a lot of horseplay that reminds me of the old

days in Olmsted Falls. Remember John Bonsey and Scowley Folk and the resin strings and the cabbages we threw at doors? Well, a good many cabbages will be thrown by this man at many respectable doors—not because he feels it is an act of justice but because it is so much fun. He likes to do it on a parlor scale; broad, never really witty (you couldn't call it witty) and seldom even funny, but bold and cheerful and exuberant. Sam Rosenman is "Sammy the Rose" and Morgenthau, Jr. "Henry the Morgue." There is teasing and loud laughing at teatime, which is a rite he follows but which is quite strange to my Ohio sensibility.

The man's energy and vitality are astonishing. I've been amazed with his interest in things. It skips and bounces through seemingly intricate subjects and maybe it is my academic training that makes me feel that no one could possibly learn much in such a hit or miss fashion. I don't find that he has read much about economic subjects. What he gets is from talking to people and when he stores away the net of conversation he never knows what part of what he has kept is what he said himself or what his visitor said. There is a lot of autointoxication of the intelligence that we shall have to watch. But he gets a lot from talking with people who come in. A typical approach to a big problem is "so and so was telling me yesterday." Another is "now *we* found in dealing with the *state* so-and-so that we had to deal with such-and-such."

This quality seems to give Tugwell some worries because he wants people to show familiarity with pretty elementary ideas. But I believe that his [Roosevelt's] complete freedom from dogmatism is a virtue at this stage of the game. He will stick to ideas after he has expressed them, I believe and hope. Heaven knows Hoover is full of information and dogmas but he has been imprisoned by his knowledge and God save us from four more years of that! If we can't get a President with a fluid mind we shall have some bad times ahead.

The frightening aspect of his methods is F. D. R.'s great receptivity. So far as I know he makes no effort to check up on anything that I or anyone else has told him. I wonder what would happen if we should selfishly try to put things over on him. He would find out—but it would be too late. This means a hell of a responsibility on me.

As I look back at what I have scribbled here I see I haven't conveyed any sense of his gallantry, his political sophistication, his lack of the offensive traits of men who have a bloated sense of personal destiny. But then I know you get that from the speech. When I was working on it with him I was trying to suggest the ideas, words, and phrases that would make that picture of him over the radio and would fix the image in the public consciousness. He was trying to reach the underdog and I scraped from my memory an old phrase "The Forgotten Man," which has haunted me for years.

> If you had asked me what he stood for rather than what he is I could tell you more accurately. But that can keep. I am going up to Albany Thurs. A.M. after my class to help on the speech he is to make at St. Paul. If we get through in time I shall go on to Cleve. for the week end and we can talk it over. I shall wire or telephone. Best to Jim and Mother. . . .

I got to Cleveland that week end of April 16th. But the rag-chewing about "what he stood for" never did come off because, toward midnight of the 16th, I was routed out of Cleveland by a telephone call from Albany asking me to board the Governor's train in Detroit the next morning. The news that the Insull empire was cracking seemed to call for some last-minute additions to the speech Roosevelt was to deliver in St. Paul on the 18th, and so I crawled out of bed and made for the railroad station.

It was, perhaps, just as well that the moment passed without any exposition of the Roosevelt program of April, 1932.

As I understood it from talks and from fairly close study of his policies and utterances as Governor, it went something as follows:

F. D. R. had a fairly concrete power policy whose basic tenets were (1) the inalienable property right of all the people in the sources of water power (this, of course, was part of T. R.'s conservation policy); (2) the duty of government to see that this power was produced and distributed at the lowest possible cost to the people; (3) the applicability of the mass-production concept to electricity. Here was a subject to which Roosevelt had given more painstaking study than he had to any other single one.

His power policy was, in a sense, part of a larger policy which had included the conservation of both land and water. Roosevelt had advocated reforestation, land utilization, the relief of the farmers from an inequitable tax burden, and the curative possibilities of diversifying our industrial life by sending a proportion of it into the rural districts. The central problem of agriculture—the paradox of scarcity in the midst of plenty—he saw as a problem of conservation. In so far as he had any short-term policy on agriculture, he had expressed it in what seemed like a vague endorsement of the McNary-Haugen plan.

He was, in theory, a low-tariff man. "It is time," he had said, "for us to sit down with other nations and say to them: 'This tariff fence business, on our part and on yours, is preventing world trade. Let us see if we can work out reciprocal methods by which we can start the actual interchange of goods.' "[3] . . .

[3] Address before the New York State Grange, Albany, February 2, 1932.

He was, as Woodrow Wilson said of Jefferson, a "patron" of labor. In the state he had fought for legislation regulating the issuance of injunctions in labor controversies, the extension and more rigid application of the eight-hour day on public work, improvement of the workmen's compensation law and of factory inspections, and a variety of other labor measures.

He was concerned with the poignant plight of the unemployed and had championed a relief and public-works program with national implications. New York had been, in fact, the first state to appropriate money for relief. His program was peculiarly interesting in that its administration was highly decentralized. Such aspects of unemployment as the difficulty those over forty found in getting jobs seemed particularly vivid in his mind.

He was searching for a "workable" unemployment-insurance program and was a firm believer in the benefits that would flow from the establishment of the old-age pension system he had initiated in New York.

He had talked indignantly about the "usurious" interest rates that small borrowers had to pay and had expressed a determination to prevent mergers and consolidations in industry which were made solely for the purpose of selling watered stock.

These policies, near-policies, and mere leanings we have since been told are the roots of Mr. Roosevelt's national program. Yet I confess that I saw them as only the soil in which such roots might flourish if they were planted there.

Ernest K. Lindley, the best historian of the Roosevelt regime to date, has pointed out that "Mr. Roosevelt did not recruit his professorial advisers to provide him with a point of view; he drew them to him because their point of view was akin to his own." That is perfectly true. It is also true that "Mr. Roosevelt had developed his political philosophy long before the depression began and long before he met any member of his brains trust . . . [that] long before the presidential campaign of 1932 Mr. Roosevelt had emerged as the leading Democratic exponent of a modern liberalism of which the kernel was readiness to use the power of political government to redress the balance of the economic world."[4]

But if that readiness in itself constituted a national program, then a

[4] *The Roosevelt Revolution—First Phase,* by Ernest K. Lindley. Copyright, 1933. Published by Viking Press, Inc., New York; p. 7.

man's intention to build a house constitutes the work of the architect, of the contractor, and of the carpenters.

This is not to deny that Roosevelt *had* a political philosophy. He believed that government not only could, but should, achieve the subordination of private interests to collective interests, substitute cooperation for the mad scramble of selfish individualism. He had a profound feeling for the underdog, a real sense of the critical unbalance of economic life, a very keen awareness that political democracy could not exist side by side with economic plutocracy.

These things were a state of mind and heart thoroughly familiar in the United States. They were the heritage of a series of economic and social crises that began in 1873, the bywords of a progressivism that for over sixty years had preached the need for controlling the increasing concentration of economic power and the need for converting that power to social ends. These were the purposes that had activated Bryan, Altgeld, Tom Johnson, old Bob La Follette, and, to a degree, T. R. and Wilson. They had drawn to the support of these men the Edward Bellamys, Walter Weyls, Herbert Crolys, Louis Brandeises, Charles Van Hises, the young Walter Lippmanns of their day. They were part of the intellectual equipment of every mute, inglorious liberal in America, and, though there is no evidence that Roosevelt acquired them in Groton or Harvard, in the New York legislature or in the Navy Department, there is no doubt that he had made them his own by the time Al Smith persuaded him to run for the Governorship.

But this realization that the democratic program was still unfulfilled and this desire to carry it forward were not enough for a man to bring to the Presidency of the United States. They might have been in 1912, or even in 1924. By 1932 long neglect had made the chronic ills of our society acute and dangerous. A President could no longer approach them in leisurely fashion, with merely a humane outlook and a fragmentary understanding of what was wrong. He had to know how the philosophy of progressivism had been enlarged, documented, and made explicit. He had to decide how and where to apply it. He needed a specific program.

And in April that program had yet to be devised.

4

"Agriculture," which, in our list, we included under "Conservation," came first—and not because we were taking up things alphabetically. The obvious beginning of our discontents in this country was the persistence of the delusion that the nation could prosper while its farmers went begging.

There was another reason why "Agriculture" came first. The scene of Mr. Roosevelt's first political victory was the rural districts of Dutchess county, and from that day forward it was Louis Howe's cardinal principle to concentrate on the farmers in planning a campaign.

At any rate, "Agriculture" suggested Rex Tugwell to me, and so Rex was the first person I asked in to meet Sam and "Doc" O'Connor.

Rex, I knew, had done a study on the subject for Al Smith in the 1928 campaign and had carried on his researches for the four years that followed. He wasn't a close personal friend, yet I knew him well enough to be sure he would get along beautifully with Roosevelt. He was ignorant of politics. But he was a first-rate economist who had pushed on beyond the frontiers of stiff classicism, and his original and speculative turn of mind made him an enormously exhilarating companion. Rex was like a cocktail: his conversation picked you up and made your brain race along. At the same time there was a rich vein of melancholy in his temperament—frequently finding expression in the doubt that any politician could or would take steps to relieve the paralysis creeping over our economic system. And that gave his presentation of ideas a certain moving, emotional quality.

"Doc" O'Connor, whose dearest friends could hardly call him either impressionable or progressive, reacted startlingly to the experimental meeting with him in March. When Tugwell had left, after an exposition of his beliefs about what had to be done for agriculture, O'Connor turned to me and remarked with something akin to awe, "He's a pretty profound fellow, isn't he?" Rosenman guessed he'd do, too, in more prosaic language. And so the decision was made to take him to see the Governor.

The second recruit was Lindsay Rogers, also of Columbia. But his career in this connection was tumultuous and short-lived. Rogers had advised on tariff during the Smith campaign in much the same way that Rex had advised on agriculture. The Governor's various speeches, in preparation during the early days of April, had to contain a short statement on tariff that would not later stand in the way of any farm policies that might be adopted. I therefore asked Rogers to send me a memorandum on the tariff which I could show the Governor and which might be used in the writing of the Governor's speeches, and I received one from him on April 2nd. Thus innocently began an episode so nightmarish that I still get gooseflesh when I think back to it.

On Friday, April 15th, I called Rogers on the long-distance telephone and spoke to him for eighteen minutes, explaining that three sentences on the effects of the Hawley-Smoot tariff were being taken verbatim from his memorandum and put into the speech Roosevelt was to make at St. Paul on the following Monday. Then, because I wanted to avoid any slip-up, I read him the entire passage from the speech relating to the tariff—including his sentences—and asked for his comment or criticism. There was none.

The speech, including this passage, was duly delivered by Roosevelt on April 18th, and for the next three days generally friendly editorials and messages poured in.

Picture, then, my dismay when I opened the *New York Evening Post* on April 22nd and was confronted by the following item, which appeared under the bold-face title, "A Deadly Parallel."

"We quote below two extracts from political speeches of the moment. One is from the speech made by ex-Governor Alfred E. Smith at the Jefferson Dinner in Washington on April 13; the other is from the speech of Governor Franklin D. Roosevelt at St. Paul on April 18:

SMITH	ROOSEVELT
The consequences of the Hawley-Smoot bill have been tremendous, both directly and indirectly. Directly—American foreign trade has been steadily dwindling. . . . Indirectly—the high schedules of the Hawley-Smoot bill caused European nations to raise their own tariff walls not only against us but against each other.	The consequences of the Hawley-Smoot bill have been tremendous, both directly and indirectly. Directly, American foreign trade has been steadily dwindling. Indirectly, the high schedules of the Hawley-Smoot bill caused European nations to raise their own tariff walls, and these walls were raised not only against us but against each other.

"Smith apparently said it first. Did Roosevelt copy it from him? If so, how and why? Or did some 'ghost writer' get mixed up? Or did both Smith and Roosevelt take the words from some Democratic campaign book?" . . .

There it was—simple, incontrovertible, stupefying—like one of those dreadful dreams in which you suddenly discover that you have appeared in a ballroom without your trousers.

The next afternoon Rogers came to my office and explained. It seemed that when he had given me the memorandum on April 2nd he had forgotten to mention that he had submitted an identical statement to Al Smith for use in a speech scheduled for March 31st. This hadn't been mentioned because Smith had failed to use any part of the memorandum then. It seemed further that, on April 11th, Rogers had dictated in the office of Mrs. Henry Moskowitz a page of discussion on tariff for Smith's use in his Jefferson Day speech, and had had before him, while dictating this page, the original memorandum he had sent to both Roosevelt and Smith. It appeared, finally, that Rogers had forgotten to tell me, at the time that I made the long-distance call to him, that Smith had used parts of the memorandum he had given me. Rogers claimed that I had not read him the particular passage in question when I spoke to him on the telephone—a point that it would have been bootless to argue. He added that he was, of course, "terribly sorry" about the whole mix-up.

Al Smith had meanwhile told the papers that he himself had written the sentences used by Roosevelt. Papers all over the country picked up the story. Cartoonists went to town about it. And for three days everybody except Roosevelt and his staff had a good belly laugh.

Actually, the duplication was of no particular importance: the tariff policies of Roosevelt and Smith, as set forth *after* the three controverted sentences, differed in both form and substance. It would have been easy to show that Smith had been mistaken when he claimed the Rogers sentences as his own. But to have attempted any rebuttal would simply have prolonged the life of the story.

Eventually the furor died down. But it had been humiliating for Roosevelt, and I felt that, being responsible for the introduction of Rogers' material and having failed to note myself that Smith had used it, I was also responsible for the embarrassment that it caused. I should not have blamed Roosevelt for a minute if he had said good-by to me and my works at that point. In fact, there was a stinging feeling around my neck while I calmly waited for the ax to fall.

I did not know my man. He did not ask for, but he got, a full explanation. He heard it in silence, smiled ruefully, and said he supposed we'd better put the incident out of our minds. So I came to know one of the loveliest facets of Roosevelt's character: he stood by his people when they got into a jam—sometimes even when they got him into a jam. (I had yet to learn that this endearing virtue in a man could be a failing in a President.) We resumed, precisely as though the episode had never been.

But minus Rogers. Rogers, perhaps out of a feeling of delicacy, perhaps because he felt that Al Smith would carry the convention again, withdrew from active service. He was consulted several times in the summer and autumn of the year and was always helpful, but his relationship to the Roosevelt candidacy was never intimate again.

Meanwhile, even before Rogers began to fade out, Adolf A. Berle, Jr., had been initiated. Berle had had a whirlwind career as an infant prodigy in Harvard College and Law School. Someone has been so unkind as to suggest that he continued to be an infant long after he had ceased to be a prodigy. But I always found that the slightly youthful cockiness and brashness to which this strained epigram referred was more than compensated for by the toughness of his mind, his quickness, his energy, and his ability to organize material well. What particularly commended him were the facts that he had already done some distinguished work on the subject of corporate finance and was then engaged, with Gardiner C. Means, an economist, in an extensive piece of research on the nature and control of corporations in the United States. (This last, first published as *The Modern Corporation and Private Property* during the summer of 1932, was an analysis of one aspect of the problem.)

When I asked Berle to join us in preparing material on "credit and corporations" for Roosevelt's use, he bluntly replied that he had "another candidate for President." I did not press him to tell me whom he had in mind and, as a matter of fact, never did find out. It was his technical assistance that was wanted, not his political support, which carried not the slightest weight in any case, I remarked. He nodded energetically, laughed, and enlisted.

There were other recruits in those first few weeks—among them Professor Joseph D. McGoldrick, who was later to become comptroller of New York City; James W. Angell, economist son of Yale's President; Schuyler Wallace, who was to do some admirable studies on administrative reorganization; and Howard Lee McBain, who, throughout 1932, occasionally advised on questions of constitutional law. All, it has been wryly noted, were members of Columbia University's faculty. Possibly there was a trace of provincialism in this circumstance. But, in the main, it was the result of very practical considerations. What was being done in those early April days was wholly experimental. It might or it might not prove to be what Roosevelt needed. It was going to require the outlay of time and money by each man invited to serve, and there was to be no compensation or hope of compensation for any of them. I could not very well expect mere acquaintances to take part in such a venture.

Besides, I had to summon these people quickly. It was essential that they be close enough to each other to meet and exchange ideas almost daily, at first. I had to know them, as human beings, well enough to judge whether they could attract the Governor's interest and adjust themselves to his habits of work. I had to be sufficiently familiar with their immediate ranges of interest to know precisely how to employ their talents.

There were dozens of men of equal caliber throughout the country, inside and outside universities, whom I knew and whom I might have asked in. Many of them were later brought in, as a matter of fact. But at that stage of the game they were ruled out by one consideration or another.

There is one point here that I think deserves further emphasis. When I asked Rex, Adolf, and the others to serve, I also asked them to refuse if they had any hope of getting even their expenses paid, much less of getting a fee of any kind. It was true that men engaged in this type of work in the campaign of 1928 had been paid rather liberally, but I was determined that there be no repetition of the practice. While I did not doubt the professional disinterestedness of the 1928 job, I wanted to avoid the slightest taint of jobship in this affair. I wanted our independence, our honesty, our interest in ideas to be above the faintest suspicion, protected, even against ourselves, at a material cost most of us could ill afford.[5] Only one person demurred at this condition and, needless to say, the invitation to serve was at once withdrawn.

It would be futile to trace the processes of selection, natural and otherwise, that brought some of the original group I had tentatively named to Sam Rosenman into increasingly intimate contact with

[5] The rule about expenses was broken in my case alone before the election, but not until September, 1932, when Roosevelt asked me to accompany him on his campaign trip to the Far West. By that time the drain of long-distance telephone charges; of railroad fares to Albany, Hyde Park, Washington, and Chicago; of extra clerical assistance throughout the spring and summer had so depleted my modest resources that I was compelled to let the Democratic National Committee pay for my railroad tickets and Pullman accommodations. By September, too, my staff, which consisted of two young women, was handling each week literally hundreds of letters, addressed to the Governor, which were sent to my office by the Governor's secretariat and the Democratic National Committee because they involved "policy matters" and could not be answered in routine fashion by subordinates. Outlays for stamps, paper, and the rental of an extra typewriter were also paid thereafter by the National Committee.

After the election, we began to be reimbursed for all traveling expenses and long-distance charges incurred in the President-elect's service and, from December through March 4th, the Committee paid part of one assistant's salary.

But at no time were we paid any fee or retainer for our own services, and our total expenses far exceeded the trifling amount by which we were reimbursed.

Roosevelt and that relegated others to indirect contribution through us. Three or four of the men were too busy on other things to give much time to the work. One or two didn't get on well with all the others. One proved to be unexpectedly pedantic and, once he had spoken his piece, could only repeat it, with variations. Another's stuffy manner so obviously annoyed the Governor that he was tactfully kept away from Albany. Several, while they were experts in their own fields and were helpful on specific questions, could add almost nothing to the general give and take of ideas or to the shaping of a broad, coherent program.

All this was discovered by a system of trial and error—a system not nearly so wasteful as it sounds because Sam and I took no one to Albany who wasn't worth at least one evening's intensive pumping. And the amount of intellectual ransacking that Roosevelt could crowd into one evening was a source of constant astonishment to me.

The routine was simple enough. Sam, "Doc," and I would take one or two men on the late-afternoon train to Albany, arriving in time for dinner. The talk at table would be pleasant, casual, and generally inconsequential. But once we had moved out of the dining room to the study which adjoined it—a frowzy room, which I considered the most hideous in the dingily baroque Governor's Mansion—random talk came to an end. Roosevelt, Sam, or I would throw a question at the visitor, and we were off at an exciting and exhausting clip.

The Governor was at once a student, a cross-examiner, and a judge. He would listen with rapt attention for a few minutes and then break in with a question whose sharpness was characteristically blurred by an anecdotal introduction or an air of sympathetic agreement with the speaker. Sooner or later, we would all have at the visitor, of course. But those darting questions of Roosevelt were the ticks of the evening's metronome. The intervals between them would grow shorter. The questions themselves would become meatier, more informed—the infallible index to the amount he was picking up in the evening's course.

It was my business to learn too. But my questions were not solely directed to that end. I watched the Governor, noted his reactions, and supplemented his questions to make sure that every idea or bit of information worth using was hammered home. I was trying to avoid, more than any other single thing, a synthetic education. The stuff had to become part of Roosevelt's equipment. Otherwise, somewhere, sometime, the thing that every politician fears like death would happen—a bad break in the exposition of fact or policy in extemporaneous remarks. Otherwise the process would be nothing more than a glorified cram course designed to get him by the test of the election and promptly forgotten thereafter.

By midnight, when the time came to dash for the train to New York, Sam, "Doc," and I would be done in; the visitor (who would not realize for some days, in most cases, that he had been squeezed dry) would look a trifle wilted; and the Governor, scorning further questions, would be making vigorous pronouncements on the subject we had been discussing, waving his cigarette holder to emphasize his points.

This performance was repeated again and again through the spring and summer. We took dozens of people up to Albany or Hyde Park, sometimes with the idea that they were good for only one shot, and sometimes, as in the case of Ralph Robey (an economist-journalist of great ability and independence), because we felt they could be consistently helpful in advising us and hoped that they would become more or less attached to the little general staff that had meanwhile taken shape.

That development—the close association of Tugwell, Berle, Rosenman, O'Connor, and myself—was formally acknowledged late in April. Just before he left for the conference of Governors in Richmond, Virginia, which began on Monday, April 25th, Roosevelt asked me to serve as chairman of this group. We were in his little sitting room at his house on 65th Street in New York City, and he was giving occasional directions about the packing of his things to McDuffie, his colored valet, arranging some papers on a small table before him, and talking to me at the same time—a proclivity I had come to understand.

"It seems a shame," he said, "that I'm going to have to be away for almost a month. But if I don't get to Warm Springs now, I can't see my way clear to it until after the election, and I need the rest before I go into a campaign. Why don't you fellows go ahead, just as though I were here, seeing people and getting stuff together? Then you might send down a memorandum for me to study"—he laughed—"so I don't get too far behind on my homework."

"Good. But who, specifically, are 'you fellows'?" I cautiously asked.

"Well, Sam, of course. And 'Doc,' I suppose. You know, 'Doc's' got a pretty level head on his shoulders. And Rex, and Berle. Rex could go on with his farm thing, though he'd be good on other things too. Berle could work up something on debt and finance; you know—R.F.C. and mortgage foreclosures and the stock market. And you put in whatever you want to and pull the whole thing together so it makes sense politically. Which makes you chairman, I guess, of my privy council."

Either the phrase "privy council" particularly struck his fancy or my involuntary reaction to it, a wince at the thought of what an unfriendly newspaperman might do with the phrase if he got hold of it, made Roosevelt decide that he had struck good teasing ground. At any rate, he repeated it, shaking with laughter. And—now the baleless secret is out—thereafter referred to us as the "Privy Council" until September, when Jimmy Kieran, the *New York Times* man covering him, employed the name "brains trust." By that time the private joke had worn a little thin, and he gladly switched to the newer label.

5

The day after Roosevelt left for the South, Rex, Adolf, and I met in my office at the University and, crowded between the bookshelves, the file cases, and the typewriter tables, laid out the work of the next three weeks. It was an ambitious program.

We would each take the responsibility of preparing memoranda on a number of topics. Some of these we would farm out to other men, some we would prepare ourselves; but in every case we would be responsible for the accuracy of the material, whether it came from ourselves or from others. We would meet and discuss what we were doing while the work was in progress. Meanwhile, besides, I would prepare a broad philosophic statement—perhaps in the form of a draft speech from which paragraphs might later be taken and expanded for use in particular speeches—to precede the detailed and specific memoranda on agriculture, tariff, banking, finance, money, international debts, power, relief, railroads, governmental economy, and presidential powers.

Wild days and nights of work ensued. Berle got in Louis Faulkner and a number of other young men he knew downtown to work with him on the problem of how to loosen frozen credit and scale down the intolerable burden of accumulated debt. Tugwell went to work on the tariff and on an analysis of farm remedies proposed in the 'twenties. With Henry Morgenthau, Jr., who was then Chairman of Governor Roosevelt's agricultural advisory commission, he also prepared some elaborate "notes" for a farm program. Frederick C. Mills and Jimmy Angell contributed ideas on prices and money. McGoldrick and McBain prepared a memorandum on presidential war powers (we already foresaw the possible need for the exercise of emergency powers by the President). Fred Telford, recommended to me by Mark Graves, Roosevelt's state budget director, undertook to prepare a preliminary study of the federal budget. So it went.

There were conferences, drafts, redrafts, editings, and coordinatings.

By May 19th, the day that Sam Rosenman was to leave for a visit to Warm Springs, we had by no means all the data we had planned to gather, but a very respectable amount of it was ready. It was clipped together and dispatched to Roosevelt via Sam.

It may easily be argued that this material foreshadowed not only most of the campaign speeches but much of the New Deal itself. But that isn't accurate. What its preparation really did was to make us pull ourselves together and put down on paper a good many of the notions that we had been batting around in conversation with the Governor. It gave our thinking, to date, a local habitation and a name.[6] At last we could see, in black and white, the outlines of the national program that we had been sketching out in talk. We could take note of the holes in our thinking and get to work filling some of them up.

What was taking shape was distinctive in three respects.

First was what we might have called the "Look Homeward, Angel" interpretation of the depression: we proceeded on the assumption that the causes of our ills were domestic, internal, and that the remedies would have to be internal too. How unorthodox this was at the time may be judged by the amount of bitterness with which we were called "nationalists" by older economists.

Second was the belief that there was need not only for an extension of the government's regulatory power to prevent abuses (stock-market regulation and the abolition of child labor, for instance) but for the development of controls to stimulate and stabilize economic activity ("planning" for agriculture and the concentration of greater powers in the Federal Reserve Board, for instance). The former, designed to curb

[6] This last is literally true. For the phrase "a new deal," which was publicly introduced in the speech of acceptance, I first used in the general philosophical statement that prefaced this series of memoranda, thus: "Unlike most depressions this one has as yet produced only a few of the disorderly manifestations usually attendant upon such times. Wild radicalism has made few converts. This is due to an orderly and hopeful spirit on the part of people who nevertheless . . . want a change. To fail to offer real change is not only to betray their hopes but misunderstand their patience. . . . Reaction is no barrier to the radical. It is a challenge and a provocation. It is not the pledge of *a new deal* [italics mine]; it is the reminder of broken promises. Its unctious [*sic*] reassurances of prosperity round the corner are not oil on troubled waters; they are oil on fire." . . .

economic power and special privilege, did not depart in principle from the lines of policy laid down in the administrations of Theodore Roosevelt and Woodrow Wilson. But the latter carried us pretty far from ancient moorings.

Third was the rejection of the traditional Wilson-Brandeis philosophy that if America could once more become a nation of small proprietors, of corner grocers and smithies under spreading chestnut trees, we should have solved the problems of American life. We agreed that the heart of our difficulty was the anarchy of concentrated economic power which, like a cannon loose on a frigate's deck, tore from one side to another, crushing those in its path. But we felt that the remedy for this was not to substitute muskets for cannon or to throw the cannon overboard. We believed that any attempt to atomize big business must destroy America's greatest contribution to a higher standard of living for the body of its citizenry—the development of mass production. We agreed that equality of opportunity must be preserved. But we recognized that competition, as such, was not inherently virtuous; that competition (when it was embodied in an employer who survived only by sweating his labor, for example) created as many abuses as it prevented. So we turned from the nostalgic philosophy of the "trust busters" toward the solution first broached in modern times by Charles Richard Van Hise's *Concentration and Control.*[7]

I doubt that Roosevelt did more than glance through the memoranda of May 19th at Warm Springs. He was at work putting the finishing touches on a fine speech that Ernest Lindley had drafted for him—that speech which was to call for "bold, persistent experimentation"—and three short days after he had delivered it at Oglethorpe University he left Warm Springs for New York.[8] But he was to become familiar enough with the substance of our memoranda in the weeks after his return.

[7] This work, published by Macmillan in 1912, had a considerable influence on the thinking of T. R. and colored his campaign speeches to a marked degree when he was running in 1912. It may also be considered the forerunner of such books as Tugwell's *Industrial Discipline and the Governmental Arts,* Columbia University Press, 1933; Jerome Frank's *Save America First,* Harper, 1938; and, of course, Berle and Means' *The Modern Corporation and Private Property,* Macmillan, 1933.

[8] This speech was delivered on May 22nd. The story goes that I contributed to it, but that is not the fact. At Roosevelt's request, I merely sent down several pages of notes on James Oglethorpe, in whose honor the University was named. These were scattered and of no particular use in the final draft. The general introductory statement to the memoranda of May 19th was not intended for use at Oglethorpe, but was definitely designed as a source of ideas for the acceptance speech and subsequent speeches.

6

The excursions to Albany and Hyde Park were resumed late in May. Now "Doc," who was busy with his law practice, could no longer always accompany us, and sometimes Sam's duties as a justice of New York's Supreme Court limited, to a small degree, the amount of time he could give to political activity.[9] Thus, more often than not, it was Tugwell, Berle, and I who would make the journey, either by ourselves or with an expert in tow.

The economic jam-sessions took place once or twice a week. But I would frequently be asked to stay over for the day following one of them or, if my own work made that impossible, to come up separately on another day.

These private conferences between Roosevelt and me were for two purposes—to begin putting together an acceptance speech and to talk over a political situation that was swiftly becoming a major threat to Roosevelt's nomination, the Walker affair.

Judge Seabury's investigations into the administration of New York City had brought out certain facts pertaining to Mayor Walker which were the signal for renewed demands that Roosevelt remove Walker. But the investigation closed on June 1st without a formal request from Seabury that Roosevelt take action and, until such a request was made, the Governor could legally take no steps.

For two days the press howled for Walker's head. For two days we pondered how best to act. Then the Governor challenged Seabury "to stop talking and do something." . . . On June 8th Seabury sent the evidence against Walker and a demand for his removal to Albany. And Roosevelt, as he had with Sheriff Farley, asked Walker to reply to the accusations against him.

This bold course—the only possible course ethically and politically, though it cost Roosevelt many votes in the New York State delegation—was shaped, it is important to remember, amid the distraction and the tenseness of the preconvention month. I played only a small part in this process, but it was at my suggestion that Roosevelt asked Martin Conboy, a New York City lawyer, to act as his counsel in the Walker hearings of August. The choice of Conboy, who was, like

[9] Sam had been appointed on March 11, 1932, to fill a vacancy caused by the death of Justice Mullan. But he had not taken office until after the "thirty-day bill period" had passed.

Walker, a Catholic of Irish extraction and a member of Tammany and who, unlike Walker, had been grieved and outspoken about the goings-on of the Hall, was a political coup. This was wholly aside from the fact that Conboy was to do a superlative job in coaching Roosevelt in the facts and law of the case before and during the hearings.

But in early June it was impossible to foresee that things would pan out well, and the days that we spent were harried beyond imagining. The time, consumed by worry, by political jockeying, and by the amenities a candidate must observe toward his visitors, was only less conducive to the preparation of a statesmanlike acceptance speech than it was to a wise, just handling of the Walker affair.

Nevertheless, a speech had to be written and, somehow, that, too, had to be squeezed in.

It had been the Governor's intention for a long time to accept the nomination before the convention itself instead of awaiting the customary formal notice at his summer residence. His plan offered two great advantages. He could begin at an early date the ambitious task of selling to the people a political program involving much that was unorthodox and, equally important, he could at once dramatize himself as a breaker of custom, a daring, resolute champion of action, establishing a bold contrast with the country's picture of Hoover as timid, hesitant, irresolute. The idea of a plane ride was born of necessity. He could not very well keep the convention waiting until he got from Albany to Chicago by rail.

But a speech of acceptance was an important utterance in the life of a candidate—perhaps the most important. It was not to be dashed off at the last minute. Its preparation was the work of weeks. Hence, immediately after his return from Warm Springs, the two of us began a conversational review of the ideas that had been presented to him in the meetings at Albany and in the memoranda of May 19th. From these two or three talks I was able to get a general notion of what ideas he wanted to emphasize and what to play down. Then, because it was obviously impossible for him to find a quiet moment to dictate a draft speech, and because I knew his preferences, he asked me, early in June, to prepare a speech memorandum containing an exposition of the ideas he wished to make his own—a statement couched in the language of speechmaking rather than of economic discourse.

The result was a document in speech form approximately nine thousand words long. While it was taking shape, I consulted him frequently by telephone and in person. I also showed parts of it to Rex,

Adolf, Sam, and Louis, asking for their advice on one point or another. But the physical job of writing, I understood from Roosevelt's procedure in separating it from the general meetings, he did not wish me to share with the others, and I was scrupulously careful to respect his wishes.

When I had finished, in the third week of June, I took the document to Albany. The Governor read it with care, making penciled corrections here and there and indicating, in the margins, points that he wanted to strengthen, passages to "boil," as he phrased it, and things that should be omitted for the sake of brevity. This draft I took back to New York, where I revised it in accordance with his instructions.

When I took it to Albany on my last trip before the convention, Roosevelt asked whether I hadn't planned to go on to Chicago to see the "show" there. I told him that I had, that I was really eager to go, but that I should be only too glad to stay in the East if I could be of the slightest service to him.

"No, no," he said. "You go ahead. Sam and I can work this over now."

It was agreed that probably the best thing I could do then was to go West and get Louis and some of the other boys used to what the speech was going to say.

And so I left for Chicago, with a copy of the draft in my pocket.

7

The center of the convention, for me, was 1702 at the Congress Hotel—Louis Howe's suite. True, there were hours spent in the convention hall itself and in the room at the Drake that Jesse Straus had made available to Rex and me. There were talks with Straus, his son Bob, with Harry Hopkins, who was chairman of the New York State Temporary Emergency Relief Administration, and with dozens of others who wandered in and out of the Straus suite. But most of the time was spent in Louis' corner apartment at the Congress.

I don't believe that Louis set foot outside his rooms during the entire period of the convention. There, in the inevitable confusion that washes over every outpost of a political convention, the doughty little man worked, worried, suffered, triumphed. Except that he threw his coat aside occasionally when he took a nap, I don't think that he had his clothes off during the entire week. It was a moment when his fondest ambitions, the fruits of a lifetime of labor, hung in the balance. And his nerves were raw with the strain, his body racked by illness.

The most vivid picture that I have of those days is that of Louis at the moment Roosevelt's name was put in nomination. The convention was in an uproar. Over the radio came sounds of singing, marching delegates, blaring bands, and the futile poundings of Senator Thomas J. Walsh's gavel. Louis was lying on his bed, doubled up with suffering from his chronic asthma. For hours he had been sending directions to Arthur F. Mullen (the Roosevelt floor manager) at the convention hall, through his faithful and competent secretary, Margaret Durand, whom he always playfully called "Rabbit." Looking at that moment of victory like a man to whom happiness could never come and whose wasted body could hardly be expected to harbor the breath of life much longer, he groaned out between coughs, "Tell them to repeat 'Happy Days Are Here Again.' "

I never knew whether Louis' intense activity was especially important. Jim Farley, after all, was the field marshal, attending sessions of the convention and negotiating with delegates there and in his own apartment. Probably Louis' chief contribution was made in keeping in touch with such party leaders as Senators Hull, Wheeler, and Byrnes and in counseling with Farley and Ed Flynn ("Boss" of the Bronx and political adviser to Roosevelt and Farley). For the rest, the milling about that went on in his apartment seemed to have little enough to do with the actual political management of the convention. Yet that was the place for me because it enabled me to maintain a line of contact with Farley and Flynn and contact, by direct wire, with Roosevelt and Rosenman in Albany.

Through the first, I was able to follow the story of the attempt to win over the delegations indispensable to Roosevelt's nomination.

Through the second, I was able to learn what was being done with the copy of the draft acceptance speech I had left in Albany. When Roosevelt and Rosenman had finished their work on it, Rosenman telephoned it to me and I had a stenographer take it down. I was enormously relieved when I saw the text. My one fear had been that it would be transformed beyond recognition into the usual meaningless generalities. But there had merely been a reduction in length. The substance remained. The peroration (*i.e.,* the last five paragraphs) was new, but it had been and remained customary for me to make no attempt to draft a peroration for any speech of Roosevelt's. He always preferred to do that part of a speech in longhand, by himself.

During the agonizing six days of the convention my chief job was to get Louis to approve this speech. As I have suggested elsewhere, I had seen Louis constantly during May and June, kept him informed of what I was doing in Albany, and, in general, explained the shape our thoughts were taking. From those talks he had grown reasonably familiar with the ideas expressed in the acceptance speech, and, contrary to the impression of political wiseacres, he had no objection to them.

But though he admittedly did not demur at the philosophy of the speech I showed him, to my amazement, he rasped that the speech simply wouldn't do, simply wasn't appropriate to such an occasion. There followed, then, a fearful tirade which reached a crescendo with the shout, "Good God, do I have to do everything myself? I see Sam Rosenman in every paragraph of this mess."

So he spit it out—at last—the thing he really felt. It wasn't jealousy, solely, though clearly he resented not only Sam but the rest of us who were gathering around his "Franklin." It was the simple, primitive desire to play a major role in the crowning oratorical triumph of his idol's career.

In such a situation it was difficult, despite a long friendship with Louis, to do much with him. I explained that Rosenman had really had very little to do with the writing of the speech, but to that Louis bitterly replied that he knew better, that he had too much respect for my judgment to believe that I could have "perpetrated" this speech. "I don't expect Sam to understand, but *you'd* know it would go fine under the trees at Hyde Park and be a complete flop at a convention," he snapped. I argued that, convention or no convention, it was essential that a measured, comprehensive statement go to a country wallowing in the depths of a depression. But it was impossible to make Louis abandon the pretenses (1) that the speech was unsuitable and (2) that it was unsuitable because Sam had worked on it. And it would have been dangerous to have pressed the matter too insistently, because then all his unspoken resentment against me would have flared up. I could merely keep my fingers crossed while, over and over again, he threatened to write "a whole new speech" himself, and the hours whirled by without his making a move to begin.

On the morning of July 1st we all turned into bed, worn out by the all-night session of the convention. As the many personal accounts of the convention have since revealed, there was no joy in the Roosevelt camp that day. It seemed probable that when the convention was resumed and another ballot taken, a pretty general crack-up of the Roosevelt forces would occur. There was no great liking for the Roosevelt movement on the part of a good many state leaders, and at the first sign of weakness it would crumble.[10]

There was nothing I could do in that sector, and after a few hours' sleep I returned to the Congress. Rex and I found the place full of hell and desperation. We first went to "Doc" O'Connor's rooms. "Doc" was there with his brother, Congressman John, and a number of his associates from New York. The air was blue with cursing at the New York delegation. Tammany was more confident than ever of the defeat of Roosevelt. "Doc" was frankly pessimistic. He said, "Well, we'll have the Governorship six months more anyhow and, boy, will we make those damned Tammany fellows wish they hadn't played this game!" Gloom reigned in Howe's room too. Things were so desperate that I could not even suggest that Louis think of an acceptance speech to be delivered by a man whose nomination, at that moment, seemed highly doubtful.

Rex, Harry Hopkins (whom we picked up at Louis'), and I started for the convention. Rex and Harry, both thoroughly imbued with the prevailing pessimism, felt that the case was hopeless. We did not take a taxi at the Congress, but walked to Wabash Avenue and proceeded in a northerly direction two or three blocks. As we passed a newsstand I picked up a paper in which appeared the one column that is probably the best known of Heywood Broun's many and probably the one that he would like most not to have written. I was still boiling with indignation over Broun's reference to Roosevelt as "the corkscrew candidate of a convoluting convention" when we got to the Stadium.

The tenseness of the scene we found there is almost indescribable. The Chicago politicians had apparently been planting great numbers of leather-throated mugs in the galleries for the purpose of shouting down the Roosevelt defenders on the floor. The night before, the flotsam and jetsam of this mob had trickled down from the gallery into the box seats beside the arena and now they had boldly preempted some of these places. One almost had a sense of impending physical violence as these ugly personages unflinchingly outstared one. On the floor the delegates were red-eyed, haggard, taut, as McAdoo rose dramatically to announce that California was giving her forty-four votes to Roosevelt, and as Texas followed with her forty-six.

[10] Louisiana, Minnesota, and Mississippi were expected to lead an exodus from the Roosevelt ranks.

I have heard many accounts of the circumstances back of this break, but, after matching together all the fragments, I am convinced that the two persons who deserve more credit for the negotiations than anyone else were Sam Rayburn of Texas and Tom Storke of Santa Barbara, California. Arthur F. Mullen also materially helped win over Garner through Congressman Howard in Washington.

As soon as we could get out of the postnomination bedlam of the auditorium, we returned to the Congress, where we joined up with "Doc" and perhaps fifty other celebrants. But in the midst of the jollification I bethought me of Louis and his threats. I dashed to his apartment and, sure enough, found that he was already making good on them. He had actually summoned enough energy out of the crannies of his frail anatomy to set to work dictating an entirely new acceptance speech. And there was no stopping him.

Now was my moment for black despair—not because I had any vested interest in the text that had come from Albany, but because I honestly believed that no mere political gibberish designed to sweep the weary delegates to their feet would do.

I left and, after a sleepless few hours, returned to Louis'. He would not let me look at his speech, but, having got it out of his system, he felt more affable and so consented to give me a vague idea of what was in it. From what he said I gathered that it was little more than an elaboration of the party platform the convention had adopted, with a few banal sentences spun around each section.

While he was telling me this, B. M. Baruch and General Hugh Johnson appeared and, after a cursory introduction, Louis whisked them into another room and banged the door shut.

Who Johnson was, I had no idea. Nor had I met Baruch before. But I knew that he had been among the supporters of Al Smith and had also been friendly with Governor Ritchie of Maryland. I was, I regret to say, in no frame of mind to admit at that moment that his appearance at Louis' headquarters that morning was a gesture of loyalty to the party ticket, that it had not the slightest character of selfishness, that it was the act of a good sport. I was suspicious of his motives, his philosophy (about which I had accumulated a fine store of misinformation), and his possible influence. As I stared gloomily out of the window at the street below, I saw visions of party compromise and expediency flowing in to engulf the work of building a new party faith around the successful candidate.

It was at this unhappy moment that Jesse Straus tapped me on the shoulder and said: "Can we let Baruch see the acceptance speech? We want to be nice to him because he can contribute a good deal to the campaign."

All the pent-up feelings of the past seventy-two hours broke loose then. I turned on poor Jesse, yanked the speech out of my pocket, flung it at him with the words, "Please do! It wouldn't be a regulation campaign, would it, if the nominee didn't tack and trim? This happens to be what Franklin Roosevelt believes and wants to say. But I'm sure he wouldn't be the first man to cave in under pressure."

Straus simply looked bewildered (he told me later that these remarks were quite incomprehensible to him) and disappeared into the room into which Louis and the others had gone. Perhaps twenty minutes later Baruch emerged, beaming, and held out his hand. He had read both speeches, he said, and infinitely preferred the Albany text. In fact, he thought it was magnificent. I could have wept for surprise and relief. And when he asked whether I would go and show the speech to a good friend of his, sheer gratitude led me to say "Yes."

It was thus that I met Herbert Bayard Swope, whose friendship was to be one of the warmest and happiest relationships of my life. At the moment that I first saw him, this colorful man was seated majestically in a brilliant bathrobe eating one of his notoriously late breakfasts. Joe Kennedy, whom I had met at the Governor's Mansion in Albany, and Hugh Johnson were looking on languidly.

I explained why I had come, sat down, and read the speech to them. When I finished, Kennedy spoke up and said, "I think it is a very bullish speech. What do you think of it, Herbert?" Thereupon Herbert rose from the table and paced up and down the room nervously. He said, "It is a typical Roosevelt speech—liberal in tone, catching, forceful. But it leaves itself open to the charge of having ungenerous characteristics. It doesn't so much as mention the people in the party who have been consistently loyal Democrats. It isn't calculated to start the Governor off with the good will of a united party."

I knew that Swope was speaking out of the disappointment he felt over the defeat of his friend, Al Smith, and that he hoped that there would be some mention of Al. I explained that a number of party leaders had been mentioned in the draft and that their names had been dropped out in the course of the revision of the speech—whether by Rosenman or Roosevelt or both, I did not know. But I was reasonably sure that this had been done only to avoid the hurt feelings that would inevitably be caused by omissions. Any attempt to list all the party leaders was obviously impossible.

This seemed to satisfy Swope, and when I left him and the others I was really more cheerful. It was heartening to know that now four people in Chicago, outside of Rex and myself, liked the speech.

But that still left me with the problem of Louis and *his* speech. I tried desperately to get Louis to talk to me about it, but he flatly refused. He was too busy, he said.

Pretty disconsolately, then, I went out to the airport to meet the plane in which the Governor's party was arriving. There I found Louis with his draft, as evasive as ever. In the midst of the tumult that surrounded the plane after it landed, I got to Rosenman and told him what was up. He said that the Governor had a copy of the speech as finally revised, in very minor degree, on the plane, and that he would try to get word to him to make no changes.[11] Meanwhile, Louis got into Roosevelt's car, sharing, as he had every right to, the triumph of that trip from the airport to the Stadium. The rest of us followed.

But Louis had no chance to confer with Roosevelt in the car. Its path led through screaming, shouting, deafening crowds, and the Governor was so happy and so busy waving at his admirers that Louis could not engage him in talk. Apparently, therefore, Louis decided on one of the most desperate and, it seems to me, foolish courses that I have ever known. He undertook to get Roosevelt to accept his speech sight-unseen at the very moment before Roosevelt was to address the convention. I have heard this story more than once from Roosevelt himself and its purport is this:

After the Chairman had introduced Roosevelt, had announced to him the decision of the convention, and had completed a brief speech of his own, Louis handed Roosevelt his draft of an acceptance speech. Roosevelt, thoroughly aware of what the moment meant to Louis, took the document, extracted the other from his own pocket, and laid the two beside each other. While the convention was cheering madly, he glanced over the first pages of the two speeches, removed the first page from his own draft, replaced it with Louis', and began to read.

Meanwhile, I had pushed my way through the mob to the back of the hall and taken out my copy of the speech. As Roosevelt's high, clear

[11] All sorts of legends surround this trip to Chicago. They range from the story that Roosevelt wrote the acceptance speech, in its entirety, during his flight from Albany, to the story that, as the plane went along, page after page of the overlong draft was flung to the winds. Both are, obviously, untrue, as an examination of all the documents extant on the subject would show.

voice began to pronounce the words, I followed anxiously. The ideas were those of the Albany draft: the phrasing was unfamiliar. Louis, the little devil, had merely rephrased the introduction of the other text (which, of course, was what made it possible for Roosevelt to substitute Louis' first page for his). After a minute or two I began to hear the familiar sentences of the Albany text. So the speech went to the country—one page of Louis' redraft and the remainder the draft I had carried around all week.

As the speech drew to a close, I was poignantly aware of what was happening. The philosophy developed by the little group that I had brought together was now, in substance, the official policy of the standard-bearer of the party. In the American system the pronouncements of the party nominee rank equally with the party platform. In fact, whenever there is a conflict, the nominee's version of party orthodoxy prevails. The die was cast. The doctrine of a potentially great political movement had been proclaimed. Come what might, so far as I was concerned, not even Louis' anger could blot out this moment.

CHAPTER II

"GAYLY THE TROUBADOUR"

THESE latter-day minnesingers, the muckrakers, the goo-goos, the debunkers, have created a romantic tradition about American politics so popular that it has colored the political reporting and biography of two generations. Even the most pragmatic of observers in 1932 could not sweep altogether out of his consciousness the whisper that there was a "System" that corrupted men in public life, eroded their primeval "goodness," made timorous, acquiescent opportunists of them all. Tugwell, Berle, and I never spoke of it to one another, but each of us, I know, in his innermost being was watching for it to materialize out of the political ectoplasm around us. We were certainly not like the newly elected colored alderman who prayed, "O Lawd, keep me from temptation. But if de traction company tempts me and ah fall, let it be a big, fat temptation that ah fall to." It was simply that we would have enjoyed the chance to rebuff a "sinister" influence or two with righteous indignation.

We were doomed to disappointment.

On the night of July 2nd, or, rather, in the early morning of July 3rd, I learned my first lesson on the subject. It was the end of that day in which Roosevelt had flown to Chicago, delivered his acceptance speech, addressed the National Committee after a dinner meeting, and greeted individually the hundreds of well-wishers who swarmed through his rooms at the Congress all evening. Louis Howe and Jim Farley went off to bed around midnight, and shortly after, at a sign from Roosevelt, I eased the last of the visitors out of the apartment. I reached for my own hat, and was smilingly told to sit down a while: it seemed that Roosevelt was "not even a little bit tired." The "while" stretched into an hour and a half, for he began to talk of his plans for the campaign and, before we had finished, I had pages of notes on the trips and speeches he intended to make. We had even discussed in detail what the topics of the speeches were to be.

"A week from Monday I'll be starting off with some of my boys on a cruise along the New England coast," he said, finally. "You'd better go ahead, just as you have been, on the half dozen big issues, and have something ready when I get back." And then he suggested that I might be able to tell him "what got into Louis this week."

I did, as sympathetically as possible. Roosevelt nodded understandingly. "Yes, Louis can be difficult. He can't bear to let anyone else have a direct line through to me."

"Yet Louis surely doesn't want to take personal charge of the group that's working on policy."

"No, no, of course he doesn't. He wants to work on the other end."

The point was worth pressing. "Then you mean to go on keeping the policy job and the other separate?"

"Definitely," he said.

"And I'm to head up through to you on policy?"

"Yes."

"And authorization for the same piece of work won't be scattered around? This isn't Louis, now, I'm thinking about. It's Jim Farley and the senators and the contributors."

There was no "smiling assent, which may mean anything or nothing," but a moment of silence and, then, the unequivocal, "There'll be no drafts or suggestions or proposals that aren't cleared through you. I give you my assurance."

It was a promise that was to be kept without exception.

But immediately, within the week, it was confirmed. Jim Farley, with whom I had become acquainted in Chicago, called on the telephone when I returned to New York and asked me to come down to the Biltmore Hotel for a "heart-to-heart" talk with him. This big, genial, straightforward man went directly to the point. The Governor had told him, he explained, what I was to do.

"I just want you to know that I'm interested in getting him the votes—nothing else," he said. "Issues aren't my business. They're yours and his. You keep out of mine, and I'll keep out of yours." And, so far as policy was concerned, Jim meant that no matter what the candidate decided to campaign on, from the Lord's Prayer to the Communist Manifesto, Jim would try to get the votes.

"All right," I said.

We shook hands on it. Each of us was to keep the promise made to the other. There was never the slightest suggestion of interference on policy matters from Jim Farley and I never meddled in matters relating to political organization.

Louis, on the other hand, could not be bothered with striking attitudes—even gracious ones. But when we met again, back in New York, there was every evidence that Roosevelt had spoken to him. "When this campaign really gets under way," he said, "there are going to be hundreds of cranks and boobs, et cetera, coming in here to pester me with ideas about everything under the sun. I think I'll send them along to you." That was Louis' grudging way of making the *beau geste*—an official renunciation of one of the major jobs he had always done for Roosevelt. He reneged but once—and then, I think, inadvertently. At any rate, his expression of regret was, for him, profuse. He wrote to Roosevelt after it: "Sorry I injured Moley's feelings and upset your orderly plans on speeches—I was in error." . . .

The behavior of the big campaign contributors would have been even more disconcerting to a Lincoln Steffens. Far from demonstrating the Steffens thesis by attempts to influence the policies of the candidate, they were either, as in the case of Bernie Baruch and Will Woodin, in wholehearted sympathy with the line the "brains trust" was taking or, as in the case of Dave Hennen Morris, completely disinterested. The outside limit of "practical interference" was the sending of advice and suggestions about local conditions under which Roosevelt would speak—suggestions which were often welcome and helpful and which, when they were not, could be thrown aside with impunity. Illustrative of the many excellent letters we received is the following, from a heavy contributor and active worker before Roosevelt's speech in Pittsburgh in October:

> Dear Dr. Moley:—
>
> At the suggestion of . . . made over the long distance telephone, I am sending you the following with the request that you call the matter to the attention of Governor Roosevelt at his earliest convenience.
>
> We are expecting great results from the effect of Governor Roosevelt's speech in Pittsburgh. While there is no doubt it will be one of the most important of his campaign speeches to the nation at large, it will be especially important to Pennsylvania as it will help tremendously to cinch the victory in this state.
>
> Pittsburgh is the center of the Steel Industry of this country. Every man and woman in this particular section, whether he realizes it or not, actually lives, thinks and talks in terms of steel mills, steel tonnage, etc., because the steel industry so completely dominates this section. When these tremendous mills are in full

blast, all other troubles and worries in Pittsburgh fade out because the population is busy and working at good wages. Today, these mills are almost completely idle, their great stacks stand like monuments to a greatness that has gone, and the laboring population here is actually in the throes of despair.

In view of this statement, which I am emphasizing above, I feel it would be to great advantage in many vital ways if Governor Roosevelt, in his speech here next Wednesday, would take a few moments to touch upon certain phases of the local situation. It could be done as if it were extemporaneous if he desires. Of course, I am not suggesting any change in either topic or subject matter of his prepared speech. . . .

May I suggest that Governor Roosevelt preface his remarks with praise for the great captains of industry and capitalists whose brain and resources have built these great mills and done so much for Pittsburgh, and praise the thousands of workers whose skill and labor have supplied the energy to operate these mills. Then, after giving full praise and placing credit for all this, express in contrast the great sadness of heart which is felt at finding all these mills quiet and all these thousands and thousands out of work. . . .

I urge that the Governor say, as a climax to this portion of his talk, that it is one of his chief and major concerns to aid these people, employer and employed, to get these mills back into operation and the people at work. . . .

You will see the strategy of my suggestions when I call to your attention the following: For several weeks certain workers of the opposition have been endeavoring to get money from wealthy Republicans here. In times past these same parties in Pittsburgh have contributed tremendous sums to Republican campaigns, but it is different this time. Many meetings and conferences of Republicans have been held here with discouraging results and little money has been obtained thus far. . . .

The showing of an interested, friendly attitude towards this great Steel Industry by the Governor in his speech, as I have suggested, will have a two-fold beneficial effect. It will please the Republican capitalists here who are holding back their financial support to the Republican campaign and, no doubt, will stiffen their determination to make little or no contribution, and in addition it will especially please the thousands of voters here whose income directly and indirectly depends on this industry. . . .

Yours very truly,

Beyond the offering of such advice—which, to repeat, was invariably considered on its merits only—the "practical" men did not intrude. Jesse Straus, for example, got us a suite in the Roosevelt Hotel, asked whether his son Bob, couldn't be helpful to us, and then left us strictly to our own devices. Will Woodin quietly and modestly told us that he'd be glad to give us any information he could on railroads and banking ("the only two things, outside of music, I know a little something about") and then did not reappear until we asked for his help two months later. Bernie Baruch presented us with a copy of a memorandum he had sent to Roosevelt on the necessity of keeping our policy group separated from political headquarters, with the services of Hugh Johnson, and with a magnificent draft speech on the economics of Hoover which he and Johnson had prepared. Baruch's contributions to the party's war chest were no concern of ours, but we gradually came to look upon his generous intellectual contributions with admiration, respect, and gratitude. To us he eventually became just a "brains truster," and one of the best at that.

As our fears about the self-interest and conservatism of these men vanished, with it went the last of our delusions that "fat cats" or "machine" politicians were, in the very nature of things, inevitably bent on influencing party policies for their own special ends. *Noblesse,* apparently, could *oblige.* Paradoxically, our problem turned out to be that of getting practical men to give us the benefit of their experienced judgments rather than that of resisting their influence.

2

We, on our side, must have been the source of some surprises too. One might have supposed that, as professors, we would have neat, logical, systematic ways of doing things, wholly aside from the question whether what we did was any good. But the confusion that prevailed at political headquarters was more conspicuous than the loose-jointed disorder of our work only because headquarters was open to public view.

During most of July we had no real place of meeting. My little Columbia office could not actually hold more than three or four visitors—and then only if I chased out my secretary and assistant, who would be obliged to sit around in halls or empty classrooms for a few hours carrying on their work there as best they could. Into this bottleneck flowed letters, manuscripts, and telephone calls by the hundreds each week, and a steady stream of people with "ideas" for the campaign—visitors and communications chiefly referred there by Roosevelt's office in Albany and by Farley and Howe in New York. So the work simply had to be scattered. Sometimes we met in my apartment or in Berle's office or Tugwell's, sometimes we interviewed people in the lobby of the Biltmore or Roosevelt hotels; the preparation of the detailed material on the topics Roosevelt had outlined in Chicago was done in any place we happened to find ourselves; and the huge bundles of letters were divided up among us.

The business of handling correspondence, as a matter of fact, proved more of a chore than any outsider could imagine. Louis insisted that it was politically important that as many letters as possible go out over the Roosevelt signature. In the Governor's office at Albany was what could only be described as a letter-writing mill. Letters were dictated by various people and signed by someone who was expert in imitating Roosevelt's signature. Early in the summer another person with this peculiar gift was found, and a mill of the same sort was set up in New York under Louis' general direction. Theoretically, these machines did not handle letters that dealt with policy. They were supposed to send out merely amiable acknowledgments and pass along to us letters calling for more complicated answers. But every time I looked over the stacks of replies they turned out I would find what seemed to me dangerous commitments to this policy or that, and I often felt that if the Republicans could have got hold of any considerable number of the letters handled in this manner they might have had a field day. There is no doubt that contradictions of all sorts were sent forth over what purported to be Roosevelt's signature.[1]

I made off, of course, with as many of these as I could lay hands on and added them to the piles of letters shipped to us in the first place. We undertook to answer them with great care and check them for consistency and prudence before we sent them upstate to be signed by the candidate himself. But since we were all sadly in need of space and equipment, we could scarcely handle them with efficiency or dispatch.

But it was not only the lack of physical facilities that made system out of the question. We found that out when we set up shop in the Roosevelt Hotel suite made available late in July. The apartment consisted of a sitting room, a dining room, and a bedroom. The bedroom was kept for the use of important out-of-town collaborators. The dining room was transformed into a conference and workroom for us. In the sitting room were installed Bob Straus and John Dalton of the Harvard Business School. These two young men not only sifted a good deal of

[1] The custom of having other people sign Roosevelt's letters was abolished when Roosevelt entered the White House. But it is probable that the autograph dealers will be flooded for over a hundred years with the signatures penned by Louis' "experts" during the campaign.

the material that came in and interviewed casual visitors, but dug up statistical information and prepared short memoranda under our direction on various occasions.

Yet these were only the vestiges of order. The nature of the work itself precluded systemization. We were at once working up the material for specific speeches, pushing ahead with the broad economic education of ourselves and Roosevelt, adopting or rejecting thousands of ideas that poured in on us, and trying to observe the elementary political maxim that no one who voluntarily offered suggestions or plans, however silly, to the candidate must be sent away unhappy. Expertness in at least one field, clearheadedness, cool judgment, unfailing accuracy, good humor, exquisite tact, an iron constitution, and the ability to write well were the minimum requisites for such service. Since none of us possessed all of them, we had to shift about, making up for one another's deficiencies as well as might be.

It wasn't methodical. Beyond the fact that it all tied in through me to Roosevelt, there was no consistency. Beyond my fortnightly reports to him stating who was preparing what and when it would be ready, there were no blueprints. But it worked anyhow, and that was all that mattered.

Here, for instance—and this will illustrate our technique, or lack of one—is how one of the major speeches of the campaign, that on agriculture, was prepared.

During the early sessions of the "brains trust" at Albany and in the memoranda of May 19th, Rex Tugwell had discussed at length a new plan for the relief of agriculture which was being developed by a number of agricultural economists throughout the country. Late in June he was assigned to go to a meeting in Chicago, sponsored by the Giannini Foundation for Agricultural Economics, examine the plan in detail, and report back. He did. And out of that trip came the discovery of M. L. Wilson, a professor in the Montana State College at Bozeman.

Immediately after the convention we invited Wilson to come to New York. Rex, he, and I sat in my office for the better part of a day while he explained in detail what the "Voluntary Domestic Allotment Plan" (the name of the new scheme) was, the extent of its support among farm organization leaders, and its political and economic possibilities. When he had answered most of our arguments, we decided to take him to Albany. Roosevelt was persuaded. But that was only the beginning.

Wilson visited New York two or three times during July and early August, and we carried our discussions further. Finally, in mid-August we asked him to prepare a memorandum which might be the basis of a speech and to go over it with Henry A. Wallace, the editor of *Wallaces' Farmer and Iowa Homestead,* before sending it to us. Wallace was friendly to Roosevelt. We knew he favored the plan; but we were eager to have his detailed suggestions on substance and language, for there was no one more familiar than he with the tastes and prejudices of the great farm area whose traditional Republican allegiance Roosevelt had to destroy if he was to be elected.

On August 23rd I received the manuscript and the following letter from Wilson:

> Dear Dr. Moley:
>
> I was unable to see Mr. Wallace until today. We went over my manuscript very carefully. He commended it quite highly and had only two important suggestions to make. I shall refer to his suggestions in the course of this letter.
>
> We are agreed as to the logic, the point of attack, and the attitude taken in the copy which I am sending you. It lacks punch, clarity and in some places the movement is too slow. I am not a sufficiently accomplished writer to correct these defects. I hope, however, that you can correct these deficiencies. . . .
>
> An introductory section is designed to show that agriculture is not a narrow or class issue.
>
> The speech proper starts with the discussion of Equality for Agriculture and the reference to the prices of things which farmers buy and purchasing power of things which they sell. This savors a little of the old McNary-Haugen dogma and is designed to attract the attention of the great mass of farmers who have been influenced by the "Equality for Agriculture" Movement for the past eight years. You of course know that this discussion has reached the ears of practically every farmer in the United States. The strategy of the speech is that it is addressed to the type of farmer who may possibly be influenced to switch his vote from Republican to Democrat. Now, this class of farmer in the corn belt and wheat belt is by heredity a Republican; even in spite of the campaign for "Equality for Agriculture" he voted for Hoover four years ago. But even so—this phrase "Equality for Agriculture" has a sort of magic appeal for him; it is fixed in his sub-conscious mind and carries both a hope for better times and a resentment against the President and his so-called Eastern Republicans. It is my judgment that there are hundreds of thousands of farmers this year who will switch their votes providing this "Equality for Agriculture" idea is properly stimulated. . . .
>
> The paragraphs dealing with the explanation of the agricultural depression perhaps can be condensed. They are designed to give a

statesmanlike approach to the attack on Mr. Hoover which follows in the Historical section. . . .

Now, Mr. Wallace suggested that at this point a section should be introduced which shows that the Hoover speech leaves the farmer in a rat hole, so to speak, with no possible avenue of escape. He thinks this is a most important point—that it should be dramatized to the limit. . . . Mr. Wallace's assistant wrote out a little idea using the figure of speech of a farmer being in the bottom of a huge pit. I am attaching his first attempt to formulate the idea to this letter. . . .

I have given very careful and thoughtful attention to the wording of the section on the Voluntary Allotment Plan or the method of handling the surplus. I weighed every phrase in this section. Mr. Wallace approves it wholeheartedly. Perhaps it might be condensed. However, it is the one constructive thing in the speech that will be listened to most carefully. It must be convincingly worded so that his listeners feel that he has a workable plan and is earnest in its advocacy. . . .

I assume that the section on Land Use Planning will be prepared by someone else. I am afraid that too much of the speech will be given to the policy and experience in New York, which is of little interest west of the Allegheny Mountains. Mr. Wallace also concurs in this. . . .

The summary which I am attaching to this copy was written by Mr. Wallace. It, in my judgment, is more valuable as a suggestion than anything else. You know much better how to include this than I do. . . .

Hastily yours,
M. L. Wilson

With the Wilson and Wallace memoranda in hand I began to bring together and correlate the work of many others. Henry Morgenthau, Jr., and his assistant, Herbert E. Gaston, had prepared memoranda on the planned use of land, on oppressive farm taxation, and on the burden of farm debt. Meanwhile I had told Hugh Johnson that an agriculture speech was simmering on the stove.

Johnson had, by now, become a fixture of our little group. Baruch had dropped him into our midst casually enough; but, once there, he exploded, like an elaborate fireworks display, into a series of enchanting patterns. We had a preview of all the color, spirit, and versatility that were later to fix the eyes of the country on him, and it captivated us.

Johnson loved to dash off speeches—particularly scathing analyses of the Hoover policies—and loved even more to read them aloud with gusto. The night that we first took him to Albany he began declaiming the memorandum he and Baruch had prepared on the economics of the Hoover regime. I had heard it twice before, and so I escaped to the second floor of the Mansion to get a nap. I should have known better. The mighty roar of Johnson's voice carried through the walls and ceilings as though they were those of a Japanese house. Occasionally there would be a pause, and Roosevelt's loud laughter would ring out. It sounded as if they were having the time of their lives. I gave up the ghost, finally, and rejoined them. We missed the train back to New York that night, borrowed pajamas (all of us but Hugh, who went through an impressive business of flinging open all the windows, dashing cold water over himself, bouncing onto the unopened bed, cavalryman fashion, and dropping instantly into a noisy sleep), and acquired an indefatigable recruit.

When I asked for his suggestions on agriculture in August, he characteristically responded with a complete manuscript of a draft speech which contained much excellent material.

This mass of stuff I laid before Roosevelt. He then dictated an introductory passage intended to portray him as a friend of agriculture, several pages on the reorganization of the Department of Agriculture, and the like. At that point it became my job to correlate his dictation, Wilson's memorandum, Wallace's supplementary statement, Johnson's proposed speech, and the material provided by Morgenthau and Gaston.

Into the draft went passages from all this material. When it was completed, it was passed around for criticism. Berle contributed a couple of sentences on the farm-debt problem and the phrase "political skywriting." Tugwell, Johnson, Morgenthau, and Gaston went over it in detail and made many amendments. M. L. Wilson sent it back with further suggestions, among them the expression "the shadow of peasantry," which lent itself to effective oratorical expansion. Roosevelt added the phrase "half 'boom' and half 'broke.' " I borrowed from Maitland's immortal *History of the English Law* the "seamless web" idea. Several farm editors, notably Clifford V. Gregory, editor of *The Prairie Farmer,* and a senator or two made helpful corrections.

When the speech was finally delivered under Topeka's blistering sun on September 14th, it was a first-rate document—substantively and strategically. It laid down a set of specifications that forecast the New Deal's farm policy. More than any other single speech in the entire campaign, it captured the votes of the Middle Western farmers. Finally, it outlined the Domestic Allotment Plan without mentioning its name—outlined it so delicately that the urban voters, editors, and newspapermen accepted its broad propositions as generalities too vague to require examination. It won the Midwest without waking up the dogs of the East.

And this speech was the direct product of more than twenty-five people!

Imagine the same careful process going on in six or seven different fields: Berle and I working with Will Woodin, Joseph B. Eastman of the Interstate Commerce Commission, Ralph Budd of the Burlington, Walter M. W. Splawn (then special counsel to the House Committee on Interstate and Foreign Commerce), Donald R. Richberg (counsel of the Railway Labor Executives Association), and a half dozen others on the draft of a railroad speech for Roosevelt; Hugh Johnson, Fred Telford, Ralph Robey, Schuyler Wallace, Alexander Sachs, and Paul M. Mazur (both of Lehman Corporation), Aubrey Romine of Standard Statistics, and Swagar Sherley (former Chairman of the House Appropriations Committee) at work on finance; Kemper Simpson (Senator Costigan's expert on tariffs), Charles W. Taussig (a molasses manufacturer), and Senators James F. Byrnes, Key Pittman, Thomas J. Walsh, and Cordell Hull contributing ideas on tariff; and so on and on. Imagine it all going on at the same time, many of the men shifting about, serving now on this, now on that aspect of the work. Consider the differences of opinion and temperament that inevitably cropped up in such groups, the crucial decisions on policy and political strategy that had to be made, the endless meetings, telephonings, draftings, and checkings it all entailed, and you get a picture vaguely hinting of the swirling chaos, the dizzying turmoil of July and August.

3

Late in August, Roosevelt sent the following letter to Newton D. Baker, Owen D. Young, Bernard M. Baruch, Melvin A. Traylor, Guy A. Thompson (then President of the American Bar Association), Colonel Edward M. House, and Senators Pittman, Walsh, Robinson, Hull, and King:

> Dear ——:
>
> Between now and the end of the campaign a good many matters for immediate decision will arise—matters relating to issues and policies of various kinds—and I am asking a small group to hold themselves in readiness for consultation. This will not be in any

> sense a formal advisory committee but only a few people whose judgment I value.
>
> Professor Raymond Moley, of Columbia University, an old friend who has been assisting me in many ways, is acting as a sort of clearing house for me. This part of my task has nothing to do with those who are engaged in the strictly political management of the campaign, but has in a sense a more personal relationship. It would help me in a very practical sense if you would give me your thought on matters from time to time, and if Professor Moley calls you up or writes to you on any specific point, I hope you will feel that it comes from me and that you will confer with him.
>
> Always sincerely,

All of the men to whom this letter was addressed were notable figures in the party. Even if they had had little to contribute to our work, the move would have been a shrewd one. In the case of Baker, particularly, it was the first gracious gesture made by the candidate to the man who probably would have been nominated had Roosevelt failed. In the case of the others it was a not-too-obvious device for enlisting the good will and cooperation of the wise old leaders of the party who, had there been no "brains trust," would themselves have been Roosevelt's policy-making council.

I welcomed it because it dissipated any possibility of resentment on their part against what we were doing. But it was chiefly important because it opened up for me, as liaison officer between the group of nonpolitical economists I had assembled and these tried party leaders, vast stores of learning that would otherwise have been completely inaccessible. The generous response to the Roosevelt letter comprised contributions that ranged all the way from Baker's penetrating letters on foreign affairs to the lessons in craftsmanship some of the senators unconsciously gave every time they opened their mouths.

One such lesson is particularly vivid. I was about to show one of the senators the draft of an important speech prepared for the candidate. He waved me away. "Now before we get talking about the substance of this thing," he said, "remember this: our man is going to be talking in an open field; his speech is going to be broadcast, but there won't be auxiliary microphones spread around to pick up applause; there'll have to be a helluva lot of cheering—and loud cheering—if the speech isn't going to sound like a dud to people listening at home. I'd construct this speech so the Chief gets a cheer at the end of the first four-hundred words, another at the end of the second four-hundred, then six-hundred later. After that you don't have to worry. The crowd'll be in such a state, they'll yell for anything."

This was hardly the approach I had expected from the party's senatorial expert on the issue with which the speech was concerned. It left me reeling for a few seconds. But when I had recovered my balance, I was able to listen and learn.

The senators knew such tricks of the trade—dozens of them—that never get described in the textbooks and that are, nevertheless, as much the stuff of American political life as the activities of Bosses Murphy and Hague. And they were completely unselfish in passing on the lore they had patiently amassed through the years.

Yet the new function I was called upon to play was no young ladies' finishing-school affair. It brought me face to face at last with those deep-seated rifts which are at the heart of party politics. It plunged me into those processes of clash and compromise whose mastery is the art of statesmanship.

Viewed in the light of hindsight, the most ominous of these battles during the campaign centered in the tariff issue, an apple of discord that had disrupted the Democratic party for a generation.

The premonitory rumblings began sometime in August when I asked Charles W. Taussig to go to Tennessee and get Senator Hull's tariff ideas. Taussig's vague attachment to our group was even then the source of misunderstanding. He had first met Roosevelt on the return trip from Warm Springs in May, when he found that the Governor's car was attached to the train on which he was traveling, sent in his card, and was invited in for a short talk. Roosevelt had told me to get in touch with him, some weeks later, in terms which led me to believe that Taussig was an old friend whom he wished me to consult regularly. And so I included him in many of our conferences, trying, so far as possible, to give him occasional assignments suitable to his somewhat specialized capacities. Despite his willingness and amiability some of the members of our group were extremely impatient with him, failing, it seemed, to see in him those qualities of usefulness that Roosevelt had divined.

Taussig returned from Tennessee and presented a draft tariff speech based on Hull's ideas. We would have been idiotic to expect anything but the advocacy of tariff reductions in the light of Hull's congressional record and Southern loyalties. But we were stunned by the extremity of the major recommendation—that Roosevelt come out for cutting all tariffs by a flat ten per cent.

Now all of us were perfectly familiar with the theoretical argument for free trade. I am certain that we would have agreed, if we could have wiped out a hundred years of history, that tariff barriers should not be erected, just as we would have agreed that the Indians who were induced to sell Manhattan Island for twenty-four dollars' worth of knives and trinkets got a raw deal. But that having been said, we could no more see the practicability of lopping off a great chunk of the tariff wall in 1932 than we could of inviting the Indians to take back Manhattan.

Indiscriminate tariff reduction would have benefited the cotton growers, to be sure, while it would have wiped out hundreds of thousands of industrial workers, miners, cattlemen, and all others who, for better or for worse, had by then come to live under the protecting shadow of the tariff. Moreover, it was impossible to put under way those immense economic readjustments designed to help create balance between agriculture and industry, stability and security of livelihood, and adequate domestic purchasing power—the essential objectives of the New Deal—at the same moment that one embarked on a crusade to restore free trade.

It was not that tariff reduction was per se incompatible with the economics of the New Deal that was taking shape. But there was a crucial question of timing and method that those who adhered to the Hull school of thought blandly ignored.

There were groans of anguish in our rooms at the Roosevelt while the Hull-Taussig draft was being read, and a babel of argument when it was finished. Hugh Johnson offered to prepare an alternative draft, summoned in the stenographers, and paced up and down the apartment for half the night dictating it. It was, in essence, a proposal for the gradual reopening of the channels of commerce by skillful bilateral negotiation. Foreign outlets for our most oppressive domestic surpluses were to be secured by a series of "old-fashioned Yankee horse-trades" admitting those foreign products which would least disturb the domestic system.

I put the two drafts before Roosevelt early in September and asked how he would like me to proceed. He knew where my choice lay, but this was no question anyone else could decide for him. He read the two through with seeming care. And then he left me speechless by announcing that I had better "weave the two together."

It was, for once, an impossible assignment. I explained. "Well, then," he said, "let it go until we get on the train. We'll see what we can do about it there."[2]

A week went by on the train while we worked on all sorts of other things. Bellefontaine, Indianapolis, Jefferson City, Topeka, Goodland, Limon, Denver, Cheyenne, Laramie, Ogden, Pocatello, Butte, Everett, Portland swept past—and still no decision. At last, as we neared San Francisco, just six hectic days before the tariff speech was to be delivered at Sioux City, he found time to reexamine the two drafts and a sheaf of letters commenting on them from men to whom I had sent the two copies—notably Lindsay Rogers, Senator Costigan, and M. L. Wilson.

Wilson's letter seemed to impress him deeply. It pointed out that the reaction to a horizontal tariff reduction proposal in the West and Middle West would be immediate and devastating. There was a strong sentiment there for tariff *increases* on certain commodities! Hoover himself was planning to take advantage of it by a vigorous defense of the tariff at Des Moines. He would hold the corn and wheat belts if Roosevelt slipped up at Sioux City.

Roosevelt read this letter two or three times. Then he looked up and said: "You'd better get Tom Walsh and Key Pittman [both of whom had joined us on the train] to work with you on the speech."

"You know what that will mean?" I asked. Walsh and Pittman were both high-tariff men, and, though I was overjoyed by this statement of his, I could not, in honesty, permit it to pass without being certain he understood its implications.

His face became utterly expressionless. "We'll see," he said.

I was in the Palace Hotel in San Francisco the next morning, just after arranging to have Walsh stop off with me for two days at Santa Barbara for preliminary work on the speech, when Taussig suddenly appeared. He had, he informed me, come from talking to Mr. Roosevelt, and Mr. Roosevelt had invited him to board the train and travel back East with him. I had known that Taussig would be in California for some sort of conference when we passed through. But this invitation was at once a surprise and a signal for trouble. Yet there was now nothing to do but ask Taussig to join Walsh and myself at Santa Barbara.

[2] Roosevelt's major campaign trip, the swing through the West, began on September 12th and ended on October 3rd. He made two other trips, a Midwestern and Southern trip, October 18th to October 26th, and a New England trip, October 29th to November 1st.

The grizzled old Senator snorted as I described the sequence of events that accounted for Taussig's presence. When the three of us sat down to work in Santa Barbara, he glared at Taussig and bluntly announced that we would use as a basis of work the Johnson draft. If he expected so much as a murmur of objection, he was outwitted. Taussig looked innocently at the Pacific and said that he was agreeable.

Walsh pushed the Hull-Taussig draft aside, picked up a pencil, and began to edit the Johnson manuscript. Later on Walsh leaned back in his chair, fixed his eyes on Taussig, and said, "You know, I hardly see how you can help us further. We have this"—pointing to the draft he was conspicuously ignoring. "If I were you I'd just go back to San Francisco." There was no beating around the bush. It was a command to leave.

I have always regretted the brusqueness with which Walsh spoke then. But when he had made up his mind, he was no man to trifle with. As one of the greatest warriors in the Democratic party, the man who, with the elder La Follette and Wheeler, had discredited the Harding Administration and who, but for the death of Harding, might have driven the Republicans from office, he spoke with the voice of authority. Taussig reddened and left us. It was the last we saw of him on that trip, despite the Roosevelt invitation.

Walsh and I worked on. We rejoined the Roosevelt train at Williams, Arizona. This gave us two days to finish up the speech, and he, Pittman, and I fell to in earnest. But Taussig's dismissal was on my conscience. It was as though, in departing, he had left behind a ghost. I had never set eyes on Cordell Hull. But his silvery presence, hurt and resentful, sat in the swaying compartment with us as we rode.

No speech in the campaign was such a headache as this. Not satisfied with the moderation of Johnson's statements, Walsh then proceeded to write into the speech long theoretical arguments answering the long theoretical arguments of the Hull-Taussig draft. Pittman came to the rescue here by boldly striking them out. It would have been courting assault for me to have done so. I knew that even before Walsh roared at Pittman, "Why, you're throwing all my stuff in the wastebasket!" Pittman, lean and gray, and as canny as the old man, in his way, simply smiled sweetly and said, "You know —— well, that's just where it ought to go, you old so and so." Walsh bristled fiercely for a minute. Then he laughed, and the battle was won.

We showed Roosevelt the finished product. He rearranged it somewhat, made a few additions, and, when he had sent away the stenographer, smiled at me gayly. "There! You see? It wasn't as hard as you thought it was going to be."

I allowed that I wouldn't have thought it would be hard at all had I known he was going to ignore the Hulls of the party, substantially, and merely throw them a couple of sops in the form of statements that some of the "outrageously excessive" rates of the Hawley-Smoot tariff would have to come down.

"But you don't understand," he said. "This speech is a compromise between the free traders and the protectionists." And he meant it too!

I reflected that it would take greater persuasive powers than even he possessed to sell this idea that the speech was a compromise to the low-tariff Democrats. I, for one, could see in it only the clear inference that Roosevelt had reaffirmed Al Smith's abandonment of the historic Democratic position of "tariff for revenue only" and come out for the principle of "protection"—despite the incidental criticism of the kind of "protection" the Republicans had provided in the Hawley-Smoot Act.

I was yet to learn the uses of self-deception.

So, apparently, was Cordell Hull. Word drifted up from Tennessee later that he was profoundly grieved by Roosevelt's tariff stand. But the poor man did not learn what heartbreak could really be until after March 4th, when he began to live with Roosevelt's tariff policies.

The story took an ironic turn almost at once. Hoover demanded that Roosevelt specify what tariffs he felt were too high. So many hundreds of telegrams came in from farmers and processors asking whether the reference to "outrageously excessive" rates in the Sioux City speech applied to the duties on this commodity or that, that Roosevelt himself decided to temper his statement on the Hawley-Smoot tariff. And so, in Baltimore, he turned his phrase around. "I know of no effective, excessively high tariff duties on farm products. I do not intend that such duties shall be lowered," he said, rebutting the attack the Republicans were making throughout the West and Middle West.

There was more word eating to come. Immediately, the barrage from the East and Northeast began. Did Roosevelt mean to suggest that the tariffs on manufactured articles were too high? In Boston, at almost the tail end of the campaign, the candidate manfully finished the job: "I favor—and do not let the false statements of my opponents deceive you—continued protection for American agriculture as well as American industry."

If this was "compromise" Cordell Hull was Senators Pittman and

Walsh. Yet Roosevelt continued to believe that it was. So began seven years of evasion and cross-purposes on the tariff.

But for the student of statesmanship the process was instructive.

4

Some years ago Edward G. Lowry, a talented Washington correspondent, spoke of Bryan as the greatest of American troubadours, the modern Raimbaut d'Aurenga.[3] A new claimant arrived to contest the honor in 1932, for almost obscuring the import of his speeches was the image of Roosevelt, the troubadour, that emerged from the campaign.

It was announced in July that Roosevelt's campaign trips in the autumn would be made for the purposes of "looking, listening and learning." That, of course, was a springe to catch woodcocks.

To Roosevelt a good cause does not justify any trip: a good trip justifies any cause. Campaigning, for him, was unadulterated joy. It was broad rivers, green forests, waving corn, and undulating wheat; it was crowds of friends, from the half dozen who, seated on a baggage truck, waved to the cheery face at the speeding window to perspiring thousands at a race track or fairground; it was hands extended in welcome, voices warm with greeting, faces reflecting his smile along the interminable wayside. These are the things that ever and ever renew the life of the troubadour. What has "learning" to do with friendship and happiness? Travel is to make friends and influence people. And travel is in the blood of the *Reise*-Roosevelts.

From early morning, when Gus Gennerich or Marvin McIntyre wakened him to announce that he must hurry to appear on the back platform at the next station, until late at night, as the train puffed away from the last stop, he never wearied or lost his good humor. Between September 12th and November 7th he traveled about thirteen thousand miles, made sixteen major speeches and sixty-seven second-string speeches—not to mention innumerable back-platform appearances—talked to hundreds of people who boarded the train to ride from one station to another—governors, senators, mayors, obscure county politicians, farmers, miners, mineowners, tradespeople, local bankers, newspaper owners, reporters, manufacturers, welfare workers—and never stopped having a wonderful time.

[3] *Washington Close-Ups* by Edward G. Lowry. Houghton Mifflin Company; Boston, 1921; p. 42.

Such campaign trips, like our national political conventions, have no counterpart anywhere else in the world. Their next of kin is the traveling circus. But while countless stories and plays have brought the public behind the scenes with the bareback riders, clowns, and lions, life on the train of a presidential candidate remains pretty much of a mystery.

The lean and wiry McIntyre, whom I had first met in Louis' rooms in Chicago, and whose appointment as political secretary to Roosevelt Louis had since secured, was the harried general manager. He arranged the train's schedule, assigned the sleeping quarters, made appointments, greeted visitors, and handled the press, charging madly up and down the length of the train scores of times each day while his towering assistant, Arthur Mullen, Jr., lumbered after him. With his hands full of telegrams, papers, tickets, mimeograph stencils, and press releases, Mac must have run twenty miles every day we were traveling.

One or more members of Roosevelt's family was always on the train. That, needless to say, is *de rigueur*. The well-groomed candidate no more appears without a visible symbol of his happy family life than he appears with his shirt off. Mrs. Roosevelt, Anna, Jimmy, and Jimmy's wife, who were all, at one time or another, with us, accompanied F. D. R. to the big meetings and stood with him when he made his brief rear-platform talks. His "This is my *little* boy, Jimmy," in fact, never failed to get a laugh from the crowds who had waited patiently at forlorn depots "just to get at look at the next President," though it did seem to us kibitzers that Jimmy grew depressed after the fifteenth or twentieth performance.

There was, naturally, a car for the candidate and his family. There were several cars almost filled with newspapermen, cameramen, radio announcers, and representatives of the telegraph companies. There was a car for "visiting firemen"—those dignitaries whose status called for some days of jaunting with the candidate as compared with the four- or five-hour allowance accorded the lesser band-wagon riders. And there were two cars for the more or less permanent members of the troupe.

These included Jim Farley, who joined us at Salt Lake City and left at Los Angeles; Joe Kennedy; Charles C. Pettijohn, a veteran of the movie industry, who watched over newsreel relations and, at every stop, made contacts with motion-picture distributors and exhibitors to win their good will for the candidate; Judge Robert S. Marx of Cincinnati, taken along as a good-luck token because he had traveled with Roosevelt on the campaign trips of 1920;[4] Key Pittman and Swagar Sherley, whose chief job was to protect some of the less experienced of us against mistakes; and two wizard court stenographers, George A. Glendon, Jr., and Henry Kannee, who not only prepared the press releases, but took down every speech, prepared or extemporaneous, as Roosevelt made it, for "the record."

There were two others in our car—old Jack Cohen, a veteran newspaperman, publisher of the *Atlanta Journal* and, for the nonce, a senator from Georgia, and Breckinridge Long, an Assistant Secretary of State under Wilson. Their role was frankly to surround the visitors with a friendly, all-embracing spirit of welcome. They were both glorious entertainers—quick to laugh at the other fellow's stories, possessed of an incredible stock of anecdotes themselves, smooth, keen-witted, and amiable.

My job didn't permit of many diversions, and I was often torn with envy of the conviviality that went on in the other rooms of the car. Far into the night I would hear the gay voices of Breck, Jack, Swagar, some of the newspapermen, and the "visiting firemen." Those were tantalizing sounds to a weary struggler over the complexities of railroad debt, budgets, or what not.

The notion that Roosevelt's speeches were shaped around the things that he learned on the trip is so much fiction. Occasionally a Governor Dern would make a suggestion that lent itself to embroidery in the introductory remarks of a speech—a pleasant reference to some local tradition or achievement that delighted the audience. But the fact of the matter is that I brought on the train almost finished drafts for many of the major speeches and very elaborate memoranda for seventy-five per cent of the others. It was the entire product of two and a half months of labor by the "brains trust"—a product, I hasten to add, about which Roosevelt had been constantly consulted.

This is not to suggest for a minute that there were not endless additions and revisions on the train, endless pullings apart and whippings together. No political speech can ever be finished until the moment when the mimeographers throw up their hands and announce that they positively cannot get it ready in time for the newspapermen.

For the weeks on the train, circumstances kept me a virtual pris-

[4] Like most politicians, Roosevelt was intensely superstitious. His desire to have Judge Marx on the train is one instance. Another was his insistence on wearing the same hat throughout the entire campaign.

oner in my compartment, which was piled high with reference books and memoranda. I would escape only to go look for Sherley, Pittman, or Walsh, to slip in and out of Roosevelt's car, next door, or to speak to the newspapermen. I so rarely got to the public meetings at which F. D. R. spoke that I valued the reporters' comments on each speech. They were exceedingly good, too, in helping me predetermine public reactions to various ideas and statements. This service I tried to repay by giving them "background" on the subject matter of the speeches whenever they wanted it.

I have been asked, perhaps a thousand times, whether I was not, on these trips, what is conventionally called Roosevelt's "ghost writer." The honest answer is "No." The term is utterly unfair as applied to the course we followed. There are many who claim paternity for speeches Roosevelt made in 1932. No one, except Roosevelt, is in a better position than I to say they exaggerate and distort the part they played.

My job from the beginning—and this continued for four years—was to sift proposals for him, discuss facts and ideas with him, and help him crystallize his own policy. At the end of this process we were generally in agreement. But when we were not, and after I had stated my case as well as I could, it was my business to see that his ideas were presented as attractively as possible. Memoranda supplied by Tugwell, Johnson, Berle, and others were liberally used. Yet hardly a sentence remained unchanged when it went into the finished product. (I had sworn "Never again!" after the Lindsay Rogers episode.) I constantly tried to induce Roosevelt to dictate as much as he possibly could between speeches and appointments. I then spun together the pertinent material, as in the agriculture speech. This new draft Roosevelt would pencil over with comments. The draft would shuttle back and forth, back and forth, between us until the language of the original memorandum prepared by someone or other was almost completely obliterated.

If anyone is able to determine with exactness what I contributed to this cooperative process, he will be doing a great deal more than I can. The job wasn't that of "literary secretary": that term doesn't cover the function of counseling on policy; helping to shape substance; watching out for inconsistencies, plain errors of fact, and political boners. Nor was it that of "brains truster," for that term leaves out the technique of knowing how to put a speech together—the physical two-man job of final preparation. There isn't a label to describe our unique personal relationship.

No one can quite realize the dreadful feeling of responsibility that this entailed. Roosevelt instinctively trusted the people with whom he was associated. His mind, while it was capacious and while its windows were open on all sides to new impressions, facts, and knowledge, was neither exact nor orderly. Deep in his heart, I think, he knew this, because he seldom trusted himself to say in public more than a few sentences extemporaneously, though I doubt that he would admit that he is often inaccurate in casual conversation. I labored with the tormenting knowledge that I could not afford to be wrong. There was too much at stake. For a man who hated hard work, who could hardly be called a fact hound, no better form of torture could have been devised. The flagellants lack ingenuity.

One incident I remember clearly illustrates the conditions under which I worked. The evening before we arrived at Topeka the speech on agriculture had been completed and mimeographed. Its great length made it necessary that it be given to the newspapermen early so that they would have time to get it out over the wires for the afternoon papers. I have already indicated the immense amount of work and checking that had gone into it. Well, that evening Arthur Mullen, *père,* Democratic National Committeeman from Nebraska, brought into my cubicle a man named Murphy. Murphy seemed to be deeply interested in the farm problem. As a friendly gesture, I let them examine the press release. When he was halfway through, Murphy remarked, "This speech is full of inaccuracies." I asked him to state what he thought was inaccurate. He pointed to three or four passages which were statements of policy. I told him that those questions had been decided, but that if there were any errors of fact I would be glad to see that they were changed. He then announced that a figure in the speech, an index of farm prices, was incorrect. I checked the figure by means of a telegram to the Department of Agriculture and found that it was right.

Late that night Murphy sought to continue the argument in the dining car. He had given me a few bad hours and I asked him with a certain amount of acerbity to leave me in peace—a regrettable move, because the next day he sought out Roosevelt at the very instant the party was leaving the train, and told him that the fact in question was wrong. Roosevelt's speech had gone to the press. He was about to deliver it. No more upsetting remark could have been made to him. He looked nervously at me, and I assured him he needn't worry. He did, of course. Before he read the sentence containing the figure, he halted for one breathless moment.

The figure was never questioned again. I never saw or heard of Murphy again. But there were Murphys underfoot all through the campaign, and they made life no easier.

Those days on the trip were tense with excitement and rich with color.

There were frightening moments, as when Roosevelt's open car was literally mobbed by friendly people while he was on his way to the hotel in San Francisco and an overenthusiastic admirer nearly twisted his arm off by holding on to his hand when the car moved forward.

There was drama, as when we battled with Senator Walsh to get him to strike out of his remarks introducing Roosevelt at Butte a reference to "the golden calf" which might have precipitated the inflation issue; or when, after locking horns with Pittman, Walsh, Dill, and the others who wanted to "do something for silver" en route to Seattle, I got Roosevelt to say "there are many ways of producing the results desired without disturbing the currency of the United States."[5]

There was suspense, as when we crossed the line into California and, remembering Charles Evans Hughes' fate in 1916, suspiciously waited for something disastrous to happen. We were jittery when two archenemies, William G. McAdoo and Justus Wardell, whom McAdoo had just defeated in a bitterly contested senatorial primary, boarded the train at almost the same moment. And, still remembering Hughes, we bit our lips out of sheer nervousness as Roosevelt spoke the sentences designed to induce Hiram Johnson, who had not yet declared himself, to come out for him.

There were moments of ecstatic relief, as when McAdoo and Wardell came smilingly out of Roosevelt's car; or when Hiram Johnson, taken completely by surprise, responded to Roosevelt's remarks with a gallant declaration of support.

Once or twice I was deeply moved, notably as I heard Roosevelt deliver his now famous speech to the Commonwealth Club in San

[5] Roosevelt, however, insisted on deleting the preceding sentence which read: "So far as . . . my policy is concerned we cannot submit to any plan which includes the remonetization of silver." During the struggle with the bimetallists on the train, I kept in constant touch by telephone with Johnson and Baruch to test the Eastern reaction to various possible statements on money. I believe it is generally known that all of us who were included in the "brains trust" were "sound-money" men.

Francisco.[6] But there was a moment less public and, to me, even more impressive. We were at work on the speech to be given at Milwaukee. Roosevelt had dictated long passages on the dairy industry, inland waterways, and other subjects that seemed wholly uninspiring, although it had been my idea that, as a gesture of friendship to the La Follettes, he talk about general progressive ideals and about the University of Wisconsin, of which the people of the state are enormously proud. When the Roosevelt dictation was transcribed, he offered to read it aloud to Mrs. Roosevelt, McIntyre, Pittman, myself, and one or two others, and abide by our judgment. He did. Almost all of us found it dull. "Very well," he said, tearing up his draft and tossing it into the wastepaper basket. "We'll do one on the University." It was a brave and splendid thing to do. And I thought, "If he can only hold tight to that modesty and that honesty when he gets to be President, if he can only keep free of false pride and listen to unselfish advice, he will be a very great man."

Often there were episodes of pure comedy. One came as I sat in an automobile with Jim Farley and a strange little man, pink with excitement, suddenly leaped on the running board and yelled, "Why, *you* remember me, Jim! I ain't seen you for thirty years." It was true. It was a voice out of Farley's boyhood. Anyhow, Jim *always* remembered the people who began with "You remember me, Jim!" Nothing would do but that the little man must ride with us in the candidate's procession, to be gaped at and cheered by the crowds on the sidewalks, while Jim brought him up to date on the news of Grassy Point, New York.

There was another that came at the end of the frenzied twenty-hour day that began at the northern border of California and brought us to San Francisco—the day of McAdoo, Wardell, Hiram Johnson, and

[6] So much has been said about the origins of the Commonwealth speech that I think it is only fair to describe them. Roosevelt had originally planned to deliver merely a brief and unimportant greeting to the Club, which was meeting at noon. Knowing that it was an association of extraordinarily intelligent men devoted to the nonpartisan discussion of great public issues, I urged him to make a major speech there—to sum up, in fact, his political philosophy. He agreed. The idea of such a summary had come from Dalton and Bob Straus early in August, although they had no idea of how it should be done or where delivered, and I had asked Berle to make a draft of the ideas we had all been discussing from April through to September—the ideas that were the basic chart of thought by which Roosevelt had been guided. Berle sent a fine draft to me while I was on the train, after going over it with Baruch and Johnson. Pittman and I worked on it, on and off, as did Roosevelt himself. It passed through the same mill that every other speech went through, and was not finally completed until the early morning before it was delivered.

the arm twisting. It was two o'clock in the morning. For three hours we had been putting the last touches on the Commonwealth speech. At last it was finished, and I was ready to drop in my tracks. To my amazement, then, Roosevelt leaned back in his chair and said, "Now let's talk about what the steps ought to be after I go into office on March 4th." Thereupon he began to outline with extraordinary prescience some of the things that he actually did do in those eventful days of March and April. This went on for some time. Finally, when I could ward off the numbness of sleep no longer, I blurted out, "Don't you think you ought to go to bed now?" I wished the people who expressed concern over his health in those days could have seen him at that moment—alive, happy, energetic. "But I'm not tired," he answered. I was desperate. Looking ominously about the room, I intoned lugubriously, "Do you realize that this is the room in which Harding died?" I was wrong: my fellow Ohioan had departed this life on another floor. But the effect of my verbal bogeyman was instantaneous. Roosevelt wilted. And then, of course, realizing what had happened, we both shook with laughter. "All right. Go to bed, go to bed, you Jeremiah, and I'll read the newspapers until I get sleepy," he said.

But Louis Howe was the cause of the most hilarious incident of the entire Western trip. It seems that after we had left New York, on the 12th of September, Baruch and Hugh Johnson had prepared a broadside on the budget and federal finances. They enlisted Louis as an enthusiastic supporter of the idea that Roosevelt should deliver such a speech when he reached Chicago, and Louis began arguing with Roosevelt about it by long-distance telephone and telegraph at Williams. He did not stop arguing until we reached Chicago and F. D. R. ordered him, face to face, to "hush up" about it. But that was after he had sent me an eight-thousand-word telegram containing the text of the speech (a copy of which had already reached me by mail), numberless supplementary telegrams, and been told by Roosevelt nine or ten times over the telephone that he did not wish to make such a speech, if at all, until later in the campaign.[7] The comedy resulted from one of Louis' calls.

[7] F. D. R. was frankly reluctant to launch an attack upon Ogden Mills on the basis of a memorandum from one source, however trustworthy. Mills was in possession of all the facts on federal finance; he was a master of his subject, a dangerous fighter, and a resourceful campaigner. He was, moreover, about to make a swing across the country himself, and such a speech from Roosevelt at that time would obviously have given Mills more of a hearing than he would otherwise have got. It was elementary strategy to compel Mills to attack the positions which Roosevelt had already occupied and which he was certain he could hold.

Such telephone calls always interrupted the stage management of a rear-platform talk. Ideally, these platform talks had to be begun almost at the moment that the train stopped and the crowd assembled on the tracks, and be concluded at the moment the train started to move. There could not be a delay at either end without ruining the desired effect. So, whenever a stationmaster rushed on the train with a telephone to attach in Roosevelt's private car, there was bound to be a mix-up.

Louis had tried to get Roosevelt on the phone at two or three stops in a row. Eventually, feeling that Louis must have something urgent on his mind, Roosevelt arranged to make a short speech at the next stop, turn the platform over to Breck Long, retire into the car, and let Breck talk while the telephone conversation went on. The whole thing proceeded as scheduled. Breck began his talk. I was inside the car and did not know what he was saying, but I could hear the sound of his voice through the door and see his gestures. All went well for five minutes. Then Breck began to run out of material. Louis was apparently arguing about the budget speech, for a change, and Roosevelt was explaining, in full detail again, why he wasn't willing to make it. I began to realize that Breck was in a dreadful situation. He was obviously leading up to one climax after another, expecting on each occasion that the train would start. Occasionally he would glance around into the car with a look so agonizing that I was reminded of some of Doré's figures of lost souls in the lower regions of Hell. Still the conversation went on. Still Breck fidgeted, shouted, gestured, and threw his anguished glances back into the car. Twenty minutes must have passed. Breck was slowly losing not only his voice but his crowd. He had long since lost any conception of what he was saying when Louis was choked off and the train started.

As we hit the home stretch of the Western swing—the longest and most arduous single campaign trip of modern times—there was, for me, even an O. Henry ending.

All of us who had gone through the entire trip, except Roosevelt, were exhausted by the work and strain. The smoke of the riotous torchlight parade in Chicago had completed our physical demoralization. Our throats and our eyes still ached as we pulled out of Detroit, the last stop. Morgenthau, Louis Howe, and some of the others had boarded the train in Chicago. And now, as the train moved eastward, Roosevelt called a council of war: we must plan the next phase of the campaign—the work for October.

I looked around at the faces—those of the fellow travelers gray with fatigue, the others fresh and rested. Suddenly I realized that Louis was missing. I went to the other end of Roosevelt's car and found him talking with Mrs. Roosevelt. I do not know whether Roosevelt forgot to invite this faithful Achates or whether Louis was simply staying away from the conference to show his distaste for all us interlopers. I pleaded with him to join us. Finally he yielded.

But I would have been something more than human if there hadn't flashed into my mind at that second the picture of the days in February and March when a man who wanted to be useful had to run the gantlet of Sam Rosenman and Louis Howe.

5

When I got back to New York on October 3rd, I had to take on, in addition to the work for Roosevelt, the teaching of my classes at Columbia. It was the beginning of a tumultuous academic year during which, no matter what else was going on, I met my classes regularly—except for one week in October when I went on the second campaign trip.[8]

Things began to move faster now at the "brains trust's" headquarters. Tugwell had returned after a retreat caused by his hay fever in August. Hugh Johnson and Berle were on the job. Two senators, Key Pittman and Jimmy Byrnes, who had been wonderfully helpful on the trip, became regular members of our group at my invitation and made our spare bedroom their camp while they were in New York. Taussig reappeared, harboring no grudges, it seemed, about his California experience.

We sat down and took stock.

The public as a whole and careless newspaper commentators, of which there were many, did not see in perspective the speeches Roosevelt had delivered between April and October. The ideas they contained had so often been shrouded by studied generalities that their translation into action, after March 4th, was to come as something of a shock. Hoover and Mills were among the few articulate outsiders who perceived the boldness and coherence of the political and economic proposals that Roosevelt had made, and people weren't much

[8] This, needless to say, was the way I earned my living. But, aside from that, I genuinely loved teaching.

interested in their horrified outcries. Yet many of the main lines of the New Deal had already been publicly forecast.

We had, half-unconsciously, created a new kind of political oratory. Each major speech contained a well-matured exposition of policy. And if those sections of each speech were put together, they formed, in combination, a sweeping program of reform and experiment.

As we summed up these policies—Tugwell, Berle, Johnson, Pittman, Byrnes, and I—we concluded that three major issues remained on which the candidate must declare himself—government finance; industry, labor, and relief; international relations. The rest of the speeches would be mere restatement and, perhaps, but only perhaps, rebuttal.

After further consideration Roosevelt decided to sidetrack the idea of a speech on foreign relations. The Republicans had scrupulously avoided the issue. Public interest in it, during the fall, was at a low point. It seemed needless to raise the question. A declaration of what I understood to be Roosevelt's views on the subject was likely to cost him more undecided votes than it would make for him. He was already sure of the West and Middle West, where his views on foreign affairs would be immensely popular. There was no advantage in alienating those Eastern elements which would shy at his policies.

The speech on government finance—the subject of Louis' persuasions all through the West—Roosevelt at last decided to make at Pittsburgh. A pledge of thoroughgoing conservatism on fiscal policy—that statement has been used to taunt him with increasing frequency as the years have passed. Suffice it to say that he was wholly aware of its implications when he made it. He knew the alternatives because, while none of us, then, was a member of the "borrow and spend" school, we had honestly presented its arguments to him. So far as it is possible for anyone to be positive of anything, I am sure that the speech, as delivered, represented Roosevelt's wholehearted views on government finance.

There remained the occasion for statements on industry, labor, and relief. The first of these was October 6th, when Roosevelt spoke of cooperation within industry to achieve "regularization and planning for balance"—the idea that foreshadowed N.R.A.

Three weeks later, in Boston, came the promise that "no one shall be permitted to starve": where states were unable to carry the burden of relief, the national government would step into the breach. More, there was a promise of "temporary" work in the national forests, on flood prevention, and the like; of a coordinated system of employment exchanges; of "advanced planning of public works"; and of "unemployment reserves" (*i.e.,* unemployment insurance).

The Boston speech of October 31st completed the program of the New Deal. When it was over, with three exceptions, every important venture from 1933 to the summer of 1935 had been outlined.[9]

I might well have concluded then that my work was done except for the battles that had raged over the drafting of that Boston speech.

There had been no essential difference among us as to the ground the speech should cover. But there had been violent disagreement as to the way it should be phrased.

Berle and Tugwell were for a detailed elaboration of the industry-labor program and a sharp attack upon those in government and industry who had countenanced the abuses that existed. Pittman, Byrnes, Johnson, and I were for a general statement of the program and for a moderate approach. We felt keenly the weariness of the public as the campaign drew to a close. By all the signs, we felt, Roosevelt was as good as elected. The time had passed for sounding the tocsins. This was the moment for the dignity and conciliation that befitted a President-elect.

We argued for days about this. It was the one and only major engagement within the "brains trust." We let off steam by writing drafts. There were drafts and drafts and revisions of revisions of drafts crammed into my suitcase when I left the others to their arguments and went off to Boston, determined to prepare a semifinal statement which might well have been entitled "Discretion Is the Better Part of Valor."

Happily, Roosevelt concurred. The speech was knocked into shape the day before it was delivered. All seemed to be well until the evening of the speech. And then the identical issue—the issue of conciliation *vs.* knife throwing—reappeared in another guise.

It was an hour or two before Roosevelt was to go to the meeting. A number of people were in his hotel suite—Jimmy and his wife, Joe Kennedy, Felix Frankfurter, some friends of the Roosevelt children, Mary Cushing and Kay Halle, McIntyre, and myself. There came an urgent call from Louis, and there went through my mind what must have been the 1932 equivalent of "That man's here again!" Louis was excited. Hoover's speech at Madison Square Garden was about to come over the air. Louis understood he was going to make some unpleasant

[9] These exceptions were (1) the abandonment of gold, (2) the "borrow and spend" policies, and (3) the use of the N.R.A. as a quick recovery measure.

references to "The Boss." "Franklin" ought to listen to the speech and answer it in his own.

This sounded like foolish advice, and I was relieved when Roosevelt said he had no intention of listening to the speech, but that the rest of us ought to. I left him alone in his bedroom and went into the sitting room with the others. We turned on the radio and listened, as Hoover proceeded to make one of his most spirited attacks upon Roosevelt. McIntyre and I felt that this was the strategy of desperation and would not make the slightest dent in Roosevelt's strength. Jimmy and Frankfurter disagreed: an immediate answer in kind ought to be made, they said. Each of them rushed to a corner of the room and began dashing off sentences for insertion in the speech.

This kind of thing was dangerous in the extreme around a man of Roosevelt's impulsiveness. Mac and I went into the bedroom and found F. D. R. raging over what he had heard through the half-opened door of his room. "I simply will not let Hoover question my Americanism," he snapped at us, when we begged him to ignore the extravagances of Hoover's remarks. Just before he went out the door, Mac and I made a final desperate argument. We told him that we had been through weeks of campaigning with him; our judgment had been tested again and again; we implored him to make the high-minded, serious speech he intended to make, without descent to the level of bitter personalities; we begged him not to destroy the tone he had agreed to sound this last week of the campaign.

He made no answer, but simply stuffed in his pocket the scribbled notes Jimmy and Felix had handed him.

Mac and I went back to our bedroom, each of us flopping down on a twin bed with the despair that is part of a sense of defeat. We turned on the radio, finally. And our hearts rose as we heard the speech through to the end. Roosevelt had taken our advice.

But this narrow escape made me feel that I ought to stand by through election night. Above everything else, I wanted to be certain that the picture of gallantry, of friendliness, of statesmanship was not blotted out by demagogic attacks, by adolescent personalizings. It was a serious operation on the economic system that he had proposed to direct, not a witch hunt under economic beds.

So the last week of the campaign—in stunning contrast to that of the campaign of 1936—sounded the note of moderation, of consecration to the responsibilities ahead. The speech at the Metropolitan Opera House before an assemblage of Republicans-for-Roosevelt, the speech at Brooklyn—the scene of the second of three temporary reconciliations with Al Smith—the speech at Madison Square Garden contained no talk of "match" and "master." And the very last speech of the campaign, made at Poughkeepsie among Roosevelt's own neighbors on election eve, perhaps best expressed the mood of modesty, humility, and generosity with which he went to the country in 1932. It spoke of the "understanding and tolerance" which had come to meet him everywhere; of the hope that he might, "in some modest way," bring America's unity of purpose to practical fulfillment; of the fact that *he* wasn't important; of the fact that he was merely "the humble emblem" of a "general human purpose." Inferentially, this speech gives a better picture of Roosevelt as I knew him in 1932 than any other speech of the campaign.[10]

He was utterly calm on election eve. I stayed the night with him at Hyde Park. We were, to all intents and purposes, alone. All of the family, all but a few of the servants and one of the secretaries had gone to New York. There was no excitement, no horseplay, no petty sense of impending personal triumph. We sat before the open fire and talked quietly of the campaign, of the gathering economic storm clouds—the tumbling prices, the mounting unemployment.

As I watched the play of the firelight on his strong, mobile face, I reflected that my adventure was at an end. I had not taken part in it to taste the sweets of victory that would come the next day. I had worked those long months to justify to myself the expenditure of a lifetime's efforts to learn, to earn the right to learn more, to see how the common good might be served through a better understanding of political forces. The long lesson was over. I had much to ponder, to rationalize, to order in my mind, perhaps to write out for others who might want to read. I did not dream, that night, of any personal participation in the power that was implicit in the great, orderly political revolution of November 8th. I had the sense of a job well and faithfully done. I was ready to resume my normal pursuits.

That the group I had assembled and over which I had presided was more than a perfectly natural way to implement the efforts of a candidate for office, I did not for a moment believe. It was simply a group of informed people doing, jointly, what a group of informed people ought to do in such circumstances. Its job was obviously over.

[10] This speech, conspicuous by its absence from *The Public Papers and Addresses of Franklin D. Roosevelt* (Random House, New York, 1938), is reprinted in Appendix A.

I was quite clear about that. There could be no place in a free government for an integrated group of people possessed of power and devoid of official accountability. The traditions of our government provided for presidential advisers with appropriate official status. No doubt the men with whom I worked would, if they chose, be enlisted in the service of the government. That was a bridge to be crossed later.

But I felt sure about myself. I wanted no office.

Of course, I would be glad to help. There were odds and ends in my work for the Governor to clean up.

This last reservation was to involve me, in the weeks ahead, to a degree that I could not have imagined.

Whether it would have been wiser never to have made it is a matter of pure speculation. Until this moment I have never wasted the time to ask myself the question.

CHAPTER III

"A PACKHORSE IN HIS GREAT AFFAIRS"

HERBERT HOOVER has carried the burden of so much blame in the past ten years that one more straw will not break his back. He probably never thought of himself as being responsible for my presence in Washington, and perhaps I would have wound up there in any case. But the fact is that he was the proximate cause of those circumstances that nibbled away my resolution to call the association with Roosevelt a day.

When I came to the 65th Street house on the morning of November 9th to clear up the last bits of unfinished business, the household was just awakening. Stacks of telegrams had piled up on the first floor: new ones were being brought in from time to time by messengers. Gus Gennerich sat there alone, attempting to sort them out. After I had spent a while with him poking around among them, I went up to the Governor's room. He had finished his breakfast and lay abed contemplating the President's telegram of congratulations. We talked about the reply that ought to be made to it, and, following Roosevelt's suggestions, I scribbled one out on the back of a telegram envelope.

After a time the beaming friends and party leaders began to turn up. By noon the house was bursting with triumphant good-fellowship. Even old Colonel House, whose function at luncheon was to play rabbit's foot to the new Uncle Rastus, was infected by the spirit of the place. "You know, Governor," he said cheerfully, "some of your speeches during the campaign were so good that they sounded almost like Wilson's." It was the supreme compliment of which he was capable.

In the midst of such amiable confusion we prepared a brief message for broadcast to the nation. When it had been drafted and delivered, I thought I had written a final "finis" to the story of the past eight months. Roosevelt left for Albany. And that Wednesday evening there began for me one of those dreamlike reposes into which a man falls when a long, grueling job is suddenly ended and vacation time is precipitately upon him. I met my classes, smoked my pipe, and otherwise invoked the gods of quiet. It was an interlude of infinite peace.

Early Sunday morning, November 13th, it came to an abrupt end. There was a call from Albany. Roosevelt had just received a long telegram from President Hoover asking for a conference on the foreign debts.[1] Would I come up immediately and discuss the subject?

That, though I was wholly unaware of it, was the beginning of the end of my calm plans.

It was, at the same time—and this alone is important—the prelude to a fateful struggle between two schools of thought in this country. The prize of the struggle was to be the foreign policy of the United States in the face of a war-infested and war-ridden Europe. The struggle itself, in all its labyrinthine ramifications, would be one of the distinguishing characteristics of the Roosevelt Administration. That I was to be caught up in it would certainly be the least of its drama.

But all this lay in the future. On November 13th I knew only that the moratorium on foreign debts to which Congress formally agreed in the winter of 1931, at the recommendation of Hoover, had expired; that on December 15th payments of $95,550,000 from Great Britain and of $19,261,432 from France would, among others, be due; that on Thursday, November 10th, two days after the election, the British and French ambassadors had called on the Secretary of State, Henry L. Stimson, to ask for a review of the entire question of the debts and, pending such a review, for a postponement of the installments due on December 15th; that the British and French notes had been dispatched to President Hoover, who was resting in Palo Alto, California; and that, almost immediately, Hoover had decided to return to Washington.

The President's telegram took us completely by surprise. We could not remember any other case in which an outgoing President, during the interregnum, had asked for the advice and assistance of his successful opponent. And as we talked over the problems the Hoover proposal raised, Sunday afternoon and evening, we concluded that the President could scarcely have chosen a field in which there was less probability of sympathetic cooperation between the two administrations.

Broadly, the situation seemed to us to be something like this:

[1] This telegram was dispatched at San Bernardino on November 12th and received at Albany on the following morning.

The World War had been financed in large part, both before and after 1917, by the billions of dollars of loans we had made and credits we had granted the Allies. At the end of the war the Allies had proposed to draw from Germany, in the form of reparations, at least enough to pay back what they owed us. This fantastic burden of debt Germany could not discharge, even if she was permitted to export goods which competed with their own. At the same time we had found that our farmers and industrial producers could not continue to find expanding markets abroad as Europe's production reached and exceeded prewar levels. Hence we had *lent* Europe the money to buy our products, or, if you will, to pay us what she owed us.

This jerry-built structure had begun to crumble the instant we ceased to make foreign loans, and the aftermath of its disintegration was political and economic crisis in Europe and the collapse of the system of international economics which had, up to that time, prevailed.

Those who believed that such a collapse must mark the end of civilization, those to whom the gold-standard and free-trade ideals were the twin deities of an unshakable orthodoxy—the international bankers, the majority of our economists, and almost every graduate of every Eastern university who had dipped into the fields of foreign relations or economics—had undertaken to discover a remedy for it. By common consent they had settled upon the reparations and the war debts. If these were canceled (these particular debts among all debts—public and private) or traded for general European disarmament or British resumption of the gold standard or what not, we would root out the cause of our troubles, they had announced. And so ponderous were the arguments that buttressed this formula in the Atlantic states—in academic and presumably "intellectual" circles, at any rate—that it was actually unrespectable not to accept them. There and in Europe, the more vociferously they were championed the more passionately they were believed. Only their prospective dupes, the majority of American citizens, stubbornly refused to swallow them.

President Hoover's moratorium, recommended in June, 1931, could fairly be considered a kind of offshoot of these arguments. In the light of this fact it was not illogical for us to infer that he was edging up to some sort of proposal to readjust the foreign debts. On the other hand, Hoover was firmly pledged against cancellation of the debts. His telegram stressed that point, but added his belief that "we should be receptive to proposals from our debtors of tangible compensation in other forms than direct payment . . . [and] that substantial reduction of world armament, which will relieve our own and world burdens and dangers, has a bearing upon this question."

Beyond this, Hoover did not discuss specifications. And so the exact nature of his proposition was vague in our minds.

But there was nothing ambiguous about the suggestion that Roosevelt should share with him the responsibility for action on the December 15th problem. And if anything was clear to us that Sunday night in Albany, it was that Roosevelt must not be saddled with that responsibility.

It wasn't that we felt the slightest doubt of Hoover's excellent intentions in asking for a conference. We certainly didn't look upon this proposal as an attempt to embarrass Roosevelt politically, though we couldn't help but appreciate the explosive nature of the package that had been left at his door. But we were agreed that the heart of the recovery program was and must be domestic. We believed that that program would be jeopardized by the reaction in and out of Congress if F. D. R. became involved in complicated negotiations with foreign nations. We were profoundly certain that the foreign protestations of inability to pay were in large part untrue. Even if they were not, we knew of no trade for the war debts which seemed advisable—as advisable, at least, as keeping the debts alive to remind our debtors that they were going to find it pretty difficult to finance another war in this country. And, finally, it would be dangerous for Roosevelt to assume responsibility for such a matter. He had no access to the official records of what had gone before and he would have no control over the negotiations which followed.

All these reasons determined the reply to President Hoover's message of November 12th, which was sent off on Monday, November 14th. In it Roosevelt accepted the President's invitation, suggested that the meeting be "wholly informal and personal," and added pointedly that he hoped the President himself would confer with the members of Congress without his interposition since "the immediate question raised by the British, French and other notes creates a responsibility which rests upon those now vested with executive and legislative authority."

I returned to New York after this message was sent. On Tuesday Roosevelt held a press conference and announced that he would meet Hoover on November 22nd on his way to Warm Springs. On Thursday, at his request, I returned to Albany.

When I got to the Governor's Mansion, I received the astonishing news that he had decided to have me accompany him to the conference with the President. The job of preparing his data for the conference, then, rested with me.

I spent the next three or four days consulting with various people in New York. For obvious reasons I found myself pretty much alone around Columbia on this question. In fact, the very day the British and French notes were published in the American press, a pretentious report was issued by a group of American economists, with what seemed to be carefully calculated timing, presenting voluminous arguments to support the theory that to cancel or drastically to reduce the debts would be beneficial to the United States. I was besought by some of my colleagues to exercise whatever influence I had to persuade Roosevelt to accept these findings. But, of course, I could lean heavily on Ralph Robey, Rex Tugwell, and Adolf Berle, who agreed with me in opposition to traditional internationalism.

As a result of our talks I drafted a series of questions that I thought might help Roosevelt in the Washington conference. For his convenience they were put on small cards—one to the card—which he could consult unobtrusively during the discussion.

These questions were designed to determine the cause of the President's anxiety to do something about revision at that moment. Until we had explored that, we could not rightly make any final judgment or commitment.

Particularly, we wondered why, when Great Britain had failed to include provision for the debt payment in her budget, the Hoover Administration had made no attempt to bring up the issue; why, although there was a provision in the debt agreements that questions concerning adjustment of the debt should be brought up ninety days before payment was due, this ninety-day period had passed without some discussion between our government and the debtor governments concerning the question. We wondered whether the Hoover Administration, wishing to keep the debt question out of the campaign, had tipped off our debtors to withhold their requests until election day had passed; whether there had been any implied promise that if Hoover were re-elected, with a fresh mandate from the people, he would be able to overcome congressional scruples on the debt question.

Finally—and this was the core of our doubts and misgivings—we wondered if there was any truth in the rumor that the President had promised Laval or MacDonald, when these gentlemen visited him, that he would attempt to bring about a complete readjustment of the debt situation. Men close to Laval openly made this claim. Considering the customary mendacity of French diplomats about matters affecting French vital interests, we weren't disposed to place much credence in it. Still, it was significant that the British seemed to believe it. (I was later flatly told by three of the highest British officials that such had been the import of President Hoover's conversations.) At any rate, this unknown factor loomed so large in our reckonings that on one of the cards Roosevelt himself scribbled—not for the purpose of asking the direct question, presumably, but to remind him of the situation during the conference—the notation "secret agreements by Pres."[2]

When we arrived in Washington on November 22nd, we found the studied courtesy of the official reception a wry antidote for the warmth of the crowds in the streets. On the drive from the station to the White House we were accompanied by Warren Delano Robbins, F. D. R.'s cousin, who at that time held the position of Chief of Protocol. A delicate touch, that—which did not escape Roosevelt. Captain Walter N. Vernou, the President's naval aide, resplendent in gold braid and cord, also rode with us.

Roosevelt, his bodyguard, and I came up from the first-floor entrance of the White House in the elevator and went through to the Red Room. There stood President Hoover, grave, dignified, and somewhat uneasy. He greeted Roosevelt. I was presented to him. F. D. R. hailed the alert and always faintly arrogant Secretary Mills with a cheery "Hello, Ogden." We settled ourselves—Hoover alone on a red divan, Roosevelt next to him in a chair, I next to Roosevelt on another little sofa, and Mills facing us. Everyone smoked somewhat nervously, President Hoover on a fat cigar.

There were a few preliminary pleasantries. Roosevelt said to Mills, "The only thing I objected to in the campaign was the fact that the Republican National Committee printed a picture of your private golf course and said it was mine." Mills smiled a moment and then said sweetly, "Well, Franklin, the misinformation seems to be pretty general. The course isn't any more mine than it is yours. The sole satisfaction I've got out of it in recent years is that of paying dues to the club that owns it. I can't remember when I played it last."

What followed rates description if only because of the conflicting impressions that the public has been given about it. After the con-

[2] See Appendix B for the complete list of the questions Roosevelt took into this conference.

ference President Hoover was reported by a Washington columnist to have said furiously that "Moley did all the talking." Mr. Roosevelt, somewhat forgetfully, has said in his published papers[3] that "no tangible suggestion" on the debts was forthcoming from President Hoover. William Starr Myers and Walter H. Newton, in their all-but-official record of the Hoover Administration, describe a very concrete proposal by President Hoover, add that Roosevelt "appeared to agree with the program," and then insist that his subsequent action was "very disappointing"—so disappointing, in fact, that the nationwide "discouragement" and "apprehension" it produced helped to bring on the banking crisis.[4] Secretary Mills, the third person present at the meeting, is dead; his own written impressions of what transpired, if they exist, have not been published. There remain my own notes, written out that same night, while memory was still fresh.

Hoover plunged into a long recital on the debt question. He spoke without interruption for nearly an hour. Shyness, at the beginning, seemed to make him fix his eyes on the beautiful seal of the United States woven into the red carpet. After a while he began looking at me as he talked—a circumstance about which I had no more reason to be pleased than the inanimate carpet. He obviously found it hard to overcome the profound personal disappointment of the election, for he glanced at Roosevelt only occasionally, and then turned his eyes away again.

Before he had finished, it was clear that we were in the presence of the best-informed individual in the country on the question of the debts. His story showed a mastery of detail and a clarity of arrangement that compelled admiration.

His administration had observed four principles with respect to the debts, he said.

First, they were not political debts, but substantially honest business obligations. In so far as we had contributed money to the cause of "making the world safe for democracy," the reductions achieved during the Coolidge Administration had wiped out these obligations.

Second, the United States had and should consider each country as a unit and each debt as an independent transaction in dealing with debt questions.

Third, the debts and the reparations were not related, so far as we

[3] *Public Papers and Addresses of Franklin D. Roosevelt; op. cit.;* Vol. I, p. 867.

[4] *The Hoover Administration—a Documented Narrative.* Charles Scribner's Sons; New York, 1936; pp. 283 and 288.

were concerned. As a nation we took no responsibility for the fixing of the reparations, and we could not admit the contentions of the European countries that we should let them off to the extent that they had let Germany off.

Fourth, we must take account of professed and proven inability on the part of any of our debtors to pay us.

And then Mr. Hoover moved to one of those plausible generalizations into which he so frequently fell. Either cancellation *or* default, he said, would shake international credit. And that would cause economic shivers to pass through this country.

He did not add what was unquestionably in his mind at that point —his complete rejection of the Roosevelt theory of the depression, and his firm belief that the depression throughout the world had been arrested in the middle of 1932 and that this country, as well as all others, was on its way to a substantial recovery as early as July 1st. To have said that at the moment, of course, would have brought out into the open a fundamental difference of opinion between Roosevelt and himself. But the mere fact that the argument remained unspoken did not make the moment less awkward.

There was a pause. Then Hoover cleared his throat and continued. While *both* cancellation and default ought to be avoided at all costs, we could not insist upon payment without extending some hope of revision or reexamination unless we wanted to force the European nations to establish a united front against us on economic questions. The price of this policy would be "grave repercussions" both here and abroad.

At this point Roosevelt took out the little cards and interjected a number of the questions written on them. Hoover and, occasionally, Mills replied. There is nothing about the substance of their answers that isn't now a matter of public record, available to students of the subject. But, at the time, their answers were helpful and informative, particularly in so far as they indicated the resentful, not to say bitter, attitude of both Hoover and Mills toward the French and their feeling that England would face a grave difficulty in meeting the December 15th payment.

When Roosevelt had finished with his questions, Hoover took up his discussion once more. He described in detail how Congress had come to dominate the debt question. He expressed the belief that if he negotiated an agreement of any kind with our debtors Congress would refuse to approve it. His hands were tied by Congress.

And so, at last, he came to the nub of the matter: he would like to have the Debt Commission reconstituted. Perhaps it should consist of three senators, three representatives, and three members appointed by the President. He offered to permit Roosevelt to name or at least to participate in the naming of the executive members. Thus negotiations begun in the closing days of his own administration could continue, uninterrupted, into Roosevelt's administration, as they would have to if they involved the questions of capacity to pay and the lack of uniformity in the settlements that had been made with England, France, Italy, and the other countries.

When Hoover reached the end of his recital, F. D. R. nodded his head in partial agreement. Obviously, the European countries ought to have a better opportunity to present their claims. "I see no reason why the old legal maxim that a debtor ought to have access to the creditor shouldn't prevail," he said. And then, turning to me, "Don't you think so, Ray?"

I answered, "Yes, even a horse trader does that," and dropped into silence again.

"Well, then, where do we go from there?" Roosevelt continued to look at me. Clearly he wanted to hear my reaction before he went further.

I said, then, that it seemed to me that the appointment of such a commission as the President suggested, played up dramatically as it would be by the press, would precipitate so much uncertainty as to the future that a stoppage rather than an acceleration of business activity would result. The problem was incredibly complex. No satisfactory settlement could be negotiated in a short time, or perhaps for many years.

At the same time, it seemed wise to relieve the tension between us and the foreign nations by some sort of continuing process of negotiation. That suggested to me the ordinary channels of diplomatic intercourse. Up to that moment the debt question was very largely within the province of the Treasury, a fact attested by the presence of Secretary Mills rather than that of Secretary Stimson at this conference. What prevented the State Department from taking an active hand in these questions over the next few months? What bar was there to exploratory discussion between our foreign-affairs office and European representatives? And then, somewhat impertinently perhaps, I added that what little knowledge I had of the constitutional powers of the President led me to believe that there was no way that Congress could deprive him of his power to carry on conversations with the representatives of foreign governments. Therefore, there was no need to ask Congress for permission to negotiate with foreign powers on debts.

It seemed to me that it would be best to insist upon the payment of the December 15th debt installments and to say, at the same time, that the channels of diplomatic intercourse were open to suggestions for revision. I added that, in my opinion, Mr. Hoover's four principles ought to be approved by the new administration. In short, the Roosevelt policy might well be the acceptance of Hoover's four points, with the addition of a fifth to embody the idea of constant negotiation for revision through action of the Executive.

This was sheer improvisation. I had never discussed the formula with Roosevelt. But he took it up at once.

Hoover and Mills were visibly annoyed. They had hoped that Roosevelt would prove receptive to Hoover's general conclusions about the dreadful urgency of the problem. They had hoped that he would go along on the Debt Commission proposal.

It was all very polite. There were no table poundings, no raised voices. But the talk after that was tense, and the tug of war unmistakable.

The afternoon was drawing on. By now the light through the heavy red draperies shone only dimly on the portraits of Grant, John Adams, Madison, and Thomas Jefferson. Hoover seemed to decide, finally, that the time had come to make the best of things. He suggested that since he and Roosevelt had blocked out certain opinions on which they agreed and others on which they disagreed it might be desirable for them to issue separate statements of policy.

It was decided, then, that he would issue a statement after having communicated its contents to Roosevelt. Roosevelt would issue a statement subsequently, outlining his views. Perhaps the preponderance of agreement between the two statements might indicate a sufficient degree of harmony to reassure the country. For the moment, a brief noncommittal note could be given to the newspapers. Hoover wrote one out on the pad and read it to us. Roosevelt approved and then asked that Secretary Mills confer with me after the Hoover statement was prepared.

With that the general conference broke up. Roosevelt and Hoover remained alone for a few minutes. Mills and I, having agreed that we would meet the next day at the Mayflower Hotel, parted amiably enough. But I left the White House with an overpowering impression of the strained atmosphere of the meeting.

Unquestionably, Hoover liked and respected his Secretary of the Treasury, but he had stiffly called him "Mills" during the entire afternoon. Mills' attitude toward Hoover seemed to be the grudging deference of a proud and imperious man toward a superior officer. Whatever the relations between Roosevelt and his close associates have been, they have certainly included nothing of the bristling formality that cloaked the devotion of these two men.

Further, it was clear that you could have scoured the country without finding two people who distrusted Roosevelt—as a human being and as President-elect—more than that pair. I take it that I was regarded with contempt that changed into cold anger as the afternoon passed.

On the other hand, I admitted to myself that I had been somewhat nettled at Mills before the meeting because of a crack he had taken at me in a press conference: he was making preparations for the meeting, he had said, and he hoped "the professor" was studying too. And I knew I was not alone in my sensitiveness. Mills was the one adversary in the campaign of 1932 of whom Roosevelt was leery. He was never afraid of Hoover's speeches, but both Louis and I knew that his reluctance to meet Mills head-on, in debate, had been one of the chief reasons for the postponement of the speech on government finance until the last days of the campaign.

Later, in March, I was to spend many days in intimate contact with Mills at the Treasury. There my respect for him was augmented by a feeling of personal affection. During the years before his untimely death, I saw him frequently. To the end he was a brave man, a challenging, outspoken adversary and a loyal friend.

But when he came to my room at the Mayflower Hotel the morning after the conference, it was hard to see the lovable qualities of this intellectual hedgehog. He announced brusquely that he had Mr. Hoover's statement prepared for release, and I, immediately, took him to Roosevelt's apartment. Of these two men, Hudson Valley neighbors, Harvard classmates, implacable political enemies, Mills was grave and tense, Roosevelt gay and nonchalant. After the amenities had been satisfied, Mills sat down, opening a typewritten manuscript. "Well, Ogden," said Roosevelt facetiously, "you must have sat up all night working on that." Mills' face hardened. Without looking at Roosevelt he said, "This is a very important document," and proceeded at once to read the statement. Roosevelt made no comment about it, said that he had been unable to complete his own statement (he had spent the evening in an exceedingly important conference with the congressional leaders on his domestic program) but would finish it on the train that afternoon and release it toward evening.

Mills rose to go and said good-by to Roosevelt. I walked to the door with him. As we reached it, and Roosevelt turned to other things, Mills whispered to me, "I wish you would do what you can to impress upon Mr. Roosevelt the seriousness of this matter and the need of his developing a constructive policy about it." It was for all the world like a schoolteacher urging a mother to make her naughty child do his homework. I simply remarked that it seemed to me we had a formula worked out—a formula that Mr. Roosevelt felt was constructive.

That formula was given to the press the same day, as Roosevelt's train sped south toward Warm Springs. It was, in essence, the one outlined during the conference—insistence on the payment of the December 15th installments, acceptance of Hoover's four principles, and the substitution of the idea of continuing diplomatic negotiation on debt revision for the Hoover proposal to revive the Debt Commission.[5]

I heaved a sigh of relief when it was turned over to the newspapermen. Within its small compass, and taken in connection with the Hoover statement, it etched out a debt policy that has remained unchanged to the present time. It maintained the integrity of the debts as living obligations which, from that day to this, have prevented the use of the United States as a war treasury by Europe and have done more to stave off a general war than a dozen alliances or a score of diplomatic notes.

But viewed wholly apart from the debt question, the statement was of profound importance because it was the first spectacular step Roosevelt took to differentiate his foreign policy from that of the internationalists. It served notice on the League advocates, the pro-sanctionists, and those who desired a revival of foreign lending that Roosevelt was likely to be no Herbert Hoover or Henry Stimson on foreign affairs. It was a warning that the New Deal rejected the point of view

[5] I had prepared a draft of the statement late the night before. It was put into final form while the train was passing through Virginia. Baruch assisted in this process.

of those who would make us parties to a political and economic alliance with England and France—policing the world, maintaining the international *status quo*, and seeking to enforce peace through threats of war.

If we had any notion that the struggle with those who would turn F. D. R.'s attention away from domestic matters would not be bitter, we had shed them before the end of November. The kickback in the Eastern papers, after Roosevelt's statement of November 23rd, was sharp.

It was instructive, besides, because it was the first application of the strategy New Deal critics were to use from that time on—attack upon those around Roosevelt, rather than upon Roosevelt himself. I got all its impact that time. Of course, Roosevelt's decision to have me accompany him to the conference with Hoover had caused a revolution in my own public relations. Such anonymity as I had enjoyed vanished with the announcement of that decision: pallid "human-interest" stories burgeoned in the newspapers. But there was still another abrupt change as soon as Roosevelt's attitude toward the European debts became known. The assumption seemed to be that Roosevelt didn't quite know what the meeting with Hoover was all about and that he might have been taken into camp or made to see the light (depending on how you looked at it) if only I hadn't been around. There was editorial comment about "impractical professors" and "provincial academicians"—playing Svengali, presumably, to his pitiable Trilby. Less pleasant, foreign news-gathering agencies and particularly the offshoots of the French foreign office began an industrious circulation of personal stories.

All this, on the whole, was more amusing than not. At least it seemed amusing then, because throughout those days I cherished the delusion that my participation in the debts affair was nothing but an unanticipated epilogue to my story.

2

It was at Warm Springs that Roosevelt first offered me a job in his administration. He led up to the subject by talking about his secretariat. He had decided, he said, to make Louis Howe his Secretary. Louis would occupy a back office at the White House and be what he most wanted to be—a "man of mystery." Marvin McIntyre and

Stephen Early would handle his engagements and press relations respectively.[6]

That left the post of Administrative Assistant to the President. (Held during the Hoover regime by French Strother, a magazine writer, its duties seemed to consist chiefly of trimming verbal Christmas trees—touching up the President's speeches and messages.) But, F. D. R. continued, he thought Louis would be unhappy if I should be given that job and so he had decided to drop the office altogether.

I was stunned by the casual assumption implicit in this statement. I explained: I thought I had made it clear many, many times during the campaign that I wanted no office. I wanted to think, teach, write, and speak as a free agent, reaching an audience, however small, that accepted me on the basis of what I had to say, rather than because I was a part of a governmental machine. Impartiality and forthrightness were the price that had to be paid for such freedom. It seemed to me that honest teaching and writing about public affairs precluded not only White House cupbearing and administrative paper-shuffling, but party goose-stepping.

Only recently Jim Farley, in describing what seemed to him, as a good party man, a serious defect in me, inadvertently defined the quality I was trying to describe. He said that I "found it hard to work in harness with other people." Had he said that I resisted (and finally renounced) public office because I recognized that in my chosen profession there was no place for a man who could *wear* a harness, he would have stated almost precisely what I said to Franklin Roosevelt in the simple bedroom of the cottage at Warm Springs on a late November day in 1932.

I concluded my little speech by adding that I had put my hand to the plow twenty years before when I gave up public office and began to teach in a university. I had no desire to turn my eyes back. That being true, Louis' anxieties, the pother of newspaper speculation about what I was going to "be," and Roosevelt's own meditations were all needless.

Roosevelt's answer was the answer of a shrewd politician. It carefully skirted the fundamental question and yet it undermined my

[6] It was characteristic of F. D. R.'s way of doing things that McIntyre and, I believe, Early did not learn until they received their commissions that the Hoover arrangement—three secretaries with equal rank—had been discarded, and that they were to be assistant secretaries, with Louis enjoying the exclusive right to the title of Secretary to the President.

resolution to stick to my professional last with every emotional indirection in the political armory.

"Of course you wouldn't want to be tied down to an administrative job," he said. "But that isn't my idea. I've been digging through the Congressional Directory and I find that the office of Assistant Secretary of State is the only one of importance that seems completely free of statutory duties. If you took that title—and you'll have to have some sort of official status—you could go on just as you have been. You could work in your own way, giving me confidential assistance. Your responsibility would be directly to me. There'd be no entanglements either with my secretariat or with any of the Cabinet.

"Don't you see? You've got to have a job with enough prestige to make it possible for you to deal with people of importance for me. But that's all the title has to mean. Nothing else has to change. We just continue. I don't have to tell you that I've found it easier to work with you than I have with anyone else. And I don't have to remind you that I've got an immediate problem.

"I'm still Governor of New York and I face a terrible couple of weeks before January 1st finishing up that job. Meanwhile the debts thing may crop up again, and I've got to get some legislation from this Congress.

"I have no Cabinet yet. I can't call in many people for advice and help without inviting speculation about whether I'm going to appoint them. That will embarrass them and me. You know my intellectual commitments. You know most of the people that we've got to put to work. I'd counted on you to keep in touch with the State Department on debts for me, and to get the ball on legislation rolling."

There was more in the same appealing vein. It was, so far as I was concerned, an unprecedented expression of personal confidence. I was more deeply touched than I like, now, to admit, and I wanted to answer without cavil.

I thanked him. He had, I explained, described the only role I could conceivably play in his administration. My whole association with him had been fine and decent. I had learned much from it. Both affection and gratitude compelled me to go ahead for the moment and help out, as he wished. But it would be best to let the matter rest there, and decide definitely about the appointment sometime later.

He understood, he said. And so we left it.

But the pleasure that came with this first spoken recognition that

I had served usefully was not unmingled with pervasive doubts during the long hours on the train back to New York.

The potentialities of the job that Roosevelt had so lightheartedly described were obvious. No one in the administration would have a more intimate relationship with the President. No one, except himself, would have more to do with making policy. The size of the job would be limited only by my own capacities; the burden of responsibility, only by my ability to bear it.

But when you carry a load you must be sure of your footing, and I was painfully aware that the ground around high places is slippery. Everything—assuming that I accepted the job—would depend upon the constancy, the unswerving faith, the sympathetic understanding, and the retentive memory of the principal in this relationship. I could confidently count on bitter jealousies and merciless criticism from others.

There went through my mind, then, a passage from an extraordinary letter that Sir Francis Bacon wrote to Sir George Villiers when Villiers became the intimate of James I.

> Kings and great princes [the old serpent had written] even the wisest of them have had their friends, their favourites, their privadoes, in all ages; for they have their affections as well as other men. Of these they make several uses; sometimes to communicate and debate their thoughts with them, and to ripen their judgments thereby; sometimes to ease their cares by imparting them; and sometimes to interpose them between themselves and the envy or malice of their people; for kings cannot err; that must be discharged upon the shoulders of their ministers; and they who are nearest unto them must be content to bear the greatest load. Remember then what your true condition is: the king himself is above the reach of his people, but cannot be above their censures; and you are his shadow, if either he commit an error, and is loth to avow it, but excuses it upon his ministers, of which you are first in the eye; or you commit the fault or have willingly permitted it, and must suffer for it: and so perhaps you may be offered a sacrifice to appease the multitude. . . . Remember well the great trust you have undertaken: you are as a continual centinel, always to stand upon your watch to give him true intelligence. If you flatter him, you betray him; if you conceal the truth of those things from him which concern his justice or his honour . . . you are as dangerous a traitor to his state, as he that riseth in arms against him.

I was pondering the meaning of this advice, as I sat at lunch on the day after the train left Atlanta, when a friendly voice interrupted me.

"My name is Sam Rayburn. We met at Warm Springs."

Sam and I were soon talking earnestly across the table about the future of the administration. And then, completely without warning, Sam peered about as if to be assured of privacy, leaned toward me and murmured, "I hope we don't have any —— —— Rasputin in this administration."

It was a long stretch from the sinuous Chancellor of James I to the mystic monk of Nicholas. Yet the connection was clear. It was almost as if Sam had reached inside me and dragged my perplexity into the open.

His next words were only partly reassuring. It developed that he was not referring to me. But the party leaders who had helped nominate and elect Roosevelt had no intention of putting up with "palace politics or palace politicos."

This, from an authentic interpreter of that vast conglomerate known as congressional opinion, was significant confirmation of my doubts about the job that was mine for the taking. In the months ahead Sam was to be my guide and ally in a dozen forays. But never was advice more gently or shrewdly given than on that December 3rd.

Meanwhile, though I was to hold my decision in suspension for the next two months, the offer from Roosevelt had marked the beginning of a new phase in my relations with him.

I was no longer "head of the brains trust," for—as I had determined it should on election eve—the "brains trust" had ceased to exist after November 8th. Specifically, Tugwell, Johnson, Berle, and I never met as a group from that day on. I was to see them individually many times on Roosevelt's work. But their contributions no longer became part of a unified product—a draft speech or a recommendation on policy offered to him as a group suggestion.

Nor was I any longer primarily occupied with the preparation of speeches and the methodical presentation of economic ideas.

The time had come to begin translating policy into action. My authorization seemed to make me Roosevelt's *de facto* minister for the moment.

It was essential that Roosevelt get as much of his program as he possibly could through the lame-duck Congress that convened on December 5th. As Lindley has cogently pointed out, Roosevelt "had at most one year in which to defeat the depression. The new legislation which he needed was more than Congress, at its habitual pace, could enact in three years. He also wished to avoid calling a special session of the new Congress until he had had at least five or six weeks after his inauguration to install his administration and get a firm hold on the government."[7]

Roosevelt had already put Swagar Sherley and Lewis W. Douglas to work on the subject of governmental economy and reorganization.

Before I left Warm Springs I had arranged to have Wallace, Tugwell, Morgenthau, and M. L. Wilson meet in Washington. There the strategy on the farm bill, which ought to have been passed before the spring planting season, was laid out.

The next two weeks, back in New York, were devoted to handing out other assignments and getting things moving.

Berle, H. Parker Willis, and others began to draft farm-mortgage relief legislation. Will Woodin, Berle, Eastman, and others went to work on bills to expedite bankruptcy proceedings—particularly as concerned the railroads.

I interviewed Samuel Untermyer, who had been counsel of the famous Pujo Committee and who, for years, had advocated stock-exchange regulation, and, after several meetings, asked Charles Taussig to get material from him on the subject.

All the excitement, the man-killing pressure of the pre-election days began again. There were telephonings, temperaments, conferences, crises. The big push was on. Foreign debts and debtors seemed remote, unreal, hardly worth thinking about.

3

But almost before we could realize what was happening, the debt question became part of a violent skirmish between the outgoing and incoming administrations.

The British paid in full and the French defaulted on December 15th.[8] One might have been forgiven for assuming that the issue had

[7] *The Roosevelt Revolution; op. cit.;* p. 47.

[8] This was after many notes had flown back and forth between the State Department, the British Foreign Office, and the Quai d'Orsay.

On November 23rd, the day after the first conference with Hoover, Secretary Stimson handed to the British and French ambassadors replies to their notes of November 10th. These, which were practically identical, stated succinctly that Congress alone had the authority to modify the amounts or method of payment of debts. The President had no authority to suspend the December 15th payments but he was "prepared to recommend to Congress that it constitute an agency to examine been put away on ice for the moment. Yet that was to underestimate the opposition. What happened was that the debts began to be associated subtly, swiftly, skillfully, with other questions of foreign policy.

All of us had jotted down in our mental future books the fact that there was a World Economic Conference somewhere in the offing. The decision to call such a conference had been made at the Lausanne get-together in the summer of 1932, and we knew that two representatives appointed by Hoover, Edmund E. Day and John H. Williams, had worked with the Preparatory Commission of Experts at Geneva during the autumn. President Hoover had spoken of the Conference during the meeting with Roosevelt, had mentioned the fact that no date for it had yet been set, and had let the matter go at that. There was no attempt on his part, during the meeting, to associate the debts and the

---

the whole subject." The notes then firmly answered the contention that the world-wide depression had made debt payment difficult by pointing out that we, too, had suffered serious hardships because of the depression. The United States had made no commitments whatever prior to the reduction of the German reparations at Lausanne. (This denial was carefully elaborated in the note to France, for President Hoover feared that the debts might be overhauled in such a way as to favor unduly those who had reduced the reparations.)

On December 1st there came back from the British government a long and persuasive answer. It argued again that our insistence on payment was likely to "accentuate the gravity of the present crisis and to compromise fatally all efforts to counteract it," and concluded with the veiled threat that if war-debt payments were to be resumed the United Kingdom would have to strengthen its exchange position through measures further restricting British purchases of American goods.

The French note followed along with Great Britain's, adding only a vehement argument to the effect that suspension of the December 15th payment was "the normal, equitable and necessary sequel" to the Hoover moratorium.

On December 7th Stimson replied to Great Britain and on December 8th to France. To Great Britain he was most sympathetic, explaining that the President appreciated the practical difficulties of making the December 15th payment and he was "confident that Congress will be willing to consider any reasonable suggestion made by your government which will facilitate payment." The President was "prepared, through whatever agency may seem appropriate, in cooperation with the British Government, to survey the entire situation," for there were "important avenues of mutual advantage" that might be explored. The reply to the French was substantially the same, but was couched much more curtly.

In its third note, on December 11th, Great Britain offered to make the December 15th payment in gold, but proposed that the payment be considered "as a capital payment of which account should be taken in any final settlement."

To this offer Secretary Stimson replied the same day. Payments could not be accepted, he insisted, with conditions that existed outside of the agreement. Finally, the British, on December 13th, agreed to pay. But they reserved the right to bring up later their proposal of December 11th.

Meanwhile Premier Herriot tried to persuade the Chamber of Deputies to follow the British course. He failed, and the Herriot government fell.

forthcoming Conference. And there seemed to us nothing urgent about a consideration of the problems that would be raised by it.

But the moment that I saw the report of Day and Williams to the State Department on the preliminary work of the agenda committee, I was alarmed. The report indicated that out of the meetings of experts was going to come an internationalists' agenda—a program for a return to an international gold standard, for the sharp writing-down of international debts, and for measures of international "cooperation" wholly incompatible with the inauguration of the New Deal's domestic program. Obviously, Day and Williams, who were serving as America's technicians, or experts, ought to be informed of the incoming administration's purposes before the agenda was put into final form.

On December 16th Rex Tugwell and I joined Roosevelt on the train at Poughkeepsie and traveled with him to New York. I told him of my fears, in which Rex concurred, and urged him to see Day and Williams at the earliest possible moment. He would, he said. And Rex was instructed to get hold of the two men, discuss Roosevelt's program with them at length, and then arrange an appointment for them with Roosevelt.

But the Day and Williams report bore fruit even before Rex could turn around. A key paragraph in that document read as follows:

> One important development in the intergovernmental situation is indispensable: a definitive settlement of the war debts must be clearly in prospect, if not already attained, before the Commission comes together again. To have this question overhanging the next meetings of the Preparatory Commission would be to cloud the discussion with such suspicion and ill-feeling as to preclude any effective progress. With a satisfactory debt settlement in hand, or in the making, and with a willingness on the part of two or three of the principal powers to assume initiative in working out a program of normalization of the world's economic order, the next meeting of the Preparatory Commission may be expected to yield highly important results. . . .

This was the germ of the long telegram which, without knowledge of the press, President Hoover sent to Roosevelt late in the afternoon of Saturday, December 17th. The problem of the debts, he said, could not

> be disassociated from the problems which will come before the World Economic Conference and to some degree from those before the Conference on World Disarmament. As the economic situation in foreign countries is one of the dominant depressants of prices

> and employment in the United States, it is urgent that the World Economic Conference should assemble at as early a date as possible. The United States should be represented by a strong and effective delegation. This delegation should be chosen at an early moment in order that it may give necessary consideration and familiarize itself with the problems. . . .
>
> While we must not change our established policy of dealing with each debtor separately . . . and while the decision heretofore reached not to consider the debt question at the coming World Conference is a wise one, it seems clear that the successful outcome of the World Economic Conference will be greatly furthered if the debt problems can be satisfactorily advanced before that conference, although final agreement in some cases may be contingent upon the satisfactory solution of certain economic questions in which our country has a direct interest and the final determination of which may well form a part of the matters coming before the Economic Conference.

Hoover wound up by urging Roosevelt to join with him in the selection of a delegation which would negotiate on debts and which would give "coordinate consideration" to, and advice about, disarmament and questions coming before the Economic Conference. Hoover suggested that the personnel of this delegation include members of Congress and possibly some of the old or new members of our delegation to the Disarmament Conference.

It would be impossible to overemphasize the importance of the issue raised by the Hoover telegram—the question whether consideration of the debts was to be confused with consideration of the Economic Conference. All the debtor nations desired joint consideration of the two. All of them hoped to establish the notion that the two could not, in fact, be considered separately. And this was true because they were determined to maneuver the United States into purchasing, by large reductions in the debts, economic and financial agreements that might possibly flow from the Economic Conference. In short, it was not alone agreements on trade, prices, and the rest that they desired as such, but agreements of this kind *plus* the bonus of debt reduction. They were set on making that the price of their cooperation on world economic matters if they could—which looked to us like asking a man to pay admission to a gambling casino.

When it was later made clear to the debtor nations that they could expect no such deal, they changed the basis of their demands and held out for another kind of bonus—currency stabilization. But in the winter of 1932-33 our problem was to make them understand plainly that we saw what was up and refused to be out-traded. And our immediate task was to resist the efforts of their sympathizers in this country to persuade us that there was an inseverable relation between debts, world economic recovery, and disarmament.

For we simply did not believe that it was true. We did not believe that the debts were a stumbling block either to peace or to recovery. We were profoundly sure that if there was a genuine desire for disarmament, disarmament could be achieved without regard to what was done about debts. And if Franklin Roosevelt can be said to have had any philosophy at all, that philosophy rested on the fundamental belief that the success of concerted international action toward recovery presupposed the beginnings of recovery at home. He did not believe that our depression could be conquered by international measures. He certainly did not believe that reduction in the debts or even the partial opening of international trade channels would rout it.

The more we'd considered what might come of the Conference, as a matter of fact, the less importance it seemed to have to the United States. There was the vague possibility of minor adjustments in trade and monetary relations. But the academic language of the agenda in preparation in Geneva offered no real prospect of substantial benefits to this country.

And so the reply to Hoover's message of the 17th[9] was a polite refusal, stressing, above all things, the fact that Roosevelt looked upon the three questions of disarmament, debts, and economic relations as requiring selective treatment. The Hoover disarmament policies he believed might well be pursued. The debts, he repeated, could be dealt with through the existing machinery of the diplomatic service, supplemented, if necessary, by presidential appointment of special agents. As to the Economic Conference, there was no reason to submerge it in conversations relating to disarmament or debts. There was a "relationship, but not an identity." Roosevelt further "respectfully" suggested that the appointment of the delegation to the Economic Conference and the final determination of its program be held in abeyance until after March 4th.

On December 20th the President returned to the fray with another telegram. He was not, he told Roosevelt, attempting to determine the nature of the solution of the problems he had outlined, but to set up

[9] This reply was sent on December 19th. Some hours before it was received, Hoover sent a message to Congress following, in substance, the lines of his telegram of the 17th.

the machinery for their consideration. He disclaimed any desire to commit Roosevelt to his own views. But he thought Mr. Roosevelt would agree that debts, disarmament and economic problems "require coordination." . . . He would be glad to have Roosevelt designate Owen D. Young, Colonel House, "or any other men of your party possessed of your views and your confidence"—that not too delicately suggested that he hoped it wouldn't be I—to sit with officials of his own administration in an endeavor to see what steps might be taken "to avoid delays of precious time and inevitable losses that will ensue from such delays."

Roosevelt's reply went forward the next evening. Patiently, tactfully, it explained that he was unwilling to be led to do, by indirection, what he did not intend to do directly.

> I think perhaps [he telegraphed the President] the difficulties to which you refer are not in finding the means or the willingness for cooperation but, rather, in defining clearly those things concerning which cooperation between us is possible. . . .
>
> . . . for me to accept any joint responsibility in the work of exploration might well be construed by the debtor or other nations, collectively or individually, as a commitment—moral even though not legal, as to policies and courses of action.
>
> The designation of a man or men of such eminence as your telegram suggests would not imply mere fact-finding; it would suggest the presumption that such representatives were empowered to exchange views on matters of large and binding policy.
>
> Current press dispatches from abroad already indicate that the joint action which you propose would most certainly be interpreted there as much more of a policy commitment than either you or I actually contemplate.
>
> May I respectfully suggest that you proceed with the selection of your representatives to conduct the preliminary exploration necessary with individual debtor nations and representatives to discuss the agenda of the World Economic Conference, making it clear that none of these representatives is authorized to bind this government as to any ultimate policy.
>
> If this be done, let me repeat that I shall be happy to receive their information and their expressions of opinion. . . .

In brief, Roosevelt flatly refused once again to be committed to the foreign policies to which Hoover, doubtless because of his wholehearted belief in their soundness, stubbornly wished to commit him.

On December 22nd the President handed the entire correspondence to the press, together with a statement showing that he was enraged by Roosevelt's failure to knuckle under. That, at least, was Roosevelt's interpretation of the President's blunt "Governor Roosevelt considers that it is undesirable for him to accede to my suggestions for cooperative action on the foreign problems outlined in my recent message to Congress. I will respect his wishes." . . .

The interchange ended with Roosevelt's indignant statement that he was willing to cooperate and had proposed a method to that end which was consistent with the incoming administration's policies: the President was free to adopt it or not, as he saw fit.

Thus, for the moment, ended the Hoover-Roosevelt relationship.

4

But where President Hoover ostensibly left off, there were others—to whom Mr. Roosevelt was less allergic—ready to step in. Their entrance was to bring the third act of this drama to a climax. And its incidental effect was to open up for me whole vistas of Roosevelt's mind and character whose existence I barely began to suspect during the campaign.

On the same day that Hoover released the correspondence between F. D. R. and himself, Norman H. Davis returned from Geneva. Davis was delegate of the United States to the Disarmament Conference and also a member of the Organizing Commission of the World Economic Conference. These were the most recent of a series of appointments to the endless commissions, committees, councils, and delegations the United States had been dispatching to Europe since 1917. As minor architect and chief American maintenance man of the toppling structure erected at Paris in 1919, this handsome, white-haired Democrat was the darling of the internationalists in both parties. (Hence his usefulness to the Hoover Administration.) Nicholas Murray Butler and James T. Shotwell were no more zealous champions of the internationalist theology than he.

On landing, Davis announced to the reporters that the final meetings of the Preparatory Commission for the Economic Conference would take place in January, and that the Conference itself would be held in London in April.

Meanwhile Tugwell had followed instructions—conferred with Day himself and arranged for a conversation between Day, Williams, and Roosevelt. Day, Williams, and Tugwell had visited Roosevelt on Sunday, December 18th—a bit of news that completely escaped the press. And Roosevelt had told Day that it was his desire that the London

Conference be delayed as long as possible—certainly long enough for his own domestic recovery measures to take hold.

Day may or may not have agreed with Roosevelt's reasoning. I suspect that he was less impressed by it than by his own feeling that a conference held before something was done about the debts was bound to be a failure. But whatever his personal judgments in the matter, he was a good soldier. He went to Washington determined to get authority to postpone his and Williams' trip abroad for the meeting of the Preparatory Commission of Experts.

It was at this point that Davis landed and made his statement. Further, Davis telephoned Roosevelt, whom he had known well since the Wilson days, and made an appointment to see him on Monday, December 26th. He then communicated with Day and arranged two appointments with him—one before and one after the projected visit to Roosevelt. Finally, when Day met with Stimson and Davis in Washington and begged them to cooperate with Roosevelt by working for a delay of the Conference, Davis was adamant.

Both Day and Tugwell were considerably upset by this turn of events. Day was confounded by Davis' announcement of a time schedule before consultation with him, disturbed by Davis' clear intention to act, thenceforth, as intermediary between himself and Roosevelt, and puzzled by Davis' insistence on the time schedule he had announced. Tugwell feared that there was more to Davis' tactics than met the eye.

Just before this imbroglio I had gone to Cleveland to spend the Christmas holidays with my family and to recover fully from a brief illness. With Roosevelt's permission I had asked Rex to act for me vis-à-vis Day and Davis. So, accidentally, I was spared the unseemly scuffling outside closed doors that service in Roosevelt's interest seemed to require for the next few days.

Rex, precisely as I would have done, called Roosevelt on Christmas morning and described the situation to him. Roosevelt suggested that Tugwell bring Day and Williams to Albany on Tuesday, the 27th. He would ask Davis to stay overnight at the Mansion. Perhaps if he, Tugwell, Davis, Day, and Williams sat down together, they might get matters straightened out. So it was left.

But on the following day, December 26th, Davis had a conference with Day, during which he so strongly objected to Day's and Williams' projected visit to Albany that they yielded to his arguments. Tugwell, alarmed by Davis' interference with Roosevelt's orders, then went to Albany himself.

When he arrived there, he found Davis closeted with Roosevelt. He was told by a secretary to come back at nine-thirty the following morning, December 27th. This he did, and found Davis in Roosevelt's bedroom.

Roosevelt apologized for not having included Tugwell in the conference of the night before. He had wanted to make up his mind about the merits of what Davis had to say, he said, by seeing him alone. And then, in Davis' presence, he told Rex that he had changed his plans and had decided not to see Day and Williams again. Instead, Davis and Tugwell were to go to New York and see them. The two men were then, in effect, dismissed. Rex was given no opportunity to remonstrate, to remind F. D. R. of what he had told Day—and why—or to ask for enlightenment about this sudden change of front. Davis seemed to have the upper hand at the moment.

The outcome of the discussion that followed in New York was a compromise between the Tugwell and Davis positions. Davis had his way about the meeting of experts: Day and Williams were to sail on December 28th. But Tugwell succeeded in upsetting the Davis idea of having the Conference itself in April.

This arrangement was far from satisfactory. It left Day and Williams to go off to Europe without a complete picture of the policies of the new administration. (The interview of December 18th with Roosevelt had permitted only the briefest discussion of the need for broadening the agenda of the Conference.) It failed to dispel the impression, naturally fixed in the minds of foreign diplomats, that the United States was satisfied that the Conference should take place in the near future.

But in the light of all the curious circumstances it was the best Tugwell could do. He at least prevented agreement that the Conference be held in April. And as we look back at the Conference now, after six years, it is clear that it could have been a greater fiasco than it was only if it had been held in April or May.

A word must be said here of Davis' course. It is possible to see in it no more than a man's effort to save his own face. Perhaps Davis had agreed to the January-April time schedule with the other diplomats without discussing it with Day and Williams. Perhaps he was determined to see it through for that reason.

But it seems likely that he was moved by a purpose far less trivial.

Davis was, after all, our delegate to the Disarmament Conference, which, for almost a year, had been dragging along at Geneva, achieving nothing because of the reluctance of most of the well-armed powers to admit that the idea of limiting armaments had any reference to them. League enthusiast that he was, it seems probable that Davis' heart was so set on making the Disarmament Conference achieve something that he was trying to meet the European diplomats more than half way on other matters. Perhaps Mr. Davis sincerely believed that if holding the Economic Conference in April—when discussions were bound to be confused with talk of debts and were bound to complicate Mr. Roosevelt's domestic program—would bring the Disarmament Conference to a successful conclusion the results would be worth more than the price we paid for them.

At any rate, he succeeded, somehow, in modifying Roosevelt's plans. Day and Williams sailed for Europe on the 28th.

That was the situation I found when I returned from Cleveland. What had happened was not fatal, but it was disturbing. And even more disturbing was what I recognized as a concerted effort to involve Roosevelt in the debt question again.

It began on New Year's day with the suggestion to me by Emmanuel Monick, Financial Attaché of the French Embassy,[10] that the French government would like to make some sort of debt payment, but would be unable to explain such action to the French people unless it could point to some "new fact" that would justify a retreat from the default of December 15th. Perhaps Roosevelt might secretly suggest such a "fact." I correctly judged, as later events proved, that this E. Phillips Oppenheim byplay meant nothing because the French had not the slightest intention, at that time, of making any debt payment, and I so advised Roosevelt.

Three days later the same vague proposition was put to Roosevelt by an old friend of his—one of the partners of a great banking firm.

Sometime between, by the most improbable of coincidences, Norman Davis also reported this same veering on the part of the French. What was even more interesting was that Davis suggested, then, that F. D. R. ought to see Secretary of State Stimson to talk over this matter and that Roosevelt cottoned to the idea at once.

On January 6th he invited the Secretary to lunch with him at Hyde Park. I was not asked to attend—a curious fact in the light of his conversation with me at Warm Springs.

[10] At an informal meeting requested through a mutual friend by Monick.

The meeting that took place between the two men on January 9th lasted approximately five hours. When Secretary Stimson emerged from it he was completely noncommittal, passing off the questions of the newspapermen with the pleasantry that he had enjoyed "a delightful lunch." And no one could have dreamed at that moment how strongly this suggested the gentle purr of the cat that has swallowed the canary.

The evidence of what had happened was to appear fragment by fragment over the next weeks.

On January 11th, in a statement made at his 65th Street house, Roosevelt endorsed President Hoover's request to Congress for power to join with other nations in embargoing the shipment of arms.

On January 16th Secretary Stimson, in stating once more to the European foreign offices and the League of Nations his position with respect to Manchurian recognition, indicated broadly that there would be no disposition on the part of the new administration to change it.

The next day, January 17th, Governor Roosevelt, without consulting any of us, issued a statement saying that "American foreign policy must uphold the sanctity of international treaties." This, quite without significance in itself, when read in connection with the previous statement of Stimson, definitely committed him and his administration to the maintenance of the Stimson doctrine in the Far East. It meant that the incoming administration accepted the formula that the United States would not recognize political changes achieved by an "aggressor." It bespoke acceptance of such inchoate definitions of the term "aggressor" as then existed. It implied approval of the theory of collective sanctions and approval of the fallacy that, as "neutrals" in a foreign war, we ought to discriminate against one side or the other by embargoes and similar measures. It was, in essence, wholehearted acquiescence in the Hoover-Stimson rejection of the traditional American concept of neutrality, of disinterestedness, impartiality, and nonparticipation in foreign quarrels. Finally, it endorsed a policy that invited a major war in the Far East—a war which the United States and England might have had to wage against Japan had England not refused to go along with Stimson.

But all this was not the end of Stimson's accomplishment on January 9th. Roosevelt casually announced in the midst of these developments that he had agreed to meet Hoover on the war-debts question once again.

Meanwhile Day and Williams were carrying on in Geneva and the news drifted back that, in the second session of the Preparatory Commission's meetings, Professor Williams had said that he personally believed that a debt settlement was the chief contribution that the United States could make to the Conference. He had also volunteered the suggestion that the Roosevelt administration would offer a more liberal policy with respect to tariffs. This, according to the *New York Times* correspondent, "was Geneva's first serious information of President-elect Roosevelt's policy on anything."

All these incidents—the Williams' *gaffe*, the endorsement of the Manchurian and arms-embargo policies, the agreement to confer with Hoover on debts again, the blandishments of the French, the delicate activities of Norman Davis—indicated that Roosevelt was letting himself be pushed into an impossible position. The dangers of contradictory commitments were already apparent.

To say that I was sick at heart over what was happening would be the epitome of understatement. I was also completely baffled. Was Roosevelt really ignorant of the implications of what he was doing? Or was he in process of achieving one of those "compromises" between what he had led me to believe he thought and what he thought the Davises and Hulls of the party would like him to think? Or was this simply to prove to me—who, God knew, required no such proof—that he was dependent on no one kind of advice, on no adviser at all, in fact? Or was it something of all three?

Rex and I tried to find the answer. On January 18th we spent hours with Roosevelt at the 65th Street house explaining, as a starter, why we felt it was a tragic mistake to underwrite the Hoover-Stimson policy in the Far East. Rex, always more fluent and excitable than I, elaborated the argument with all the clarity and passion of which he was capable. I listened intently, trying to discover from F. D. R.'s reaction what had motivated him.

We might as well have saved our breath. Roosevelt put an end to the discussion by looking up and recalling that his ancestors used to trade with China. "I have always had the deepest sympathy for the Chinese," he said. "How could you expect me not to go along with Stimson on Japan?"

That was all. It was so simple, so incredible, there could be no answer. One could either pack up and go home or stop crying over spilt milk and try to prevent the spilling of any more. The damage, so far as the Manchurian and arms-embargo policies were concerned, had been done. There remained the debt and Conference policies to fight for. And, at that moment, there was born in me a blazing determination to fight for them.

And so when Roosevelt asked me that day, "Have you any engagements for the 20th—because I'd like you to go with me to the Hoover meeting?" nothing could have kept me from accepting—not even my desire to free myself of a situation into which I had been drawn unwillingly, in the first place, and which had been made increasingly ambiguous by Roosevelt himself as the weeks had passed.[11]

I frankly saw no need for another conference with Hoover. The peg on which Stimson had hung the meeting was the repeated requests the British government had made to the State Department, through its Ambassador, Sir Ronald Lindsay, for a reconsideration of the debt issue before March 4th and for a preliminary discussion of the problems slated for consideration at the Economic Conference.

But it did not require any mind reader to call the turn the meeting would take. I knew that it would involve the broader question that Roosevelt and Hoover had threshed out in their December correspondence—the question whether Roosevelt was to be jockeyed into a policy of trading off the debts for some unrelated consideration which might or might not be of value.

Less than a month and a half remained before Roosevelt took office. What was the hurry to do something about debts and the Economic Conference before that date? Undoubtedly the British were eager to take advantage of the favorable opinion created here by their full December 15th payment and, realizing that negotiations with the outgoing Hoover Administration were useless, were attempting to draw Roosevelt into them. More than that, they wanted to establish, if possible, the theory that unless debts were settled there could be no possibility of agreement on other economic questions. But we could take in good part this natural attempt of the British to out-trade us without falling for it. And what was there to be gained by rushing into a conference with people who had championed the substance of the British proposals even before the British had made them?

I had yet to learn how far Messrs. Stimson and Davis were prepared to go and what inroads had already been made.

[11] I stress the fact that Roosevelt asked me on the 18th to accompany him because, subsequently, gossip columns out of Washington, apparently sympathetic to Norman Davis, stated that it was really Davis who had been asked by Roosevelt to accompany him to the meeting with Hoover and that my inclusion was the result of my own request on the very eve of the meeting. The precise opposite was the case, as will be seen shortly.

Roosevelt explained: After talking things over with Stimson and, from time to time, with Davis, he felt that the British request for a review of their war debts was not wholly unreasonable. Though it would complicate his domestic program to discuss debts so soon after his inauguration, nevertheless the fact that the British had paid on December 15th merited a friendly hearing of what they had to say. Besides, the British were probably entitled to special consideration because we had been less lenient with them than with any of our other debtors in the debt settlement. Finally, he had become convinced that the work of the forthcoming Economic Conference might be greatly furthered by preliminary exploration of points of difference and of possible agreement. There was no reason why there should not be such preliminary exploration.

But this, he assured me, was as far as he had gone in conversation. And before we boarded the train to Washington, on January 19th, he had agreed with me that (1) any debt negotiations which took place would have to be conducted, on our side, by Roosevelt-appointed officials—and after March 4th; (2) there must be no linking of debts and the Economic Conference: the two sets of negotiations might be concurrent, but they must be separate.

I was careful to point out that not only Hoover and Stimson but Davis as well, if given the opportunity, would urge another course. He laughingly told me not to worry: he felt as strongly on the question as I did.

Yet I could not help but worry when he added, then, that Davis would come along on the train, even though he made the further announcement that there would be no connection between his train talk with Davis and his call on Hoover later in the day and even though later, when specifically asked by the reporters whether Davis was to accompany him to the conference, he answered in the negative. And what happened later was amply to justify my fears.

After we arrived in Washington, Stimson came to see Roosevelt at his hotel. When they had talked alone briefly, F. D. R. called both Davis and me into the conference. There was some general discussion then of the British proposals, but nothing definite was agreed upon.

On the next morning, the 20th, the difference in point of view that had been smoldering between Davis, Rex, and myself burst into flame when he and Rex met in Davis' room at the hotel. They heatedly disagreed on the question of whether the debt conversations and discussions of other matters should be linked. I also had a brief talk with

Davis in which we argued the same question. Davis then went to Roosevelt and asked him point-blank if he would like to have him accompany him to the White House. To my dismay F. D. R. good-naturedly said that he could come if he wanted to. And so Roosevelt, Davis, and I set off for the conference.

Almost immediately, of course, the discussion centered upon the British proposals, and at once it became clear that Stimson, who, with Mills, accompanied the President, was assuming that Roosevelt had agreed with him as to the course to be followed.

There was, first, the assumption that discussions with the British should begin at once. Every argument conceivable about the need for immediacy was advanced after Roosevelt quietly repeated what he had said in his message of December 19th to the President—that he wished all discussion to be held in abeyance until after March 4th. But despite all argument Roosevelt stood firm, and, at last, Hoover was forced to concede this point.

Then there was the assumption that the new administration would receive representations on both debts and economic matters indiscriminately. Stimson seemed to believe that Roosevelt's agreement was in the bag. Hoover, Mills, and Davis, however, showed their hand by arguing the point. Roosevelt, who seemed to be enjoying this high-powered barrage, leaned back in his chair and said nothing. I soon found myself participating in the discussion. If Mr. Hoover felt that I had done a good deal of talking in the first conference, he certainly had occasion to think so at this one. But I was prepared to support what I understood to be Roosevelt's point of view with all the force I had—the more so since Davis, who was there by Roosevelt's grace, lacked the sensibility to keep from chiming in with the Hoover, Stimson, and Mills arguments.

Finally, after what seemed to be hours, Roosevelt put an end to this unequal debate. Firmly, unequivocally, he indicated that discussions of the debts and of other matters must be separate. There was nothing the others could do but yield.

Without a word President Hoover picked up a pad and started to write out the statement he would give to the press. As he proceeded, there was some little discussion as to its wording. But its text, as finally devised, indicates that there was no doubt as to Roosevelt's position—that it was thoroughly understood there was to be a clear demarcation between the two sorts of discussion with the British.[12]

[12] See Appendix C.

At the end of the meeting Stimson brought up the question of the form of statement he should make to the British government. Because of the fact that this statement would pertain to conferences that would not be held until the new administration came in, it must, of necessity, be a joint product. Roosevelt agreed. But he was taking the train South that afternoon. He told Stimson, therefore, to meet with me and prepare the statement, adding that I would have full authority to commit him to whatever I agreed upon. I then made an appointment to meet Stimson that afternoon at his office. So the conference ended.

We all returned to the hotel for lunch. Immediately after lunch, and shortly before Roosevelt was to leave for his train, while I was alone with him, Stimson telephoned. He had, in the interim since the end of our conference, composed a statement to be submitted to the British. This statement, which he read over the telephone, he attempted to have Roosevelt approve there and then. As he talked, Roosevelt indicated to me what the call was about. We agreed by sign language that he should tell Stimson to hold up the statement until I had a chance to see it.

I have always felt, and I think with justification, that Secretary Stimson attempted to catch Roosevelt in the midst of the hurry of departure and get him to agree, in substance, to what he had refused to agree to as late as that morning. It was not a pleasant conclusion, but it was none the less inescapable.

Rex Tugwell accompanied me to the State Department then, and, when I saw that Stimson had with him his Assistant Secretary of State, Mr. Harvey H. Bundy, and his Economic Adviser, Mr. Herbert Feis, I asked Rex to stand by.

After what had just happened, nothing could surprise me—even Stimson's blithe reading of a statement which, despite the clear understanding that had been reached in the morning and embodied in President Hoover's statement, linked the debts and other economic problems. I indicated to Stimson that the draft was wholly unsatisfactory. I could not agree to any statement that did not provide separate treatment of the two questions.

We then attempted to draft a new statement which would meet my objections, and, meanwhile, Rex tried to explain why, in our judgment, it was important to keep the matters separate. Stimson showed great indignation at this point and said testily to Rex that what he was proposing was likely to tear down everything that he, the Secretary, had been working for throughout his term. This little outburst was apparently an accumulation of irritation at the fact that his final efforts to commit Roosevelt to his point of view were being thwarted.

Stimson then went on and stated flatly that, when he had discussed the matter with Roosevelt, Roosevelt had said that the two questions were "twins." I remarked that they might be twins, but they were not Siamese twins.

Stimson's temper did not improve at this point, and when Rex made the suggestion that we delay the whole matter and consult Roosevelt again, he said that time was essential—that he intended to meet the British Ambassador soon, and then to have a press conference.

We went back to the work of draftsmanship. Again and again, as we struggled over the sentences, Stimson insisted that he knew Roosevelt's opinion better than I did. "In fact," he said, "I have the *aide-mémoire* of a telephone conversation in which the Governor agreed to joining the negotiations."

I insisted that there must have been some misunderstanding on one side or the other. I was perfectly clear as to Roosevelt's intentions about the procedure to be followed in this matter, and I was perfectly clear about what Roosevelt had agreed to that morning. If Stimson was unwilling to wait and consult him when he got off the train, my say as to his intentions would have to be final.

In the end, his good humor slowly returning, Stimson gave way, and we agreed on a formula. The statement to the British said that Mr. Roosevelt would be glad to receive early in March, "a representative or representatives of the British government" to discuss the future of the debts.

Separated from this, and in another paragraph, the statement indicated that Mr. Roosevelt would be glad to receive representatives "also" sent to discuss world economic questions in which the two governments were mutually interested.

The document thus definitely distinguished the two sets of negotiations, and when Stimson and I initialed it, I felt that the battle had been won.

Secretary Stimson evidently felt that way too. He told me frankly that he had been compelled by my insistence to follow a course with which he was not in agreement. Therefore he intended to leave a memorandum in the State Department files registering his mature judgment that another course would have been preferable.

I spared him the retort that it was a matter of no importance to me what he chose to leave in the files so long as the President-elect had been saved from a commitment that would have been dangerous. We parted in the most agreeable fashion imaginable, the Secretary assuring me that he would be delighted to "cooperate" with me and inviting me to "keep in touch" with him.

The net of that day's dueling was that Roosevelt had been committed no further than he had determined to be committed when we boarded the train the day before. I had also been able to defend a principle that had, during the critical moment, become even more important to me than any personal plans of my own or any personal devotion to Roosevelt. And that day, considered in the light of the preceding three weeks, had etched a few indelible lines in my mental picture of Roosevelt—lines that were to deepen as time went on.

5

Those satisfactions, such as they were, proved to be the only ones the sequence of events afforded.

On the 21st there appeared in the *New York Sun* a long "dope" story to the effect that the Democratic leaders were eager to have Davis supplant me in all contacts with the State Department. The next morning I was shocked to read a story in the *New York Times*—a semi-official story—giving a thoroughly inaccurate account of what had happened in the meeting with Stimson, announcing it had ended in a "temporary 'deadlock' " and adding that Stimson had delivered the reply to the British verbally.[13]

There was only one way to handle the situation. I telephoned F. D. R. immediately and gave him an accurate account of the Stimson negotiations. Roosevelt approved thoroughly what I had done and suggested that I call Stimson not only to check on the report that Stimson had transmitted the invitation to the British orally but to inquire also how it was that inaccurate stories of our meeting had leaked out of the State Department.

I then told him of the gossip in the *Sun* and added frankly that there

[13] That the blame for this error rested with the official source of the news and not with the *Times* was shown two days later in a signed dispatch by Arthur Krock, chief of the *Times* Bureau. Commenting upon "a certain furtiveness among the [State] departmental officials," he added, "For example: Last Friday the press was informed that the communication to Ambassador Lindsay had been 'oral.' It now appears that whatever words Mr. Stimson used were accompanied by a written document. With perfectly straight faces, officials at the department explained today that in diplomatic parlance, that was really oral, its contents having been 'verbally' outlined at the same time."

was genuine doubt in my own mind as to whether he did not prefer to have Davis take over on foreign affairs in the weeks before March 4th. I should be glad to withdraw without any hard feelings.

Roosevelt laughed heartily. He assured me that the story was "planted"—probably by overenthusiastic supporters of Davis, who would like to see him appointed Secretary of State. And then he said what follows, which I quote from my journal of that day:

> I am through with Norman Davis. The incident is closed so far as I'm concerned. When he got off the train we said good-by and no mention of a future appointment was made. In the matter of debts you are my sole representative. . . . I also want you to go ahead and get Rex and two or three others to begin preparing the stuff I'll need for the preliminary economic discussions with the foreign representatives after March 4th.

I told him that I would come to Warm Springs in a week or so to talk over that and a good many other questions. Meanwhile I would go to Washington to check over the replies Stimson would be sending to the other nations that had made requests similar to that of the British.

I called Stimson then. He expressed deep regret over the newspaper accounts of our meeting—and quite properly so, since the material for them must have come from his Department. (Rex and I had left Washington after the meeting without any contact with the press.) There followed his assurance that the *Times* story was incorrect in saying that he had transmitted the statement verbally to the British Ambassador: he had, he said, handed to the British Ambassador the memorandum which he and I had initialed. We then agreed that I should stop by the State Department late that week to go over the replies to Italy, Czechoslovakia, and the rest.

This I did, on January 26th. And aside from a minor set-to with Stimson over the rude tone of the reply he proposed to send to the French, everything went smoothly enough.

On that same visit to Washington, I had a meeting with Senators Joseph T. Robinson, Pittman, and Hull and talked over with them the charges the Republican Arthur R. Robinson of Indiana had made on the floor of the Senate about our handling of the debt negotiations. I gave the three the entire story, informed them that Roosevelt had not yielded an inch with respect to the debts, and received their assurances, in return, that they were satisfied with what had been done.

This conversation also dispelled the confusion that had resulted in their minds from a series of newspaper stories that had appeared during the days immediately preceding—stories that represented us as being nonplused by Great Britain's response to the American note of January 21st. Using as their springboard, first, the January 24th speech of the Chancellor of the Exchequer, Neville Chamberlain, at Leeds and, second, the British note of January 25th, these stories had it that Great Britain had rejected a Hoover-Roosevelt offer to use the debts for trading purposes.[14]

Now *we* knew there had been no such offer made, and hence there could be no rejection of it. Hoover and Stimson knew we had flatly refused to authorize what would have been, in substance, the making of such an offer. The British government knew it. And all newspaper readers who had carefully examined the text of Hoover's statement of January 20th must have realized that we had insisted upon a sharp separation of debt conversations and economic conversations.

The facts were simple enough. The important aspect of the Chamberlain speech was not what was said, but what was left unsaid. True, Chamberlain had boldly taken the position that the settlement of the debt to the United States must be both small and final. But any good trader would take that position before getting down to real business. The significance of the speech lay in the fact that Chamberlain had abandoned the British demand that we yield on the debts in return for economic concessions—had abandoned the notion of a *quid pro quo* debt discussion.

That interpretation of his speech was completely validated by an examination of the British note of the following day—which, by implication, distinguished debt talks and other conversations. The news in that situation was not that "Britain Bars Trading in Debt Parley," but that Britain had finally given up the ghost when she realized that the President-elect simply *would not consent* to any trading.

And any vestiges of doubt as to the validity of this interpretation were finally dispelled by Chamberlain's frank and friendly talk to the American newspaper correspondents on February 2nd. While he did not minimize the differences of opinion between the two countries with respect to the debts, Chamberlain indicated clearly then that the British were not going to tie up questions of the debts with other

[14] The *New York Times*, for example, said that Britain's reply was "a rejection of the Roosevelt-Hoover proposal that war debts and related economic questions be discussed here for concurrent action with a view to affecting the trade of a debt concession for something in the sphere of currency stabilization, reciprocal tariff arrangements, or the like."

international economic questions at the forthcoming conferences in Washington.

It was, of course, a demonstration of the skill that so often characterizes British diplomacy that the English saw they must retreat while there was still plenty of time to retreat in good order. Acceptance of our policy that there would be no trade on debts was the only possible basis of negotiation with the new administration, and it had come with far better grace from them than it had from Hoover, Stimson, and Davis.

In pursuance of this realistic *volte-face* the British Cabinet asked Sir Ronald Lindsay to return to England—presumably to give them his own impressions of the President-elect, of American public opinion with respect to the subjects of the forthcoming negotiations, and of the way they ought to go about presenting their case to the United States. Immediately on hearing this news, Roosevelt suggested to Stimson that it might smooth the way to a better understanding of his policies in England if Sir Ronald came to Warm Springs and had a talk with him. At best the indirect transmittal of his views through the State Department had been none too satisfactory for any of the principals.

Hence Sir Ronald's flight to Warm Springs on the 28th of January.

No one could have been better suited, from the British point of view, for the task of sounding out Mr. Roosevelt. The two men had known each other, of course, since the days of the Wilson Administration. But more than that, Sir Ronald was exactly the type of man to attract the friendly, frank, and open side of Roosevelt. Good-humored, kind, and direct, he always suggested the wholesomeness of roast beef with the sophisticated tang of Worcestershire sauce.

It is interesting to note that, while the papers were buzzing with rumors as to what specific propositions were being sent back to England through the Ambassador, for the most part the conversation at Warm Springs was a friendly and not very definite chat about all manner of things. Yet Lindsay's perceptiveness was never better illustrated than by his ability to size up the situation in the midst of these sociabilities. That became evident soon after his return to England, when, with every day that passed, the British grew less eager to discuss the debts and concentrated on preparing for the economic discussions.

Meanwhile, suffice it to say for the course that was followed:

(1) The argument that debts needed immediate settlement was predicated on the belief that the alternative was default. That this was not

the fact was demonstrated by England's payment in full on December 15th, by France's hints that she could pay if we made it worth her while, and by examination of the budgets of our debtors—whose expenditures for armaments in most cases far exceeded the amount of the installments due us that year.

(2) The argument that we could have persuaded Great Britain to return to the gold standard in the winter of 1932-33 or even to stabilize at that time if we had made concessions on debts was obviously illusory.

(3) The argument that debt payments involved an insurmountable transfer problem overlooked the fact that the nationals of both England and France owned vast amounts of securities and other property in this country which could have been utilized, within limits, in making the transfer. Theoretical objections to the transfer of gold at that time have been shaken by the hard fact that great quantities of gold have come into the United States from England and France, anyhow, since then.

(4) The argument that agreement on currencies, tariff barriers, and the like presupposed a settlement of the debt question was abandoned, for all serious purposes, by the foreign nations themselves long before the London Conference. The history of the Conference, which we shall examine later, indicates that debts were not a subject of negotiation there and that agreement on other matters was quite within the realm of possibility nevertheless.

(5) The facts that the debts have continued to stand and the failure of our debtors to pay them have, from 1932 up to the present day, acted as a bar to further European loans. Thus the maintenance of the debts as living obligations has served not only to notify Europe that we did not propose to underwrite another European war but to check any tendencies we might have to repeat the mistakes of the 'twenties—to rely for "prosperity" upon an unreal foreign purchasing power while we overlooked the insufficiency of our domestic purchasing power.

In any event, Lindsay's visit to Warm Springs concluded our debt dealings until some time after the inauguration. No one, from that point on, continued to press debt revision as indispensable. That particular engagement in the struggle to keep the Hoover-Stimson foreign policies from being forced upon Roosevelt had been won, though those of the Hoover-Stimson-Davis persuasion had gained strategic advantage elsewhere that would be used to the full later.

6

I have not attempted to conceal the fact that the Hoover-Stimson-Davis affair produced a marked change in my own psychology between the middle of December and the end of January. As I came face to face with those forces—external and internal—that threatened to impair the fundamental integrity of the New Deal even before it got under way, mere willingness on my part to be of temporary service to Roosevelt had become an Irishman's instinctive squaring off to battle for the thing in which he believes. With every attack, every setback, every sign of confusion of policy, my desire to go about my own business seemed less urgent.

But there was more than this to the transformation. It would have been foolish to deny that, by February 1st, the outlook on the domestic front was even more grim than it had been during the blackest moments of the fight over foreign policy.

Things were going badly in a sharply divided Congress. It was already possible to foresee that precious little of the new legislation that was needed would be got through the lame-duck session.

The farm bill that had emerged from the House on January 12th was almost a travesty of the plan Roosevelt had described during the campaign. Its hopeless inadequacy, and the obvious dislike of "Cotton" Ed Smith, ranking member of the Senate Committee on Agriculture, for the Roosevelt farm policy, accurately foretold the final result—no satisfactory farm legislation by March 4th.

Farm-mortgage relief was the subject of continuous wrangling. There were numberless bills in both Houses that included some sort of provision for extending federal credit for that purpose. But their very profusion suggested that agreement on any one bill would be impossible.[15]

Legislation to relieve bankrupts of intolerable fees and legal delays was muddled beyond belief. Within the Roosevelt ranks Berle and Frankfurter were at loggerheads over the form it should take. In Congress there were squabbles about the constitutionality and the soundness of several bills—argument embittered by the question whether farm-mortgage relief, in one form or another, should be included in such legislation.[16]

[15] No farm-mortgage bill actually passed the lame-duck Congress.

[16] A bankruptcy law, however, finally squeaked through in the last days of the 72nd Congress.

The Senate and the House were deadlocked on the amount of alcoholic content in beer that constituted an intoxicant. Even the passage of a resolution repealing the Eighteenth Amendment—pledged by both parties—seemed doubtful at January's end.[17]

The platform and campaign pledges on budget balance and economy threatened, too, to go aglimmering. There had been a major rumpus over new taxes in December, agreement on a tax plan between Roosevelt and the Congressional leaders early in January, and a forced abandonment of the plan by the leaders almost immediately afterward.

And there seemed to be only the barest chance that Congress would grant the President extraordinary powers to do what Congress itself was unwilling to do—cut costs drastically.[18]

In short, by February 1st it was clear that any bits of New Deal legislation that might be wrested from the dying Congress would be so much velvet. A special session would have to be called very soon after the inauguration—whether or not such haste was theoretically desirable.

But the chaos in Congress did not begin to suggest the confusion and despair of the depression-racked country outside. The story of sagging farm-commodity prices, of farmers banding together to protect their homes against foreclosures and tax sales with rifle and shotgun, of the creeping paralysis of industrial activity, of the growing number of the unemployed, of the vanishing credit of the states, cities, and towns that were trying to feed them, of the staggering public and private indebtedness—the story in all its terrifying detail has been told too often to need elaboration here. The point is that it was practically impossible to avoid knowing, by the turn of the year, that the most acute economic crisis in the country's history was coming to a head. The business indices, the constant reports of Woodin and Baruch, the desperate letters of thousands upon thousands of normally self-reliant men and women—all heralded the collapse.

Only a monstrous egotist could, under such circumstances, have

[17] After losing its first test in the House, it was brought up in the Senate in a form that Garner privately called "a welch on the Democratic platform." Only in the closing days of the session was a resolution that conformed to the platform finally got from Congress.

[18] This authorization was finally passed on March 1st as a rider to the Treasury-Post Office Appropriations bill. Though I was credited, at the time, with the devising of the scheme that thus enlarged the powers of the Executive, the fact is that the idea was current in the East in the early spring of 1932 and was generally discussed at Albany and Hyde Park in April, 1932.

given himself over to soul searchings about whether it would be better, wiser, safer, to plunge ahead into the maelstrom or to scramble back to the rim of things and look on objectively. It was a time for muffling doubts and ignoring the minatory fingers of affectionate friends. If Roosevelt failed, in the weeks to come, no one's dreams of individual salvation would be worth a damn in any case. If he wanted me still, I would stand by until the storm abated.

I landed at Warm Springs on the night of February 1st with only one request—that I be permitted to hold any office Roosevelt chose except that of Assistant Secretary of State. For during the preceding weeks I had seen those mysterious processes that had led Roosevelt to believe, in the campaign, that he had achieved a "compromise" on the tariff come out into the open. I had learned that he had offered the first place in his Cabinet to a man who personified the philosophical opposition to the New Deal policies.

CHAPTER IV

WILD SWANS AND FAITHFUL DOGS

ONE of the best yarns in H. H. Kohlsaat's chatty memoirs[1] is his story of how McKinley came to appoint his Secretary of the Treasury. It seems that McKinley had confided in Kohlsaat at the end of January, 1897, that he was desperately looking for a suitable Secretary of the Treasury. A couple of days later Kohlsaat called McKinley on the telephone from Chicago and told him he had found him a Secretary of the Treasury—Lyman J. Gage, with whom he was in the habit of walking to work in the morning.

"Have I ever met him?" McKinley asked.

Kohlsaat reminded him that Gage had been present at a reception he had attended in Chicago.

"Oh," said McKinley, "did he have white whiskers?"

"Yes," said Kohlsaat.

"That is an inspiration," McKinley answered.

And thus did the "advance agent of prosperity" fill the great financial office in his administration.

I have never been able to think of the selection of the Roosevelt Cabinet, in 1933, without recalling this story. There was always casualness, although there were no whiskers.

Contrary to tradition, the chief political architect of Roosevelt's November victory not only did not guide, but scarcely sat in on the process of Cabinet making. For some curious reason that I have never been able to understand, Jim Farley was not invited to put forward a list of his own. He was merely informed of Roosevelt's decisions and allowed, in some instances, to discuss the invitation with the prospect.

My situation, far more justifiably, was like his. I wasn't asked, but told about the Cabinet. Yet I was permitted to look on to a much greater extent than he, and I was asked to act as intermediary in far

[1] Kohlsaat, *From McKinley to Harding—Personal Recollections of Our Presidents.* Charles Scribner's Sons; New York, 1923; pp. 55-59.

more cases. Louis Howe, on the other hand, had a couple of fixed ideas on the subject and actually succeeded in selling them to Roosevelt. Except in one case, I merely enjoyed Roosevelt's confidence and served as negotiator.

These privileges were not to be underestimated. For if Roosevelt's final selections failed to indicate much about his future policies to the country at large, to one who was seeking to understand him rather than seeking a clue to policy the process of selection itself was magnificently revealing.

There was, for one thing, Roosevelt's spirited disdain of most of the political rules that usually govern such things. He considered himself under direct obligations to no man so far as Cabinet appointments were concerned. Neither recognized party leadership nor active campaign support figured heavily in his calculations.

This might have suggested to a logical mind that he wanted to surround himself with the best possible advisers he could get, whether they were "big names" or relatively obscure men. But nothing in his conversation indicated any such desire. Certainly the Cabinet as it finally took shape did not even remotely hint of it.

There was another possibility—the chance that he might want a Cabinet which, regardless of ability or political status, would be wholeheartedly sympathetic to his policies. But except in the consideration of the Treasury appointment, the question of general sympathies was never brought up. Nor was there, on the other hand, any extensive attempt to balance the political and economic philosophies of the Cabinet members.

So far as I could see, there was neither a well-defined purpose nor underlying principle in the selection of the Roosevelt Cabinet. It was shaped by a score of unrelated factors. And in some cases it almost seemed as though happenstance played only a slightly smaller part than it did in the Kohlsaat story.

Roosevelt wanted to give some recognition to the Republican progressives. He vaguely recognized the need for a kind of geographical representation in the Cabinet. He seemed to resent all those, except Josephus Daniels, who had outranked him in the Wilson Administration. This eliminated such men as Newton Baker and McAdoo from the running. He happened to like Senator Walsh. But he ignored several men whose stature was comparable to Walsh's, because he had an automatic disposition to pooh-pooh the qualities of those the public rated as "big." He believed that he could entrust a good deal of power to subordinates like myself without complicating his relations with his Cabinet. He wanted to be the first President to appoint a woman to a Cabinet post. (He first thought of Ruth Bryan Owen and later switched to Frances Perkins, his own Labor Commissioner in New York State.) He loved the sea and could not have imagined anyone in the Navy post who would not be highly susceptible to suggestions from him. These, and a half dozen other impulses, half thought out, half sensed, determined the ingredients of the rather savorless Cabinet pudding that was ultimately dished up to the public.

This is generalization, of course. Perhaps the historians of the future will be able to discover in the Roosevelt Cabinet some delicate pattern overlooked by me. If so, I wish them well. My contribution to their search is the unvarnished report of what I know about the official family's selection.

2

The first long talk I had with Roosevelt on Cabinet personnel took place in the little study at Albany in the early evening of December 23, 1932. He had decided, he said, to begin by selecting someone for the State Department. The rest of the Cabinet could be "more or less" fitted around that man.

He talked desultorily of the qualifications of Senators Key Pittman, Cordell Hull, and Joe Robinson; of Newton Baker, Owen Young, Bernie Baruch, and Robert W. Bingham of Louisville. It was clear he had come to no final decision. But there were indications that he had already eliminated most of these men from serious consideration. Baruch could be better used elsewhere, he felt. Joe Robinson was needed as Senate leader. Robinson's supreme desire was a Court appointment, in any case. Baker simply wouldn't do. Pittman he liked, but Pittman would emerge as Chairman of the Committee on Foreign Relations in the Senate if Swanson should come into the Cabinet. As such, his power and influence could be as great as that of the Secretary of State.

There remained Bingham, Young, and Hull. Of Bingham, Roosevelt frankly said that he knew little or nothing except the facts that Bingham was publisher of the *Louisville Courier-Journal,* that he had contributed substantially to the campaign fund, and that Colonel "Mouse"—a pet name for old House—had repeatedly recommended him. It seemed that Bingham's very obscurity, so far as national politics was concerned, intrigued him. He spoke laughingly of the "stiff dose for the international bankers" Bingham's appointment would be.

But such conversational high jinks were not to be taken seriously (though it is surprising how often they are by people who don't know Roosevelt well). Soon after there must have been some checkup on Bingham that satisfied Roosevelt of Bingham's inadequacy for the job. At any rate, I never heard F. D. R. mention him in that connection again.

Of Hull, he spoke in completely different terms. Hull was Louis Howe's idea, originally, I knew. As far back as 1928 Louis had told me of his boundless admiration for him in explaining why he thought Hull would be the perfect candidate for Vice President on the Democratic ticket that year. All through the spring and early summer of 1932 he'd overlooked no opportunity to speak well of Hull, who had been influential among the Southern party leaders in supporting Roosevelt for the nomination.

The effect of this was cumulative. By August, when Hull's name first came up in conversation between us (this was at the time F. D. R. sent out his letter about me to the elder statesmen of the party), Roosevelt was unconsciously using Louis' very words to describe his own feelings about Hull. He spoke of Hull's dignity and his high-mindedness. This was repeated on the December night we talked of Cabinet possibilities, with the added comment that Hull's appointment would be pleasing to the old-line party leaders. There was not the slightest evidence that Roosevelt saw the fundamental conflict between his New Deal and the beliefs of the older Democrats, the basic incongruity of his own program and Hull's Adam Smith economics.

Young's chances were less good than Hull's, I gathered. Roosevelt recognized his ability, intellectual distinction, and great hold on the respect of the public. He mentioned the fact that Young was one of the few prominent industrialists with relatively liberal ideas. Besides, Young's appointment would be reassuring to the business community. But, in some almost imperceptible way, I got the sense that he didn't feel he could run around in his mental carpet slippers in Young's presence, while he undoubtedly could in Hull's. And I would have been willing to give odds that Young wouldn't be asked to serve when he added casually that Young's connections with the utility business (which, by the way, were wholly unblameworthy) would "make progressives mad."

Yet the matter didn't seem to be by any means settled when I left the Mansion that night, and I was really surprised when, a week and a half later, Louis Howe (with whom I continued to swap notes on "The Boss'" activities all through the interregnum) told me that Young was definitely out.

It was then that I learned that, much as Louis admired Hull, he was uneasy about this decision of "Franklin's." In the preconvention period, he confided, there had been a moment when a number of victories by Al Smith and Garner put a chock under the wheels of the band-wagon. At that moment Young had loomed up on the Democratic scene as an exceedingly likely compromise candidate. Subsequently, Young withdrew his name from consideration. Louis told me that he felt the amenities required that Young be given "the refusal" of the office of Secretary of State.

Whatever Louis' feelings in the matter, this wasn't done. I think it was sometime during the second or third weeks in January that Hull was offered the post.[2] At any rate, on January 22nd Roosevelt told me over the telephone from Warm Springs to keep "the gentleman from Tennessee" informed of what I was doing on foreign affairs.

Orders were orders, however inexplicable. I called on Hull on January 27th.[3] I had met him only once before, when he came to the 65th Street house with the other congressional leaders on the night of January 5th to confer with Roosevelt on the legislative program. But he had talked so little then that it had been impossible for me to get any impression of him as a person. It developed that this, in itself, was characteristic. But I was impressed by the kindliness and gentleness with which this gaunt, inarticulate man received me and heard the story of the negotiations with the Hoover Administration. His few comments indicated neither agreement nor disagreement with the course we had followed. There was just an H. B. Warner air of infinite patience and long-suffering.

I came away with the hope that Hull's capacity for bearing pain was

[2] Meanwhile Young, who was greatly embarrassed by the constant mention of his name as a Cabinet possibility in political "dope" stories, had already sent a private letter to F. D. R. through Will Woodin indicating his disinclination to serve in the Cabinet because of the failing health of his wife. I am certain that Young would not have accepted a public office at that time even if he had been offered one. But I have always considered it unfortunate, in the light of what Louis told me, that the gracious gesture was not made, and that, later, after Mrs. Young's death, when Young became available, he was substantially ignored by the administration.

[3] This visit with Hull alone took place earlier in the day than the conference with him, Joe Robinson, and Key Pittman, referred to on page 102. It was a talk with the potential Secretary of State, while Hull attended the later meeting with the others in his capacity as senator.

as great as it seemed to be. For the tariff episode of the campaign left little doubt in my mind that acceptance of the State Department job at the hands of Franklin Roosevelt would result in either bitter frustration for the lifelong champion of tariff reduction or a complete double somersault by Roosevelt—and it never occurred to me that there was much likelihood of the latter.

One way or the other, there was bound to be turmoil. And I had nothing but pity for the guilelessness that might lead Hull to walk with eyes wide open into a difficult, perhaps an intolerable situation.

Several days later these reflections were substantiated in a wholly unexpected way. I was approached in Washington by five prominent Democratic senators, individually.[4] They understood, they said, that Hull was being considered for Secretary of State. Since I was going directly to Warm Springs, would I convey their views on the subject to the President-elect? They assured me that, fond as they were of Hull, they couldn't "see" him in that job. He knew little about foreign affairs generally and was so set on the idea of tariff reduction it was unlikely that he could ever acquire a broad view of them. "Why, it's an open secret that he's got only one string to his bow. And every time he makes his speech on tariffs, he clears the floor of the Senate," one of them said. Further, his appointment made absolutely no sense in the light of Roosevelt's announced tariff policies. For good measure, they added that Hull was unable to handle men well. Two of them requested that I tell Roosevelt that, while they would be glad to see Hull in the Treasury, they looked with serious concern upon his possible appointment to the State Department.

This was ticklish business. I told each of the senators that I would convey his message without any personal expression of opinion. But, lest there be any misunderstanding, I determined to do it over the telephone from Washington in the presence of at least one of them.

I did that, telling F. D. R. in whose presence I was speaking and reporting precisely what I had been told. Roosevelt listened in silence. When I had finished, he said, "So . . . Well, you tell the senators I'll be glad to have some fine idealism in the State Department."

That was pretty definitive. His "Dutch was up." I knew his answer would have been the same if the five senators had pleaded with him on bended knees.

[4] Three of these men have since died. But because the others are still active in public life and because it might gravely affect their relations with the present administration, I do not feel free to mention their names. These will, however, be found in my papers when they are made available.

It was my third experience at broadcasting storm warnings into the figurative void. But I certainly didn't propose to ignore them myself. The job Roosevelt had asked me to do was hazardous enough as it was. I was no professional daredevil, spoiling to pitch camp on a mound of dynamite sticks.

And so on February 3rd, when we were alone at the swimming pool in Warm Springs, I told Roosevelt that, though I was willing to go on as he had asked for the time being, I would take no job at all, or the humblest in his giving, rather than take nominal office in the State Department. Under the best of circumstances my situation would be anomalous. No Secretary of any department was likely to be overjoyed at having an Assistant who saw the President more often than he, who knew the President's mind better, and who was asked to handle matters of which the Secretary knew nothing.

But to house me, who would do well enough as a symbol of the new order, with the living embodiment of what the New Deal was not would be tempting providence. Anything would be better than that. And then I added dryly, to make my point unmistakable, "Why, if I were in the Philippines, I could almost serve you better than I could in the State Department." Meaning, of course, that the handicap would be no greater if I were in South Africa or the Mongolian Desert or the middle of the Pacific Ocean.

To my utter astonishment—for Roosevelt was usually quick at catching shades of meaning—he shot back, "No, no. You'd be eight thousand miles away. I need you here."

I sheepishly explained. I hadn't the remotest intention of asking for the Philippines job. I was merely saying facetiously that I could be half a world away and do the kind of confidential work he wanted done no worse than I would across the street from the White House, if I had to contend with the natural resentment of a boss-in-name-only. That was not to imply that I didn't like Hull as a man. In fact, I was greatly taken with his gentleness and simplicity. But it would take a saint to bear such a cross. And I preferred not to bank on the saint in any man.

The answer came, "Hull knows all about it. There'll be no misunderstanding with him if he takes the job. You're going to work with *me*."

I stubbornly repeated that even if Hull had been warned that there'd be a large and reluctant fly in his ointment, it was asking too much of a human being to expect him to relish having it there.

But F. D. R. was not to be budged. The job of Assistant Secretary of State, because of its lack of statutory duties, was the one job that would do. I was to forget my worries and the "false alarms" of Felix Frankfurter and other good friends whose size-up of the situation coincided with mine.[5] Surely I didn't doubt his word? Everything was going to be all right.

Then, later, when he saw I was still unconvinced, he undertook to reassure me by dictating to me a brief statement as to my duties. They were to include *the handling of "the foreign debts, the world economic conference, supervision of the economic adviser's office and such additional duties as the President may direct in the general field of foreign and domestic government"*!

Possession of this slip of paper, I knew, was not going to level any of the hurdles I foresaw. But when Roosevelt added that I might keep it for my own protection and use it if it became necessary—a possibility he could barely imagine—I saw that I had no alternative but to give in.

I saw Hull next on February 8th, to carry out Roosevelt's order to "get a definite answer from Hull." We didn't speak, then, either of my appointment or of the Roosevelt tariff policies. But there was no indication that he felt anything but the same kindliness toward me that he showed at our first private meeting. He said somewhat awkwardly (Arthur Krock has explained that he sometimes talks "in cascades of words, rushing murkily over tangles of syntax"[6]) that being Secretary of State entailed heavy social responsibilities.[7] That would cost a lot of money. And since he was both a man of modest means and hated entertaining, he wasn't sure he ought to accept.

I assured him I didn't think he needed to feel any concern about the "social" question. But I would get in touch with Louis Howe and

[5] It was about this time that Felix sent me the following letter:

Dear Ray:

> Your tasks at best will not be easy in the days and months ahead, and you are, therefore, entitled to have your status left in no equivocation and to have it as clearly defined as the nature of your duties will demand. That means publicly and candidly declared. Of course F. D. R. is fine and sensible and generous about all these matters, but others are involved, and as time passes men's feelings of good sense and disinterestedness become frayed and fatigued. That's a situation easy to guard against at the outset, and it is to the public interest that it be guarded against, not the least to the interest of the new President himself. . . .

Yours as always,
F. F.

[6] *New York Times,* December 29, 1938.

[7] Perhaps he had in mind Krock's bantering about how he would have to "get a big house with butlers and footmen," if he became Secretary of State. See *We Saw It Happen.* Simon & Schuster; New York, 1938; p. 17.

with F. D. R., who was then cruising on Vincent Astor's yacht, and report back.

Louis, back in New York, decided that the only sensible way to solve Hull's problem was to get as Under Secretary someone who would do the entertaining in his place. I talked to Hull about this. He seemed to be satisfied. And so Louis and I radioed to F. D. R. on February 11th in a simple code he had suggested before leaving Warm Springs, ". . . further conferences on Tennessee project [Hull] indicate possible adoption provided some other food supplying and consuming means can be found."

Howe had William Phillips in mind as the "other food supplying and consuming means." But obviously this was a decision that had to wait on F. D. R.'s return. So the matter of Hull's acceptance hung fire.

Meanwhile a very curious thing had happened. Stories began to appear in Washington gossip columns that I was sponsoring the Phillips appointment because I thought I could "control" Phillips. It was said too, that I could not "control" Sumner Welles, who had also been spoken of as candidate for the Under Secretary's post.

The fact was that Welles wasn't under consideration by either Roosevelt or Louis except for the post of Assistant Secretary in charge of Latin American Affairs and, while F. D. R. was at sea, Louis had been instructed to make a careful study of his record to determine whether that post should be offered. I had nothing to do with either Louis' decision about Phillips or the researches about Welles. It was a matter of complete indifference to me which was chosen to do what within the Department. I knew neither. I knew only that both were experienced in the diplomatic service, both were well-to-do, both were friends of Roosevelt, and neither, by any stretch of the imagination, knew what the New Deal was all about.

So the stories, which were palpably untrue, weren't, in themselves, annoying.

But when they were followed up with others—to the effect that I was to be "planted" in the State Department as Roosevelt's "man" for the same reason that William R. Castle, Jr., had allegedly been "planted" by Hoover in Stimson's bailiwick—all the alarms in my political firehouse went off. Hull wasn't going to like this. And I couldn't say that I blamed him.

Yet it was neither his fault nor mine. It was the first of the inevitable consequences of the situation Roosevelt refused to face. It would be repeated so long as we were both in the State Department or, perhaps, so long as my status was not publicly cleared up.

And so I marched down to Louis' office with the statement F. D. R. had given me. It remained now to have this statement given to the press. I wanted advice as to when and how to do it.

I found dear old Josephus Daniels with Louis and, knowing his experience and reputed finesse, I put the problem to them both. I received, I'm sorry to say, the worst political advice I ever got. They both told me to ignore the stories, that publication of the statement F. D. R. had dictated would create more confusion than there was already. Anyhow—this, when I protested—it would be entirely out of order for me to hand it out in F. D. R.'s absence. I must do nothing until he returned.

I stupidly did not realize the implications of Louis' position until I took the matter to Roosevelt on the 18th of February—the day after he got back to New York. "Oh, that!" he said. "Yes, Louis's been telling me about it. I really wish you wouldn't make the statement public. . . . By the way, I've decided on Billy Phillips for Under Secretary, and I'm sure now Hull will accept."[8]

It was on hearing this answer that I decided to stay in Washington only a month. I made a record of the decision, too—in letters to several friends (sent on February 18th) and in a verbal statement to the newspapermen (made on March 2nd).

3

The invitation to Carter Glass came from Roosevelt at his most unconventional—when he was doing what everybody expected of him. It was, actually, compelled by an almost unanimous party opinion. Glass had been Secretary of the Treasury. He was the party's "works" on banking and finance, and his appointment would be reassuring at a time when the already shaky credit structure of the country seemed to cry out for reassurances.

The offer was first made in January. Roosevelt saw Glass briefly in Washington on January 19th and urged him to accept. But their talk was hurried: F. D. R. was preoccupied with the chief business in hand that day—the debt talk with Hoover—and Glass, sensitive and proud, was not the man to obtrude his own problems at such a moment.

[8] Hull's appointment was announced on February 21st.

No decision was reached. And so, before Roosevelt left for Warm Springs, he instructed me to carry on the negotiations with Glass—to find out what was making Glass hesitate, and to report back to him.

On January 27th Glass and I met in his office. Characteristically, Glass began by saying that he would have liked to speak to the "Guvnah" at length about the Treasury offer. It was too bad the opportunity hadn't presented itself. However, perhaps it would help if he talked frankly to me.

It was impossible not to find this faint touch of petulance endearing. I found myself listening first with great sympathy, and then with profound respect for his canniness. Here was a man who didn't buy pigs in pokes.

He wanted to know, first, he said, whether he would have a free hand in selecting the personnel in the Treasury. Particularly, he wanted his old colleague, Russell Leffingwell, as Under Secretary. If Roosevelt felt that Leffingwell's Morgan connection was an insuperable political obstacle, he would yield. But, in general, he wanted to be free to choose his assistants.

Second, he was worried about Roosevelt's policy on the gold standard. Inflation was an issue on which he could not and would not yield. And if there was any possibility of a resort to it, he wanted to be "a roaring lion in the Senate."

I repeated this conversation to Roosevelt next day over the telephone.

"Make it perfectly clear to him that, so far as subordinates go, we simply can't tie up with '23' [Morgan & Co.]," F. D. R. said. And, "So far as inflation goes, you can say that *we're not going to throw ideas out of the window simply because they're labeled inflation.* If you feel that the old boy doesn't want to go along, don't press him."

Three days later, when I went to Washington, I visited Glass at his home and told him, referring to my notes, what F. D. R. had said—all, of course, except the important stage direction at the end.[9] Glass yielded on the question of appointments. He would not insist on Leffingwell, he said, and he was sure that, as reasonable men, Roosevelt and he would be able to agree on other appointments. As to inflation, I was to tell Roosevelt that he was "not against inflation *in*

[9] Wherever I acted as intermediary, I always made notes of conversations. This was simply a matter of caution—to protect not only myself but the two principals in each case.

vacuo, but just you bring me any specific measure providing for inflation and see if I can't punch it full of holes."

But then there appeared a new element in the picture. He was reluctant to enter the Cabinet because of his wife's ailing health and his own frail condition.

I urged him to see his family doctor in Virginia as soon as possible and get a decision as to whether he could stand the burdens of the office.

When I saw him next, he definitely said that he could not accept. He did not bring up the question of inflation directly. But I knew it weighed heavily in the scales because he phrased his refusal this way: "Even if there were no other objection, my own health and the heavy social burden that would fall on my wife would preclude my acceptance." He would send Roosevelt, through me, a letter declining the offer. This he did on February 8th.

I received his letter of declination and its gracious covering letter with a profound sense of relief.[10] Throughout these negotiations I

[10] I am delighted that the care with which I tried to conduct these negotiations, as well as the accuracy with which I remember them, has been attested substantially by Glass, through his official biographers, his secretary, Rixey Smith, and Norman Beasley. Glass' letter of February 8th, to me, with its significant second sentence, appears in this work (*Carter Glass.* Longmans, Green & Company; New York, 1939; p. 332) as follows:

"My dear Mr. Moley:

"I am sending you the letter to the President-elect, under seal and registered, and will be obliged if you will communicate my decision to Mr. Roosevelt. You have been very kind and patient to hear my story and I derive infinite satisfaction from the fact that you seem to concur in my conclusions.

"Hoping for you the best of good fortunes and happiness, believe me,

"Sincerely yours

CARTER GLASS."

Glass' letter to the President, dated February 7th, also reproduced in the Smith-Beasley book, reads:

"My dear Franklin:

"I shall never be able to tell you the measure of my appreciation of the honor which you have done me in inviting me to take the responsible post of Secretary of the Treasury in your cabinet. It grieves me to find that I am unable to requite your confidence and kindness by complying with your wish. I have very earnestly considered the matter in all its important aspects, prompted by a compelling desire to be of service to you and to the country. You may be sure it has caused me genuine distress to reach the decision indicated.

"Aside from the fact that the reaction to the suggestion among my colleagues in the Senate has been positively averse to me leaving this body, the unanimity of protest from Virginia by press and representative men has been emphatic. Without any intimation from me as to my own concurring conviction, my associates in the Senate and public sentiment in Virginia unite in the judgment had resisted an almost overwhelming impulse to advise this sensitive, frail, and conscientious man to refuse the post. I did not know the exact nature of the President-elect's monetary plans. But I knew his experimental, tentative, and unorthodox temperament. And I guessed that if Glass accepted, there would, within sixty days, be a head-on collision between him and Roosevelt, after which would come an embittered, futile retirement for Glass. I coveted, for the unbroken and uncompromised and uncompromising warrior, years of usefulness in the Senate.

I sent Glass' letter to Roosevelt through one of his secretaries, who was going to Miami to meet him when he landed.

Meanwhile Louis and I sent a radio message telling F. D. R. the news. And meanwhile, because time was getting short and we knew that Roosevelt had no second choice in mind, Louis and I began to think of possibilities.

Late one afternoon in Louis' paper-strewn office on Madison Avenue I suggested the name of Will Woodin. Louis cocked his head, in the way he had when he was turning an idea over in his mind. Then he nodded his approval. Will Woodin would be "swell." He was highly respected by big business, and yet he was a strong Roosevelt supporter. Failing Glass, Louis could think of no one whose appointment would be more reassuring to the "big boys."

What Louis said was perfectly true. But what I was thinking about was F. D. R.'s "you can say we're not going to throw ideas out of the window simply because they're labeled inflation."

I've grown pretty weary, in the years since that February, of hearing Will Woodin described as "faunlike" and "elfin." One would think, to read the accounts of him, that he went dancing through

---

that I can better serve you and the country where I am than by a transfer to the Treasury. I trust you may, upon mature reflection, reach the same conclusion, keeping always uppermost in mind that I shall ever be ready to serve your administration to the full extent of my capabilities.

"That you may clearly realize that I have tried hard to overcome various difficulties of an almost insuperable nature, I may state that, at the last, hoping to allay the fears of my immediate family as to the effect of the proposed transfer on my health, I sought the frank professional opinion of my regular physician. His letter I am sending to you in strictest confidence.

"I am sure you will experience no difficulty in securing a Secretary of the Treasury upon whose vision, courage and strength you may confidently rely.

"With fervent good wishes for you and your administration and a further expression of gratitude for your kindness, believe me

"Faithfully yours,
CARTER GLASS"

directors' meetings wearing a conical hat, like one of Thomas Mackenzie's leprechauns, and playing on little pipes. The fact is that he was an extraordinarily hard-headed businessman and had an industrialist's (as opposed to a banker's) flexible mind. That rare combination of flexibility and hardheadedness, plus his absolute personal loyalty to Roosevelt, were his essential qualifications for the job.

But the Glass appointment was like King Charles' head. It kept popping up.

In a day or two we learned that Bernie Baruch, Admiral Cary Grayson, and other old friends of Glass' were imploring him to reconsider. Louis and I both felt that it would be best for him and F. D. R. to let the first decision stand. We wanted to tell that to Roosevelt and we wanted, besides, to tell him of our idea about Woodin. But we had agreed on no code name for Woodin before F. D. R.'s departure and we knew someone was sure to pick up the message if we radioed the facts directly. It was Louis who thought of the indoor swimming pool then being built on the White House grounds for Roosevelt's use, and concocted the following near-gibberish: "Prefer a wooden roof to a glass roof over swimming pool. Luhowray."

We later learned that F. D. R. had roared with laughter over our message once its meaning dawned on him.

The last talk about the appointment between Roosevelt and Glass is generally supposed to have taken place during Roosevelt's train trip home from Miami. But the question was not yet settled on February 19th, when F. D. R. called Glass from the 65th Street house. Glass said that "Cary" [Grayson] was sitting beside him, and that he was still undecided. By then there was no possible doubt about what he was thinking, because he added that if *he* didn't accept the job he'd like to see a sound-money man in the Treasury—Swagar Sherley, for instance.

Roosevelt was noncommittal. He turned to me after the conversation and said impatiently that he wished to God Glass would finally decline definitely: he was sick of this she-loves-me-she-loves-me-not business.

A little later Glass telephoned me and repeated what he had said to F. D. R. Sherley was at the 65th Street house at that very moment. I told Glass that I'd talk to him and to Roosevelt. When I'd finished the conversation with Glass, Sherley and I went into a back room and talked for a few minutes. Sherley came straight to the point. Glass had talked with him before mentioning him to Roosevelt, and

Sherley had indicated his unwillingness to accept if the job were offered. He clearly didn't want the job; he didn't even want Mr. Roosevelt to consider him for the job.

I reported this to Roosevelt, who then called Glass and got from him a definitive "No."

As soon as this was over, F. D. R. said, "Now call Will Woodin and bring him over here at eleven tonight."

At ten-thirty that night I called for Will. We went to 65th Street. The offer was made. Will asked for twenty-four hours to think it over. This was granted, and he left for home. The next day he accepted what was to be one of the most heroic jobs in the administration.

4

All this may suggest that there are certain fixed rules of etiquette to be observed on the receipt of an offer of high office—that a nice amount of blushing, stammering, swooning, and rushing off in confusion to the nearest gazebo is in order. It almost began to seem that way in February of 1933. No Elizabeth Bennett ever dodged her Darcy more tantalizingly than some of the men asked to serve by Roosevelt put off their answers. Old Tom Walsh kept us on tenterhooks for almost a month.[11] Swanson of Virginia, who was actually chosen as much so that Harry Byrd could be appointed to the Senate as for any other reason (and an ironic piece of business that maneuver proved to be), had a hard time deciding whether or not it would be best for him to stay in the Senate. Henry Wallace deliberated for some days before he accepted.[12] Berle refused the place on the Federal

[11] One of the things that figured in the Walsh negotiations was whether he would accept Felix Frankfurter as Solicitor General. Walsh refused to be persuaded that Felix would make a superlative Solicitor General. He kept insisting that he did not "want somebody in there who will lose cases in the grand manner," until Roosevelt yielded. After Walsh's tragic death Felix was asked several times, through me, to take the Solicitor's job, but refused, for the same reason, presumably, that he refused judicial office in Massachusetts—his desire to continue his teaching.

[12] My relations with Henry Wallace during 1932 were in the main at second hand. But both the men from whom I learned about him regarded him highly. Before the summer was over, Rex had completely sold me the idea that I participate with him in urging the appointment of Wallace as Secretary of Agriculture. I did. But I am sure that F. D. R. would have appointed him anyhow, and so I don't feel that, as in Woodin's case, my interposition made a difference. Roosevelt knew Wallace only very slightly. But he liked him, and he recognized that Wallace was one of the most distinguished men in the corn belt. That, and the facts that he was an outstanding Republican who had supported Roosevelt and a champion of the farm

Trade Commission I was directed to offer him, though he later accepted a temporary berth in the R.F.C. that made it possible for him to work on railroad legislation during the "Hundred Days" with some show of authority. And Frank Murphy turned down the F.T.C. Chairmanship, thus blasting my hopes for a reinvigoration of that dormant body. (His ambitions, he said, were either the Attorney-Generalship—which I told him had already been offered Walsh—or the Governor-Generalship of the Philippines—which was promised to Homer Cummings. As things worked out, he ultimately realized both ambitions.)

But there was at least one case where Cabinet office was sought. Henry Morgenthau, Sr., had dreamed for months of seeing young Henry in the Cabinet. His choice was Agriculture. It was soon made clear by F. D. R. and Louis that this was out of the question.

Jesse Straus, President of New York City's great R. H. Macy store, had been an outstandingly loyal and active Roosevelt supporter. Long before the convention he had carried on, at his own expense, a nationwide campaign of publicity for the Roosevelt candidacy and he had devoted time and energy to the making of converts through personal contact. In 1932 he had organized and largely financed the Roosevelt Business and Professional Men's League, which did valiant work during the campaign.

And so, after the victory, it was not surprising that there was talk of Straus for the Commerce post and that Straus himself, when word dribbled back to him indirectly that the job was all but his, was delighted that he would probably get the place held by his distinguished uncle under T. R. For weeks most of us took it for granted that the thing was settled.

Exactly how the works were gummed up, I don't know. But Louis

policies the New Deal had adopted, made him an ideal man for the job. F. D. R. sent a letter to him at Des Moines before he left Warm Springs. I kept in touch with Wallace by telephone until Louis and I were able to radio: "Corn Belt [Wallace] in the bag."

Shortly after, Wallace met Rex and asked him to come with him as Assistant Secretary. Rex had entertained doubts similar to mine on the subject of public office. Wallace's confidence in him, his own liking for Wallace, the big chance of helping set up the new farm program, and his concern about the international aspects of the program won from him a qualified decision. He decided to take the post for three months and then go to Europe on a tour of study and observation. Destiny filed different orders, however: the three months lengthened to more than three and a half years—of fame, of bitter and unmerited criticism, and of courageous and intelligent thinking.

did tell me that McAdoo had insisted that Roper, who was his floor leader in the convention of 1924, be given a Cabinet place and that Roosevelt had yielded.

Other things being equal, this was a change of heart to which Roosevelt was entitled. But, at the very least, Straus was entitled to have the news told to him by Roosevelt himself.

At this point Henry Morgenthau, Sr., rushed into the picture by telling Jesse that there was to be no Cabinet appointment for him, and asking whether there was anything by way of another post Jesse would like. Jesse was disappointed. But his hurt and fury over the way in which the news had come to him knew no bounds. It took hours of diplomacy to mend the breach, and to arrange for a friendly meeting between F. D. R. and Straus, at which the offer and acceptance of the Ambassadorship to France was achieved.

Fortunately for Henry, Jr., Roosevelt didn't believe in visiting his own wrath upon the second generation.

The Interior post went begging for weeks. It was first offered to Hiram Johnson, who declined. Bronson Cutting, a progressive Republican whom F. D. R. had known for years and who, like F. D. R., was a product of Groton and Harvard and an "aristocrat" turned liberal, was the second choice. I was delegated to get his answer after my visit to Warm Springs early in February.

I never knew Cutting well, but the remembrance of my meeting with him at the Carlton in Washington is one of the most vivid of that winter. He was a man of deep passions and great daring, but outwardly so taciturn, so inarticulate, that there was none of the easy conversational give and take that characterizes most practical politicians. One had the sense that he had an aesthete's rather than a nob's disdain for the first-name-calling-on-first-meeting, the hand pumping and backslapping that are the devaluated currency of political intercourse.

We discovered, after a time, that we had had a major experience in common. Both of us had migrated to New Mexico around 1910 for the same reason—tuberculosis. And then Cutting began to tell me of his career. He had had a much longer pull than I before he approached recovery, and clearly he was still, at forty-four, uncertain how much more severely he could tax himself than he was already doing in the Senate. That was one factor in his decision.

But I detected also, in his refusal of the Interior portfolio, something less than complete confidence in Roosevelt as a progressive leader—a reservation that burst into active opposition later in the spring in the fight over cuts in the veterans' payments.

I've often speculated about Roosevelt's subsequent hostility toward Cutting. I've wondered if he didn't find it easier to stomach opposition from men whose background was not like his own. Cutting shared almost all his political and economic views. Intellectually and politically the two men should have harmonized and, in those occasional moments when they disagreed, generosity and tolerance should have tided them over. But Roosevelt could never forgive Cutting's disagreement in May, 1933. Roosevelt claimed that Cutting made unpleasant remarks about him in the course of the debate on the veterans' issue. But I still wonder whether Roosevelt's inordinate bitterness did not stem from an antipathy to a class of people that was even more intense than his sympathy for the reforms to which he and Cutting were both dedicated.

After Louis and I radioed the news of Cutting's declination, nothing was done about the Interior for nearly three weeks. Meanwhile there had begun a chain of circumstance that was ultimately to come as close to duplicating Kohlsaat's McKinley story as any other incident in American history of which I know.

Late in January or early in February Roosevelt had asked Johnson, La Follette, and Cutting to name two men of their general persuasion to work with me on the debts and on the preparation for the preliminary economic discussions with the foreign nations that would take place in the spring. On February 10th Cutting called me from Washington and reported that the group had decided on Harold Ickes of Chicago for the first job and ex-Senator John J. Blaine, a La Follette man and former Governor of Wisconsin, for the second.

I got in touch with Ickes and, on my invitation, he came to New York on February 21st. The next morning I took him to the 65th Street house. So far as I knew, my bringing of Ickes to Roosevelt that morning marked their first meeting.

Ickes said nothing in the ensuing conversation that "sold" him to Roosevelt. In fact, Harold hardly said more than a word or two while F. D. R. expounded his views on the debts. At noon Ickes returned to his hotel to await my call for another meeting.

At midafternoon F. D. R. told me he had a Secretary of the Interior.

He had, it appeared, spoken to Ickes alone and tentatively about the Interior job. Shortly after, he had telephoned Hiram Johnson to ask him about Ickes. Johnson spoke warmly and sympathetically of

Ickes' abilities. That evidently decided Roosevelt. Ickes, Roosevelt added, was "coming to see me tonight."

And then he laughed—because, I think, he felt a small-boy delight with the look of stark incredulity on my face.

"I liked the cut of his jib," he added. I couldn't help but think that the calendar had as much to do with it. The inauguration was less than a week and a half away. Perhaps he had had visions of a vacant Cabinet chair.

That evening, when I returned to the 65th Street house, I found a man and a woman sitting in the little reception room. Neither knew the other from Adam. "Since you will eventually meet, anyhow," I said, "give me the pleasure of introducing the Secretary of the Interior to the Secretary of Labor."

5

The lesser appointments, with few exceptions, were discussed only en bloc in early February at the Warm Springs conferences of F. D. R., Jim Farley, Ed Flynn, Frank Walker, and Louis.

Flynn was an ace on matters of appointment. A man of education, fine tastes, and quiet demeanor, he had ruled the Bronx's cosmopolitan masses as an austere and streamlined "boss" for years. While Farley went in quest of national delegates, it was Flynn, Roosevelt's Secretary of State in New York, who had kept the political home fires burning. Flynn wanted no office for himself (although the job of Collector of the Port of New York was offered him and went, eventually, to his lieutenant, Harry Durning). But the laws of the Medes and Persians endowed him, as a matter of course, with a ranking membership in the purely political councils.

Walker had served as Treasurer in the campaign of 1932. A businessman with a yen for politics in general and nothing short of adoration for Roosevelt in particular, he, too, eschewed political office. But he would as soon have traded his place in the inner circle as Harold Vanderbilt would have given up cup racing.

These two men, together with Jim, Louis, and, of course, F. D. R., made a major decision at Warm Springs. Realizing that more could be got out of the special session of Congress if the distribution of political plums was held in abeyance until the faithful had demonstrated their capacity to vote as desired, they determined to hand out as few jobs as possible until the session was over. Patronage would be used, if not as a club, then as a steel-pointed *pic.*

The results of this policy were to be fruitful enough in terms of legislation. But it produced an administrative situation unparalleled in modern times. We stood in the city of Washington on March 4th like a handful of marauders in hostile territory. Though thousands upon thousands of Democrats had marched down Pennsylvania Avenue, only a scattering of us were in office. There were, on the executive side, the President, ten Cabinet officers, two or three Under and Assistant Secretaries like myself, and a few secretaries and clerks immediately attached to these officials. Most of us were completely ignorant of the detailed workings of the great departments of which we were a part. We had become, by the grace of the electorate, the nominal chieftains of the army of officeholders, but they were, by the grace of their knowledge, our actual masters. A considerable proportion of them had been appointed during the preceding twelve years of Republican rule. It was no British Civil Service—competent and completely nonpolitical. What we called the Civil Service was, in the main, merely a mass of Republican political appointees frozen into office by act of Congress.

A process of adjustment had to begin—long, painful, and often unsuccessful. For some of the most mediocre and futile Topazes are still at the head of various divisions and bureaus, as they were in 1933, thanks to the protective coloring lent by their very timidity, inconspicuousness, and ineffectiveness.

As the weeks ran on in March, the city of Washington became a mecca for the old Socialists, single-taxers, utility reformers, Civil Service reformers, and goo-goos of all types, who at last perceived that a new political era was at hand and who took it to be a kind of crusade which the discontented of every variety were invited to join. Their eagerness to enlist was accentuated, in many cases, by their simple need for a job. That a government composed of men who could agree on neither the nature of our economic disease nor the character of the treatment would be the last blow for the stricken country never occurred to them. Each wanted to put on his surgical mask and rubber gloves and go to work.

Old Frederick C. Howe is as good an example as any. Howe came to see me a month or so after the inauguration. Thirty years before, I had literally sat at his feet as a youngster listening to political speeches in the Tom Johnson days in Cleveland. Howe was a state senator and one of Johnson's favorite boys in that earlier and more localized New

Deal. I had read his books—burning, eloquent books—on reform. So had thousands of others. The debt of progressivism to such men could not be forgotten. But as he sat in my office misty-eyed at the thought of joining a new cause just as twilight began to steal over his lifetime of labor and frustration, I reflected that it wasn't going to be easy to find a useful place for a man of such specialized talents.

Fred Howe, like many others, landed in one that was far from ideal. As consumer's counsel in the A.A.A., he innocently scared the daylights out of businessmen with talk which, after his many years of gentle agitation, came quite naturally to him. His spiritual confrères did likewise. But reform was in power now, and room had to be made for them.

Not much better administrative material was available from the ranks of those who had served under Wilson or under various Democratic state governments in the past. Most had been out of regular administrative posts for years and had made a living at law, if they were lawyers, or at lobbying, or promotion, or in modest business undertakings.

Some of these had been skilled administrators. But, on the whole, their enforced separation from public office during the years of Republican feasting had left them pretty rusty. Dan Roper, for instance, had been a crisp, natty, deft administrator under Wilson in the Post Office Department and as Commissioner of Internal Revenue. But the years of inaction had taken their toll. He could not keep up the pace set by those, like Ickes, who were aglow with the new faith.

There were also scores of new political figures—men and women who had been Democratic party workers during the years of Republican rule. Yet they were for the most part without experience in public office and with little comprehension of what the New Deal was about. To them March 4th was an entry into a luscious promised land achieved not by the force of ideas, or even because of the failure of Republicanism, but because of party regularity. And they had been regular—a little while. Some of the saddest failures and a few near-scandals in the past six years have resulted from the appointment of such men to office. Too many of them had neither the aptitude for responsibility nor the finesse to disguise their ignorance.

In short, the Republican party had close to a monopoly of skillful, experienced administrators. To make matters worse, the business managers, established lawyers, and engineers from whose ranks top-drawer governmental executives so often come were, by and large, so partisan in their opposition to Roosevelt that he could scarcely be expected to tap those sources to the customary degree.

This difficulty, a very real one, was unnecessarily heightened by Roosevelt's refusal to admit how many exceptions there were to the generalization. In the days of 1933, when things were getting under way, I found from personal contact that there was an astonishing number of first-rate men in business and in the professions who were willing and eager to help the New Deal, in office or out. But Roosevelt could not bring himself to trust them. He was clearly suspicious of recognized eminence, perhaps because he distrusted the whole system under which men of his generation had attained eminence in business and law, and perhaps because of some deeper distrust in himself.

He didn't, on the other hand, have the same objection to the advance guard of bright young lawyers—among whom was Tom Corcoran—that had already descended upon Washington during the last days of the Hoover Administration. And so it was possible for us to use a good many exceedingly well-schooled young men that slow business in the legal profession had thrown on the market. Felix Frankfurter had been recommending promising lawyers to Presidents and Justices for many years. Quite naturally, it became routine not only for me but for a number of the others to talk with him about men. Before long, he had placed Nathan R. Margold as Solicitor in the Interior, Charles E. Wyzanski, Jr., in Labor, Jerome N. Frank in the A.A.A., and Dean G. Acheson in the Treasury—the beginning of an infiltration that was to take on an extraordinary character only when a number of those he placed became what they themselves have come to call "a well-integrated group."

Meanwhile I had ample opportunity to observe the difficulties of building an administration out of human materials so heterogeneous—some earnest but inept, some long on ideas and short on industry, some experienced but rusty, some with almost otherworldly standards of honesty, others blind to the fine line that separates party loyalty from a sordid neglect of the public interest. It was easy to see that efficiency could not be expected. Tolerable muddling was inevitable. I knew that this had been the fate of so many crusading movements swept into office during a crisis, that it was so sure to tarnish some of the New Deal's hopeful sheen, that I used to talk of it at great length to F. D. R.

Beyond all this, there was the eternal problem of welding into a workable whole the abilities and energies of two kinds of men—those who represent the two great truths—"one of which," says Maurice Magre in his *Kingdom of Lu*, "rushes straight to heaven, and another which seeks its nutriment in the soil, an ideal Truth and a practical Truth, Truth like a wild swan and Truth like a faithful dog."

It wasn't always pleasant, as the years passed, to hear the wild swans and the faithful dogs speak of each other. And only the most haphazard efforts were ever made to moderate their differences.

To that flagrant neglect may be traced some of the angriest wrangling in the party now. But it is the quality of mind that made it possible, in the first place, which is responsible for the infinitely more important confusion of policy that has been Roosevelt's greatest failure.

6

Once in the State Department, I found myself having a lot more to do with the diplomatic appointments than I would have chosen. But Hull announced that he wasn't particularly interested and, except in one or two instances, proceeded to keep hands off. This left the ball to Billy Phillips, who soon showed a preference for Social Registerites and career boys ("cookie-pushers," the newspaper men had dubbed them) so overpowering that Jim Farley raised the roof a couple of times and finally insisted that Phillips consult with me before he made any moves. What Jim's idea of "consultation" was may be judged by the fact that he thereupon turned over to me his complete file of diplomatic prospects. The job of battling with Phillips then became mine.

There was much to commend in the State Department's career service. For the most part the men and women in the lesser jobs of the diplomatic and consular service were adequately trained and personally cooperative. But imagination and a real understanding of public opinion in America were rare. More important, a deep-rooted sense of inferiority to the superlative technicians in the British service had given their judgments a strongly pro-British tinge. In the course of the years this service had, as any bureaucracy does, embodied its individual fears and prejudices in thousands of minute decisions that, taken together, had slowly formed a gigantic coral reef of major policy. It was not that there were sacrosanct and immutable ways of doing things.[13]

[13] Red tape, of course, was characteristic of every aspect of the Department's workings. The classic story about this goes back to the time that Joe Cotton was in

It was that there were patterns of thought that had grown steadily more rigid in the preceding two decades. To whip together this service, give it self-confidence, and refresh it from the wealth of educated men and women that can be recruited in this country would have been a job worthy of even Secretary Hull's energies had he been willing to use them that way.

Situated as I was, I could do little more than the routine business of seeing that Phillips did not ignore every last one of the campaign contributors—contributors in terms of money and services.

Conspicuous among the latter was Claude Bowers, a distinguished journalist and historian whose charming lack of tonishness gave Phillips an attack of horrid misgivings. Bowers had wielded his pen for years in behalf of the Democratic party, which he sincerely believed was the vessel of liberal thought in the United States: he had spoken eloquently at scores of party gatherings and had given literary assistance to perhaps half a hundred Democratic chieftains. But it required the successive efforts of myself, Farley, and Roosevelt to persuade Phillips that Bowers ought to get his heart's desire—a foreign post where there was quiet and leisure for writing. Belgium or Spain looked like suitable spots. F. D. R. opined that the informal atmosphere of Madrid, under the new Republic, was a shade preferable. Then, superstitiously thinking of Brand Whitlock, who had also once sought urbanity, leisure, and quiet and who had wound up in an invaded and devastated Belgium, Roosevelt definitely decided on Spain. I never had a happier assignment than taking the news to Bowers. But Phillips had the last laugh, after all—that is, if he thought of this sequence of events as he read the dispatches from Spain between July, 1936, and March, 1939.

Despite himself, though, Phillips often found that I had my uses. There was, for instance, the famous case of Mayor Jim Curley of Boston. Billy and Jim were citizens of the same center of culture. But otherwise they were universes apart. Curley was determined to go to Rome as Ambassador and presented unimpeachable claims to the job in the shape of a record of early, energetic, and powerful support of the Roosevelt candidacy. Jim Farley was not inclined to disallow them.

the Department. One day a cable was received from the American consul in a tiny South American country which announced with great indignation that the consul had been gravely insulted, and which asked what should be done. Cotton read it, flipped it aside, and said, "Cable him to 'Laugh it off.'" Hours after word came to Cotton's office that his instructions could not be cabled. "And why not?" cried Cotton. "There is," he was told, "no such word as 'laugh' in the Department's code."

And the correct Under Secretary came almost tearfully to my office one day to beg for help.

I don't suppose he expected such a barbarian as he took me for to understand just why he thought Curley wouldn't do. But when I allowed that Rome wasn't the place for Curley—not because of his social inadequacies, but because of other limitations—Phillips did not choose to look a gift horse in the mouth. I agreed to ask Farley to refuse Curley Rome and proffer him Poland, if Phillips would not object to Breck Long for Rome. Farley was persuaded, Curley decided Massachusetts needed him more than Poland, and the President appointed Breck Long to Italy.[14]

There was, some time later, another case in which Phillips had to yell for help. When it was planned to move Sumner Welles, who had been appointed Assistant Secretary of State in Charge of Latin American Affairs, to Cuba and bring Jefferson Caffery back from Central America to take Welles' place, it was discovered that a dreadful obstacle stood in the way. Caffery, able and likable, was a relative of that John M. Caffery of Louisiana who was an avowed enemy of Louisiana's boss. Neither Phillips nor Farley, not even the President himself, could get Huey Long to consent to the move (Long's feud with F. D. R. had already begun). But Huey had taken a fancy to me—because, I think, he sensed that I approached him with neither fear nor loathing—and it was I, at last, who had to beard him.

It came off very well, as a matter of fact. After several hours of grave conversation about the University of Louisiana—which was Huey's pride and joy—I explained the situation. Huey rumbled so alarmingly that I almost wished I hadn't brought out my verbal red cape. And then, as suddenly, a beatific, Ferdinandish calm came over him. "All rightie," he said. He would try to forget about Caffery's relative and, since I asked it, have a talk with "Jeff" Caffery himself. If "Jeff" wasn't "too terrible," Huey would let the thing ride. And so it went.

In time Phillips developed such a horror of politics that he would bundle all political comers off to my office before they had a chance to contaminate his. One of the most amusing of the diplomatic appointments thus became my business. And it left me the possessor of a story so whimsical as to compensate, in part, for the wear and tear of the routine skirmishings.

[14] The job of Assistant Secretary of State had already been offered to Breck and refused by him because he would not work under Phillips. They had been together in the Department under Wilson, and I discerned a mutual distaste of long standing. Long, incidentally, was to do a magnificent job in Rome.

One fine day a heavy contributor marched into my office and announced that he had a favor to ask. And I was to mind that it was the one favor he was asking for his contribution. His tone suggested that there was forthcoming if not a peremptory demand for confidential information then at least appointment to the Court of St. James's. I braced myself and prepared for the worst.

It developed that my caller, Mr. X, wanted a ministerial post in a small country for a young friend of his, "a teacher of history or something." I said, with immense relief, that I would have the matter looked into and then, in the rush of business, proceeded to forget about it until a day or two later, when I walked into the airport to take a plane to New York and found Mr. X and his protégé lying in wait for me.

There were introductions. Before I knew what was happening Mr. X had deposited in the plane seat next to me the young man, who promptly began to shout at me, over the roar of the motors, an account of his life and ambitions. It seems that he was a professor in a small Southern college. He planned to write a book on the arid history of the country to which he wanted to be sent. There was little or no diplomatic work to be done at its capital, and he would have a wonderful opportunity to follow his scholarly pursuits. He then overwhelmed me with a painstaking and surpassingly dull lecture on the writing of history in general and of his history in particular. After about three quarters of an hour of this, when I had reached a point where I had all I could do to keep awake, Mr. X whisked my tormentor away and sat down beside me.

"Well," he said, "how do you like him?"

"All right," I answered without enthusiasm.

"Can he be sent to ——, do you think?"

"Why, yes," I said. "That's easy. But, in heaven's name, tell me something. How come this interest in history? Where did you find this man? I should think you'd be about as interested in him as you'd be in the *Encyclopaedia Britannica*."

Ensued the following good-humored speech from Mr. X: "I have," said he, "four"—or perhaps it was five or six—"children. A wonderful doctor brought them into the world. And I've always wanted to do something for him—you know, more than just paying his fee—to show him exactly how grateful I am. But he's always refused extra presents. Until," Mr. X went on, "it occurred to me that I might give him the benefit of my contribution to the party. So I asked him whether there wasn't something the administration could do for him. He had a brother, he said—this fellow here. That's the story."

I looked at Mr. X with visible astonishment. "And that's all you want—this minor post for your wife's doctor's brother?"

"That's all I want," said Mr. X.

We investigated Mr. X's wife's physician's brother and found, as I had judged, that he'd do very nicely indeed. Jim Farley's eyebrows arched higher than Billy Phillips' when he was told of this quixotic affair. Which, needless to say, was settled to everyone's satisfaction.

The only appointment, out of perhaps a half dozen others in the State Department, in which I took any personal interest was that of William C. Bullitt. Yet that isn't quite accurate. My desire to see Bullitt appointed sprang less from an interest in him than from a wish to see Roosevelt right a wrong I believed Bullitt had suffered at the hands of the Wilson Administration.

Bullitt had been sent to Russia by Wilson. He had reported back to Wilson his belief in the stability of the Bolshevik regime, had split with the Wilson Administration when it proceeded to act on the false assumption of the regime's instability, and had subsequently told the facts about his mission to Senator Lodge's Foreign Relations Committee. For this "disloyalty" he had not only been roundly denounced by Wilson partisans but thereafter been cut politically dead by the party chieftains.

I had heard that story, of course. But I never gave Bullitt a thought until the late months of 1932, when stories began to appear in the papers telling of his current visits to various high European officials and suggesting that he was engaged on some sort of mysterious business in behalf of Roosevelt. I knew that Bullitt was a friend of Roosevelt and it seemed barely possible that there was something to the stories. But F. D. R. assured me that this wasn't the fact, and so I dismissed Bullitt from mind.

I was introduced to him, finally, by F. D. R. in February. After a rather intelligent discussion of foreign affairs at the 65th Street house, he asked me to stop by at the Yale Club for some further talk. There he told me of his 1919-20 adventure, of the years in Europe that had followed, of his sympathy for the Roosevelt policies, and of his desire to return to the diplomatic service. He impressed me very favorably, and it seemed to me that simple justice called for his being given a chance to resume the career cut short twelve years before. Strictly speaking, it wasn't my business; but I have fairly morbid sympathies for the underdog in such cases.

I spoke to Roosevelt about it, shortly after. He was inclined to be dubious about whether Bill should be given an appointment. I didn't press the matter, and things drifted along until March when, not long after the administration got under way, Bullitt appeared in Washington and established himself near my rooms in the Carlton Hotel. Bill managed to see me often there and in my office. And he was always welcome, for I found him interesting, informed, and helpful. He spoke again and again, during these visits, of his desire to fit in somewhere, and it seemed to me that he would be eminently suitable for either of two places open in the Department—the Assistant Secretaryship and the position of Special Assistant to the Secretary.

I had, by this time, clearly made out the values and the limitations of Bullitt. He was pleasant, keen-minded, idealistic, and widely informed. On the other hand, he had a deep and somewhat disturbing strain of romanticism in him. Foreign affairs were, to his imaginative mind, full of lights and shadows, plots and counterplots, villains and a few heroes—a state of mind that seemed to me dangerous, if not constantly subjected to the quieting influence of some controlling authority.[15] But there would be the kind of control he needed in both the jobs I had in mind, while Bullitt, in either, would be in a position to help infuse new life into the career service.

For what seemed like a long time, I reminded the President almost daily that there was an obligation of sorts to Bullitt—with no noteworthy results, I admit. At last I prepared a little memorandum about Bill's appointment and several others, which the President initialed. Armed with this, I went to Phillips, who thereupon showed more emotion than I knew he was capable of. He bitterly reminded me that Bill had been "disloyal" to the Wilson Administration. I answered that the years had shown that, on the point of difference between Wilson and Bullitt, Bullitt had been right: it seemed to me that loyalty to one's country superseded loyalty to a President; that it was a man's duty, under such circumstances, to pass up official position and take a public stand.

After the customary tussles Phillips and I finally agreed. Bullitt should be Special Assistant to the Secretary rather than Assistant Sec-

[15] This trait disturbed others who had known him in the war days fifteen years before. For example, when Bill met Felix Frankfurter in my room in April, Felix asked him, "Well, Bill, have you learned to keep your shirt on yet?" "Absolutely," answered Bill, "it is nailed down this time."

retary, as the latter appointment, which required senatorial confirmation, might involve the raking up of old scores. Bullitt's commission was made out. My assistant was sent to the White House with it. The President's eagerness to make the appointment may be gauged by the fact that my assistant was kept waiting through three whole mornings before F. D. R. signed it.

My defense of Bullitt's course in breaking with Wilson came back as a faintly melancholy memory in 1937, when, after my unequivocal public opposition to several of the newer Roosevelt policies, Bill, the new Ambassador to France, again occupied rooms near mine in the hotel I make my home. On this occasion—and how unlike 1933 it was—I was honored by neither a visit nor a message. La Rochefoucauld covered the case fully three hundred years ago, of course: "On ne trouve guère d'ingrats tant qu'on est en état de faire du bien." Yet I wouldn't undo anything I did in the Bullitt matter. That kind of experience—through which most people go not once, but dozens of times—has a way of teaching one nothing. And it's probably better that way.

CHAPTER V

THE FIGHT FOR SOLVENCY

WHILE in a large sense the economic prostration of 1933 could be traced back to the neglected infections of 1920-29, in the immediate sense the collapse began on February 14, 1933, when the Detroit bank crisis led Governor Comstock to declare an eight-day bank moratorium in Michigan. There had been runs on banks all through January and early February, of course. Between February 1st and February 15th, the withdrawal of gold and currency had increased from five to fifteen million dollars daily. Louisiana had had a banking holiday just two weeks before the Detroit crisis. But it was the news from Detroit that jolted the nation into panic. Before the week had passed—the week in which it became clear that the Michigan panic could be neither stemmed nor localized, despite enormous loans from the R.F.C.—we had a pretty definite idea of just what we were in for. And in the course of that agonizing week there were, for me, two haunting moments.

The first came on the night of February 15th at Miami, after Zangara had shot at Roosevelt. It was Louis' excessive caution that was responsible for my presence in Miami that night. Louis had insisted that the full account of my negotiations with Cabinet prospects could not be set forth in a letter to F. D. R. or confided to an intermediary. I must go to Miami myself to meet Roosevelt, he said. And so I went, joining Roosevelt on Vincent Astor's *Nourmahal* just as he was finishing the last dinner of his cruise.

As soon as my messages were delivered, we all started for the official reception, which was to be held in Miami's water-front park. Vincent Astor, Kermit Roosevelt, William Rhinelander Stewart, and I were in the second automobile behind that of the President-elect. It is one of those improbable coincidences that never seem believable afterward that Astor turned the conversation to the subject of an attempted assassination as we passed through the crowds in the streets. He remarked how dangerous it was to subject a public figure to such risks. It would be easy, he said, for an assassin to do his work and escape. Night was falling. The crowd was large. An assassin would be swallowed up in it. I answered that we had passed through such throngs in the twilight so many times in the preceding months that I'd lost consciousness of the danger it involved for F. D. R. We were still talking about it when we stopped at the spot where Zangara began firing.

Roosevelt was saved only by the quick action of a woman who jostled Zangara's arm and deflected his aim. But five others were wounded. One of the victims, with a surface wound on his forehead, was put into our car. Zangara was thrown on our trunk rack, and three policemen held him down. I had hold of the belt of another cop, who rode on the running board of the car as we rushed to the hospital behind F. D. R. and the wounded Tony Cermak. We waited at the hospital for a few anxious hours for word about Cermak's condition. Then, when we learned that he seemed to be weathering things, we all returned to the *Nourmahal* for the night.

Roosevelt's nerve had held absolutely throughout the evening. But the real test in such cases comes afterward, when the crowds, to whom nothing but courage can be shown, are gone. The time for the letdown among his intimates was at hand. All of us were prepared, sympathetically, understandingly, for any reaction that might come from Roosevelt now that the tension was over and he was alone with us. For anything, that is, except what happened.

There was nothing—not so much as the twitching of a muscle, the mopping of a brow, or even the hint of a false gaiety—to indicate that it wasn't any other evening in any other place. Roosevelt was simply himself—easy, confident, poised, to all appearances unmoved.

F. D. R. had talked to me once or twice during the campaign about the possibility that someone would try to assassinate him. To that extent, I knew, he was prepared for Zangara's attempt. But it is one thing to talk philosophically about assassination, and another to face it. And I confess that I have never in my life seen anything more magnificent than Roosevelt's calm that night on the *Nourmahal*.

The companion picture came four days later in the early-morning hours of Sunday, February 19th. We had all gone, in the evening, to the Astor Hotel, where a group of New York City political reporters, called the Inner Circle, was giving its annual jamboree. During one of the skits put on by the Circle's members, Roosevelt passed me an envelope under the table and signaled me to read what was in it. I opened it as unobtrusively as possible and saw, to my astonishment, a letter in President Hoover's handwriting.[1] Circumstances made it impossible for me to read it carefully, but a glance was enough to tell me the news it brought. The bank crisis was getting out of hand.

We had all expected that to happen, just as Roosevelt had expected that someone, someday, would take a shot at him. It had been clear for nearly two months that wholesale deflation, in its most excruciating form, was running its course. It had been clear that falling price levels and diminishing economic activity were rapidly making the burden of debt intolerable. It had been clear that a widespread withdrawal and sequestration of gold would mean the obliteration of the banking system. We had known that banks were being forcibly liquidated, that huge business concerns were finding the going hard, that wages were plummeting, that hundreds of thousands of unemployed were roaming the streets. The only question in our minds had been how long the credit structure and the human beings on whose confidence it rested could stand the strain.

But the letter from Hoover announcing that the breaking point had come somehow made the awful picture take on life for the first time, and nothing I had imagined eased the shock of that reality. I looked up at Roosevelt, expecting, certainly, to see some shadow of the grim news in his face or manner. And there was nothing—nothing but laughter and applause for the play actors, pleasant bantering with those who sat at table with him, and the gay, unhurried, autographing of programs for half a hundred fellow guests at the dinner's end.

I thought then, "Well, this can't go on. The kickback's got to come when he leaves this crowd. This is just for show. We'll see what happens when he's alone with us."

But when we got back to the 65th Street house—Roosevelt and three or four of us—there was still no sign. The letter from Hoover was passed around and then discussed.[2] Capital was fleeing the country. Hoarding was reaching unbearably high levels. The dollar was wobbling on the foreign exchanges as gold poured out. The bony hand of death was stretched out over the banks and insurance companies.

[1] This letter was written on February 17th and delivered directly to Roosevelt by a Secret Service man on February 18th. A curious circumstance connected with it is that, in addressing the envelope, Hoover spelled Roosevelt's name "Roosvelt"—as good an indication as any of the tremendous strain under which he was laboring when he sent it.

[2] The existence of this letter was not mentioned in the press, so far as I know, until two years later. The text of the letter then appeared in *The Saturday Evening Post* in a series of articles written by Myers and Newton, and later appeared in *The Hoover Administration; op. cit.;* p. 338.

And Roosevelt was, to all appearances, unmoved.

It was not until I left the Roosevelt house at two o'clock that Sunday morning that the curious parallel occurred to me. Here were two sequences of stimulus and reaction—Roosevelt alone with his friends after the attempt on his life, and Roosevelt alone with his friends after hearing the news that the banking system was mortally stricken. And the responses had been alike!

I wondered, then, whether the Hoover letter might not have had another reception if Hoover hadn't gone on, after reciting the stark news, first to state that he had had the depression fully in flight by the summer of 1932 and that it had been halted by agitation for money tinkering and by the publication of R.F.C. loans and such like; then to imply that "steadily degenerating confidence" caused by fear of Roosevelt's policies was the real cause of the crisis; and then to tell the President-elect that all that was needed was a statement from him "to restore confidence." The statement was to give the country "prompt assurance that there will be no tampering or inflation of the currency; that the budget will be unquestionably balanced, even if further taxation is necessary; that the Government credit will be maintained by refusal to exhaust it in the issue of securities."

The tone of the letter was truly extraordinary. For one thing, it asked Roosevelt, in effect, to accept the Hoover thesis about the origin of the depression which Roosevelt had torn to shreds during the campaign.[3] For another, it assumed that Roosevelt would succeed—where Hoover had repeatedly failed—in hornswoggling the country with optimistic statements which everyone knew weren't justified. It invited Roosevelt to make a promise that could not honestly be made, for things had already gone so far that the temporary suspension of specie payments seemed inevitable. It scrupulously avoided mention of the circumstance that none of the budgets Hoover himself had made up had balanced or were likely to balance. And, finally, it wholly disregarded the fact that, while the citizen who was rushing to the bank to draw out his money may have known vaguely about the gold standard,

[3] Hoover himself recognized this fact, when he wrote to Senator David A. Reed on February 20th: "I realize that if these declarations be made by the President-elect, he will have ratified the whole major program of the Republican Administration; that is, it means the abandonment of ninety per cent of the so-called new deal. But unless this is done, they run a grave danger of precipitating a complete financial debacle. If it is precipitated, the responsibility lies squarely with them for they have had ample warning—unless, of course, such a debacle is part of the 'new deal.'" (*The Hoover Administration; op. cit.;* p. 341.)

he was primarily concerned about the soundness of the bank in which he had his money.

This last, a transcendently important factor in the situation, was confirmed when Roosevelt asked the people to put their money back into banks on March 12th. They did—not because he promised the things Hoover asked him to promise on February 17th, but because they had been given assurances that the banks that were reopened would be safe.[4] That completely refutes Hoover's theory that Roosevelt could have stemmed the bank panic by the making of a statement about the currency.

But I found, as the days passed, that it was a mistake to attribute Roosevelt's extraordinary calm to resentment at the unreasonableness or futility of the Hoover proposals. Even when he had got whatever there might have been of that out of his system, even when he had answered Hoover to the effect that "mere statements" could accomplish nothing at such a time, his mood persisted.[5] It was not that he shared Louis Howe's disposition to regard the crisis as a kind of wonderful lark.[6] He listened to Will Woodin's reports of meetings with Secretary Mills and the leading bankers of New York earnestly enough. He talked over with Will and with me all the proposals the bankers had to offer. But from these things he would turn to conferences with Cary Grayson on the details of the inaugural parade or to sittings for

[4] One of the claims made in *The Hoover Administration* by Myers and Newton is that Hoover for three years had carried on a vigorous campaign for bank reform. Then follows the implication that he had chosen Senator Glass to prepare and introduce a bill embodying certain reforms. John T. Flynn, in *The New Republic* of December 4, 1935, had this to say about it:

"I followed that legislation carefully from beginning to end. And this is the first I ever heard of Hoover's lifting a finger for it. Professor H. Parker Willis, of Columbia, acted as technical adviser to the Banking Committee in preparing that bill. He knows its history as well as any man. He has embodied it in a book—'The Banking Situation,' published in 1934 by Columbia University. Professor Willis says what everyone at the time knew to be true, that not only did Hoover do nothing to support the Glass bill but actually 'retarded it and prevented its passage,' to use Professor Willis' words."

[5] Supposedly because of an oversight by one of Roosevelt's secretaries, his reply to Hoover's letter was not sent until eleven days had passed. This was unfortunate so far as courtesy was involved. It had no significance beyond that. Its earlier delivery would have meant nothing in terms of policy so far as either Hoover or Roosevelt was concerned.

[6] A "human-interest" story in the *New York Times,* whose import was that the people in Detroit were taking the bank situation there as a joke, apparently impressed Louis so deeply that all through the next two weeks he referred to it by way of minimizing the importance of the problem and by way of assuring us that the panic would subside naturally.

the artist who was painting his portrait as though each activity were of equal importance.

The fact is that I found it impossible to discover how deeply Roosevelt was impressed with the seriousness of the crisis. Between February 18th and March 3rd I detected nothing but the most complete confidence in his own ability to deal with any situation that might arise—a confidence fed by the scandalous inability of the bankers to suggest any practicable measures for blocking off the panic.[7] It was Will Woodin and I who tore our hair over the reports of the mounting gold withdrawals and the growing number of bank suspensions and who sat up night after night pondering the possible remedies. Roosevelt went serenely through those days on the assumptions that Hoover was perfectly capable of acting without his concurrence; that there was no remedy of which we knew that was not available to the Hoover Administration; that he could not take any responsibility for measures over whose execution he would have no control; and that, until noon of March 4th, the baby was Hoover's anyhow. Typical was his answer to the complaint of the bankers that the revelations of the current Senate investigation into banking methods were destroying public confidence. "The bankers should have thought of that," he said, "when they did the things that are being exposed now."

When we arrived in Washington on the night of March 2nd, terror held the country in grip. Twenty-one states had total or partial bank holidays. The Federal Reserve Board's weekly statement showed the loss of $226,310,000 in gold. And President Hoover and the Treasury officials were near exhaustion from a week of conferences, proposals, counterproposals, and stubborn efforts to "dodge the deep damnation of the banking crisis"[8] by persuading Roosevelt to act jointly with the administration.

Those efforts had begun on the 28th of February and ranged all the way from the repetition of the request for "a declaration even now on the line I suggested" (made in a letter from Hoover dated February 28th) to a proffer of "full co-operation" with the President-elect "in any line of sensible action" to meet the situation. The catch, obviously, was what constituted "sensible action." Up to the night of

[7] The bankers at first backed the Hoover idea that a statement from Roosevelt would do the trick. They then threw their support behind the idea of huge loans from the R.F.C.—an idea that died aborning when it was pointed out that the R.F.C. had at its disposal only a fraction of the amount needed to take care of banks already badly shaken. Their other suggestions were equally useless.

[8] This phrase is that of John Flynn. It appeared in the article cited above.

March 2nd there was no indication that the two men could ever agree on that point.

But that night, shortly after we were installed at the Mayflower, word came through Woodin that, for the first time, proposals had been made which called for grave consideration. Representatives of the Federal Reserve Board and Treasury were asking that Roosevelt approve the issue of a proclamation closing all the banks. Hoover himself felt that this was not necessary if Roosevelt would approve a proclamation of emergency powers under a section of a statute of war days, the Trading with the Enemy Act, enabling him to control withdrawals of currency and gold.[9] Would Mr. Roosevelt agree to either of these proposals?

At once the congressional leaders of the party were summoned to the hotel, and, in the long hours that followed, the whole question of Roosevelt's responsibility in the situation was threshed out. The final consensus was that there was no need for joint action or approval by Roosevelt to make either proposal effective. President Hoover was free to proceed as he thought best. That was the word sent back to the White House. The message was not, as reported by Myers and Newton, that Roosevelt *refused to approve* either proposal.

There the matter stood until midafternoon of the next day—Friday, March 3rd. All through the morning, apparently, Hoover felt that the situation had taken a turn for the better.[10] But after lunch, when the reports of devastating gold and currency withdrawals began to pour in again, the decision seems to have been made to approach Roosevelt once more.

I have never been able to understand why the attempt to stage the "approach" should have been made in the queer way it was unless Hoover was still laboring under the delusion that F. D. R. could always be pushed around at will provided you got him off by himself. That theory may be wrong. But here's the story for what it's worth.

Roosevelt was scheduled to call on the President at four o'clock for the traditional preinaugural visit. Certainly none of us dreamed, when

[9] Roosevelt had been apprised of the contents of the Trading with the Enemy Act some weeks before this.

[10] This was certainly not the feeling of most of those at the Treasury. But it would appear that Hoover and Mills were more optimistic, according to Myers and Newton. "Secretary Mills," say Myers and Newton (p. 365), "reported to President Hoover that the banks in the larger centers had taken various measures which he felt would prevent any general closing over the inauguration and that the President-elect's inaugural address might give the necessary assurances to stop the monetary panic. In the afternoon, however, the situation took another turn for the worse, partly due to further withdrawal of balances held from one bank to another." . . .

he left the Mayflower, that the call would involve anything but a formal exchange of courtesies. The moment he had left I lay down on a couch in his apartment. I was dead tired, and it seemed as though I had a whole heavenly hour to catch up on my sleep. But my nerves were taut. For one reason or another I couldn't get my mind off Roosevelt's copy of the inaugural address, which was being guarded so carefully in my pocket that I didn't even take my coat off before I stretched out. I tossed and turned for some fifteen or twenty minutes and then, just as I was about to drift off into unconsciousness, the telephone rang.

It was Warren Robbins. F. D. R. had asked him to call. He told me that Ike Hoover, the veteran chief usher at the White House, had whispered to Roosevelt as he entered the building that Hoover was planning to bring in Secretary Mills and Eugene Meyer, Governor of the Federal Reserve Board, the moment the social amenities had been disposed of. I was to come to the White House at once—immediately. And the minute Mills and Meyer appeared, Roosevelt would ask President Hoover courteously that I be sent for.

I rushed over, needless to say, and arrived just in their wake. I don't believe that Hoover has figured out to this day the apparent miracle of my appearance about fifty seconds after he had "surprised" F. D. R. by producing Mills and Meyer, and F. D. R. had formally asked that I be summoned.

At any rate, I was in at the beginning of the tense discussion. The two proposals of the preceding night were made again. Roosevelt repeated the substance of the message he had sent through Woodin.

The President demurred. He still felt that a bank-closing proclamation was unnecessary and that a proclamation controlling foreign exchange and withdrawals would be adequate. But—and this was an important point—as the President-elect doubtless knew, the second course would necessitate the use of emergency powers under the Trading with the Enemy Act, and it was extremely doubtful whether this Act was still valid. His own Attorney General, Hoover continued, was inclined to think not. The use of some of the powers under this Act, then, might subsequently be disavowed by Congress. That would create a hopeless tangle. Mr. Roosevelt's assurances that Congress would not do this were indispensable. Otherwise Hoover could not proceed.[11]

[11] In any fair consideration of the Hoover-Roosevelt exchanges on the bank crisis it should be remembered that Hoover and his chief advisers were concerned about the possible political turn which a new Democratic Congress might give to his acts.

In short, Hoover was asking for an assurance and a commitment in terms of absolutes.

Perhaps it was the look of utter weariness and defeat on Hoover's face that made Roosevelt refrain from answering as sharply as he might have. He said quietly that he had looked into the Act himself. He had asked his own Attorney General designate, Senator Walsh, for an opinion on the status of the Act and, before his death, Walsh had reported that in an emergency he would rule that the needed exercise of powers was valid. Homer Cummings, who had been drafted to take Walsh's place the day before, was now studying the question. But for himself, Roosevelt had every reason to believe that the requisite authority still existed. Beyond that, he could not go.

The way was open for Mr. Hoover to act alone. If he decided to invoke the emergency powers, the incoming administration would regard his action with the greatest of sympathy. But, said Roosevelt, the risk of subsequent congressional disavowal would be no jot or tittle smaller whether he, Roosevelt, invoked the emergency powers or Hoover invoked them.

The meeting broke up shortly after five o'clock with F. D. R.'s "I shall be waiting at my hotel, Mr. President, to learn what you decide."

The hours after that, until one o'clock the next morning, were a blur of talk in the Roosevelt suite. Woodin, Glass, Jesse Jones, and Hull were there for a while. The telephone rang constantly. Party leaders were calling to check up on the situation and tender advice. Thomas W. Lamont called from New York to recommend that no action be taken: it was thought by the leading bankers there that the banks could pull through to the next noon and possibly, then, with Roosevelt in office, a sweeping change in psychology would take place before Monday. Hoover called to say he had the same word from both New York and Chicago, where the bankers were also in session, and had finally decided to do nothing.[12] Still the talk went on. We were all, by then, indescribably tense—even Roosevelt.

He doubtless felt that if his invocation of the Trading with the Enemy Act proved disastrous Congress would jump at the chance to blame him for invoking it and refuse to validate his action.

12 Myers and Newton (p. 366) describe this conversation as follows:

"Finally, at 11:30 that night, from a conference meeting in the White House, President Hoover telephoned to President-elect Roosevelt, who was in conference with his advisers at his hotel in Washington, and asked for their conclusions. Mr. Roosevelt stated that Senator Glass, with whom he was conferring, was opposed to national closing, that the Senator believed the country should go temporarily onto a clearing-house scrip basis. Mr. Roosevelt believed that the governors of the

To meet this danger [of] radicalism by ~~Toryism~~ Reaction is to ~~court~~ invite disaster. ~~Toryism~~ Reaction is no barrier to the radical. It is a challenge and a provocation. It is not the ~~promise~~ pledge of a new deal it is the reminder of broken ~~promises~~ promises. Its unctuous reassurances of prosperity round the corner are not oil on troubled water, they are oil on fire.

THE "NEW DEAL"

The phrase "New Deal" first made its appearance in connection with Mr. Roosevelt's program in his acceptance speech on July 2, 1932. It was suggested to him by Mr. Moley in a memorandum six weeks before. A portion of Mr. Moley's rough notes for that memorandum, including the phrase, is reproduced above. (See page 23) the foreign debts, the world economic conference, supervision of the economic adviser's office and such additional duties as the President may direct in the general field of foreign and domestic government.

Dictated by FDR as my duties.

DUTIES

Because he wished to clear up the ambiguity certain to characterize his position if he should hold the office of Assistant Secretary of State while working for the President directly, Mr. Moley asked Mr. Roosevelt to dictate a statement describing his duties. The page shown herewith is a reproduction of that statement as dictated to Mr. Moley on February 3, 1933. (See page 116)

THINGS TO DO
FOR F.D.R.

Pages reproduced herewith are from Mr. Moley's notebook. They list matters he had been directed by Mr. Roosevelt to take up in Washington on February 7 and 8, 1933. These directions, in the main, refer to appointments to the Cabinet. The initials "F. F." refer to Felix Frankfurter, suggested to Walsh for Solicitor General. (See Chapter IV)

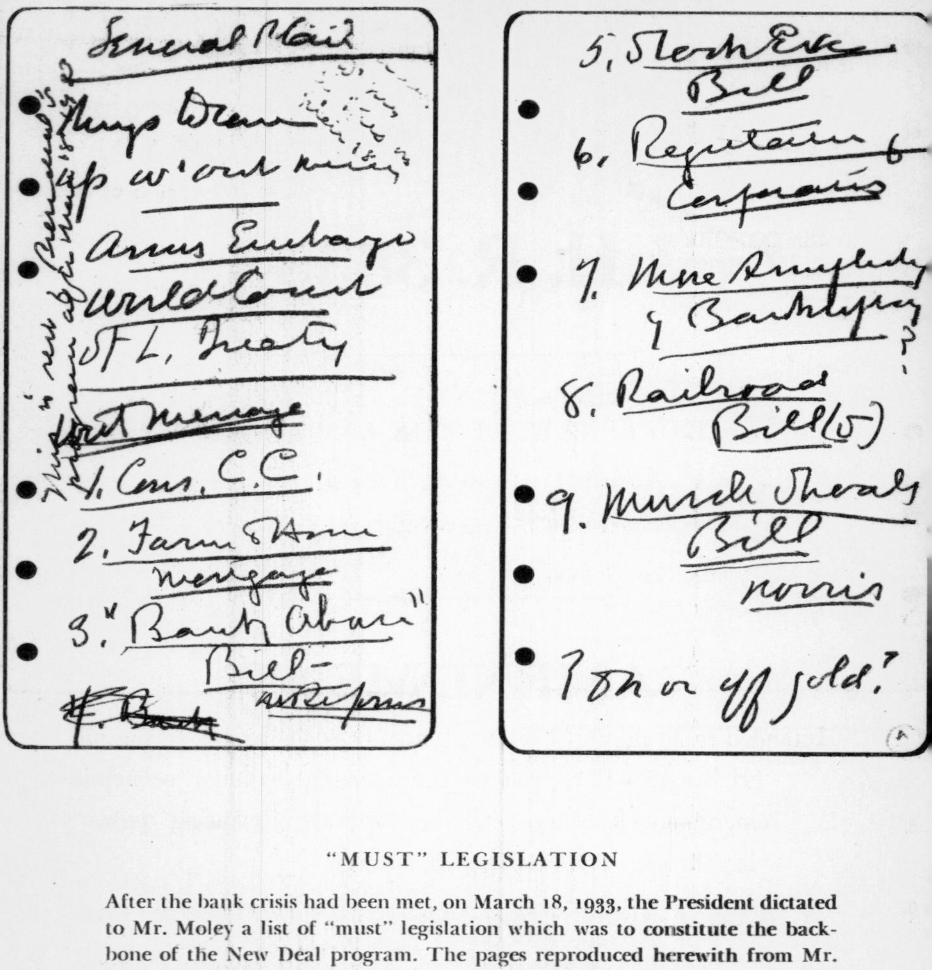

"MUST" LEGISLATION

After the bank crisis had been met, on March 18, 1933, the President dictated to Mr. Moley a list of "must" legislation which was to constitute the backbone of the New Deal program. The pages reproduced herewith from Mr. Moley's notebook shows the list of measures as taken down by him from the President's dictation. (See Chapter VI)

MONEY CONTROLS (*opposite page*)

Among the most controversial of the important measures passed by the Hundred Days' Congress was the Thomas amendment, which gave the Executive the power to regulate the gold-content of the dollar and other vast monetary controls. The accompanying illustration shows a portion of the first page of the Thomas amendment with the President's penciled directions to Mr. Moley to secure its revision and passage. This document was handed to Mr. Moley on the night of April 18, 1933. (See page 159)

Ray Moley – Byrnes
Thomas
Treasury

73D CONGRESS
1ST SESSION

H. R. 3835

IN THE SENATE OF THE UNITED STATES

APRIL 11 (calendar day, APRIL 12), 1933

Ordered to lie on the table and to be printed

AMENDMENT

Intended to be proposed by Mr. THOMAS of Oklahoma to the bill (H.R. 3835) to relieve the existing national economic emergency by increasing agricultural purchasing power, viz: On page 43, after line 5, insert:

PART 6—FINANCING—AND EXERCISING POWER CONFERRED BY SECTION 8 OF ARTICLE I OF THE CONSTITUTION: TO COIN MONEY AND TO REGULATE THE VALUE THEREOF

SEC. 34. Pursuant to the policy stated in this Act, and for the purposes of raising commodity prices, meeting the existing deficit in the Federal Treasury and expenses of maturing obligations and the expenses of the Federal Government, the President is hereby authorized, within his

Asst. Secretary Moley is sailing tomorrow for London at the request of the President. He will act in a sense as a messenger or liaison officer on this short trip, giving the American delegates first hand information of the various developments, Congressional etc. in this country since the delegation left and conveying the Presidents views of the effect of these developments on the original

SAILING ORDERS

instructions given the Delegation before they sailed.

Asst Secy Moley will stay in London only about a week and will then return to give the President full information of the Conference up to that time.

SAILING ORDERS

When the President decided that Mr. Moley should go to the London Economic Conference, Mr. Roosevelt was at sea on the schooner *Amberjack*. At the President's suggestion Mr. Moley flew to Nantucket, was conveyed by destroyer to the *Amberjack* and, after a conference, received in the President's own handwriting these specific instructions as to his duties in London and the purpose of his visit. The President's statement was immediately released to the press on June 20, 1933. (See page 237)

Prof Raymond Moley left by sea-plane after a 2 hour visit on the Amberjack, & returned straight to N.Y. (He goes on the U.S.S. Bernadou to Nantucket & gets the plane there U.S.S. Bernadou will then rejoin us at Provincetown)

SAILING ORDERS

At one o'clock Hoover telephoned again. Mills, the Treasury people, and some Federal Reserve Board officials were still at it in the Treasury. He had just wanted to keep Roosevelt informed. F. D. R. thanked him and suggested that they both "turn in" and get some rest.

I said good night then, too, and left the apartment to go back to my own rooms. But when I stepped out of the elevator into the Mayflower lobby, there was Will Woodin, who had left us some time earlier—presumably to go to bed. He smiled when he saw my face. "Don't say it," he said. "I really tried very hard. But I couldn't even get to the stage of undressing. This thing is bad. Will you come over to the Treasury with me? We'll see if we can give those fellows there a hand."

We found Mills; Arthur Ballantine, the Under Secretary; F. G. Awalt, the Acting Comptroller of the Currency; Eugene Meyer; and one or two others haggard and red-eyed in the Secretary's office. They were still going over the bank figures for the day, and they told us, when we arrived, that it was their mournful conclusion that the banks would have to be protected against runs that morning whether the New York and Chicago bankers themselves realized it or not. They had been calling the governors of all the states that had not already suspended or restricted banking operations and had induced them to agree to declare brief holidays. It remained only to get hold of Henry Horner of Illinois, whom they hadn't yet been able to reach, and to persuade Herbert Lehman of New York to overrule the bankers who were urging him to hold off.

Will's and my contribution was the suggestion that they call Lehman back and put the thing to him again in a more forcible way. Lehman was called again—and again. There were seemingly endless conversations with George L. Harrison, Governor of the New York Federal Reserve Bank, who kept pointing out what the commercial bankers in New York did not yet realize—that the gold withdrawals were becoming unbearable. Sometime in the midst of all this I fell asleep. The next

States would take care of the closing situation where it was necessary. He said he did not want any kind of proclamation issued. The President asked if he could repeat Mr. Roosevelt's statement to the men assembled with him at the White House, and did so."

I was, of course, not actually listening on the telephone to the conversation of the two men. But I did hear Roosevelt's end of the conversation and Roosevelt's summary of it, for the benefit of all of us there, the moment he had hung up. And neither what I remember nor what I noted down at the time jibes with the foregoing description.

thing I remember was Will's waking me with the words, "It's all right, Ray. Let's go now. Lehman's agreed."

I rubbed my eyes and looked at an unforgettable picture. Mills sat behind the desk of the Secretary of the Treasury, Woodin on the other side. The long days and nights after, Woodin was to sit behind the desk and Mills in front. Otherwise nothing was to change in that room. Mills, Woodin, Ballantine, Awalt, and I had forgotten to be Republicans or Democrats. We were just a bunch of men trying to save the banking system.

We stood up then, and walked through the echoing halls past the soft-footed watchmen and the deathwatch of reporters and photographers who were to snap pictures of the same group of us, in the same clothes, bowed under the same weariness, for a week of nights.

2

When Roosevelt took the oath of office on the steps of the Capitol at eight minutes past one that Saturday, he had already decided on three swift moves—to invoke the powers of the Trading with the Enemy Act,[13] call the new Congress into special session before the next week's end, and summon leading bankers of New York, Chicago, Philadelphia, Baltimore, and Richmond to a meeting in Washington Sunday. But that left a list of transcendently important questions still unanswered: what day to fix for the meeting of Congress, whether the Federal Reserve Banks could be closed by presidential proclamation, what steps must be taken to restore confidence on the part of the nation's depositors before the banks were reopened, and what remedial plan to present to Congress.

The first question was answered on Saturday night. Will gave F. D. R. his assurance that, come what might, he would have emergency bank legislation ready by Thursday morning. It was agreed, then, that Congress should be called to meet on that day, the 9th.

The second question was answered around two o'clock on Monday morning, after hours of argument with Federal Reserve Bank officials who continued to harp on the dubiousness of the President's authority to close the Reserve Banks. Will Woodin had gone on listening pa-

[13] The little ritual that took place in the first Cabinet meeting on Sunday which involved F. D. R.'s turning to Cummings and asking, "How much time will you require to prepare an opinion?" and Cummings' replying, "Mr. President, I am ready to give my opinion now," was nothing but a formality.

tiently; but when I could bear the pro-ing and con-ing no longer, I broke in with the remark that if two Secretaries of the Treasury and the Governor of the Federal Reserve Board couldn't order the closing of the Reserve Banks, who, in God's name, could? Meyer left the room to call George Harrison in New York again. When he was through speaking, he rejoined us with the announcement that all the Reserve Banks would close.

Meanwhile, late Sunday, after F. D. R., Woodin, Cummings, and I had worked over it, the proclamation of emergency powers declaring a four-day bank holiday and an embargo on the withdrawal, transfer, or domestic use of gold and silver had been made.[14] And meanwhile, too, at ten o'clock on Sunday morning, four interminable days and nights of conferences with the bankers had begun.

These men had been called in on the theory that they could help Will decide how to answer the last two major questions. But the resulting babble of tongues was so deafening it was a marvel that Will wasn't totally confounded by it.

I suppose the most distracting element in the situation was the fact that the nerves of most of the participants were near the cracking point even before the meetings began. Illustrative was the case of Berle. With Woodin's approval I had invited him and Ralph Robey of "brains-trust" days to participate in the conferences at the Treasury. I was having breakfast with Ralph in the hotel dining room on Sunday morning when Berle came upon the scene and called me out into the lobby.

"What," said Berle, "is that man doing here?"

I answered that I had asked Robey to come down from New York because I felt that the job was too big "for Woodin or for you or for me or for fifty of us put together."

Thereupon Adolf blurted out, "There is too much Colonel House business going on here."

I felt as though someone had thrown cold water in my face, but, realizing that Adolf was probably too excited to be taken seriously, I laughed and said good-naturedly, "Oh, come, come, Adolf. You wouldn't be meaning me, now, would you?"

"I simply said there was too much Colonel House business going on," he snapped. "You can make of that what you want."

Rather than answer roughly, I turned on my heel and left the hotel for the Treasury, convinced that Berle would muffle this strange new

[14] A draft of this proclamation had been prepared by Mills and Ballantine.

feeling he was showing toward both Robey and me, and convinced that the two men would come to the Treasury, as planned. But this did not happen. I was shocked, later, to see Berle appear at the Treasury without Robey, and to learn that Robey, bewildered and annoyed, had gone back to New York.

Early the next morning, after I had gone to bed, Berle came bursting into my room in a state of great agitation. The substance of his disquisition was that we would certainly not be able to work out a scheme for reopening the banks in the next three days, and the climax came with his statement that nobody was making sense except Ogden Mills. This was too much! There was nothing to do but persuade him to go away and stop encroaching on the miserable four hours which was all I had for sleep.

The bankers had their casualties, too. Several pillars of that community went to pieces and, of those who didn't, many came perilously close to it. Melvin A. Traylor of Chicago, for instance, was possessed by the idea that the Treasury's critical refunding operation of March 15th would not succeed—that the issue of Treasury certificates would not be taken up. I ventured the suggestion that if worse came to worst, the President might ask for a public subscription. Traylor looked at me with utter amazement and said that I couldn't have any comprehension of what I was saying. And when I replied that he underestimated the extent to which Roosevelt would be able to command the united action of the people if, say, he appealed to them over the radio, Traylor shouted, "You're talking like William Jennings Bryan and his million men who'd leap to arms overnight!"

Explosions like these weren't the exception between Sunday morning and Wednesday night. And to complete the mad picture, there was furious disagreement about purposes and methods.

Some of the bankers insisted there must be a nationwide issue of scrip. Others urged that currency be issued against the sound assets of the banks. Others concentrated on the argument that the banks could not be made safe unless the state banking systems were forced into the Federal Reserve system. There was talk of the need for converting the Reserve Banks into government-owned deposit banks, talk of guaranteeing deposits, even talk of nationalizing the banking business—talk that went on and on in circles. Late Monday night, after two almost uninterrupted days of it, Will and I sat down in his rooms and took stock.

"I'll be damned if I go back into those meetings," Will said, "until I get my head cleared."

We agreed, then, that the only possible way to proceed was to try to see things in the large. Assured as we were of the loyal support and superlative technical advice of Mills, Ballantine, and Awalt, we could afford to let details go for the moment. What we needed was a comprehensive formula. And that we came close to producing before I left Will's apartment that Monday night.

It was, in essence, that we were facing a problem of public psychology more acutely than we were facing a problem of finance—that every step taken must be tested less on the basis of its ultimate desirability from a financial point of view than on the basis of its immediate effect in restoring confidence.

The corollaries of these propositions were obvious. They recognized the need for:

(1) "Swift and staccato action" (Will's phrase).

(2) The stressing of conventional banking methods and the avoidance of any unusual or highly controversial measures.

(3) The opening of as many banks as could possibly be opened within the realm of safety, since the greater the number opened the greater the probability of confidence in banks generally.

(4) The blacking out of the reputedly left-wing presidential advisers (Berle, Tugwell, and myself) during the crisis.[15]

(5) A tremendous gesture by the President and Congress in the direction of economy.

(6) A man-to-man appeal for public confidence by the President himself.

That was how we left it when I went off to bed. But the finishing touch was Will Woodin's alone.

I must explain that, because it was doubtful whether the banks when reopened would have enough currency and coin to meet minimum needs, the idea of issuing scrip had gained so much momentum by Monday night that we almost all took it for granted that it would be carried through. It was Will who tossed the scheme out the window

[15] I say "reputedly left-wing" because, strange as it may seem, we were actually supposed then to be Reds of the deepest hue and because it's important to note that no radical would have considered this program I was helping to formulate worth a row of pins. Certainly the intimate presidential advisers in 1939 would disagree violently with the conception of public confidence that Will Woodin and I shared.

and decided in favor of those in the Treasury—including Mills and Ballantine—who believed the issue of scrip was unnecessary.

Early Tuesday morning, as I came in to breakfast with him, he yelled at me with wild enthusiasm, "I've got it! I've got it!"

Not being given to cheerfulness myself at breakfast time, I looked at him pretty glumly and said, "Got what?"

"Well," said Will, "after you left, I played my guitar a little while and then read a little while and then slept a little while and then awakened and then thought about this scrip thing and then played some more and read some more and slept some more and thought some more. And, by gum, if I didn't hit on the answer that way! Why didn't I see it before? We don't have to issue scrip!"

Here Will's tiny fist came crashing down on the table.

"We don't need it. These bankers have hypnotized themselves and us. We can issue currency against the sound assets of the banks. The Reserve Act lets us print all we'll need. And it won't frighten people. It won't look like stage money. It'll be money that looks like money."

This, I can state positively, was the origin of the Emergency Banking legislation. The way in which Will made his decision was characteristic of him. Half businessman, half artist, he had succeeded in brushing away the confusing advice of the days previous and come cleanly to the simplest of all possible solutions.

We jumped up from table and made straight for the White House. Roosevelt listened to the whole plan with mounting enthusiasm. In twenty minutes we had his O.K. Then we were off for forty-eight hours of wrangling over details in the meetings at the Treasury, of bill drafting, message drafting, and conferring with the congressional leaders.

At noon on Thursday, March 9th, the new Congress met. At three o'clock the President's message was read. An hour later the Emergency Banking bill, which no one but the congressional leaders had seen, was passed by the House.[16] It went through the Senate at seven-thirty

[16] The bill itself was represented by a folded newspaper in the House because there had not been time to print copies of it. Its drafting had largely been the work of Walter Wyatt, general counsel of the Federal Reserve Board. Its final draft, which had not been achieved until the early morning hours of that day, provided:

(1) Approval and confirmation of all the proclamations and actions of Roosevelt and Woodin under the Trading with the Enemy Act.

(2) Amendment of that Act to give the President new powers to regulate transactions in foreign exchange; transfers of credit between, or transfers by, banking institutions; and the export, hoarding, earmarking, or melting of gold or silver coin, bullion or currency by any person within the United States.

o'clock that evening. Before nine o'clock F. D. R. had signed it. The sequence of bold, heart-warming action had begun.

On Friday morning the sensational economy message and bill were sent to the Capitol. This bill, giving the President drastic authority to cut more than $100,000,000 from government salaries and revise the entire pension and veterans' compensation system at a saving of over $400,000,000, had been prepared by Lew Douglas, whom F. D. R. had appointed budget director, partly on the basis of reports presented by the National Economy League, and partly on the basis of data furnished him by Alvin Brown, who was, at the time, working for Bernie Baruch. Lew, Will, and I had joined in urging Roosevelt to plunge ahead with it that week and we likewise collaborated on the draft of the accompanying message.

The bill itself was given the unusual title, "A Bill to Maintain the Credit of the United States Government." The message was designed to tell the country that the administration intended to follow sound financial policies, to avoid inflationary spending, to be just but firm with the demands of the veterans, and to move immediately in the direction of balancing the budget.

Together, they proved to be a staggering dose for Congress to down. Rebellion broke loose in the House. But the courage and determination of Representative McDuffie of Alabama, a man whose part in the early history of the New Deal has been strangely neglected in all comments upon it, saved the day. McDuffie carried the fight to the floor of the House, fought off amendments, and forced the bill through in two hours.

The psychological effect was electric. The bill, of course, had been greeted with loud shouts of approval by all articulate conservatives. But I am confident that deep down in the consciousness of the average people of the country it found a similar response. Somehow or other, whatever the justice of the case might have been, Hoover had always seemed to be an expensive President. His building program, his ex-

---

(3) The issuance of Federal Reserve Bank Notes to Reserve member banks up to one hundred per cent of the value of government bonds and ninety per cent of other rediscounted assets held by them during the period of the emergency.

(4) The progressive reopening of the banks under license from the Treasury and their operation under "such regulations, limitations, and restrictions as may be prescribed by the Secretary of the Treasury."

(5) The authorization of the R.F.C. to subscribe to the preferred stock of any national banking association, state bank, or trust company which the Secretary of the Treasury found was in need of funds for capital purposes, and the making of loans secured by preferred stock to such institutions.

pansion of certain departments, and, above all, his deficits had given the public the idea that national bankruptcy was not far off. The idea that spending was an economic blessing had few supporters. The bulk of the population was still convinced that a balanced budget was indispensable to recovery.

Meanwhile, on Thursday night, Roosevelt had extended the bank moratorium to give the Treasury and Federal Reserve officials time to reopen the banks. So began, on Friday morning, the man-killing job of checking the reports of hundreds upon hundreds of banks. All of us around the Treasury were aware of the danger—the critical and ever-present danger—that in the hurly-burly grievous mistakes would be made, that banks would be opened that should be kept closed and that banks would be kept closed that might, if they were permitted to open, weather the storm. It was clear that, despite the competence of the Acting Comptroller of the Currency, grave injustices might result unless the scales were sometimes tipped in the direction of leniency. And no one but Will Woodin could take the responsibility for tipping them.

The most dramatic decision we made involved the opening of A. P. Giannini's Bank of America National Trust and Savings Association in California. The first opinion of the responsible officials in California was that the bank should not be permitted to open. But it soon became apparent that it would be unwise to accept this judgment. We were aware that the failure of the Bank of America to reopen would mean much more than the failure of almost any other bank of this class to reopen. The Bank of America had 410 branches. With its one million depositors it was in a very real sense the bank of the common people of California. To keep it closed would shock the state beyond description.

Woodin met the problem with such courage as I have rarely seen. He directed Awalt to go over the figures with him again. When everything was taken into consideration, the two men reached the conclusion that the bank was by no means insolvent. Then ensued a long telephone conversation with a high banking official in San Francisco—a conversation punctuated by some pretty strong language on Woodin's end. It wound up with Woodin's, "Are you willing to take the responsibility for keeping this institution closed?" and the answer, from California, that the official refused to take that responsibility. "Well, then," said Will, "the bank will open." I shall never forget the look of joy on the faces of Hiram Johnson and William McAdoo when I stepped out of Woodin's office after that telephone call and told them the news.

There were a half dozen moments almost as tense, and some mistakes were undoubtedly made in the human process by which decisions were reached. But as I look back at those frenzied days, it seems to me that the country has never quite realized the extent to which Woodin, Ballantine, and, last but by no means least, Awalt helped to restore the confidence of the country by a rapid and unprejudiced approximation of the equities—social as well as financial—involved in each case.

By Sunday night, then, when the words of Roosevelt's first fireside talk began to fall on the ears of a listening nation, the emergency program, shaped on the previous Monday night and Tuesday morning, was well along toward achievement. The build-up was perfect. No one could deny that the climax was perfect, too. As simple and moving as any presidential utterance in the history of this country, Roosevelt's message to the people explaining what had been done and asking them to put their money back into the banks marked the end of the nightmare of panic.[17] To those of us who really knew what had happened that week, it may not have been the dawn. But it was most assuredly the herald of the dawn.

It cannot be emphasized too strongly that the policies which vanquished the bank crisis were thoroughly conservative policies. The sole departure from convention lay in the swiftness and boldness with which they were carried out. Those who conceived and executed them were intent upon rallying the confidence, first, of the conservative business and banking leaders of the country and, then, through them, of the public generally. Had Roosevelt turned, in those fateful days, to the type of adviser that ultimately came into prominence in his administration, it is more than likely that questions of reform would have taken precedence over considerations of safety, with a resultant confusion and delay that would have wreaked incalculable damage upon our whole economic order. If ever there was a moment when things hung in the balance, it was on March 5, 1933—when unorthodoxy would have drained the last remaining strength of the capitalistic system.

Capitalism was saved in eight days, and no other single factor in its salvation was half so important as the imagination and sturdiness and common sense of Will Woodin.

[17] The drafting of this speech has been credited to me so often that fairness compels me to state what I know about its authorship. A first draft was prepared by Charles Michelson, director of publicity for the Democratic National Committee. This was completely rewritten by Ballantine, who took it to Roosevelt. Roosevelt edited it before delivery. My sole contribution was a hurried checking over.

3

But to suppose for a moment that, once the bank crisis had passed, we thought we had achieved a permanent solution of the banking and financial problems is like imagining that Dr. James Alexander Miller, having pulled a tubercular patient through a critical case of pneumonia, would tell him that he was no longer in need of medical care. Yet that is just the kind of interpretation most of those who have written on the subject place upon the administration's course between March 13th, when the first of the banks were reopened, and April 19th, when the gold standard was suspended and Roosevelt publicly announced his acceptance of the power to inflate the currency under the Thomas amendment. The administration thought it had fixed everything, the story runs; it suddenly found it hadn't—either because it had opened too many unsound banks or because the millions of dollars of deposits frozen in banks still closed were discovered to be acting as a deflationary factor (this part of the story varies according to the conservatism of the writer); and so then it took the most attractive "out" by rushing into inflation.

Good stories—all of them—overlooking only the facts that Roosevelt recognized the need for pretty fundamental banking reform; that he was perfectly aware of the strength of inflationary sentiment in and out of Congress, and that his mind was open on the question whether the superdeflationary effects of the March crisis and the measures taken to deal with it would not require an antidote of drastic action.[18]

This certainly isn't to imply that Roosevelt himself was "sold" on the idea of inflation before or immediately after his inauguration. I can testify that he wasn't. But he was very consciously waiting to see whether the effort to preserve the monetary standard after March 13th wouldn't entail greater sacrifices in terms of sinking money incomes than the American people would bear, or should be expected to bear, and wouldn't be overwhelmed by the political forces demanding what would amount to uncontrolled inflation.

I doubt that more than a handful of economists in the United States ever realized just how compelling the force of political circumstance

[18] The proof I have to offer on these points are my fragmentary notes of conversations with F. D. R. (notes taken while we were talking). For example, on two of the pages of my daybook, recording a talk with F. D. R. on the morning of March 18th on his legislative program generally, there appear references both to banking legislation and to the gold question.

was. Their idea seems to be that, from mid-February on, Roosevelt was beset by a few crackpot congressmen and senators (who could only "be counted upon to make a certain number of wild speeches"), a few businessmen and farm leaders organized under the title "The Committee for the Nation," and a couple of starry-eyed monetary experts; that Roosevelt mistook their voice for the voice of the people and therefore grossly overestimated the demand for inflation; and that if he had pulled a Grover Cleveland, "setting his face" against currency "tinkering," he could have exploded the myth of inflationary sentiment.

The cold fact is that the inflationary movement attained such formidable strength by April 18th that Roosevelt realized that he could not block it, that he could, at most, try to direct it.

Our realization of its growing momentum was, of course, a subjective process. For me, it was associated, curiously enough, with a little tune Will Woodin composed on the piano one night late in February after he and I had listened to Senator Burton K. Wheeler and ex-Senator Jonathan Bourne, Jr., expatiate for three hours on the advantages that would come from free coinage of silver. Will had called it "Lullaby in Silver" because he composed it, he said, "to get this silver talk off my mind before I go to bed." After that night every time anyone talked to me of inflation, Will's "Lullaby in Silver" ran through my head until, by early April, the simple little tune had taken on the majestic proportions of a crashing symphonic theme in my consciousness.

But political judgments aren't made on the basis of such quirks of the imagination. The decisions of April 18th and 19th were the prosaic results of a counting of noses in the Senate.

No one doubted that inflation had a majority in the House. The only unknown was exactly how strong inflationary sentiment had grown in the Senate since January 24th, when eighteen votes were recorded in its favor. We found that out on Monday, April 17th, just before the Senate voted on Wheeler's amendment to the farm bill providing for the free coinage of silver at a ratio of sixteen to one.[19]

Immediately after that measure was introduced, a Western senator put through a call to me. He was not, he explained, convinced that

[19] It was natural that inflationary sentiment should express itself in the form of amendment to the farm bill. The main purpose of the bill was to raise commodity prices. The idea of doing this through restricted production was not only less dazzling but less familiar than the notion that it could be done through monetary inflation—a notion touted as a remedy for farm ills ever since farm products were first traded for tokens of value, and deeply rooted in the political thinking of the West and Northwest.

"sixteen to one" was sound. He wanted to support the administration if he could. But he had the "folks back home" to keep in mind and he simply couldn't afford, in any real test, to stand out against inflation. What could I suggest that he do?

I suggested that the senator watch the roll call, absent himself from the chamber until the end of the roll call, and then, if there were thirty votes for free silver, vote "No"; but if there were less than thirty votes for it, he might vote "Yes."

Several other senators called my office that day, put the same question, and got the same answer. Still others made inquiry through other channels. All told, we knew that well over ten senators either voted "No" on the Wheeler amendment or refrained from voting on it altogether, despite the fact that they were prepared to support inflation of some sort.

So, though the Wheeler amendment was defeated by a vote of 43 to 33, Roosevelt had conclusive evidence on April 17th that the Senate contained a majority in favor of inflation.

What alternative was there then? A clear one for the theorist working over his charts. But none for a President of the United States. As Walter Lippmann put it, the only questions left were "how inflation was to be produced and whether or not it would be managed and controlled."

Directly after the vote on the Wheeler amendment, Senator Elmer Thomas of Oklahoma introduced another authorizing the President to do any or all of the following things: (1) to issue greenbacks in meeting all forms of current and maturing federal obligations and in buying up United States bonds; (2) to fix the ratio of the value of silver to gold and provide for free coinage of silver by proclamation; and (3) to fix the weight of the gold dollar by proclamation.

Here were all three of the dreaded proposals for inflation bound up together in a way deliberately calculated to enlist all the inflationary support in Congress. And if there had been any doubt that it would succeed in so doing—which there wasn't—it would finally have been dispelled on the morning of Tuesday, April 18th.

Early that morning I was awakened by a telephone call from Senator Bulkley of Ohio. He gave me positive assurance that the Thomas amendment would go through as it stood unless the administration took a hand, and the most the administration could hope to achieve, he added, was congressional consent to vesting inflationary power in the President. Two minutes later Jimmy Byrnes telephoned the same message. I asked Jimmy to stop by, pick me up, and accompany me to the White House. (All through those weeks the nine-o'clock visit to the presidential bedside was routine.)

Before Jimmy left the White House that morning, it had been decided that Roosevelt would accept the Thomas amendment provided Thomas agreed to a thorough rewriting of it. Jimmy was entrusted with the responsibility of bringing Thomas around.

He succeeded. A few hours later Thomas handed F. D. R. a copy of his amendment, with the statement that he was agreeable to "minor changes" so long as the "big principle" of his measure wasn't destroyed.

That night there was scheduled a conference at the White House for discussion of the coming meetings with MacDonald and the other British representatives who were on the Atlantic en route to Washington. We joined the President promptly after dinner—Secretary Hull, Secretary Woodin, Senator Pittman, Herbert Feis, James Warburg, Budget Director Douglas, Bill Bullitt, and myself. But we never did get down to the business for which we'd gathered because, as we filed into the room, Roosevelt handed me the copy of the amendment Thomas had given him and said, "Here, Ray, you act as a clearing house to take care of this. Have it thoroughly amended and then give them the word to pass it." And then, turning to the others, "Congratulate me."

At that moment hell broke loose in the room. This was the first any of those present, except Woodin, Pittman, and I, knew of Roosevelt's decision that morning. Douglas, Warburg, and Feis were so horrified that they began to scold Mr. Roosevelt as though he were a perverse and particularly backward schoolboy. For two hours they argued the case, pacing up and down the room, interrupted more by each other than by the President's good-natured replies. Secretary Hull said nothing at all, but looked as though he had been stabbed in the back when, at one point in the rough and tumble, F. D. R. took out a ten-dollar bill, examined it, and said, "Ha! Issued by the First National Bank of ———. That's in Tennessee—in *your* state, Cordell. How do *I* know it's any good? Only the fact that I think it is makes it so." And Will, who had protested a little when he heard the news earlier, did no more than whisper to me, "What's a Secretary of the Treasury to do when he's presented with a *fait accompli*?"[20]

[20] Woodin's mature reaction to the steps taken on the 19th may be gauged by the following story told by Mr. Roosevelt in *On Our Way* (John Day Company; New York, 1934; p. 61). Says Roosevelt: "The next morning [April 20th] the Secretary came in to see me. His face was wreathed in smiles, but I looked at him and said: 'Mr. Secretary, I have some very bad news for you. I have to announce to you the

We left the White House close to midnight, and I rode with Key Pittman out to his house, making plans for the next day, before I returned to my hotel. When I reached my apartment, I found Douglas, Warburg, and Bullitt in my sitting room still violently discussing the "enormity" of the step Roosevelt was taking. The stream of talk went on for well over an hour then, and reached its crescendo with Lew Douglas', "Well, this is the end of Western civilization." Eventually the three men left, and I went to bed. Later, I heard the sequel. Neither Douglas nor Warburg slept that night. They wandered around the streets, bewailing the step that had been taken. At five in the morning they returned to the hotel and aroused Bullitt from sleep. Apparently they had to tell somebody the net result of all their travail; they had decided, at last, that they could not change the President's major decision and so they would concentrate on getting him to agree to one or two small limitations upon the powers conferred by the measure.

Early that Wednesday morning I went down to the Capitol, where, in the office of the foreign-relations committee, Pittman, Byrnes, a couple of draftsmen, and I began the two-day job of revision.[21] That morning the President announced his decision to the press.

That night the announcement was made that, henceforth, the export of gold would be prohibited. The United States had cut loose from the gold standard.

These are the facts, so far as I know them, about April 19th. Three-quarters of the explanation of what was behind them, Lindley has suggested, lay in the powerful sequence of events. But intimate ob-

---

serious fact that the United States has gone off the gold standard.' Mr. Woodin is a good sport. He threw up both hands, opened his eyes wide and exclaimed: 'My heavens! What, again?'" I'm not sure that Will Woodin was so happy as Roosevelt believed. But he was a "good sport."

[21] The Thomas amendment passed the Senate on April 28th, by a vote of 64 to 21. The House adopted it on May 3rd, 307 to 86. As finally revised, the bill empowered the President:

(1) To negotiate with the Reserve banks to get them to conduct open market operations in obligations of the federal government and to buy Treasury bills or other obligations to an amount not exceeding three billion dollars.

(2) To issue greenbacks up to three billion dollars for the purpose of retiring outstanding federal obligations (these limitations on the issue and use of greenbacks being among Lew Douglas' suggested modifications).

(3) To reduce the gold content of the dollar up to fifty per cent and fix the ratio between gold and silver.

(4) To accept silver from foreign debtors up to an amount of $100,000,000 (later increased to $200,000,000), the price of silver being fixed for such purpose at not more than fifty cents an ounce, and to issue silver certificates against silver thus received (Key Pittman's pet idea).

servation of Roosevelt during those days has always made me believe that the element of circumstance played an even greater role. Rationalizations—the business of making a virtue of necessity—came after the decisions were made. It is true that those rationalizations, in turn, were to become the intellectual bridges to a silly and futile monetary policy—the brief adoption, in October, of Professor Warren's theory that changes in the gold price would cause commodity prices to vary proportionately. But if an active, choate desire to achieve a dollar whose gold content fluctuated with the price level played any appreciable part in determining Mr. Roosevelt's course in April, he certainly succeeded in concealing it from me.

Wool has been pulled over my eyes more than once. Perhaps it was then. Yet I believed and still believe that Roosevelt did not abandon the gold standard because of any positive theories about an "adjustable" dollar, but to prevent further deflation. I still believe that Roosevelt accepted the Thomas amendment only to circumvent uncontrolled inflation by Congress. I had the feeling that Roosevelt would baffle the "wild men" more effectively than a fundamentalist could, and that he could be trusted to resist the more dangerous forms of money magic. And all but the most extreme gold-standard adherents seemed to share that feeling.

It's ironic that the one form of inflation that was at that time not feared at all—budgetary inflation—has, after six years, become the real menace to our financial solidarity, until for those who like to think of things in terms of ultimates, in terms of threats to Western civilization, it is, I suppose, as good a talking point as any.

CHAPTER VI

THE HUNDRED DAYS

SO FAR as my first hectic weeks in Washington can be said to have had any personal design at all, they were shaped by the decision of February 18th—the decision to stay in Washington not more than a month. I didn't move my family to Washington. My hotel rooms were engaged on a day-to-day basis. I had with me only a small trunkful of clothes. I continued to carry a full teaching schedule in New York—the courses I gave being, by temporary arrangement, crammed into one day. I had listed myself in the Columbia and Barnard catalogues that went to press late in February, 1933, for a full schedule of courses, normally distributed over the week, in the academic year 1933-34. I was already negotiating with two syndicates about writing for the newspapers. In short, I had not the smallest intention of running out on my fine resolution. I wanted to go home and go about my business. And when the week-end of March 18th and 19th rolled around, and it was apparent that the bank crisis was over, I so informed Roosevelt.

The conversation that ensued was flatteringly reminiscent of its two predecessors in late November and early February. I was needed. I knew the people who were working on the legislative program he had decided to push through before distributing patronage. I knew who and what were necessary to complete it. Who would help with the messages and other state papers? Et cetera, et cetera, et cetera.

" 'Who will smoke my meerschaum pipe, who will hold her white, white hand?' " I wrote, by way of summing up this intoxicating speech in my journal and by way of suggesting, too, that I was wholly conscious of the blarney-content thereof.

F. D. R.'s infectious enthusiasm about the future he was sketching out for me hadn't changed. But that my resistance to it had is indicated by his final comment on that occasion. "Well," said he, "don't forget you're enlisted for a while more, anyhow. And at the rate we've been going, a lot of things can happen to make you change your mind."

As a matter of fact, a lot of things did happen between that morning and March 31st. But they included almost as many incidents calculated to stiffen my determination as to undermine it.

There was, for instance, Will Woodin's reaction to my announcement that I was leaving. He said that he felt closer to me than to anyone else in Washington, and he reminded me of what I already knew—that he was far from well,[1] that he had as yet no new Under Secretary, and that a gigantic job still lay before him. Would I accept the job of Under Secretary?

There were elements of common sense in this suggestion. To go to the Treasury would end difficulties under which I labored in the State Department, although I would nevertheless have insisted upon leaving Washington in a very few months. I told Will that I would abide by his judgment and the President's. But Roosevelt refused to appoint me to that job when Woodin asked him to. When he turned to me and said that I'd be tied down too much as Under Secretary of the Treasury and that he didn't propose to lose my services by turning me over to Will, the melting mood induced by Woodin's importunings passed. I took it into my head to believe that F. D. R. was either laughing off our talk on the 18th or that he figured he'd buttered me into compliance. And I didn't like being either buttered or shoved around.

Yet, tempting me to stay, was the realization that the conduct of our foreign affairs by the State Department was far from reassuring. Specifically I had in mind such facts as these that follow. On March 6th I had stumbled by accident upon Norman Davis in the State Department drafting, with Hull's consent, a reply to a British memorandum on the coming debt and economic negotiations received the week before—this, despite Roosevelt's definite instructions that I was to work on everything pertaining to these negotiations. On March 12th I had discovered that, to accompany the announcement of Hugh R. Wilson's

[1] Each morning during the bank crisis Will would confide that his throat was bothering him and, before the crisis was over, Will was already under a doctor's care. When the strain of the first battle passed, he left for a few days' rest in New York. This rest seemed to clear up the pain and irritation in his throat, and he came back to work. But just as soon as he put in a week or two of hard work again, the throat complaint returned. Finally, as summer came on, he found it necessary to take more time off. He went to New York for treatment. Then, though his condition became increasingly serious, he returned to the battle in August and carried on a little while. Finally, late in the year, he gave up the fight. On May 3, 1934, he died of the ailment that had so unmistakably come upon him in the early days of March, 1933. It is not emphasizing unduly the significance of this chain of circumstances to say that Woodin was unquestionably a victim of the strain under which he had labored to restore order in the financial system of the country.

designation to attend the meetings of the League Advisory Committee on Manchuria, the career servants of the Department had prepared a statement which would have lent itself to wide misinterpretation of our relations to the League, that they had slipped it past most of their superiors and had carried it to the point where it was ready for mimeographing and release to the press.[2] And between March 13th and March 31st, eager as I was to slough off my duties, I had been unable to uncover in the Department a single person who understood and sympathized with F. D. R.'s domestic and foreign objectives sufficiently to be capable of directing the preparations for the foreign economic conversations scheduled to begin in April.

On the other hand, to counteract my feeling that the New Deal desperately needed friends in the State Department, was the knowledge that Roosevelt himself was responsible for the dearth of its friends there and—more important—that he was still sublimely indifferent to the dangerous situation he was thus creating. In spite of his professed indignation over the incidents of March 6th and March 12th, for example, he had agreed, by March 17th, to let Allen W. Dulles, an outspoken internationalist, sail off to the Disarmament Conference with Norman Davis.[3] Who was I, to try to set myself up as a dike against a flood of his own making?

Finally, in this casting up of incorporeal accounts, was the item of professional ethics—the principle that makes a managing editor who's been given his notice stay by his paper until he's actually been replaced. In the few short weeks that I'd been in Washington I had managed to get myself almost inextricably involved in the frantic business of getting pieces of legislation under way. There were a half dozen of them—a municipal bankruptcy bill, a securities bill, a railroad measure,

[2] This statement was drastically revised by F. D. R. and myself on the 12th to indicate the United States' continued disinterestedness in League affairs.

[3] Once in Geneva, Davis persuaded Roosevelt and Hull to permit him to make, in return for an undesignated limitation of armament, the following extraordinary commitment: The United States would not only "consult" other nations in case of a threatened war, but if we concurred "in the judgment rendered as to the responsible and guilty party," we would not interfere with "collective effort" made by other nations to restore peace. This, of course, was a commitment to support the League and abandon American neutrality in case of war. Congress immediately recognized it as such—even if Roosevelt did not—and at once proceeded to qualify and, in large part, nullify it by passing Hiram Johnson's amendment to the Arms Embargo Resolution of 1933. Mr. Roosevelt might have spared himself this rebuff had he pondered the meaning of letting Davis and Dulles represent the United States in Geneva.

farm- and home-mortgage relief plans—all in different stages of preparation, all requiring the most exacting study, the most delicate negotiation, and the weighing of endlessly conflicting arguments on the supposed virtues and defects of each provision in each draft of each bill. I had to admit to Roosevelt on the 28th that it would, indeed, cause confusion and considerable duplication of work if I should pull out on the 31st. I was tending so many of the irons he had in the fire that, modesty aside, my going would leave him shorthanded.

Yet, the net of all these confusing circumstances suggested that, as a matter of personal contentment and self-interest, it would be best for me to go my way. As a thinking human being, I knew that. The logical thing, the "smart" thing to do was to go. Theoretically, only the victim of political myopia, on the one hand, or the fortunate possessor of clairvoyant gifts, on the other, would have stayed.

I stayed.

I make neither apologies nor proud claims for that fact. (I can only call it a fact: it wasn't a clear-cut decision and it wasn't supine acquiescence; it was a hunch, more than anything else.) I don't pretend that I was blind to most of the heartache that lay immediately ahead. And I don't pretend either that I foresaw that, in terms of ultimate personal reputation, ultimate personal opportunity, and ultimate personal security, it was the eminently wise thing to stay. I didn't calculate it. I didn't plan it that way. I just stayed.

2

Though the political experts of the Mayflower lobby spent endless hours during the week of March 12th telling each other that the President must (1) hold Congress in continuous session and drive through his legislative program or (2) let Congress recess a few short weeks—and why—F. D. R. himself scarcely stopped to recognize he faced a choice. He allowed that the congressional leaders must be somewhat tuckered out by the winter's work. He granted that they'd all looked forward to a week or two of respite. But, he said, figuratively thumping his chest, *he* wasn't tired. *He* was full of pep. *He* was rarin' to go. The thing to do was to strike while Congress was hot.

That was all there was to what the newspapers called "the momentous decision." The leaders went through the motions of consenting on March 17th. But in the light of F. D. R.'s insistence and the immense prestige the handling of the bank crisis had brought him, they had no real alternative. On March 16th the A.A.A. bill and message were sent down to Congress, and for ninety-two days thereafter bills and messages were tossed into the congressional hopper as fast as they could be prepared.

It wasn't an office I had in those days: it was a caprice.

In addition to two major assignments in the field of foreign relations, I had a roving commission to watch over the formulation of legislation, to unravel the snarls that delayed that formulative process, to cull out of the thousand and one schemes that came pouring into Washington the few that deserved presidential examination, to work up the basic material for F. D. R.'s speeches and messages with the appropriate officials, to assume the literary role after these preparatory chores were done, to be on hand when there were such special headaches as the Thomas amendment revision to be handled, and, with Louis Howe, to "sit on the lid" when some of Roosevelt's less happy impulses threatened to break loose. But, in the execution of these jobs, I was subject to the constant risk of disavowal or repudiation by Roosevelt. I was utterly dependent on his mood, his whim, his state of mind.

The days, for me, went something like this:

7:30 Breakfast and conference. Sometimes the conference would be with Bullitt, Feis, and Warburg on the foreign economic negotiations. Generally, though, my breakfast guests were men from out of town who'd come to make suggestions on some aspect of the Roosevelt legislative program.

8:30 Join Will Woodin in the apartment next to mine and talk about the Treasury.

9:00 In the President's bedroom to discuss the business of the day. The half hour between 9:00 and 9:30 was shared with Lew Douglas. He and I'd agreed in the beginning that each was to have fifteen minutes of that time, but one of us was likely to stay through the other's session.

9:30 Stop in the Cabinet room and dictate a half hour or so for one of the speeches or messages that were in constant preparation through that spring.

10:00 Leave the dictation to be transcribed, cross the street to my office at the State Department, glance at my mail, and confer briefly with Hull, Phillips, Feis, or others on foreign affairs.

11:00 Back to the White House, there to go over the dictation with F. D. R. or to take up again the earlier conversation of the morning.

11:45 Arrive at the Treasury, to work with Woodin for a bit, or at some other department to confer on legislation.

1:00 Lunch, snatched wherever I found myself.

1:30 Nap, on a little black leather settee with the resiliency of concrete, thoughtfully provided by the State Department.

2:00 The beginning of three hours' or more appointments at my office. These were divided into fifteen-minute interviews. My callers would be not only men with legitimate business to discuss but a choice variety of panacea artists. I tried to see as many people as I could, since I was Roosevelt's unofficial sieve on policy. But time was limited and the job of listening patiently, directing people to the officials that they really ought to see, or getting rid of them entirely was work on the political rock pile. (This was the most tiring and, I believe, the least important of my jobs.) In spite of all that I could do, I was charged with being pretty difficult to get to. A story went the rounds of the columns that May: an important figure in the banking world had found it impossible to get an interview and was finally forced to ask F. D. R. to intercede and make a date for him with me. There was much half-serious chaffing about this yarn, which, needless to say, was quite untrue.

5:00 or 5:30 Conference with my staff. This time of day I dubbed "The Children's Hour"—a bit of foolishness that seems to have caught the President's fancy, for he soon appropriated it. My staff had grown six-strong since the inauguration. There were the two girls I'd brought down from New York—able youngsters who had worked with me for over two years. The one, Celeste Jedel, trained in political science and economics, was my research assistant and office manager, though she was given the Department title of Assistant Legal Adviser. The other, Annette Pomeranz, was my personal secretary. Then there was the competent Mrs. Helen Cook, long a secretary in the office of Assistant Secretary of State, who stayed with me to keep such State Department business as I did within the correct limits of the fixed routine. Next came Katherine C. Blackburn, the resourceful librarian of the National Committee, who was added to my staff at Louis Howe's request. Then there was Bobby, Jesse Straus' son, who continued to volunteer his services, as he had during the campaign, until I turned him over to Hugh Johnson when Hugh needed help in April. Finally, and by no means least, there was Arthur Mullen, Jr., the young giant who'd been McIntyre's assistant on the campaign trips. Art, a lawyer, acted as liaison between Jim Farley's office and my own, and between McIntyre, Steve and me, to keep my wires from getting crossed. He lived with me at the Carlton, and his variegated duties included sending visitors packing at 2:00 A.M. and generally seeing to my care and feeding.[4] Together, the seven of us would go over the mail, the interviews, the telephone calls, and the research, and try to plan the coming day.

7:00 Dinner, which was generally a conference time on legislation once again.

8:30 Usually back to the White House for a session alone with F. D. R. or to sit in on a conference of his with congressmen or executive officials.

11:00 or 11:30 Return to the hotel where, like as not, there were men waiting to confer who couldn't be squeezed in at any other time.

1:30 or 2:00 Bed.

But this kind of timetable no more suggests the quality of those days than a program note suggests the color, movement, and cacophony of Strauss' *Don Quixote*. Their quintessence was a series of mad leaps from one thing to another—from the problems of relief, to securities marketing, to monetary stabilization, to appointments in the State Department, to municipal bankruptcy, to the guarantee of bank deposits, and so on and on—until the tired brain rebelled against the disciplined wrenchings and contortions of the day. And always there was the ominous undertone—the consciousness of the risk of repudiation and of the risk of blundering.

3

Strangely enough, the whirl of work in March, April, and May never got me down half so much as my infrequent attempts to find diversion in Washington's polite society. Sometime in those months I'm supposed to have made the remark, "I know of no scientific proof that all work and no play makes Jack a dull boy." I don't remember saying that, but, if I did, it was probably to choke back the comment that anything was preferable to the kind of "play" official Washington afforded.

The writers of society columns and other purveyors of romantic

[4] Art was able, loyal, and tireless. He was also fabulously profane. The only sad moment in my association with him came when a priest, a friend of his family, charged me sternly with the duty, as an older man, of breaking Art of his profanity. I felt, then, that I was in conscience bound to cut off my chief vicarious release. I reckoned without Art. Despite my admonitions, he continued to curse my enemies and, occasionally, my friends, his judgments of the latter, incidentally, proving, in many cases, to be shrewder than my own.

blather have managed to keep alive the fiction that Washington society is a wonderful and mysterious thing: beauteous ladies and susceptible men eat terrapin, exchange brilliant witticisms, and bandy secrets. That is unadulterated bunk.

Chief among Washington's so-called social attractions are its dinners. Commenting on these functions and the rented potted palms that are their hallmark, Ed Lowry once said: "It was a game, mildly diverting, to scratch one's name on the underside of the fronds of the palms and then keep tab to see how many times one encountered the same palms during the winter season."[5] Fortunately, the guests at dinner parties could be identified without resort to this playful device. But they turned up no less regularly than the palms.

So did the wilted bits of conversation. If those who passed them on were attempting to influence the course of statesmanship, they had a consummate ability to cover up their tracks. One's neighbors at table (1) talked of how "the real Washington" could not possibly be understood by the newcomer; (2) asked what President Roosevelt was "really like" and actually expected more than a stereotyped answer; (3) remarked vaguely on the picture of J. P. Morgan with the midget in his lap or on whatever other irrelevancy had been blazoned on the front pages that day; (4) described the time they had met Henry Adams without showing any signs of ever having read him; and (5) asked, "And now that the ——— bill's been introduced, what's the administration's next move?"

What passed for urbane conversation was the throwing of verbal banana peels under the feet of one's fellow guests. What passed for wit was, like as not, pure shrewishness. What passed for charm was an arch look and the sprightly, "Oh, I've heard the most naughty stories about you." (After which, of course, the squirming prey was supposed to inquire what the canard was. It seems I broke all rules, one night, by countering with, "Madam, twenty-five years ago I left the small gossipy town in which I grew up. Now, tonight, I know I've come back home.")

Perhaps these people knew what they were doing, after all. One's struggles to keep a civil tongue in one's own head did, at least, keep one awake. And boorishness seemed to be the only antidote for dullness that they could contrive.

"One has no choice but to go everywhere or nowhere," Mr. Adams once observed about these affairs. But that was 1893.

Forty years later it was possible to tell Mrs. Cook to decline all but

[5] *Washington Close-Ups; op. cit.;* p. 24.

the three or four absolutely "must" diplomatic invitations that came not to me, but to the office that I held. Happily, it was possible to slip off for dinner with the Michael MacWhites of Ireland. Occasionally there was an informal visit with Bill and Mildred Herridge of Canada; an evening at the piquant, loyal, and generous Cissy Patterson's; a chat with that gentle sheep in wolf's clothing, Sir Ronald Lindsay, and with the gracious Paul Claudel. Such pleasant hours made one forget, temporarily, that Washington's society has lived with a succession of administrations, a parade of public figures, and, wantonlike, manifested toward each the same complacent self-interest. And when one was, perforce, reminded, there was always work to do.

So it was one of the minor irritations of those days to read in Frank Kent's columns that my capacities as a diner-out were omnivorous, that I was being "taken up" in a big way, and, boy, how I did love it.

Years later I was charged by ardent New Dealers with too much dining out with businessmen in New York. Both fictions still live. The composite is that of one who was cursed by the conservatives for dining as a New Dealer and cursed by the New Dealers for dining as a conservative. It seems to have been my destiny to eat at the wrong places at the wrong time.

4

I'm frank to confess that such thrusts as Kent's stung sharply at the time. I could bluff to Jack Garner that I didn't give a damn when, in the course of volunteering advice on how I should handle the press, that always succinct man said, "Stop exposing yourself or you'll get your butt spanked." But I'm sure I neither succeeded in deceiving the Old Man nor in bolstering up my own spirits.

Vastly overestimating both the extent to which people generally were interested in me and the amount of false or malicious comment that was appearing, I became sensitive to a point where I would explode over the story that I never had my suits pressed, for instance. Happily, my own staff was, for the most part, the sole audience at these exhibitions. But once in a while the outbreak would take place in public. It was then I got my first real lessons in public relations.

I learned that "corrections" revive and perpetuate printed untruths. I learned to take the raps without comment even to my intimates. (The mumbling of a few choice expletives sufficed, just as a quiet "ouch!" does with a minor bruise.) By the time a couple of months had passed,

I got hep to the fact that such injuries are largely confined to the vulnerable area known as pride. And once that salutary stage was reached, it was easy to move on to complete, heartfelt indifference.

Elementary lessons? Certainly they were. I could have told myself as much in the first place—as a matter of theory. But when I'd mastered them—in practice—I could cry, with Romeo, "Hang up philosophy! . . . It helps not, it prevails not. . . . Thou canst not speak of that thou dost not feel."

Still, there was an element of truth in the I-don't-give-a-damn remark to Garner. I hadn't the disposition to try to build myself a favorable press. I wasn't angling for any other political office, or even to keep my own. I wanted only to be spared such mischief-making fictions as the one that said I coveted Hull's post (which did incalculable damage in my relations with Hull) and such excessive personal publicity as would irritate the White House.[6]

But even if I'd had the desire or ability to play a deep game with the newspapermen, I wouldn't have had the time. Under the stress of day-to-day work, I was obliged to meet them catch-as-catch-can.

It wasn't an easy job they had those days. Many of them were men trained in the old school of Washington reporting, where a breakfast omelet with Hoover was worth a working knowledge of Keynes or Kemmerer any day of the week and to know the provisions of the Federal Reserve Act was unmanly esotericism. With economic reform bills pouring out of the White House, they needed background material desperately. I tried to help supply it, when I could, somewhat as I'd done on the campaign trips—not in press conferences, but informally. Four or five of the newspapermen would catch me as I went to lunch, or as I came into the hotel late at night, or stop by during "The Children's Hour." There'd be questions, answers, and general rag-chewing.

Some of the men came to be good personal friends—Ernest Lindley, John Boettiger, Francis Stephenson, Elliott Thurston, George R. Holmes, George Durno, Eddie Roddan, Paul Mallon, Kingsbury Smith, and, in a slightly different field, Willard Kiplinger. Others, like Ray Brandt, Ray Clapper, and Ray Tucker, I knew less well, but respected for their professional competence.

I think most of the enormous corps in Washington will agree that, one way or the other, the first months of the New Deal offered them a

[6] This last was a point on which I was warned by a considerable number of informed people.

superlative postgraduate course. But there were a few newspapermen who never cared and never learned what it was all about, although in time they picked up some of the economic patter that became familiar even to Washington's Cave Dwellers. These were the lazy ones, whose leg work seemed to consist of swapping gossip in an atmosphere of idle conviviality.

Yet such things were the exception. I can honestly say that, taken as a group, the Washington correspondents were an energetic, resourceful, conscientious bunch. What's more, I've never known a group of men and women who more scrupulously kept their pledged word. I've never been double-crossed by any of them, never had a confidence betrayed. And while I may have thought, at times, that I was getting kicked around mercilessly, I see now I was pretty squarely treated after all.

Ordinarily one learns little from the yellow pages of an old scrapbook. I have. An unemotional examination of the clippings my office made in 1933 has made me realize that the press was generally fair and accurate. The occasional bit of venomous gossip and the excess credit I sometimes got for this or that completely washed each other out. More striking still, I've seen demonstrated the essential truth of the flip aphorism that any publicity is better than none. In the long run even attacks perpetuate a man's ability to get attention for what he has to say.

But this objectivity was sadly lacking in 1933. Unlike Mr. Roosevelt, whose "temperamental equipment for the strain of public life," Lindley correctly says, "is miraculously good,"[7] I never called members of the press "liars" or the dupes of publishers. Yet I admit I often felt pretty sorry for myself that spring, and seconded Mr. Dooley's "Fame invites a man out iv his house to be crowned f'r his gloryous deeds, an' sarves him with a warrant f'r batin' his wife."

5

With some of the legislation of the "Hundred Days" I had little or nothing to do—notably the A.A.A. and T.V.A. In the preparation of other bills I played the role of liaison between the White House and the department and the congressmen immediately concerned. How delicate a job that was may be simply illustrated by description of my connection with the legislation on relief.

Early in March I was asked to dine at the Capitol with La Follette,

[7] *The Roosevelt Revolution; op. cit.;* p. 302.

Costigan, Rex Tugwell, and some others. We talked relief. The two senators favored public works as an integral part of the relief policy. They had ineffectively tried to get a works bill through the lame-duck Congress. Now they wondered whether there was any possibility of persuading the President to get behind a bill for public works. When and how should they proceed?

I explained, without committing myself on the issue of public works, that I might put the question of support squarely to F. D. R. But I had the sense that such a blunt move wouldn't help them any. They knew as well as I that he was frankly leery of the arguments for public works.[8] Yet if it was advice on strategy they wanted, rather than specific action on my part, I could make suggestions. It seemed to me that they'd do best to speak to him of it whenever the occasion offered, but to avoid pressing him too hard. Perhaps before the session was over they might get results. I reminded them of the possibility that there'd be some sort of legislation on industrial relations later in the spring. The President might agree to tie the two together then.

That, in brief, was the course they decided to adopt.

A few days later, on the 14th, at breakfast, Frances Perkins outlined the plan for grants-in-aid to the states for direct work relief on which she and Senators Wagner, Costigan, and La Follette had been working, and reported there was practical agreement on the details of a bill. Did I think, she asked, the President was ready to consider it? I promised to let her know.

At nine o'clock that day I repeated the conversation to the President. He didn't answer me directly. Instead, he began to describe an idea to which, he said, he had given a lot of thought and which he'd formulated to his satisfaction only the night before. It was the stunning idea of putting an army of young men, recruited from the unemployed, to work in the forests and national parks. I remarked that something like that had been suggested by William James in his famous essay "The

[8] Again and again, when we were formulating the plans for the campaign in 1932, Roosevelt had been urged by Tugwell and others to come out for a $5,000,000,000 public-works program. He repeatedly shied away from the proposal. This seems to have been partly because, as Roosevelt explained, Hoover, despite all his preparations, had not been able to find over $900,000,000 worth of "good" and useful projects. But it was also because Roosevelt certainly did not, at that time, subscribe to the pump-priming theory. The interesting figure of $3,300,000,000 for public works, to which Roosevelt finally agreed early in May, 1933, always seemed to me to represent a compromise between the $5,000,000,000 program that had been urged on him and the $900,000,000 Hoover figure that Roosevelt personally regarded as the probable outside limit of useful plans and projects.

Moral Equivalent of War" and asked F. D. R. whether he hadn't been influenced by the vague memory of his student days under James. He admitted there might be some connection, though he wasn't consciously aware of it. And then he went on, "But look here! I think I'll go ahead with this—the way I did on beer."

Going ahead "the way I did on beer" meant dashing off a message and shooting it to Congress without consulting anyone capable of an informed judgment. I urged delay. "Suppose," I said, "we draft a memorandum on your Civilian Reclamation Corps [that was the title he had in mind], get it to the appropriate Cabinet officers at once, and find out what they think of it?" This was a way, I saw, not only to forestall impulsive action on his part, but, at the same time, to give the Wagner-Costigan-La Follette group, through Secretary Perkins, a legitimate chance to describe its broader recommendations.

That was how the thing worked out. On the 14th a memorandum and draft bill on the C.C.C. was handed to the Secretaries of Labor, War, Agriculture, and the Interior. On the 15th they responded with a memorandum indicating that they'd considered not only the C.C.C. proposal but "the whole program of relief for industrial unemployment." "We are of the opinion," they continued smoothly, "that there are three items to be considered in this program." One of them was the C.C.C. The others? They were grants-in-aid and public works.

The whole maneuver had been so gently executed that no one's toes were trodden on. F. D. R. had been quietly prevailed upon to get advice before proceeding with the C.C.C. The Senate public-works group, all serious students of the subject, had been assured the hearing to which they were entitled whether or not the President was inclined to agree with them.

On March 15th the President asked me to have Frances Perkins, La Follette, Costigan, and Harry Hopkins (who had come down from New York) meet him in his office the next day. The meeting was arranged. I couldn't be there (the 16th was a Thursday, and Thursday was my teaching day). I was sorry, because I would have liked to see these people operate. They must have been persuasive, because when the meeting broke up F. D. R., who distrusted public works profoundly, had agreed to mention them in his message on relief.

The next four days were largely given over to consultations on details. On the 19th, Sunday, F. D. R. handed me an outline of his message, written in pencil. On the 21st the message went to Congress.

The C.C.C. passed eight days after. The Emergency Relief bill, appropriating half a billion dollars for distribution through the states and setting up a Federal Relief Administration, was finally signed on May the 12th. Between those dates I kept in touch with Bob La Follette and duly reported to the President his reminders that nothing specific had yet been done on public works. But, at the same time, I passed on to him Ralph Robey's cautions against pump priming. Ultimately, as I had vaguely foreseen, the provision for public works (about which F. D. R. continued, at heart, to be indifferent) was intertwined with the National Industrial Recovery plan (about which none of the conspicuous public-works advocates in the Senate was particularly crazy), and the two things carried each other through.

The important point of this long story centers in the question of technique. In serving as a go-between, I tried never to commit the President to the smallest move unless I was more than reasonably sure he wished it so. On the other hand, I tried never to act as special pleader for any group in matters like this. I was concerned with their getting a hearing when they clearly merited it, and with F. D. R.'s getting all the serious advice he could. And that was all.

The critic will say that personal belief and prejudice entered into this process at every point. Perhaps it did. But, recognizing the danger, I took the only course I could devise to minimize it. I conscientiously told F. D. R. just what my opinions were before I tried to act as though I hadn't any.

6

There were other pitfalls for the presidential privado. Francis Bacon's protégé didn't have to worry about maintaining good relations with Congress. Professor Frankfurter's protégés were ultimately to forget to. Somewhere in the philosophic ages between, an old-fashioned and rather wary man like myself proceeded in the belief that the Constitution of the United States still vested the legislative power in the House and in the Senate.

That meant something more than never presuming to try to force a congressman's vote. It meant never soliciting votes. It meant never discussing bills with members of the House and Senate unless it was explicitly understood as between the President and the men concerned that I was acceptable to both sides. It meant listening with deep respect to the experienced judgments of such men as Garner, Robinson,

Rainey, Byrnes, and Rayburn. And, finally, it meant acting on the assumption that they knew what they were about.

What fine distinctions this involved in practice will be suggested by the tangled history of the Securities Act of 1933.

I've mentioned earlier that, in December, 1932, I'd asked Sam Untermyer to help with the preparation of stock-exchange and securities legislation. That was done with Roosevelt's knowledge and approval. Regulation of the issuance and exchange of securities, advocated in the Democratic platform and F. D. R.'s Columbus speech, was a "must" of the first order in his program. And no one could think of reform in this field without considering Sam Untermyer's pioneer work in it.

The Pujo Committee of 1912, which investigated "the money trust," was not the beginning of Untermyer's activity, but its investigation gave this prewar Counselor at Law his first big part on the national stage. It also crystallized public hostility toward those whom F. D. R. was later to call "the money changers." Its findings gave the Wilson Administration its initial impulse. The Federal Reserve Act would probably have been impossible without the Pujo fanfare. Some of Wilson's speeches at the time actually used the florid verbiage of Untermyer. Even Brandeis' classic *Other People's Money* frankly acknowledged indebtedness to him. In a sense, Untermyer had been a colorful, voluble John the Baptist preparing the way for the solemnities of Wilson, Brandeis, and Glass.

It was natural, then, that we should turn to the old maestro for advice. And advice was eagerly and aggressively given. For two decades Untermyer had cried out for the reform of the stock exchange, and he leaped to the call when I told him that Roosevelt would welcome his help in planning the regulation of the issuance and marketing of securities.

For a while everything went smoothly enough. Untermyer fell to work. He turned down, that December, an offer from Senator Norbeck to serve as counsel for the investigation into banking and financial practices by the Senate Committee on Banking and Currency—turned it down not only because he felt the Committee lacked the authority to conduct an investigation which would serve "as the basis for constructive remedial legislation"[9] but because he was intent on the assignment Roosevelt had authorized me to give him. I was deluged with

[9] Untermyer found fault with the "superficial and insufficient terms" of the resolution under which the Committee was conducting the investigation.

letters, memoranda, and reports from him on the progress he was making.

I have an idea that Untermyer was hoping to become counsel of the investigation when Senator Fletcher assumed the Chairmanship of the Banking and Currency Committee on March 4th, and, as a matter of fact, I think that, despite his seventy-five years, he might have done a vastly better job than Ferdinand Pecora did. Pecora was like a police chief who rounds up all the suspicious characters in town to solve a jewel robbery. Untermyer would have been a Sherlock Holmes, sensing just whom and what to go after. Pecora laid about in all directions with a flail. Untermyer would have used a dart. But it certainly wasn't my business to get entangled in matters of congressional prerogative, and I carefully avoided even the hint of a commitment on the subject of Untermyer's possible appointment, though, in fairness, it must be said that Untermyer never put the thing to me directly.

At any rate, early in January Untermyer sent me a draft of a bill for the regulation of the stock exchange and the issuance of securities. It contemplated the placing of the regulatory machinery in the Post Office.[10] I told him then that it was my feeling—and Roosevelt thoroughly agreed—that to put such a comprehensive system of regulation in the Post Office Department would be unwise. The Post Office Department was essentially a service organization. The idea of sticking an immense regulatory machine into it horrified my sense of the administrative and legal proprieties. Untermyer disagreed. But, after much consultation with him and with F. D. R., I concluded that Untermyer could nevertheless be of vital assistance in the drafting of the precise kind of bill desired. With F. D. R.'s express consent I continued to keep in touch with him through February and early March.

Imagine my surprise, then, when I learned around mid-March that F. D. R. had asked Attorney General Cummings and Secretary Roper to prepare securities legislation; that they had brought Huston Thompson, ex-chairman of the Federal Trade Commission, into the picture; and that Thompson had already prepared a bill. Such mix-ups had occurred before. So far as I know, they never sprang from any desire to cause embarrassment, but from sheer forgetfulness. (One time F. D. R. absent-mindedly asked five people to do the same job and was flabbergasted when they all turned up with elaborate reports.) That made them no less embarrassing. F. D. R. was dismayed when he was re-

[10] It was Untermyer's belief that this would be the best assurance of the legislation's constitutionality.

minded of the work that Untermyer had been doing. And then he fell back on an often-used technique. Maybe if he got everybody together "around the conference table" he could soothe all injured feelings and compromise all differences.

I had my doubts. There are differences that can't be compromised. Thompson's bill provided, sensibly, that the regulatory machinery be put under the Federal Trade Commission, but otherwise it had little to commend it. It covered securities marketing only, while Untermyer's also covered the stock and commodities exchanges. It showed neither the skill at legal draftsmanship nor the knowledge of finance that Untermyer's did. Still, since Roper and Cummings had gone so far with Thompson, there was nothing else to do, and so I arranged that all the parties should meet one Sunday afternoon in March.

The peace conference in the President's study was a frost. Old Untermyer felt, and showed, a cold contempt for Thompson's work. Thompson, in self-defense perhaps, kept shooting at the Achilles heel of Untermyer's—the Post Office idea. Untermyer then got on his high horse. Not only was the Thompson bill a mess, but his own was perfect. And that, he wished it understood, included the Post Office idea.

Reconciliation was obviously hopeless. It seemed to me the wisest thing to do was to get in still a third party and start to draft a bill all over again. But the President said "No." The Roper-Cummings-Thompson group was to go ahead. Untermyer was to go back home and draft a separate exchange-control bill. This decision, when we were later alone, I protested on the ground that not only was the Thompson bill unsatisfactory but that if securities legislation was to be separated from stock-exchange legislation the latter ought to precede the former. Strictly speaking, there was nothing of an emergency nature about the securities act. But even the vague possibility that Roosevelt would cut loose from gold suggested the need for guarding against potential speculative excesses as quickly as possible. F. D. R. replied that there'd be time for both.[11]

Before the week was out, the Thompson bill had been introduced in both houses. And, before another week had passed, my office was inundated by letters, telegrams, and telephone calls about the bill. Scarcely anyone, from the most unreconstructed banker to the most ardent reformer, had a kind word to say for it. Among the men who spoke of it to me that week was Averell Harriman, a man of fine, dis-

[11] By the time Untermyer had revised his bill, F. D. R. had decided to put off stock-exchange regulation until the regular session of Congress in January, 1934.

criminating intelligence and distinctly liberal stripe. He had studied the bill and had assayed the opinions of his associates in banking and law. We agreed that it was an impossible confection.

But I took the same position with him that I did with everyone else. The bill, for better or for worse, was now in the hands of the congressional committees. My own hands were tied. I couldn't presume to interfere in any way. I could only suggest that, as citizens, the critics of the bill were entitled to communicate with Congressman Rayburn and Senator Fletcher, the chairmen of the committees concerned.

Whether or not they did, I've no idea. I only know that Sam Rayburn came to see me about the bill. He and his committee, he said, thought it was a hopeless mess—too severe in some spots, too lenient in others. I asked him if he thought it could be patched up. He snorted. "It'll have to be thrown out. That's what I want to talk to you about. I want you to get me a draftsman who knows this stuff to write a new bill under my direction. And you've got to persuade the Chief that this Thompson bill won't do."

I said that I could legitimately undertake to bring F. D. R. around. But before I went ahead on the draftsman business, it would have to be understood that I was acting directly on his, Rayburn's, authorization—not on the President's.

For all his seeming slowness, there isn't much Sam misses. He laughed appreciatively. "All right," he said, "you've got it."

A day or so later, after talking it over with Sam, I put a call through to Felix Frankfurter. There were any number of reasons why Felix seemed appropriate. Untermyer had taken a position from which he could not gracefully retreat between one day and the next. To bring him back into the picture at that moment would be adding insult to Thompson's injury.

On the other hand, Felix's legal talents were unquestioned. He had the bubbling energy and quick intelligence to get the job done reasonably fast. He would be guided by the fundamental point of view that had inspired Untermyer, Wilson, and Brandeis, and a securities act that didn't embody that point of view would be like a policeman's nightstick made of putty. (The idea of having a securities act, in the first place, was an expression of the Wilson-Brandeis regulatory philosophy.) And finally, offhand, we knew of no one except Untermyer in the private practice of law who was both competent to do the job and free of those professional connections which unconsciously influence a man either to pull his punches or, contrariwise, grow murderous to prove he isn't pulling his punches. Felix, we felt, would do his best to represent the public interest: he wouldn't fall over backwards and reject the advice of everyone who had experience in banking and finance nor would he hesitate to brave unreasonable opposition.

On Friday, April 7th, he arrived in Washington and came to breakfast in my rooms. With him he brought two thin, solemn young men he'd chosen to assist him—James McCauley Landis, a professor in the Harvard Law School, and Benjamin V. Cohen, who, he said, had had considerable experience in the drafting of state laws.

It's interesting to look back at that simple breakfast as a moment of transition in the lives of those men. It was Cohen's first contact with the New Deal, his entrance into national affairs. For Landis, it was the step onto the escalator that was to carry him to the chairmanship of the S.E.C. and, shortly afterward, to the deanship of the Harvard Law School. And it was to make inevitable Felix's appointment to the Supreme Court of the United States by Franklin Roosevelt.

But of course we didn't sit around and look into little crystal balls. We talked of the work in hand and I gave them a rough idea of what Rayburn was like. Felix was bursting with enthusiasm for the job. He explained that he would direct Landis and Cohen from Cambridge and come down to Washington when his teaching permitted and the need for his presence arose.

Where, meanwhile, should the two assistants be housed and how should their expenses be paid? I suggested the Carlton. That would make it possible for me to take care of their bills with my own. No doubt the House committee or the Democratic National Committee would reimburse me for their room and board. (There was not such faith in all Israel! As I recall it, it was two years or more before the Democratic Committee came across—and then only after a good deal of nagging. I don't know what moved me to make the grand gesture that morning. I should have realized that it would knock my already staggering exchequer clear through the ropes. But more of my personal finances later.)

Presently, breakfast over, Cohen and Landis were dismissed, and Harriman, whom I had also invited, appeared. I explained to Felix that it was Rayburn's wish that he consult with enlightened men with experience in the securities-marketing field. Both Rayburn and I felt that Harriman might well be the spokesman for that group. Felix said, "Of course." Nor did he show the slightest tendency to disagree when, to make the point stronger, I added that theory, untempered by practical knowledge, wouldn't produce the kind of legislation Rayburn had in mind.

Ensued a friendly discussion of objectives and methods. The two men agreed that the British Companies Act should be the model for their work. Harriman suggested that, since he was not a lawyer and since Felix had designated two young men to do the spade work, he, Harriman, might well name two New York lawyers, Arthur H. Dean and Alexander I. Henderson, to sit in on the drafting process. Felix seemed satisfied.

I had visions of a fair, competently drawn, workable securities act.

With the sense of a job well done, I called Rayburn and arranged to have Felix meet him at his office. And, so far as Rayburn was concerned, I intended that my contact with the bill should end there. It's true that I received a series of reports from Felix on the progress of his work. And it's true that once or twice, at Felix's request, I had to ease things up between Landis and Cohen, whose intensity, sensitiveness, and twenty-four-hour-a-day exposure to each other occasionally induced those blowups that explorers recognize as unavoidable when any two men are isolated under conditions of strain. But these things did not involve what I conceived to be unwarranted interference with the legislative process.

I scrupulously refrained from interference with the actual drafting of the bill. I did not even read it. But I felt apprehensive when I learned that Felix was not disposed to permit that degree of cooperation between Landis and Cohen, on the one hand, and Harriman and the two lawyers from New York, on the other, which, it seemed to me, was indispensable to the attainment of our objective—the protection of investors without unnecessary hampering of the process of issuing securities.

Fortunately, Rayburn did not take the same view of things that Frankfurter seemed to. After a draft had been made and the bill had been introduced, Rayburn arranged a meeting between Landis, Cohen, Dean, and Henderson. As a result, some, but by no means all, of the "bugs" were eliminated from the bill. No hearings were held by Rayburn's committee, however. The bill was hastily passed.[12]

[12] This was the first appearance of the strategy that Cohen and Corcoran were to use so often in the years thereafter—ramming a too-severe bill through one House and then using it for trading purposes in the other. Corcoran was to say of it, "When you want one loaf of bread, you've got to ask for two." And the adoption of this technique was to be one of the chief factors that undermined congressional

It was trying, during those days, to stick to my principles of behavior vis-à-vis Congress in view of the pressures that were operating. Perhaps the justification for occasional bursts of temper on my part is suggested by a simple illustration. One day during the period when Rayburn's committee was working on the securities bill, an important Democratic politician called and asked me to "do something" about the "injustices" of the bill. I was to "tell Rayburn to fix it up." I told my caller that I did not stick my nose into the internal workings of a House committee and that he ought to go directly to Rayburn. "Now don't play high and mighty with me," was his reply. "Rayburn himself told me that he was taking orders from the 'brains trust.' " I replied with some heat that I doubted seriously that Rayburn had said any such thing, that the "brains trust" no longer existed, and that Rayburn had never received any "order" of any kind from me. And he never would.

The conversation ended angrily. Such conversations often did. Yet the only possible thing to do was to refer complaints to Sam Rayburn and to assume he knew his business. The draftsmen were working under his direction. It was for him and his committee to decide whether or not to follow their advice. The legislative responsibility was his, not mine.

In the Senate a somewhat different problem presented itself. The Senate Committee had meanwhile reported out the Thompson bill. Everyone agreed that, whatever the defects of the Frankfurter-Cohen-Landis-Rayburn bill, they were as nothing compared with the Thompson bill's. The question was how to inter the Thompson bill quietly and decently. At Felix's and Sam's request—and with the approval of F. D. R. (who, by now, was more than willing to admit he'd plunged the administration into a hornet's nest when he'd rushed ahead in March)—I called Joe Robinson. Was there anything that he, as Senate leader, could do to get the administration out from under the Thompson bill?[13]

Robinson was doubtful. He could promise, at most, to hold off a vote on it in the Senate until the House had acted. For the rest, he could simply say he'd try.

confidence in Roosevelt. You can't cry "Wolf!" indefinitely. When outraged congressmen eventually began to realize that F. D. R.'s requests for legislation were not to be taken at face value, that he was continuously asking for more than he wanted or expected to get, their reactions toward the White House changed considerably.

[13] Louis Howe was given the job of applying emollients to Thompson's hurt feelings.

But Robinson came through. With infinite skill he and Jimmy Byrnes got to work. No one unfamiliar with practical politics and parliamentary procedure can quite appreciate the contrivings this operation involved. Robinson and Byrnes decided not to get the bill referred back to Fletcher's committee, but to pass the Thompson bill in the Senate and substitute the House bill in conference. The ultimate success of this maneuver was a triumph for the two loyal strategists.

For me the entire affair had been a tortuous dance on the eggs of congressional prerogative. With every step there was the possibility that I'd fall flat on my face. And there were moments when the temptation to shift the eggs around was almost irresistible.

When the Act was passed and Roosevelt signed it, I received a message from Felix which read: "Your constant help was indispensable in obtaining a sound securities bill." But I felt no little doubt about its soundness in a practical sense. I agreed that, as a long-time measure, the Act was a fine job. Yet I believed it overlooked the fundamental reality of the situation.

That reality was that the corporation lawyers of the country sincerely felt that the Act was excessively cumbersome. Whether or not this was true was of less moment than the fact that corporations and bankers believed that it was and consequently hesitated to float new issues. By so much, recovery was retarded. It's my opinion (and this is an issue no one can ever decide definitively) that a little less perfectionism in April and May, 1933, a little less conviction of rectitude, a little less pooh-poohing of the "hysterical outcries of the Wall Street boys," and a little more of the appearance of sympathy and reasonableness would have gone a long way toward serving the ends of both recovery and reform. The draftsmen of the Act argue that there'd have been no flotations anyhow in 1933. But that's like a mother who doesn't stop her little boy from reading ghost stories before he goes to bed on the ground that he'd have nightmares anyway.[14]

I couldn't help but think, too, as I told F. D. R. the day he sent Untermyer home, that stock-exchange regulation should have been given precedence over securities legislation. By May 27th, when the securities bill was passed, a dangerous speculative spree that did not

[14] Ultimately the Act, with its sister, the Securities Exchange Act, became a workable law under Kennedy, Landis, and William O. Douglas. But that was due to sensible administration and to constructive amendments in 1934.

end until mid-July was already under way, and it was, in fact, too late to get a stock-exchange bill through Congress.

7

The origins of the N.I.R.A., the most controversial of all that spring's controversial legislation, are supposed to have been "fortuitous." That's true enough of the National Industrial Recovery Act itself and the organization set up under it. It isn't true of the philosophy underlying the N.R.A.

The source of that philosophy, as I've suggested earlier, was Van Hise's *Concentration and Control,* and it was endlessly discussed, from every angle, during the "brains trust" days. In several of his campaign speeches F. D. R. had touched upon the idea of substituting, for the futile attempt to control the abuses of anarchic private economic power by smashing it to bits, a policy of cooperative business-government planning to combat the instability of economic operations and the insecurity of livelihood. The beliefs that economic bigness was here to stay; that the problem of government was to enable the whole people to enjoy the benefits of mass production and distribution (economy and security); and that it was the duty of government to devise, with business, the means of social and individual adjustment to the facts of the industrial age—these were the heart and soul of the New Deal. Its fundamental purpose was an effort to modify the characteristics of a chaotic competitive system that could and did produce sweatshops, child labor, rackets, ruinous price cutting, a devastated agriculture, and a score of other blights even in the peak year of 1928. Its chief objective was the initiation of preliminary steps toward a balanced and dynamic economic system. And if ever a man seemed to embrace this philosophy wholeheartedly, that man was Franklin Roosevelt.

That this philosophy (which had, and still has, I believe, vast numbers of adherents in this country) should have been embodied in a piece of legislation primarily designed to ameliorate the immediate effects of the depression upon businessmen and industrial workers was, I suppose, a mistake: because, while the lessons the administrators of N.R.A. so painfully learned will be invaluable to the statesmen of the future, the net effect of the confused, two-headed experiment was to discredit and delay a development which, in my opinion, is inevitable.

I freely take my share of blame for the mistakes in timing and presentation that contributed to the experiment's unhappy end.

These are the facts that indicate just what that share was:

On March 9th Hugh Johnson rode down from New York to Washington on the train with me. He was full of concern about the farm bill that was then being whipped into final form. I asked him to write down the high points of his argument and his proposals and handed him my notebook for that purpose. His notes, which I have preserved, indicate his conviction that to increase the cost of farm products *without a parallel stimulation of industrial activity* would be fatal: the farm program, possibly coupled with inflation, would increase costs so fast that a crushing burden would fall upon urban populations.

And then, as the two of us went on talking, we agreed (1) that, to relieve the situation, there must be some sort of stimulation to industrial reemployment and (2) that this emergency action would be a way to introduce the beginnings of that business-government cooperation contemplated in F. D. R.'s long-range plans.

With this conversation in mind I went back to my office and got out of my files the innumerable plans for industrial rehabilitation that had come to me during the preceding year.

There were literally dozens of these plans—outstanding among them being those of Gerard Swope, John R. Oishei, Henry I. Harriman (President of the Chamber of Commerce, who had talked at length to F. D. R. on this subject on many occasions during 1932), M. C. Rorty, Bob La Follette, Fred I. Kent, H. S. Rivitz, and Henry S. Dennison. Some of them proposed that the Federal Trade Commission be empowered to clarify and relax the antitrust laws by approving trade-association agreements on competitive practices. Some proposed an enormous public drive to stimulate increased production and consumption and, at the same time, raise the standards under which industry operated. Some proposed large expenditures on public works and the subsidizing of plant improvement and enlargement. Some proposed government loans to industry to tide it over the gap between the increased costs of employment and the pickup of purchasing power that would ultimately result. And there was every possible combination and permutation of these ideas.

This mass of stuff I turned over to Jim Warburg, who was working with me on the Economic Conference preparations. I asked Jim to go through it, get in touch with the authors of some of the more important plans, see what sense he could make out of all the talk, and report back.

Warburg fell to—interviewing, among others, Professor Moulton of the Brookings Institution, Fred Kent, and Adolph C. Miller of the Federal Reserve Board. He presented me, about four weeks later, with a memorandum advocating that the government guarantee industry against losses for a stipulated period in return for an agreement that it share in any profits of industry. He suggested further that, instead of concentrating on consumers' goods, the government make every effort to stimulate the movement of producers' goods. He reported that Fred Kent, Walter Stewart, Lew Douglas, and Adolph Miller agreed with him. His final suggestion was that the President assemble a committee, including the above-named people, and lock them in a room until they could agree upon a uniform program. And appended to this document was a draft message, for the President's possible use, which argued for the rehabilitation of industry and for specific government action toward the "regimentation" (Warburg's word) of industry.

I was not, frankly, very greatly taken by this conscientious memorandum and I laid it aside with the feeling that, regardless of Hugh's talk and mine, thinking in business and government circles on the subject had not yet crystallized sufficiently to justify any further moves at the time. This conclusion, and the reasons therefore, I described to F. D. R. that same day, April 4th. We agreed that nothing should be done as yet.

This decision went out the window on April 6th, when I was in New York. That day the Senate suddenly passed the Black Thirty-hour Week bill—an utterly impractical attempt to insure work-spreading by legislating a shorter work week. Realizing the paralyzing effect on industry such an inflexible law would have, believing that it was born of the old labor tactics of driving for concessions when the "enemy" was weakest, and fearing that the Black bill would carry in the House, the President let his hand be forced. He immediately appointed a Cabinet committee, headed by Secretary Perkins, to work out a substitute for the Black bill.

This substitute—with which I had nothing whatever to do—provided for a thirty-hour week for most industries, with a forty-hour week as a maximum. The Secretary of Labor, on a finding by himself or herself that fair wages were not being paid, might appoint fair-wage boards for each industry, which boards were to submit recommendations as to minimum wages for the industry concerned, adjusting their recommendations to particular localities where necessary. The Secretary of Labor could then put these recommendations into effect through a "directory order." The Secretary of Labor was also to be given the power to relax antitrust laws and authorize the making of trade agreements of various types.

The Perkins substitute proved almost as great a shock to employers as the Black bill itself. Miss Perkins and F. D. R. were aghast at the commotion it caused. Roosevelt was sufficiently impressed to recall our earlier conversations on Warburg's exploratory work and to suggest that I come back into the picture again. On Tuesday, April 11th, he directed me to get in touch—not through Warburg, but directly—with the various groups in Washington which we knew were working on business-government cooperation plans. Specifically, he mentioned the Brookings Institution and the Chamber of Commerce.

I did so at once. The informal conversations with people at both these places that followed in the next two days—and the news of them that leaked out—undoubtedly gave Arthur Krock the idea that the situation was further along than it really was. At any rate, he wrote a rather sensational account, which appeared in the *New York Times* on April 14th, to the effect that some form of industrial regulation was imminent. I quote that account because, while it did not give an accurate picture of what I was doing and represented me as the initiator of the plan in the President's cosmos rather than his investigator, it did describe the way our thoughts were running.

> A plan to mobilize private industry under the government [wrote Mr. Krock] for expansion in the production of articles and materials in normal demand, this expansion to be coeval with the administration's public works activities, is being developed by the President's closest advisers, and they hope to persuade him to attempt it. . . . Among the important administration advisers who are giving thought to the plan is Assistant Secretary of State Raymond Moley, who is represented as being "sold" on the general idea. If this is true, then its adoption is but one step away, since there is no adviser in whom the President reposes more confidence. With others in the administration who have been trying to evolve a coordinated program, Mr. Moley has not been content with what is known here as "holding the line." That reference is to emergency legislation, temporary measures to avert an economic debacle. The real objective of the administration is to restore normal business conditions, with people at work and domestic and foreign trade fluid once again.

In the course of the two weeks that followed April 11th I spent as many hours as I could—what with my "normal" run of work, the Thomas amendment affair, and the arrival of Prime Minister MacDonald and his delegation to begin the talks for which the preparations on this side had been entrusted to me—on the business-government cooperation plans. But by the 25th it was obvious that I couldn't get on top of this job, too. Or, at least, I couldn't get on top of it fast enough to stave off the menace of the Black or Perkins bills and the equal menace of a rapid inflationary price rise unaccompanied by any attempt to raise purchasing power in the wage- and salary-earning classes. It was that day that I walked straight into Hugh Johnson in the lobby of the Carlton Hotel. I fell into his arms and told him the whole sad story of my failure to deliver.

"Will you, in heaven's name," I said, "come over to my office and take all the material I've got and do this job for F. D. R.? Nobody can do it better than you. You're familiar with the only comparable thing that's ever been done—the work of the War Industries Board."

Hugh said he would.

We went to my office. I routed someone out of a desk, gave it to Hugh, and turned over Bobby Straus to him. Hugh took off his coat and necktie, unbuttoned the collar of his shirt, and sat down. That was the beginning of the N.R.A. From that day on, except for trips incidental to the job he was doing for the government, he didn't leave Washington for over a year. "Indeed," he says, "I never went back to New York from that day to the end of my service except to get my clothes and rarely even so much as saw my own family."[15]

After Hugh had been working feverishly for a few days, he ran into the kind of snag which I, by then, had half come to expect, but which stunned him. It seems that Roosevelt had authorized a goodly number of other people—John Dickinson (Assistant Secretary of Commerce), Senator Wagner, Secretary Perkins, Donald Richberg, Rex Tugwell, and others—to do the same job he had delegated to me and I, in turn, had delegated to Hugh. In fact, by the time Hugh had produced a rough draft bill John Dickinson had one ready too. So I suppose there would have been an N.R.A. of some kind even if Hugh and I had been sitting on the South Pole through April and May.

That's where I began to wish I were, anyhow, as I listened to Hugh and John Dickinson wrangle over the relative merits of their bills. But wishes weren't airplanes, and so one of the usual compromise ses-

[15] *The Blue Eagle from Egg to Earth.* Doubleday, Doran & Company, Inc.; New York, 1935; p. 193.

sions was staged at the White House. It was at that meeting that F. D. R. ordered all parties to get together, shut themselves up in the room, iron out their differences, and come back to him with a bill.

Out of the rough and tumble of the next few days there emerged a bill—the National Industrial Recovery bill. But with this process I had nothing to do. Except for work on the N.R.A. message, my connection with the N.R.A. ended at the White House conference.

Yet it's historically important to note a conversation between F. D. R. and myself that preceded not only the N.R.A. message of May 17th but the second fireside chat ten days earlier. In that radio talk the President used the following words: "It is wholly wrong to call the measures we have taken government control of farming or government control of industry or government control of transportation. It is rather a partnership between government and farming and a partnership between government and industry and a partnership between government and transportation, not partnership in profits, because the profits would still go to the citizens, but rather a partnership in planning and a partnership to see that the plans are carried out."

While we were working on this passage, I made a point of doing the thing I had always done with F. D. R., the thing I was to beg Tom Corcoran to do when I arranged his entree to the White House: I told Roosevelt exactly where I stood, I then reviewed all the issues involved as objectively as possible, and I asked him whether he was clear in his own mind as to the precise nature of the decision he was making. This conversation is particularly vivid in my mind because—after listening to an exposition that ranged from a description of T. R.'s "partnership" ideas in 1912, and Wilson's arguments against them, to a solemn "You realize, then, that you're taking an enormous step away from the philosophy of equalitarianism and laissez-faire?"—F. D. R. looked graver than he had been at any moment since the night before his inauguration. And then, when he had been silent a few minutes, he said, "If that philosophy hadn't proved to be bankrupt, Herbert Hoover would be sitting here right now. I never felt surer of anything in my life than I do of the soundness of this passage."

It was a statement I was to recall many times as I watched his administration lurch between the philosophy of controlling bigness and the philosophy of destroying bigness, between the belief in a partnership between government and industry and the belief in trust busting.

However, I had no way of knowing in May, 1933, that Roosevelt had not the slightest comprehension of the difference between the two sets of beliefs. He said that he did, and he acted as if he did. And we had, after all, been talking of that very difference since April, 1932.

The National Industrial Recovery Act—by now a thorough hodgepodge of provisions designed to give the country temporary economic stimulation and provisions designed to lay the groundwork for permanent business-government partnership and planning, of provisions calculated to satisfy the forces behind the Black bill and provisions calculated to achieve workable wage-hour agreements—was passed on June 13th. I blame myself for not seeing that this intertwining and jumbling of emergency and long-time policies was unsound and for not protesting it. It probably would have made no difference at all if I had. It might have been as futile as my argument that stock-exchange regulation should have priority over, or at least accompany, securities legislation. But I should like to have been wise enough to have done it.

There was only one blunder I had the perspicacity to spot—the separation of the administration of the public-works features of the bill and its partnership-business mobilization provisions. When the President proposed to cut his baby in two, Hugh Johnson recognized no Solomonlike qualities in the sovereign and cried out that to make this separation would be fatal to the purposes of the whole Act. He frankly told the President in a conference at which Frances Perkins and others were present that he would not be responsible for a truncated section of the Act. Frances Perkins dissuaded him from going home. But he took the job under protest.

I added mine to his in conversation with Roosevelt, saying again and again that the success of the Act, as drawn, presupposed perfect coordination in the administration of its public-works and industrial-recovery provisions. The President saw no reason why there couldn't be such coordination by Hugh Johnson and Harold Ickes.

What happened, of course, was that Johnson moved ahead altogether too fast and Ickes moved at a snail's pace. This was precisely the opposite of what should have happened. Public works, if they were going to do any good, should have got under way with incredible speed—even at the risk of inefficiency and perhaps occasional dishonesty. The making of codes should have proceeded slowly. (No one is more willing to admit that fact than Hugh himself.) The result was that almost all of American industry, large and small, was "codified" inside of a year, while Ickes was so cautious that an absurdly small amount of money was spent on public works during that first critical year, thus completely destroying any possibility of benefit from spending in the critical months when it might have helped.

But to have foreseen this is no excuse for being blind to even more patent omens in those days of universal gyromancy, those days when men foretold the future by watching others grow dizzy and fall.

8

There were, in the first 104 days of Roosevelt's administration, ten speeches made, fifteen messages sent to Congress, and fifteen pieces of major legislation sponsored by him—a record of sheer effort, if not achievement, that has no parallel in the history of American Presidents. Official Washington was in the grip of a war psychology as surely as it had been in 1917. None of us close to F. D. R. lived normal lives. Confusion, haste, the dread of making mistakes, the consciousness of responsibility for the economic well-being of millions of people made mortal inroads on the health of some of us, like Will Woodin and Joe Robinson, and left the rest of us ready to snap at our own images in the mirror.

Only Roosevelt preserved the air of a man who'd found a happy way of life. From March 4th, when he had reviewed his three-and-a-half-hour inaugural parade with every evidence of real enjoyment while Woodin wrestled with the question of how to open the banks, until June 16th, when Congress adjourned, I saw him lose his poise, self-confidence, and good humor but once. That was when Cutting refused to compromise in the fight on veterans' cuts. But for the rest, he was the ebullient, easy, calm man pictured in the Sunday rotogravure sections.

This phenomenon, which had seemed remarkable enough during the campaign and banking crisis, now began to take on the appearance of the miraculous. I had, fleetingly, the illusion that Roosevelt had no nerves at all.

He'd slip from one thing to another with no more self-consciousness than Penrod would turn from chasing carpenters to playing George B. Jashber. What began as a social encounter—say a swim in the White House pool, complete with splashings and duckings—would, with bewildering suddenness, be interrupted by a series of questions on the progress of the railroad legislation. What began as a serious evening's discussion on the guarantee of bank deposits (which F. D. R. distrusted), and whether or not the administration should get behind the Glass bank bill in view of the fact that Glass had accepted the guarantee of deposits to get support for the rest of the bill, would, long before a decision had been reached, become a leisurely night at home: F. D. R. would be working on his stamp collection and start telling anecdotes of his Wilson days; Mrs. Roosevelt would wander in and out to call his attention to passages in a book that she was reading; the sweet-faced Missy Le Hand and Grace Tully would appear with photographs for him to sign; Louis would stick his head in and ask wryly if he'd be breaking into this "important conference" if he told us the story of what he had said to Harold Ickes that morning.

If these quick transitions, these smooth changes of pace did not make for a maximum of efficiency in the short pull, they were certainly a clue to Roosevelt's staying power.

There were other explanations, of course. He had the successful executive's ability to keep his mind clear of "details" once he had decided on a "principle of action" together with a perfect faith that, somehow, someone would always be around to take care of "details" satisfactorily. ("Details" included such questions as whether the C.C.C. should recruit 250,000 or half a million men, whether $480,000,000 or $385,000,000 was cut from the budget, etc.) He had the faculty of emerging from three hours of fifteen-minute interviews exhilarated, where another man would be done in. And that wasn't because he followed Coolidge's prescription for disposing of visitors—"Don't talk back to 'em." F. D. R. enjoyed himself for just the opposite reason. His visitors didn't talk back to him. They couldn't. It was he who called the conversational turns, he who would discourse at length on this or that, he who would catch and hold and visibly delight the caller.

In short, he was like the fairy-story prince who didn't know how to shudder. Not even the realization that he was playing ninepins with the skulls and thighbones of economic orthodoxy seemed to worry him.

It may be argued that, with Congress jumping through the hoops, he had no reason for concern. But that isn't an accurate picture of his situation or theirs. The emergency had made recognition of his leadership and temporary acquiescence in it by Congress inevitable. History shows that in times of national crisis the power of the Executive has always waxed. Yet there was no evidence then of any disposition on F. D. R.'s part to look upon the shift of power as permanent—either as regarded discretionary control over portions of the economic system or as regarded Congress.

He took his defeats at the hands of Congress good-naturedly—except for his fury at Cutting. When Congress revolted against the overly drastic cuts in payments to veterans, he showed a willingness to compromise. When the Senate Foreign Relations Committee clipped the wings of his arms-embargo resolution, he yielded. When congressional leaders told him point-blank that no matter what he and Secretary Hull had agreed upon Congress would refuse to give the administration authority to reduce tariffs, he let the matter drop. There was a vastly greater amount of give-and-take in his attitude toward the "Hundred Days' " Congress than the country realized.

But even supposing his relationship with Congress never cost him a twinge that spring, the fact remains that he might have been excused a couple of sleepless nights as he saw his policies embodied into law.

He had abandoned the gold standard, accepted immense powers to control the nation's monetary system, and begun to move in the direction of negotiating with foreign nations for the establishment of an international standard more satisfactory than the traditional one.[16]

Through the Banking Act, investment banking was divorced from deposit banking and a deposit-insurance plan set up. But more significant still, a couple of long steps toward the unification of the state and national banking systems were authorized, and the Federal Reserve Board's activities were headed toward the exercise of credit control comparable to the monetary control F. D. R. had acquired. It required no neurotic temperament to see that these unprecedented monetary and credit controls could be utilized so unwisely as to throw the economic system completely out of kilter for the same human reasons that they might be utilized so skillfully as to help stabilize it.

Through the revision of the powers of the R.F.C., the establishment of the Farm Credit Administration and the Federal Home Owners Loan Act, the government of the United States was being made the greatest investment and mortgage banker in the world.

Through the Tennessee Valley Act, F. D. R. was not only carrying on a vast experiment in regional planning and conservation but fostering public competition with private utilities.

Through the Railroad Coordination Act, he was moving toward the establishment of a more unified transportation system.

[16] These preliminary moves toward international monetary cooperation will be described briefly in Chapter VII.

Through his program for relief, he was giving sanction to the theory that the federal government must assure all its citizens a minimum livelihood.

Through the Securities Act, he was committing the government not only to restrict irresponsible securities promotion but to exert the beginnings of control over the capital markets.

Through the A.A.A., he was to conduct an enormous "experiment" in controlling agricultural surpluses. The objective was to achieve economic balance between industrial and agricultural producers by controlling production and by taxing processors (or consumers). But underlying this whole admittedly risky excursion into new politico-economic fields was the revolutionary assumption of public responsibility for the economic well-being of the thirty million farmers and farm dependents of the nation.

And finally, through the N.R.A., he was recognizing the socially and economically wasteful effects of intense competition in labor and industry; he was abandoning the theory that the atomistic competitive solution of Wilson and Brandeis had worked or was workable; he was experimenting with government control over concentrated economic power in the interests of the wage earner, the salary earner, the consumer, and the employer.

The hazards and responsibilities this combination involved might well have given the most intrepid social explorer some qualms. But I was never conscious of a moment's doubt in Roosevelt's mind that he could wisely and safely administer discretionary powers too staggering even to be fully comprehended by the electorate at large. His courage was absolute.

And I? I was pretty much like the Mike in my favorite Pat and Mike story.

Pat, it seems, came to the hospital to visit a friend who had had a bad fall the night before. He found the injured man so swathed in bandages that he couldn't speak. But there was a mutual friend, Mike, sitting by the bedside, and Pat asked Mike to tell him what had happened. "Well, Pat," said Mike, " a few of us were havin' a little parrty last noight, y'undershtand, an' Tim here had a mite too much to dhrink. All of a sudden, what does he do but h'ist himself up on the window ledge an' proclaim that he can fly to annuther window ledge across the shtreet. An' thin he took off."

"Well f'r the luvva Gawd," exclaimed Pat, "why didn't you shtop him?"

"Shtop him?" Mike shouted. "Why, you damn' fool! I thought he *could*!"

Only about my own lot did I continue to maintain a healthy skepticism. At any rate, I was realistic enough to say to Bernie Baruch early in June—when he urged me not to go to London with the words, "Don't leave your nice warm bed. Somebody'll be in it when you get back"—" 'Bed,' Bernie? 'Bed'? You've got your figure of speech all cockeyed. This isn't a bed! This is a hot, sweaty, slippery horse I'm riding bareback. My grandfather used to be a bareback rider in a little circus in France until he was thrown. And I don't expect to fare any better than he."

CHAPTER VII

"FOR KINGS CANNOT ERR"

LET not thy left hand know what thy right hand doeth," enjoined the Savior. Mr. Roosevelt said "amen" a couple of times that spring and, for a while, it looked as though the left hand of his domestic policy and the right hand of his foreign policy were somehow managing to produce some rather passable harmony. But by May each had begun to go off on little contrapuntal excursions of its own. And the shrieking dissonance that ensued was the theme song of the World Economic Conference in London.

What happened in May, of course, had been foreshadowed by the struggle over foreign policy during the interregnum. It had been made inevitable by the appointment of Cordell Hull. For Mr. Hull, who had never made any secret of his burning faith that the salvation of the world depended upon the revival of international laissez-faire capitalism, naturally looked upon his appointment as Roosevelt's endorsement of that faith. So did all its other adherents. And yet, with every day that passed, it became clearer that Roosevelt's domestic program was moving away from laissez-faire, that it presupposed a considerable insulation of our national economy from the rest of the world. So long as the President who'd had Hull sworn in as Secretary of State five hours after he'd stood on the rostrum in front of the Capitol and solemnly announced to the American people, "Our international trade relations, though vastly important, are, in point of time and necessity, secondary to the establishment of a sound national economy," refused to see anything incongruous in these circumstances, just so long were confusion and discord unavoidable—just so long would Norman Davis be negotiating tariff truces abroad, for instance, while Henry Wallace, at home, was putting through a rise in the tariff on cotton products.[1]

[1] This actually happened early in May. Lindley summarizes it pithily thus: "When the organizing committee for the conference met in London in early May, Norman

But, all things considered, we managed remarkably well to achieve the semblance of pulling together through March and April.

We found on hand, when Roosevelt went into office on March 4th, a memorandum from the British asking when the negotiations suggested by Roosevelt in January were to begin and how they were to be conducted. As I've already noted, finding Norman Davis hidden away in a corner of the State Department composing a reply which blurred out the distinction between debt negotiations and economic negotiations we'd struggled so fiercely to establish was hardly reassuring.[2]

But that could be handled with reasonable tact. Our preoccupation with the banking crisis was reason enough for putting off a reply to the British, and by the time we got around to preparing one we could and did act as though we'd just forgotten about the Davis draft.

Possibly Davis and Hull were chagrined by the tone of the reply that was finally sent out. (It repeated that discussion of the debt owed us by the British must be completely separate from discussion of tariffs, quotas, embargoes, and currencies and it indicated that the United States did not feel there was any tearing hurry about getting down to business by suggesting that, before the British sent over special representatives, the British officials here ought to talk over the whole thing in a preliminary way with the State Department.) But they were wise enough to make no issue of the question then. The honors were about even, in any case. The Davis draft hadn't got past me, and the invitation that went forward to the British was somewhat on the tepid side. But Davis had the satisfaction of knowing that the economic talks he and Stimson had prevailed upon F. D. R. to propose were about to come off, and that in itself was an achievement of no small proportions.

I, for one, could see no great utility in pre-preliminary talks with Sir Ronald Lindsay and T. K. Bewley, his financial counselor, once

---

H. Davis proposed a tariff truce on behalf of the United States. He finally got it adopted, but the exceptions and interpretations made by the eight participants were numerous and vitiating. The British, who had just cornered Argentina's exchange in a discriminatory trade agreement, coolly went ahead with the formation of their protected trade system. Shortly afterward Mr. Roosevelt himself faced the question of the real meaning of the truce. For a day or two he withheld approval of preparations for the application of a cotton processing tax because it meant a compensatory rise in the tariff on cotton products. Then he changed his mind and gave the word to go ahead." (*The Roosevelt Revolution; op. cit.;* p. 186.)

[2] See page 163.

they got under way. Toward the tail end of March we began meeting frequently in the State Department—Sir Ronald and Bewley, Secretary Hull, Herbert Feis (the Economic Adviser in the State Department), Bill Bullitt, Jimmy Warburg (whom I'd brought in with F. D. R.'s consent in February to work as a volunteer on the Conference preparations), and a few assorted members of the State Department staff. Nothing of any practical value was discussed at these meetings, which continued intermittently through the first two weeks in April. There were endless fine generalities about tariff barriers—generalities which were meaningless in the light of our own A.A.A. program and the current British adherence to tariff protectionism. But the Secretary was very happy. He looked forward to the Economic Conference as the nation's and the world's supreme opportunity, and the enthusiasm that he brought to even these pre-preliminary talks was genuinely moving.

He had, in the course of these weeks, put his campaign idea of a general ten per cent tariff reduction to Roosevelt again, and Roosevelt had said that if some sort of tariff legislation could be agreed upon within the State Department and by the Secretaries of Agriculture, Commerce, and Labor he would send it along to Congress. That, the Secretary felt, was very hopeful. He seemed to have no doubt that we were on the road to world tariff reduction.

It wasn't for me, at that stage of the game, to suggest that getting the College of Cardinals to endorse the Communist Manifesto would be a cinch compared with meeting the conditions the President had quietly laid down. Nor was it for me to say that it seemed to Louis Howe and me that F. D. R.'s strategy was to let Hull's low-tariff talk screen the movement of the rest of the administration in the other direction. It occurred to me that it might, after all, be *my* leg that F. D. R. was pulling, and not Hull's. (It proved, eventually, to be the legs of us both.) But it was too early to figure out just what was up, and the only honest thing to do was to continue the serious preparations Feis, Warburg, Bullitt, and I were making.[3] I might write in my notebook that I had my doubts that the Conference could accomplish much with every major power headed in the direction of nationalism and self-containment, and still conscientiously work over modest

[3] These preparations had begun in February, in accordance with F. D. R.'s order (see page 102). They had, naturally, been suspended during the critical first two weeks of the administration. But they were resumed around March 20th, when Feis was assigned to work with Warburg and Bullitt.

proposals on which there was some possibility of international agreement.

So, as I say, things seemed to hang together, after a fashion, well into April. There were the meetings with Lindsay, in which we all got to know each other well. And there were the meetings of an interdepartmental committee which was laboring over tariff legislation. And there were the meetings of Feis, Warburg, Bullitt, and myself to formulate an American program for discussion.

Meanwhile there were other negotiations afoot. When Roosevelt had agreed, in January, to receive a representative to discuss the British debts, the newspapers surmised that that representative would be Prime Minister MacDonald. I don't know, as a matter of fact, whether F. D. R. had MacDonald in mind then. By early March, though, he was already talking to me of his desire to have MacDonald come over. Word to that effect was informally dropped to Sir Ronald. And on March 22nd, when Davis sailed for Geneva and the Disarmament Conference, he had instructions to stop off in London to see whether MacDonald could be persuaded to make the trip.

Now MacDonald, as everyone knew, was merely a front for as hard-boiled a Conservative Government as England had had for many a year. F. D. R. admitted that fact. But he did not agree with my contention that it might be futile to deal with MacDonald. I felt that MacDonald's Government might well refuse to support him in any debt agreement he might reach with us. F. D. R. replied that the Conservatives were "special-privilege people" and we could get nowhere with them unless we dealt with them through MacDonald, who was "a man of liberal ideas" and who, since he was Prime Minister, could not very well be repudiated.

It developed that the British Cabinet was generally of the same mind as Mr. Roosevelt on the subject of MacDonald as a negotiator for them. Only, where Roosevelt hoped, they feared.

Davis was informed that the Cabinet opposed MacDonald's possible visit to the United States almost to a man. There was some half-hearted talk about the embarrassment that might come to the Government if MacDonald made the trip without advance assurance from us that the June 15th debt payment could be postponed. But I suspect that this argument was a blind. There was every evidence, if one read between the lines of Davis' cables, that Baldwin and Chamberlain felt about MacDonald's possible trip much as the Vicar of Wakefield would have felt about sending his son to market a second time.

At any rate, the debt argument collapsed when, prodded by reminders from Washington that the debts were not to be sold for any fancy favors on England's part, Davis made it clear to MacDonald, Baldwin, Chamberlain, Simon, and Runciman that there was no possibility of an advance commitment on debts. And still, though most of the British Cabinet readily admitted that it was out of the question for MacDonald to get any debt assurances from F. D. R., the intra-Cabinet opposition to the MacDonald trip went on.

After more than a week of doubt and reluctance the Cabinet yielded. MacDonald, who believed as sincerely as Hull in the international route to recovery and who was, in fact, the father of the Economic Conference idea, was authorized to come to the United States and talk over the debts with F. D. R. This left Baldwin and Chamberlain at home where they could go on building up their protected trade system. Then, to make the situation unmistakably clear, came the announcement that Sir Frederick Leith-Ross, Chief Economic Adviser to His Majesty's Government, and Sir Robert Vansittart, Permanent Under-Secretary of State for Foreign Affairs—two of the most astute men in the British service—were to accompany MacDonald as the representatives who would separately discuss economic questions with us. In short, the idealistic MacDonald was permitted to visit Roosevelt, but in the care of two figurative bodyguards.

This was a "pretty state of things"—made to order for the gentle satire of Sir William Gilbert. But it began to shift to the realm of broad comedy when the process was repeated, move for move, by the French.

F. D. R. was eager to have Herriot represent the French for the same reason that he wanted MacDonald to represent the English. M. Herriot was known to favor the payment of the French debt. Besides, he was an old friend of Mr. Roosevelt. What did it matter that he wasn't at the time a member of the French Government? What did it matter that he wasn't representative of French opinion on the subject of debts? All the better to bargain with, reasoned F. D. R.

The French Ambassador, to whom all but the Q.E.D. of this interesting proposition was disclosed, kept his witty tongue firmly planted in his cheek while he regained his composure. Then he said: But certainly! If it pleased his Excellency, the French Government could assuredly sent M. Herriot with the expressions of its esteem the most distinguished.

And so it did. But when M. Herriot was seen to set foot on American soil it was remarked that he was flanked by Charles Rist, Economic Adviser to the French Government and former Deputy Governor of the Bank of France, by Jean J. Bizot, Adviser to the French Treasury, by Robert Coulondre of the French Foreign Office, and by Paul Elbel of the Ministry of Commerce—all hard-headed realists of the first water.

On April 21st, then, when the parade of diplomats from fifty-three foreign nations began, a fundamental cleavage was already apparent not only in the American but in the English and French ranks. The Big Three, without whose general agreement the London Conference could get nowhere, were each represented by people of two minds. And to pile Ossa on the Pelion of discord, F. D. R. had cut loose from gold and agreed to accept inflationary powers while MacDonald and Herriot were on the water, thus throwing MacDonald into an agony of apprehension about the British export trade and the French into a panic about their own ability to stay on gold. Both the British and the French were inclined to pooh-pooh the idea that we'd been forced off gold by domestic conditions and to insist that we'd abandoned gold deliberately to get into a better bargaining position on international monetary questions.

Only boundless optimism could envisage agreement on "the solution of the world's ills" (to quote M. Herriot) coming out of this farrago of purposes, philosophies, interests, and concerns. And yet, perhaps, if one didn't hope for too much, these preliminary talks might, after all, clear the way for two or three feasible accords.

2

The first fact that emerged, once the exploratory conferences had begun, was that it had been a mistake to invite men of such political stature as MacDonald and Herriot. Each was supposedly his nation's "representative" on debts—as distinguished from the "representatives" (plural) who were to discuss the economic problems on the agenda of the London Conference. But each was given to large propositions and we-must-work-shoulder-to-shoulder-to-save-the-world talk. So they began at once, in conversation with F. D. R., to discuss the rise of Hitler, the peace of Europe, the political situation of the French, the progress of the Disarmament Conference, the prospect of world cooperation to achieve economic recovery, and a good many other matters that had little to do with the debts owed us.

Mr. Roosevelt, who was nothing if not a gracious and courteous host, was hardly in a position to call a halt to these digressions. In any case, he himself was intrigued by this opportunity to drink dizzying draughts of conversational *Weltpolitik*. And even if these things hadn't been true, it would have been useless for him to insist on down-to-earth debt negotiations because both MacDonald and Herriot proved to be magnificently vague about all aspects of the debt issue. (MacDonald was actually confused about how much the British debt was and cheerfully mixed up millions and billions of pounds and dollars when he talked about it.)

F. D. R. went into these meetings (first with MacDonald and then with Herriot) equipped with a formula for the settlement of the debt question. This formula—which has never, so far as I know, been made public—was tentative. But it did provide an intelligent basis for discussion.[4]

Affectionately known among those of us who had worked on it as "The Bunny," it contemplated (1) cancellation of all interest charges on the debts owed us; (2) redetermination of the present (then) value of the principal owed by each nation with some allowances; (3) reaffirmation by the debtor of this obligation to us and the lodging of a note for the newly determined amount with the Bank of International Settlements—the note to be collaterated by bullion reserves amounting to perhaps thirty per cent of the amount owed and by a sinking-fund agreement covering the remainder; (4) agreement by the B.I.S. with the United States to apply all proceeds of the sinking-fund payments to the purchase of United States government obligations in the market, and all interest received from such United States obligations to the purchase of additional United States securities; (5) delivery by the B.I.S. to the United States of its certificate for the face amount of the note deposited by the debtor nation; (6) delivery by the B.I.S. to the United States, at the end of the plan, of seventy per cent of the face value of the certificate in bonds of the United States government at par and thirty per cent in bullion; (7) or alternatively, should commercialization become possible, anticipation of the operation of the plan by the debtor government by delivery to the United States, for cancellation, of such bonds as had been accumulated by the sinking fund, plus cash sufficient to make the sum of the face

[4] The formula was chiefly the work of James Warburg, but it was shaped by discussions with the President, Secretary Hull, Lew Douglas, myself, and others.

value of the bonds delivered and the cash proceeds of commercialization equal the face amount of the note of the debtor government.

If the British and French had any intention of paying—which I strongly doubted—this ingenious plan, summarized here only roughly, was a reasonable proposition to haggle over.

But when it became obvious that no businesslike negotiations on this basis or any other could conceivably take place between F. D. R. and MacDonald or F. D. R. and Herriot, the matter was ostensibly dropped with public joint statements (one by F. D. R. and MacDonald and the other by F. D. R. and Herriot) that the debts had been discussed in a general way, that there had been "preliminary explorations of many different routes"—although there was no plan or settlement—and that after the Argonauts had gone home, the conversations might well continue in Washington, London, or Paris.

At this moment of almost farcical impasse F. D. R. directed Lew Douglas and me to ask Leith-Ross to stay on in Washington, after MacDonald left, and to discuss the British debt with him. No one on the American side—including Secretary Hull—was to know anything about these discussions except F. D. R. himself. As for the French, they could wait for the moment. Lew and I followed instructions—with what results will be seen shortly.

Meanwhile, concurrent with the conferences that F. D. R. was holding in the White House, were the conferences of the various foreign experts and Hull, Bullitt, Feis, Warburg, and myself on tariffs, currencies, and the like in the State Department. The American proposals made at these meetings were prepared by Warburg, Bullitt, Feis, and myself, with the approval of F. D. R. They stemmed largely from Roosevelt's desire to see international action to raise the world price level.

To that end, we proposed, first, the devising of an improved international gold standard. (This immediately produced a friendly atmosphere by allaying the suspicions of the English and French that we were all set for a currency war.) It seemed to us that the gold standard could be improved by agreement upon a uniform bullion cover for all countries at a somewhat lower ratio than the average of existing ratios. Perhaps a twenty-five per cent gold coverage might be satisfactory, and perhaps there might be an agreement for the optional inclusion of a small proportion of silver in the Central Bank reserves. It was suggested, too, that the importance of silver might be further recognized by an agreement not to debase silver coinages, to stabilize the price of silver between fifty and seventy-five cents an ounce, and to prevent the dumping of large stocks of it.

This was our plan for the restoration of a revised international gold standard. It was offered with the proviso that each nation must be free to decide when and with what gold coverage it would adhere to the new standard.

Other proposals directed toward the achievement of both "stable monetary conditions" and "an increase in the general level of prices" included possible agreement to remove exchange restrictions, to synchronize national public-works programs, and to eliminate extreme tariff barriers.

To the real satisfaction of those of us who participated in these practical discussions, we approached what seemed to be a promising meeting of minds on some essentials. We were certainly not agreeing on any plans to change the face of the world, but we were achieving a degree of understanding on a few troublesome questions.

It looked as though a streamlined international gold standard were in prospect. It looked as though cooperative price-raising measures might be devised. It looked as though there might be a *de facto* stabilization of the dollar when it had sunk to its "natural" level in relation to other world currencies—a point below which it would probably not sink unless it was forced down by actual currency inflation through the exercise of the still unused powers conferred on F. D. R. by the Thomas amendment.[5]

To be sure, our own group, as well as the foreign representatives, were so sharply divided on the question of what to do about tariffs that, in these talks, nothing more than agreement on a possible tariff truce lasting the duration of the London Conference was achieved.[6] Still, even this was something.

[5] The continued fall of the dollar and the British stabilization operations—which were soon modified—left the French in an exceedingly difficult position. The French, in 1927, had devalued the franc eighty per cent, and the prospect of being forced to devalue further, thus causing millions of small investors a still greater loss in savings, was, for their Government, a terrifying one. The mere knowledge that the United States intended to return "as soon as practicable" to an international monetary standard was reassuring.

[6] Agreement to join in a movement for tariff truce was made at an evening session in which so many expressions of mutual good will had been exchanged that anything seemed possible. The next morning I met MacDonald in a White House corridor just as he was leaving his room for breakfast. He seemed disturbed and said, "I'm not so sure about this tariff truce now. In bringing it about, you people are like a man who, having finished his breakfast, says to his friend who is coming down from his room, 'Let's have a truce on breakfasts.'" I inferred that some of

Those who realized that, in spite of dreams, economic nationalism was the order of the day felt that more wasn't in the cards just then. F. D. R. himself was so delighted with these results that he arranged general meetings of MacDonald and the English experts and Herriot and French experts, respectively, before MacDonald and Herriot took their departures, so that he and they could bestow their blessings on the work that had been done in the State Department talks.[7]

With tariffs and monetary questions at that stage of discussion, there remained the question of when, precisely, the Conference should be held. Remember that the English and French during the interregnum, when they still hoped to make a debt settlement a *quid pro quo* for agreements at the Economic Conference, wished to begin the Conference early in the spring.[8] The consequence of our insistence upon separating the two big issues had been a noticeable cooling on the part of the British and French Governments on the subject of the need for haste in convening the Conference. Realists in both Governments doubtless concluded that we weren't going to play our usual role of fat boy again. That being so, and the agreements that might flow from the Conference being obviously limited by internal factors here and in Europe, they intimated that they had no desire to press us on the time question.

But MacDonald, Herriot, and Hull were of another mind. Their faith in international cooperation grew by what it fed upon. And the modest success of our preliminary talks caused this faith to suffer an acute attack of elephantiasis. Everything was so friendly, so cooperative, so hopeful! Why put off the great meeting of minds that might produce "the solution of the world's ills"?

It was with a sinking heart that I learned on the morning of April 26th that Roosevelt had agreed in conversation with MacDonald and Herriot the night before to fix the opening of the Conference on June 12th. It seemed almost incredible that this was the same Roosevelt who had enjoined Edmund Day on December 18th to try to delay the Conference opening as long as possible beyond April so that the domestic experiments of the New Deal could actually get going before we

---

MacDonald's advisers had been speaking to him during the night or early that morning.

[7] This he could do with a show of logic only because MacDonald and Herriot, the debt representatives, had wandered conversationally all over the field of the London Conference.

[8] See pages 87 and 92.

began formal international economic negotiations. But F. D. R. had nothing on MacDonald and Herriot when it came to captivating enthusiasm. When the two charmers joined forces, the third charmer went down.

So June 12th it was. And it was exactly June 12th because, as F. D. R. pointed out, the Conference ought not to meet earlier, when Congress would still be in session, and because, as MacDonald pointed out, the Conference ought not to meet later, or it would run on into the grouse season and all the British statesmen would walk out on it. What with Congress on the one side and grouse on the other, agreement on June 12th was a triumph of diplomacy.

This accomplished, MacDonald sailed away. No doubt with an eye on the dour Cabinet colleagues awaiting him in London, he said in his speech to the newspapermen that he was returning to his colleagues in the British Cabinet "as free as I was the day I left them." But his air belied this suggestion of prudence. There was in his manner a certain joyousness that comes from gamboling through the twinkling young grasses in the verdant gardens of Utopia.

Herriot, too, when he left three days later, after having presented our Secretary of the Treasury with a copy of his book on Beethoven, had a look of bliss remembered and of bliss to come. "A week ago," he said, "we might very well have wondered whether the World Economic Conference could meet at all and, in the event of its meeting, at what date it would meet. Now we know for certain that it is to begin its work on the twelfth of June. . . . On certain points we have already brought our views much nearer to each other; an excellent way of proceeding, which President Roosevelt has rightly advocated, while he launched new motions concerning the world disarmament and security." Thus, in rather awkward English, was conveyed the idea that the French, who in their panic at America's abandonment of gold were apparently willing to throw overboard the whole idea of an Economic Conference, had got enough comfort out of the conversations in Washington to go ahead enthusiastically. What Herriot looked forward to, of course, was the possibility of early dollar stabilization and of some kind of collective-security agreement.

Prime Minister Bennett of Canada, Guido Jung of Italy, Hjalmar Schacht of Germany, and the representatives of the forty-eight other nations who came and went after the English and French, through late April and May, seemed to find the now rampant optimism of

Washington temporarily contagious.[9] Encouraging joint statements on the progress of the various talks began to come pouring out of the White House. Day after day the headlines featured the discussions with the foreign statesmen. Peace—it was wonderful! Prosperity—it was going to be negotiated at London in June.

All unwittingly, as Lindley has pointed out, Roosevelt was emerging "in the eyes of the public at home and abroad as the chief sponsor of the World Economic Conference and the international approach to recovery."[10] Not only had we maneuvered ourselves into the always vulnerable position of "leadership" in European affairs but we were raising the expectations of the American public to wholly unwarranted heights.

3

The time for a sobering reaction had come—if, indeed, it was to come at all before the assured failure of the London Conference to live up to these extravagant expectations.

I was perhaps in a better spot to see the confluence of foreign and domestic policies than most of the others in the administration. I was very close to the enactment or prospective enactment of a whole series of domestic measures—the monetary program, the A.A.A. and the N.R.A. among them—which pointed unmistakably toward a more self-contained economy. I saw Roosevelt's public reputation grow by leaps and bounds as a rising business curve accompanied these moves. I saw the thrill that increasing praise gave him. In his second fireside speech on May 7th the President so completely placed his faith and confidence in his domestic program that there was no further question in my mind about his basic reactions. I knew, for a certainty, that Secretary Hull did not realize that in any actual conflict between his domestic program and a program of international economics the President would decide in favor of his domestic program. I saw that Hull was so absorbed in those problems on which he'd been working during the spring weeks that the question of correlating his ideas to the domestic program had never seriously occurred to him. I saw that the public had been misled into thinking that the main line of recovery was shifting from the United States to London. And, looking ahead

[9] Most of the smaller nations did not send special representatives, but were represented by their ambassadors or ministers in this country.

[10] *The Roosevelt Revolution; op. cit.;* p. 182.

to June, I could not help but feel that some note of moderation, of warning, was in order.

Advantageously placed or not, I was not alone in these feelings. There were dozens of other men in the administration who shared them. But I was the only one who had decided to leave the administration soon. I could best afford to take in my hands a political life I was about to forego in any case, and speak out honestly.

The President knew my plans. He knew that I had already promised the group that ultimately established *Today* that I would join them as soon as satisfactory preparations for launching a journalistic venture could be made. He knew that, meanwhile, I had signed a contract with a syndicate to write a series of newspaper articles. He knew that my weekly pieces were to begin appearing early in June, that I had to get the first two of them to the syndicate people by May 17th or 18th, and that one of those two articles frankly described the prospects of the Economic Conference as I judged them.

He not only knew of that piece, but he read it in his office on May 16th.

It was a warning against excessive optimism.[11] It described what the Conference had been called to achieve, what preparations had been made for it, and the purpose of the preliminary discussions in Washington. It predicted that the Conference might result in certain remedial agreements with respect to silver and with respect to some other relatively simple monetary questions. As to the removal of trade barriers, it advised a pretty temperate optimism.

> The problems most difficult of solution [it read] will be related to trade, the barriers against trade and the readjustment of these barriers. Tariffs and other restrictive devices are deeply rooted in the policies of the various countries and are closely integrated parts of their economic life. All of the nations, including our own, have been moving toward self-support for a long time. Industrial and agricultural life has developed in that direction with remarkable rapidity of late. Manufacturing has grown in even such remotely industrial countries as China and India. American capital and industry, by the establishment of factories abroad, have themselves gone far toward the acceleration of this tendency. The inexorable laws of cheaper production and reduced costs of transportation help. Thus a combination of forces is arrayed against extensive attacks upon trade barriers. Moderate results must be anticipated. The groundwork can be laid for many bilateral agreements and a more enlightened point of view. But we shall not have a vast new

[11] For the text of this article, see Appendix D.

commerce on the seven seas, even after a successful Economic Conference.

Finally, the article stated, the Conference promised to provide a round table at which nations could exchange ideas as to the best methods of recovery. Much more should not be expected.

When Roosevelt had finished reading the article, he approved it. More important still, he added, "As a matter of fact, this would be a grand speech for Cordell to make at the opening of the Conference."

I looked at him with astonishment, for I'd never known him to employ irony. And then the wonder really grew. He wasn't being ironical. He was in dead earnest—as earnest as he'd been the preceding September when he told me his tariff stand was a compromise. So I perceived he had returned to an intellectual region into which I could not follow.

But that was neither here nor there. The article had his imprimatur. I sent it along to the syndicate.

At about that time I received an invitation to speak over the Columbia Broadcasting network. Feeling as I did about the urgent need for deflating public expectations about the Conference, and knowing that my article wouldn't be published for at least two weeks, I decided to paraphrase the article and speak it over the radio. Except for the fact that the speech included some descriptive material about the agenda of the Conference, the two texts were almost indistinguishable.[12] I didn't burden the President with the speech, which he had substantially approved in the form of the article, beyond telling him that I was going to make it.

The speech was delivered on May 20th. It was to prove, as the weeks rolled by, the most accurate prediction about the Conference of which I know. Bold and perhaps quixotic as it was, there's nothing in my public career about which I have less regret.

But meanwhile I had to face some immediate reactions. The warning was enthusiastically received by many senators and representatives and by a part of the press. The laissez-faire press, of which the *New York Times* and the *Baltimore Sun* were examples, heartily disagreed and deeply regretted the "clash" between Secretary Hull and myself it revealed.

And the Secretary? I met him in the lobby of the Carlton a couple of mornings later. We were both setting out for the day's work—he for the State Department and I for the usual bedside conference with F. D. R.

[12] For the text of this speech, see Appendix E.

When we'd exchanged good mornings, I said (with all sincerity) that I regretted that the newspaper comment on my speech should involve talk of "clashes." We were, after all, two conscientious men both working for the same man. We were dealing not in personalities but in opinions. Hull expressed not the slightest concern over the affair, nor did he indicate in any way that he resented my speaking my mind on the prospects of the Conference with the same frankness that he had touched upon the question.

But there can be no doubt that he was deeply offended. That fact was to emerge later.

Unfortunately, this wasn't the first time our wires crossed. There'd been a shower of sparks only a couple of days before. The incident concerned the debt talks with Leith-Ross.

Lew Douglas and I, as per instructions, had asked Leith-Ross to stay behind. We had spent all of May 1st and most of May 2nd at the British Embassy discussing "The Bunny" with him. Leith-Ross had been enormously interested in the general proposition and had expressed his belief that a final settlement of the debt question might be reached on some such basis. But it was obviously going to be impossible to reach such a settlement in the few weeks that remained before June 15th when the next installment was due. That left the question whether there was to be a payment on June 15th.

Then Leith-Ross, with the air of a man who has the most repulsive and humiliating job of his life to do, announced that economic and political conditions in England made payment in June exceedingly unlikely. Financially it would be a very great hardship on the British to make the payment. (Note that he didn't take the position that it was financially impossible.) Politically it would be dangerous for the Government to ignore the strong public opinion that Britain could not and should not be expected to make full payment. And yet the British did not like the idea of default. The very word was offensive to their moral sensibilities. It ran counter to every precept of that system of financial ethics they had grown great by observing.

Was there not some way they might be tided over this potentially disastrous moment? Might President Roosevelt not persuade Congress to agree to a temporary suspension of the June 15th payment on the ground, say, that nonpayment would interrupt the negotiations for a final settlement, or perhaps on the ground that it would jeopardize the Economic Conference?

Lew and I did not need any consultation with Roosevelt to answer this series of questions. Sir Frederick would do well to put out of his mind, we said, the idea that the President was disposed to take the initiative and inform Great Britain that the United States did not expect her to make a payment on June 15th. And even if Roosevelt were so disposed—which he wasn't—there existed a public opinion here as well as in Great Britain. That public opinion would not permit the President to make such a move. Congress was in no mood to do anything but exact payment.

Well, then, Leith-Ross asked, could not the President secure from Congress general powers to deal with the debt situation that would enable him to handle the British failure to pay on June 15th not as a default but as a suspension?

We thought not, even supposing Roosevelt were moved to make such a request. We believed the British ought to take serious thought before failing to make the June 15th payment.

Then, since there was nothing further to be accomplished by consultation between us until Leith-Ross had explained the situation to his Government and laid "The Bunny" before them, Sir Frederick sailed. He would send us word soon.

Of all this Secretary Hull knew nothing—by F. D. R.'s express orders. That was the situation on May 18th, which happened, by hideous mischance, to be a Thursday, when I was absent. It was that day the "word" Leith-Ross had promised Lew Douglas and me came through from England in the shape of a cable and a personal letter to the President from MacDonald. Sir Ronald Lindsay, who had received these messages for delivery, called my office and asked for me. He was told that I was in New York, teaching. Could I be reached at once? "Yes," was the innocent reply, if it were urgent I could be summoned out of my class to the telephone. Would the Ambassador like that done?

For one fateful moment Sir Ronald hesitated. And then the pleasant, kindly man, who, no doubt, could not conceive of such a situation as existed between Roosevelt and his Secretary of State, rushed ahead. Never mind, he said; he would speak to the Secretary instead.

He did. He told Hull of the receipt of the MacDonald messages. He began to describe the substance of the messages. They concerned the debt situation and the discussions of Sir Frederick Leith-Ross, Budget Director Douglas, and Assistant Secretary of State Moley. The British Government wished to know whether a formal response to the questions raised in these discussions was awaited on this side. Hull cut the talk short. He knew nothing of any such discussions. He suggested that the British Ambassador communicate with the President.

It took Sir Ronald two days to recover from the shock of this conversation.[13] I don't know that Secretary Hull ever did. At any rate, I found him more silent and formal than usual when I returned to the State Department on Friday morning, the 19th. And his humor didn't improve as he perceived what Roosevelt was going to do on the June 15th question.

The substance of the MacDonald letter and message was a repetition of the position taken by Leith-Ross. The British Government did not consider itself in a position to meet the June 15th payment. Yet at all costs (short of payment, presumably) it hoped to avoid an actual default. Default would cause hostility in both countries: the American man on the street would blame the British for defaulting, and the British man on the street would blame the United States for forcing Britain into the position of defaulting. Couldn't a request be made to Congress for general powers to deal with the debt situation pending negotiations for a final settlement? Had President Roosevelt abandoned hope of getting powers to handle the June 15th matter?

The inference was that Roosevelt had once entertained and expressed this hope.

Now stories to the same effect had appeared in several newspapers. But if they were justified, any more than was the inference in the MacDonald communications, I had not known it. When brought face to face with the issue, Roosevelt announced to me that he had done no more than tell MacDonald that no doubt the two of them would hit upon "some way of meeting" the June 15th situation. It was, he added with a shrug of the shoulders, obviously out of the question to get Congress to give him general powers.

So there we were. Hull took the position that if something agreeable to the British could not be worked out on the June 15th matter failure would threaten the Economic Conference itself. I don't believe that he went as far as Billy Phillips, whose views on the subject were as fol-

[13] On the morning of the 20th when I arrived in my office I found the following message:

"Mr. Moley:

"The British Ambassador called this morning and asked me to give you the following message:

'I asked the Secretary of State a certain question. He referred me to the President about it. What shall I do next?'

"The Ambassador said he is at the disposal of the President or the Secretary at any time."

lows: that he had never felt more strongly about anything in his life; that he believed the British position had crystallized and was unalterable; that we must take the position that, if the British would make the concessions we wanted at the Economic Conference, we would make corresponding concessions in regard to the debts; or, if we chose to cling to our position, that we would have to say good-by to the Economic Conference. But Hull did hold that Roosevelt ought to be actively sympathetic and ought to "save" the British and the Conference.

It was with almost ominous aloofness that he watched Roosevelt's reply being drafted. That reply was dispatched on May 22nd. In friendly and amiable terms it conveyed the cheerless news: Mr. Roosevelt was determined not to let any aspect of the debt question get mixed up with the issues before the Conference; Mr. Roosevelt held to his policy of free debt discussion whenever the debtor governments desired; and, specifically, if the British Government didn't feel it was able to pay the entire amount due on June 15th could it not pay a *part* of what it owed at that time? Mr. Roosevelt assured the Prime Minister of his warmest regards. That was all.

The reaction to the almost hysterical optimism of late April and early May was now in full swing. But before a week was out Secretary Hull's faith in international cooperation and his belief in Roosevelt's enthusiasm for international action were to undergo an even more merciless pummeling.

First there was the news, communicated by Roosevelt, that a reciprocal-tariff-treaty bill which the interdepartmental committee had finally produced and on which Hull had set his heart would not be sent to Congress by the President. F. D. R. had been informed by the leaders that it could not be got through. He had decided to accept their judgment. That decision came as a stunning blow to Hull.

Then there was the news of the European and American reaction to an "appeal to the nations" Roosevelt had dispatched on the 16th in the hope of saving the Disarmament Conference from complete breakdown.

There is a story behind that spectacular gesture that calls for a little explaining.

The Disarmament Conference at Geneva was near collapse on May 12th, when Hitler summoned the Reichstag for the 17th to address it on disarmament and German foreign policy generally. In Paris, London, and Geneva the worst was feared. The Hitler speech, if intransigent, would be the Disarmament Conference's *coup de grâce*. It was felt that only a strong statement by the United States could lead Hitler to take a conciliatory position, and thus prevent an irreconcilable breach.

These sentiments, conveyed to Norman Davis by a half dozen anxious European officials, came hurtling over the cables to Roosevelt and Hull. Billy Phillips, Louis Howe, and Bill Bullitt were summoned. (I happened to be out of Washington that week-end.) Together, the five men decided to draft the kind of statement that might do the trick. In the form of a message to the heads of fifty-four governments, it urged the reduction and ultimate elimination of offensive weapons, advocated adherence to the MacDonald disarmament plan then before the Conference, and proposed that all nations enter into "a solemn and definite [one of F. D. R.'s favorite words] pact of non-aggression." This document was shown to me on Monday morning, May 15th. I was asked to go over it and "pretty up" the language. "Put the old organ roll into it" were, as I remember them, the exact words. And I was assured that the message would prove to be a master stroke. It would frighten Hitler. It would hearten the French by suggesting that we shared their desire to maintain the European *status quo*.

Actually, it did nothing of the kind. Hitler's speech wasn't truculent, but it certainly left no doubt of his position. The French were vocal in their disappointment: they had hoped for a message practically guaranteeing that we would maintain the system of "security" they had been erecting in Europe since 1919. The English were frankly cold: they made no bones about their cautious attitude toward a nonaggression pact that might interfere with their "police work" on their own African and Asian frontiers or with the operations of their cruisers protecting British interests in distant waters.

The reception of Norman Davis' "consultation" proposal[14] made six days after the "appeal to the nations," was even more disconcerting to the internationalists in this country. A low roar went up from the isolationists in the Senate. The French were dissatisfied because we had not gone further. The British remained uninterested.

The White House immediately sought cover: it seemed that the Davis "consultation" proposal presupposed speedy agreement on substantial disarmament. It was unnecessary to add that nobody, any more, anticipated speedy agreement on the question.

On May 30th the Disarmament Conference, now hopelessly dead-

[14] See footnote, page 164.

locked after fifteen months of getting nowhere, prepared to recess—a recess that was an adjournment in all but name.

This series of events, illuminating, as it did, the palpable self-interest of the British and French (which their talk of international "cooperation" had never quite concealed) and the vehement opposition to European "entanglements" in the United States, would have crushed a man of less militant faith than Secretary Hull. But there was even more grim news in store for him.

During the visits of the MacDonald and Herriot delegations, it must be repeated, there had been talk of the possibility that the dollar would be temporarily pegged when its value in terms of pounds sterling had fallen as far as it could naturally be expected to go without actual currency inflation by Roosevelt. Roosevelt had by no means actually committed himself to such stabilization, but the general idea was conveyed that stabilization was a good possibility, if not a probability, though the time and level of stabilization were left open.

What justified these broad assurances were the predictions of Will Woodin, Jim Warburg, Lew Douglas, and the Treasury experts that the dollar, if left to itself, would not sink more than eighteen or twenty per cent, which, in relation to sterling at the moment, would mean about a $4.00 pound as compared with the current quotation of around $3.50 and the old par of $4.87.

But by the 20th of May the behavior of the dollar began to cause consternation. Its gyrations suggested that it might well continue to depreciate until the pound was well above $4.00.

The American experts advanced technical reasons to support their opinion that it wouldn't. Speculative activities were responsible for the dollar's untoward behavior, they said.

F. D. R. suddenly took the position (in private, of course) that the dollar might sink to lows that the experts hadn't conceived of. He was in no hurry to stabilize until he was sure he was going to get the best bargain there was to be got. With the dollar falling as it was in the exchange markets, our stock and bond prices were leaping upward and our commodity prices soaring. New purchasing power was being created in this country, he held. This stimulating movement must not be stopped. This was recovery—not a dangerous speculative spree!

And in Paris and London the phenomenon of the dollar's continued tumble and the realization that Mr. Roosevelt would react to it precisely as he was reacting were the occasion for a wringing of hands. The French, whose adherence to gold put them in the worst fix, were the first to pull themselves together. They suggested, informally, that no plan to implement the general policy of restoring stable exchange rates and a higher and more stable level of prices—the general policy which had been agreed upon in the Washington meetings in April—could be achieved until the credit and monetary policies of France, Great Britain, and the United States were made known to one another in fairly exact terms.

The British then picked up the ball. In a cable received on May 26th they expatiated on the impossibility of the Conference's making any progress on monetary agreements unless it was clearly understood, beforehand, just how far the United States intended to let the dollar plummet. Perhaps, to avoid awkwardness at the Conference, it might be best for representatives of England and France and a representative or representatives empowered to speak for the United States government to meet, apart from the Conference, and agree on temporary currency stabilization, at any rate. To this official plea MacDonald added a personal one. He sincerely hoped President Roosevelt would send representatives to this meeting and instruct them definitely as to the rate at which he'd be willing to stabilize the dollar for the time being, at least. That was essential to the success of the Conference.

Roosevelt acquiesced—up to a point. He agreed to send over Oliver M. W. Sprague, former adviser to the Bank of England, professor at Harvard, and special adviser to the Treasury. George L. Harrison, Governor of the New York Federal Reserve Bank, and acting for the Federal Reserve Bank, was also to go.

But the President gave no definite, written instructions. Sprague was simply told to see what he could do about negotiating some sort of arrangement designed to steady the exchanges. As for the American delegation to the Economic Conference, it was told that it was free to go ahead and lay the American proposals for a revised gold standard before the Conference. But it was to keep its hands out of stabilization. It was to shun the subject as the plague.

Now Secretary Hull was far from being as interested in monetary problems as he was in tariff barriers. He had not followed the April monetary discussions particularly closely. But it required no great familiarity with these problems to see how the margin of possible agreement in London was being narrowed. Whether Roosevelt's course was justified by domestic conditions is another question—a debatable question. Of its deflationary effect on the prospects of the Conference there could be no doubt.

For almost any man, other than Hull, whom I've ever known this would have been the last straw. It would have been the signal for a showdown with Roosevelt. It would have provoked a brutally frank examination of the vast, yawning gulf that seemed to separate the two men's objectives. It would have ended with a clear understanding on both sides, if not in some workable readjustment of policies.

But Secretary Hull's confidence would admit no setbacks, envisage no defeats. His customary look of infinite sadness noticeably deepened. But the words that he spoke as he set sail for London on May 31st did not even hint of discouragement. "The fact that the entire world is in a state of bitter economic war and all the world is at present functioning on an artificial basis," he said, "affords the strongest reason for an agreement among the countries to lower trade barriers and stabilize the currency exchange, with a corresponding restoration of international finance and trade. The program as suggested by the agenda at the preparatory conference applies measures . . . that if carried out would give remedies that would be equally beneficial to all. The result of this is that . . . *there should be an agreement as to the fundamentals of the situation in a few weeks, that should equally apply to currency stabilization as well as to trade barriers* [Italics mine]."

4

So, in the two short weeks between May 15th and May 31st, had the essentially schismatic nature of our so-called foreign policy emerged. This was the prelude to the Donnybrook Fair in London.

It's doubtful whether a collection of the political geniuses of all the ages could have represented us satisfactorily under these circumstances. But the odds were a million to one that the delegation Roosevelt chose could not negotiate successfully on the basis of these confused, confusing, shifting purposes.

Heading the delegation was Secretary Hull, absolutely unreconciled to the adjustments the exigencies of Roosevelt's domestic policies were causing.

Next in rank, as Vice Chairman, came former Governor James M. Cox of Ohio, who had been F. D. R.'s running mate on the national ticket in 1920. Jim Cox, a genial, sophisticated newspaper publisher, was orthodox, not to say conservative, on monetary questions. His knowledge of tariff problems was admittedly not extensive, but he was a low-tariff man. In general, because of his commitments to the Wilson principles in 1920, he was more or less of an internationalist.

Then came Key Pittman, Chairman of the Senate Foreign Relations Committee. Key was a high-tariff man. His long study of the silver problem (as Senator from Nevada) made him not only eager to "do something for silver," but more sympathetic than any other member of the delegation to the increasingly unorthodox monetary views of Roosevelt.

Representative Samuel D. McReynolds of Tennessee, Chairman of the Foreign Affairs Committee of the House, was, like Secretary Hull, an ardent low-tariff man. He made no pretense to expert knowledge of monetary problems.

These four men agreed to serve early in May. The two other members of the delegation weren't chosen until, almost literally, the last moment. Senator James Couzens of Michigan, like Pittman, a high-tariff, soft-money man, was persuaded by Roosevelt to serve after all attempts to induce Hiram Johnson had failed.[15] Ralph W. Morrison, a wealthy Texan, was appointed on the recommendation of Jim Farley and Jack Garner the day before the delegation sailed.[16] His views on tariff and money were unknown to the President.

None of these six men had ever attended an international conference.

Lined up behind them was a small army of experts, advisers, and clerks—Bill Bullitt, Chief Executive Officer of the Delegation; Warburg, its Financial Adviser; Feis, Chief Technical Adviser; Fred Nielsen, Legal Adviser; Charles Michelson and Elliott Thurston, Press Officers of the delegation; and some forty others.

I shall never forget the last meeting of the President with most of the members of the delegation and some of the experts. The meeting was held for the purpose of handing them their "instructions." These "instructions" consisted of resolutions to be offered by the delegation at the Conference, together with some explanatory material related to these resolutions. After they had been read, a desultory discussion took place. Baruch and I were there, in addition to those attached to the delegation. There were attempts to provoke some discussion of what the policy with reference to tariffs and stabilization should be.

[15] Johnson's distrust of the administration's internationalist tendencies was so great that he wanted no part of this jaunt to London.

[16] Morrison had first been slated to go as technical adviser. He refused, however, and on May 30th the President was prevailed upon to name him as a delegate.

Hull said practically nothing. The keen-minded Baruch, realizing not only that the delegates were of different minds themselves but that the President himself had not made clear what his views were, interposed a few leading remarks. But the illumination touched off by these remarks was instantly blurred over by foggy generality. I tried to do what Baruch failed to do, and likewise failed.

Many of those present thought they knew the President's mind. They didn't. Others, who had qualms, resolutely pushed them aside. Others were apparently concerned with nothing except thoughts of the trip ahead.

I felt almost physically ill as we left the President's office. Baruch's apprehensions and mine checked to the last detail. And yet there was nothing for us to do except hope for the best. A very inchoate die, a very shadowy die, had been cast. But it was a die, and it had been cast.

I had been asked to serve as a delegate early in May, and had refused. When F. D. R. asked me why, I reminded him of my plans for leaving the administration shortly. But there were three other strong reasons, I said, for my not wanting to serve. I didn't think much of the Conference's prospects: I didn't think we could obtain from it anything of substantial value to this country. I was, as he knew, far more interested in the domestic picture than in the foreign. And the debts were still unfinished business: inasmuch as I'd been handling them for him since November, I thought it best if I saw the June 15th negotiations through. It would be impossible for me to deal with debts if I were also a member of the delegation.

F. D. R. cheerfully assented. For some two weeks that was the last that was said of my going to London except in the newspapers.

But before Hull and the delegation left, Roosevelt, sensing perhaps for the first time the heterogeneity of his delegation and the disparity between the Hull philosophy and his own domestic policies, arranged with Hull for a series of liaison men to carry verbal reports between the United States and London. Warren Delano Robbins, he who, as Chief of Protocol under Hoover, had welcomed F. D. R. at the Union Station in Washington on November 22nd, would be the first of these liaison officers. I might be the second man, leaving for London as soon as Congress adjourned and the debts were out of the way and returning after about a week. A third man would follow, and then as many, in turn, as the duration of the Conference called for.

In short, it was understood, as I bade Hull Godspeed on the deck of the liner that was taking him to London, that I might possibly see him there.

I returned from the dock in New York to a Washington as tumultuous as it had been at any moment since the bank crisis. Congress was in revolt over the veterans' payments. The N.I.R.A. bill was evoking shouts of "Dictator." There was violent pulling and hauling over the Glass-Steagall Banking Act. Prices were shooting upward to what were, in my mind, alarming heights. And the negotiations over the debts, now that there were only fifteen days left, began in earnest.

My appointments for one of those days, as I jotted them down in my journal, will suggest exactly what that involved for me.

9:00	F. D. R.
10:00	Acting-Secretary Phillips
10:30	British Ambassador
11:50	Italian Ambassador
12:00	Japanese Ambassador
12:45	Rumanian Minister
1:05	Czechoslovakian Minister
2:30	Lew Douglas
3:30	Tom Corcoran—at Frankfurter's request
4:00	Man with a money scheme, sent by Louis Howe
4:30	F. D. R. and Phillips
9:00	White House conference *re* veterans

Negotiations with the British proceeded on the basis of the MacDonald-Roosevelt interchange. The bluff and honest Lindsay now began to document the thesis that Britain deserved some sympathy from us. They had never once failed to make their payments. The total they had paid, to date, was $1,447,270,000, whereas the French, who originally had owed us almost as much as the British, had paid us only $200,000,000. Furthermore, Sir Ronald argued, a very considerable debt was owed them by European nations. How could they forgive their debtors if we were unwilling to forgive ours? (This curious use of the sacred mandate of the Lord's Prayer was not lost upon us, but we were all able to bear up under the impact of grief over the British dilemma.) And, finally, his face red with distress, Sir Ronald repeated that payment would be "difficult—very, very difficult." We must understand that British pride was involved, and yet, British pride or no British pride, he had to make this admission.

I reminded Sir Ronald that Congress, in December, 1931, had declared that it was to be "against the policy of Congress that any of the indebtedness of foreign countries to the United States should be in any manner cancelled or reduced." This clear-cut prohibition still rested upon the President. He could not seek power to postpone payments without a tremendous uproar in an already rebellious Congress. He could not even have got it while Congress was in the mood to give him power as great as that of any other President in history. We could only hope, after June 15th, to negotiate some sort of permanent settlement that Congress might be disposed to approve.

The British countered with the offer of a "token" payment of $5,000,000, to be lumped with the payment of December and considered as a payment on account toward an amount to be determined in the final settlement. If we accepted this, they hoped we would avoid any intimation that the British were defaulting.

We said "No." In the first place, the word "token" in the United States conveyed a wholly different idea than it did in England: "token," to us, meant a small worthless coin. Second, payment of $5,000,000, considering the amount due, looked a good deal like a token as a token was known in the United States: it was absurdly small.

So we dickered, like traders in an Eastern bazaar.

In the end the British came through with the offer of a $10,000,000 payment.[17] This was to constitute "an acknowledgment of the debt pending a final settlement," their note said, after a long recital of the circumstances which prevented their making a full payment. Our reply spread on the record our lingering skepticism about the British inability to pay in full. But we accepted the offer. The way was now open to an amicable adjustment of the whole matter—an adjustment which was never achieved.[18]

Concurrently, in the first two weeks of June, there were more or less graceful exchanges with our other debtors. Of these, I should say that the negotiations with the French were the most unpleasant.

Since January the French had been hinting that if some "new fact"

[17] Actually this involved an outlay of only $7,000,000 by them because they took advantage of the President's authorization (inserted by Key Pittman in the Thomas amendment) to accept up to $200,000,000 in war-debt payments in silver. The trick in that provision was that the Treasury might fix the price at which silver would be accepted, provided that such price should not exceed fifty cents an ounce. At the current price of silver in the world market the British could get by on a $10,000,000 payment with approximately $7,000,000.

[18] The following autumn, after I was out of office, the British sent negotiators who spent some time in Washington on what proved to be a fruitless discussion of the debt. Since that time, apparently, our government has sent requests for payment at regular intervals and the matter has been permitted to remain in *statu quo*.

could be conjured up on the basis of which they could save their face after their default of December the existing Government might get something through the French parliament. Shortly after the conversations with Leith-Ross on "The Bunny," Warburg and Bullitt were permitted to convey to the French representatives, informally and confidentially, the idea contained in "The Bunny." The French assured the two that this idea would be held in the strictest confidence by the French Government. A few days later a story appeared in a French newspaper containing enough of "The Bunny" to indicate that it was a deliberate plant, perhaps intended to test French opinion, but certainly embarrassing to us. Warburg and Bullitt were instructed to inform M. Henry, Counselor of Embassy, and the new Ambassador, M. de Laboulaye, that this sort of thing made decent negotiation impossible; that, in fact, we were really furious; that after all, since they were the debtors and we were the creditors, we were not in the position of having to make any propositions to them; and that now we were just going to sit back and wait for them to offer us something tangible.

The French offer of something tangible appeared in the form of a note stating that they had hoped that a new "arrangement" of the war debts might be concluded, expressing disappointment that their hope had not been realized, and announcing that therefore the French Government was "obliged to defer payment of the sum due June 15th." It added the droll touch that France by no means intended "to break unilaterally engagements entered into." Whatever this meant was not clear to non-Gallic minds. It remains a mystery to this day.

Our reply was curt. It merely noted that the French Government "has failed to meet in whole or in part the installment due on existing debt agreements." We added a dig about the failure of the French Government to meet the payment due on December 15th and its failure to show any desire even to discuss the problem. This official reply I had the pleasure of supplementing in a private conversation with de Laboulaye. With the aid of a vocabulary acquired during my boyhood in Ohio, I described exactly what Americans thought about the conduct of the French Government. It neither confessed inability to pay nor offered payment of even a small amount on account, which seemed to us completely faithless.[19] So far as I know, there is where the matter stands after six years.

There was reference, by some of the representatives of our debtors,

19 At last we had begun to understand the attitude of Hoover and Stimson toward the French and to admit to ourselves that they may have had the right idea after all.

to the transfer problem. Since debtor nations must convert into our currency the payments owed us, it was argued, and since payment of any substantial part of the debts in gold was impossible, and since we were unwilling to accept the surplus goods and services of our debtors, in repayment of their loans, by reducing our own exports and increasing our imports, we had placed insuperable difficulties in the way of payment. The facts were, of course, that the nationals of a number of our debtors had balances and owned property in this country which could have been used, within limits, in making the transfer had their nations been determined to keep up their payments. And the further facts were, as subsequent events have shown, that the objections to the transfer of gold which were made at that time were not entirely valid. In June, 1933, we had about thirty per cent of the world's monetary gold supply. We now have sixty per cent.

Most of the nations stated inability to pay. We accepted those statements after some futile effort to break them down. (There were, for instance, long discussions with the Italian Ambasador about the Italian offer to pay $1,000,000 on account. We reminded him that the payment of $1,000,000 on a total due of $13,545,438.00 would "be regarded in the United States as insubstantial"—that, in fact, it looked to us like the kind of a tip which one gave in a very unfashionable restaurant. But it was impossible to force them up.) There was, perforce, nothing to do but hope that the sad conditions our debtors mentioned would improve, nothing to do but let the whole business be a lesson to us.

The notes that flew between us and our debtors in the first fifteen days of June—and there were literally scores of them—would not have made pretty reading for those who were so sure that an era of good faith and good will in international relations awaited only a little cooperativeness by the United States. Only the British and the Finnish seemed to feel that simple honesty was an element in good will, and that neighborliness was a two-way affair. The British at least went through the motions of earnest negotiation. Finland actually paid.

Later on, in July, still hoping against hope that we might induce our debtors to take something out of their armament appropriations to pay part of what they owed us, F. D. R. decided to ask Finland to come in first to discuss a possible adjustment of the debt. He felt that the popularity of Finland with the American people would assure a favorable reception in Congress of a proposal offering Finland a substantial reduction. That might enable us to follow up such a reduction to Finland with considerable debt scalings to other countries. Much to our surprise, Finland notified Phillips, who was then Acting Secretary, that she had no desire to carry on negotiations with regard to a readjustment of her debt. She was content to pay in full. This amazing news polished off the scheme. It probably would have got us nowhere anyhow.

We consoled ourselves with the knowledge that we'd bought some rather fine insurance against further involvement in European wars. There the debt story ended.

5

Meanwhile, as this wretched business dragged to an end, the news from our delegation and our separate stabilization representatives was, almost from the first, alarming.

The delegation, divided in outlook, was no sooner on shipboard than it began to wrangle. On Saturday, June 3rd, talking to the newspapermen, Secretary Hull expressed the hope that discussion of tariffs would be given priority over other matters at the Conference. When Pittman was questioned about this by the reporters, he attempted—successfully—to get them to blanket the statement. He feared, of course, that our delegation might get too far out in front on tariff reduction and run the risk of presidential rebuke.

This deeply disturbed Hull. The other delegates began to take sides. Disorganized, undisciplined, and divided, the group made only the feeblest efforts to conceal the state of affairs from the newspapermen who swarmed over the ship. The reporters were soon speaking of it to one another as "The Funeral Ship"—a phrase coined by the quick-tongued George Holmes of the I.N.S.

The delegation arrived in London late on Thursday, June 8th. By Saturday the disagreement within the delegation attained ominous proportions. The Conference was to be organized into two large groups—the one to be called the Commission on Economic Affairs (which included tariffs) and the other to be called the Commission on Monetary and Financial Affairs. Our delegation had been given to understand that it would get the chairmanship of one of the two. Hull was for our taking the chairmanship of the Economic Commission—though he himself didn't want the post. There was strong opposition.

It was reinforced by the arrival of Cox.[20] No doubt as a result of his discussions on the boat about the problem of money with Harrison, Sprague, and Warburg, Cox was determined to get the chairmanship of the Monetary Commission. The opposition to Hull became overwhelming when the news reached the delegation that F. D. R., in Washington, had formally announced what had privately been made known to Hull days before—that he wasn't going to ask Congress for tariff bargaining powers.

Realizing, at last, that acceptance of the chairmanship of the Economic Commission would plaster the delegation with responsibility for what the Commission ultimately did, and realizing that Congress was likely to repudiate any tariff-reduction agreements, even those delegates who sympathized with Hull's point of view backed away. Hull stood alone.

To make matters more complicated, Sir Maurice Hankey, the famous secretary of the British Cabinet (particularly famous for his self-effacement and anonymity, which has always seemed to me a delightful paradox) had informed Bill Bullitt that the French and the British had decided that the chairmen of the two big Commissions ought to be the delegates of two *minor* powers. Hence it appeared, for the moment, that our delegation was engaged in a squabble over a non-existent horse.

Bullitt objected so vociferously to Hankey's announcement that the British indicated they would revert to the original plan of giving one chairmanship to the United States. But by this time Secretary Hull, despondent over the "desertions" within the delegation, announced

[20] Cox had come to England on a boat that sailed later than that which most of the delegation took. He arrived in London with Harrison, Sprague, and Warburg late on June 9th. On the day that Cox sailed I visited him in his room at the Waldorf. Walter Lippmann was there also. I had known Cox for many years, having assisted him occasionally with his speeches when he was Governor of Ohio and when I was connected with the Council of National Defense in Columbus during the war. Cox announced that he knew rather little about international exchange and sought suggestions from Lippmann and me as to suitable reading matter on that subject for his consumption on the boat. Lippmann mentioned a book. I suggested that inasmuch as Roosevelt's views on currency since May seemed to approximate those expressed by Keynes in his *Treatise on Money* it might be well for Cox to read the last chapter in the second volume of that work. I sent for the book and saw that it got to him.

I have never been able to trace any evidence of his reading the book in his later thinking. His trip on the boat seems to have exposed him to education by three strict sound-money men. He arrived at London more set than ever in his monetary orthodoxy.

that perhaps, after all, it would be better to let the chairmanships go to minor powers.

Ensued a heated argument on Sunday afternoon, June 11th, at a meeting in the Secretary's rooms at Claridge's. It seems to have been a brutal verbal free-for-all, with no holds barred. It ended in no decision.

Vague reports leaked out to the press. The Secretary, it was rumored, had stormed in his rooms that Sunday night. He had talked of cabling his resignation to Washington on the grounds, first, that the delegation would not support him and, second, that the President's formal announcement on tariff legislation had constituted a public humiliation for him.[21]

A cable from Bullitt was rushed over the wires to the President: the President must reassure the Secretary, tell him of his confidence in him. A soothing, encouraging message was prepared. Its receipt in London on Monday morning, the 12th, seemed to mollify the Secretary. At any rate, he let the delegation go ahead and insist upon getting the monetary chairmanship.[22]

By evening the Secretary had a new cause for concern.

En route to Europe he had written his opening speech for the Conference. The speech was a passionate denunciation of economic nationalism, which was decried as frenzied, delusive, and suicidal. High tariffs, quotas, embargoes, exchange restrictions, and depreciated currencies were causing "hundreds of millions of people" to starve. The belief that individual nations could, "by bootstrap methods," achieve recovery had proven "fruitless." Now the whole world was looking to the Conference to proclaim that economic nationalism was "a discredited policy." The success or failure of the Conference would signify the success or failure of statesmanship everywhere.

This address the Secretary was scheduled to deliver before the Conference on its second day, Tuesday, June 13th. The draft had been cabled to the President for "any suggestions" he might care to make on June 10th. But the President was knee-deep in the last-minute debt negotiations and the business of trying to get Congress to adjourn,

[21] On June 11th Arthur Krock of the *New York Times* viewed the President's announcement thus: "Temporarily . . . the devoted band which Mr. Hull led to London has been abandoned. It is as marooned as if it had been wrecked on one of the New Hebrides." The fact was, of course, that Mr. Hull's "devoted band" was engaged in gouging out his and one another's entrails and that the abandoning took place during the two weeks before Mr. Hull sailed.

[22] This it succeeded in doing on Thursday, June 15th, after an incredible amount of backing and filling by the English and French.

which he had hoped it would do on the 10th. He did not get to the Hull draft until Sunday, the 11th.

When the Hull draft arrived, I read it with many misgivings. But in view of my own well-known position on the question it seemed only fair that I should not in any way attempt to influence the President in his reaction or in his reply to it. I was scrupulously careful about this. I went over to the White House with Billy Phillips when the draft was handed to the President and, in Phillips' presence, explained that I would take no part in the handling of the speech.

I therefore didn't make any recommendations whatever about it. But F. D. R.'s "suggestions" were sweeping. They included a general recommendation that the speech be abridged; a series of injunctions that particular paragraphs, sentences, and phrases be "toned down"; and the order that at least one passage be recast, because it was at variance with the President's campaign speeches. Added up, they thundered, "Danger! Go Slow."

It was Monday evening, London time, before they burst upon the Secretary. His submissive mood of the morning instantly vanished. He was too distressed to make the corrections in his speech that night. It was Tuesday morning before he could bring himself to the task. But the delay had made it impossible for the press releases to be prepared before the scheduled hour. Fifteen minutes before the Secretary was to make his speech, MacDonald was notified that he would not speak until Wednesday.

It happened, as a matter of fact, to be just as well. MacDonald had made brief but unpleasant reference to the war debts on Monday, the day of the Conference's opening. Secretary Hull's failure to appear on Tuesday at the hour set for his speech was construed in London as a skillful rebuke for the unjustifiable reference to debts in the Conference.

In Washington, though, it was taken to be an indication of the muddle that characterized our delegation. And the tenor of the speech, as finally delivered on Wednesday, was the tip-off that worse was still to come. For while the Secretary had religiously embodied each specific suggestion F. D. R. had made, he had entirely overlooked the broad implications of the President's cable. The speech remained a vehement attack on "bootstrap methods" of recovery. It bespoke an "Ich-kann-nicht-anders" temper on tariffs. Obstacles had evidently only increased the Secretary's ardor. It was apparent that he'd decided to have his say in London.

And now, on Thursday, June 15th, another focus of misunderstanding in London began to light up dangerously. Sprague, Harrison, and Warburg had begun temporary stabilization talks with Montagu Norman of the Bank of England and Clément Moret of the Bank of France.[23] Unquestionably at the behest of the British and French Governments, Norman and Moret, particularly Moret, had resorted to irritating tactics. What had been a plea for temporary stabilization on May 26th had become a peremptory demand for immediate and definite stabilization on June 10th.

Sprague, Harrison, and Warburg finally made it clear that this was impossible. But I suspect that when the conversations began to turn on specific methods of steadying exchange and on specific rates they allowed themselves to appear too eager. What was required was a good show of indifference and independence to force Norman and Moret into reasonable positions.

As the conversations went on, during the 12th, 13th, and 14th, rumors flew through the exchanges of the world. On the 12th, for instance, when the pound went to $4.18, the reports were that the British and French proposed to stabilize at $3.50. The dollar alternately swooped and soared. So did stock and commodity prices.

On the 15th the dollar began to go up. The sterling rate was $4.02. Stocks fell. There were rumors that stabilization at $4.05 had been agreed upon. There were other rumors that the figure was $4.00. Governor Cox was quoted as confirming the $4.05 figure. (He later denied having said any such thing.)

Of the exact course of the stabilization negotiations we, in Washington, were completely uninformed. The report that Sprague, Harrison, and Warburg had even considered such a proposal galvanized us into action. F. D. R. at once cabled them that, while he felt sure the "wild" rumors were unfounded, he must remind them that any stabilization proposal must be submitted to himself and Woodin. This cable was followed within the hour by a demand from Woodin for a full account of the negotiations thus far. Publicly, Woodin repudiated reports that a stabilization agreement had been reached. "Various reports from London published today concerning an agreement by the American delegates to stabilization in some form," he said, "have been brought

23 Warburg, though attached to the delegation, which was not supposed to concern itself with these temporary stabilization talks, had been given special permission to sit in on them by F. D. R. following receipt of a cable from Hull requesting this.

to my attention. Such reports cannot be founded on fact. Any proposal concerning stabilization would have to be submitted to the President and to the Treasury. No suggestion of such a proposal has been received here. The discussions in London in regard to this subject must be exploratory only, and any agreement on this subject will be reached in Washington, not elsewhere."

The replies that came back from our stabilization negotiators early on the 16th confirmed our fears. Harrison, Sprague, and Warburg had evolved a plan of cooperation between the Federal Reserve Bank of New York and the Bank of England to maintain exchange rates within a spread of three per cent vis-à-vis the gold franc. This meant a dollar-pound ratio of about $4.00. They assured us flatly that agreement "much" above this point would introduce an "arbitrary factor" into the situation—meaning, presumably, that a higher ratio would be artificial and impossible to maintain without great hardship. Further, the plan provided that the Bank of England and the New York Federal Reserve Bank would each expend up to 60,000,000 gold dollars to maintain the $4.00 middle rate. There followed a strong implication that the Treasury was to guarantee the New York Federal Reserve Bank against this possible loss. It was phrased this way: if the President approved the agreement, "it would seem reasonable to presume" that the Bank was acting "for the account of" the government of the United States. Finally, this agreement was contingent upon agreement on two others:

(1) A general declaration that the British and United States governments and the banks of issue in those countries held that stabilization of their currencies on a gold basis, under proper conditions, was their ultimate objective.

(2) A general declaration that during the Conference the British, French, and United States governments and banks of issue would do everything in their power to limit fluctuations in those of their currencies which were off gold and would not, in the absence of unforeseen circumstances, resort to policies calculated to depress the exchange. (This meant that the British undertook not to use the equalization fund to affect the price of sterling and that we were to agree not to use the Thomas amendment during the Conference unless, for instance, there was a serious reaction of trade and prices.)

A council of war was summoned to the White House. Present were Will Woodin, Dean Acheson (who'd been appointed Under Secretary of the Treasury on May 3rd), and myself. It was decided that, while agreement on the $4.00 middle rate would have seemed like a good trade in late April, in mid-June it was preposterous: $4.20 would have been nearer the mark.

As I understood it, our position was that a *tentative and flexible agreement* was desirable to calm the fears of the French, Swiss, Dutch, Italian, Belgian, and German peoples that the dollar would be permitted to depreciate to a point which would force their currencies off gold.

But that did not mean falling for the extreme demands of the French and British. Our men needed to be taught to counter bluff with bluff.

That, as I saw it, was what was in F. D. R.'s mind as we worked over the reply. The proposal our negotiators sent was turned down. They were please to bear in mind, the President said, that the broad principle of ultimate return to a modified gold standard discussed at Washington in April presupposed the return of *all* nations—and not two or three only. There were sixty-six nations represented in London—not just the United States and Great Britain. What was more, the President wasn't interested in stabilization at $4.00—"at present approximate levels," he put it. And he certainly wasn't interested in binding the dollar rigidly to the pound: he would not approve "close" stabilization with such small leeway as they were suggesting.

Then came a proposal designed to jolt the French and the English into the realization that we could be as tough in driving a bargain as they. He wasn't at all sure, F. D. R. said, that there was any need whatever for an agreement based on mutual action. For his part, he would not like to go beyond an informal statement that if the pound should go to $4.25, say, the United States might consider some sort of unilateral action to keep the dollar from falling lower.

When this reply was being drafted on Friday, June 16th, F. D. R. at first intended to add that the United States would be willing to export gold to an amount between $50,000,000 and $80,000,000 to hold the dollar at the $4.25 point—an immensely important clue to his frame of mind that day. But then he decided to delete the softening words—not because they did not represent his intentions, but because he did not want to mitigate the effect of brusqueness. If he was going to give Sprague, Harrison, and Warburg a lesson and Norman and Moret a good fright, there must be no winkings to suggest he didn't mean business.

The reply completed, F. D. R. turned to me. I could see how things were, he remarked. One wouldn't think it possible that Harrison,

Sprague, Cox, and Warburg could fail to catch on to this cable on stabilization. Yet, who knew? Nobody who represented us seemed to get his drift. Obviously, it seemed that I ought to go to London. I could get away readily enough. The debt negotiations were practically finished. Congress had adjourned.[24] At most, even including the time for traveling, it would take me only a month. I could sail the following Wednesday.

In his press conference that morning, in response to a question about whether I was going to London, Roosevelt had said, off the record, that "from the very start," the plan had been for me "to go over *sometime*" (italics mine) for a week or two. He had not been more definite than this, in talking of my going, until late afternoon of the 16th.

We talked at great length during the evening of the 16th, as F. D. R. made ready to leave for a cruise on the schooner *Amberjack*. The trip to London promised to be a nasty chore, I said. I was reluctant to go. I suggested that we leave it this way: things might run more smoothly in London after these first few dreadful days, and, if so, it might not be necessary for me to go; if, however, the reports out of London didn't improve, I would go.

Meanwhile, in the event that I should go, who would stay in Washington to keep F. D. R. informed of what was happening? Woodin was not well and was planning to return to New York for medical care. Acheson alone, able as he was, could not swing such a job. What of Bernie Baruch? He'd been originally slated by F. D. R. for the chairmanship of the delegation before it was known that Hull wanted to go. He surely deserved this recognition not only because of his services to the party and to F. D. R.'s candidacy but because of his great ability. Why not ask Bernie to "sit in" as his Washington adviser on the Conference if I did go?

Roosevelt was delighted with the idea. "As a matter of fact," he said, "I not only had Bernie in mind for that job myself, but I've already spoken to him about it. He's willing. So you can go ahead with it."

There was one other point. I mentioned the fact that F. D. R. was indebted to Herbert Swope in much the same way that he was to Bernie. Swope, whom I had by now come to know intimately, had given loyal support to Roosevelt's candidacy. I thought it would make him happy if F. D. R. asked him to accompany me, should I go. I also believed Swope, an experienced journalist and student of public affairs, could be of real assistance. Could that be managed?

[24] Congress wound up a little after one o'clock that Friday morning.

I'd spoken of this during the afternoon to Louis Howe, who announced that he was "dead against" giving Swope such an assignment. When asked why he objected to Herbert, Louis had only sputtered something incoherent about not liking Swope. Louis and I'd had some rather plain words then. It was bitterly unfair to blackball a man on the basis of any such vague prejudice, I'd said. Louis could go ahead and say anything he liked to F. D. R. about Swope, but I intended to put the case to him too.

F. D. R. smiled indulgently when told of Louis' objections. He knew all about Louis' feelings, he said. Steve Early and McIntyre had expressed doubts about the advisability of sending Swope too. "But *I* like him, so let's forget about them," he added. "We'll send him word right now."

He thereupon wrote out a telegram saying that he was sending me to London "soon" (note the indefiniteness here again) and that he would be delighted if Herbert could accompany me, having, as he did, such confidence in Herbert's "judgment and wide knowledge of international affairs." Herbert answered immediately. He would regard it as a privilege to be of service.[25]

Thus preparations were concluded for my possible going—if the news from London got no better.

The news not only got no better but got a good deal worse.

Upon receipt of the Roosevelt cable rejecting the Harrison-Sprague-Warburg proposal on Saturday, June 17th, Harrison threw his things into his bag and hurriedly sailed for home. Sprague, Warburg, and Cox (who presumably had been taken into their confidence when he became chairman of the Monetary Commission on Thursday) sent a cable late Sunday expressing regret over their failure to meet the President's wishes on technical details and assuring the President that they would work for a better bargain, but begging that he endorse the proposed arrangement in principle lest the United States be charged with backing down on its implied willingness to stabilize temporarily.

In short, our stabilization negotiators were somewhat chastened. But they still held to their convictions.

Meantime our delegation to the Conference managed to get itself into a ludicrous fix. At a delegation meeting on Saturday morning it

[25] As I look back at this incident, my only regret is that it was to involve a good friend in a thoroughly unpleasant experience with me. Otherwise I would not undo it for a moment. Herbert could not have served more loyally, wisely, or faithfully. His collaboration was easily worth the tussle with Louis.

was suggested that a horizontal ten per cent tariff cut be proposed by the delegation in the Conference. The delegates, with the exception of Hull and Morrison, turned thumbs down. But it was finally agreed, in deference to the Secretary's feelings, that the idea be included in a list of topics the United States would like to see discussed at the Conference.

That afternoon, as the Secretary was getting into his car to go to a garden party at Windsor, one of the delegation's experts rushed up to him and asked him to sign a document which Hull thought was such a list of topics for discussion. He signed it hurriedly. It was forthwith sent to the Secretariat of the Conference. There it was construed as a list of proposals made by the United States delegation, mimeographed, and handed out to the press. Hull, apprised of what was happening by a frantic press officer of the delegation who reached him at Windsor, insisted that the intention of the delegation could not possibly be so misconstrued. By the time he was persuaded that it not only could be, but was being so interpreted, the damage had already been done. Europe was blazing with headlines that the United States delegation had proposed a general ten per cent tariff cut.

This was not all. Before the delegation could meet to decide what action to take (which it did on Sunday morning, when it authorized Key Pittman to issue a statement explaining what had happened) two of the delegates had talked immoderately to the press.

This brought to a head on Sunday another intra-delegation battle which centered in the question whether the delegates ought to make individual statements to the press. There had been other instances of such behavior on the preceding days. A couple of the delegates had sounded off to the newspaper men on stabilization. It was suggested by Bullitt that the delegates agree to make no statements without the Secretary's approval. One of them categorically refused: he intended to voice his opinions to the press on all matters at any time, he said, without let or hindrance.

Hull, when pressed to insist on establishing this rudiment of discipline, said that he could not give orders to the delegates: he had not selected them; therefore he could not instruct them. So the chaos deepened.

By Monday morning I was certain that F. D. R. would insist upon my going to London. I began to make ready to leave, although my misgivings were still pretty grave. In the afternoon I talked to the press and generally prepared the way for departure on the following Wednesday.[26] Bernie Baruch and Swope were with me at my office much of the day. I stayed on in the evening, clearing my desk.

At about nine o'clock I had a telephone call. It was from McIntyre and Jimmy Byrnes, who were out enjoying some sort of festivities in the suburbs. Their conversation was not completely clear, but it bore on the fact that they had been talking together and decided that it would be unwise for me to go. I told them that I was sure they were right. I suggested that they join me at my hotel a little later.

Then I left the office, went to the hotel, and, before going to my own rooms, stopped in at Hugh Johnson's. "I want to ask you one simple question," I told Hugh. "As head of the N.R.A., what is your feeling about a possible agreement to stabilize?"

"All right," said Hugh. "Here's my answer: an agreement to stabilize now on the lines your boy friends in London are suggesting would bust to hell and gone the prices we're sweating to raise. Please get me. I'm for a return to gold at the earliest possible moment. But that moment isn't now." I thanked him and said good-by, with the words that he'd confirmed what the people in the Department of Agriculture had told me earlier that day.

A little while later McIntyre and Byrnes arrived at my rooms. Very seriously, now, they announced that I oughtn't to leave Washington. With the President, several Cabinet officers, and most of the presidential secretariat away, I ought to stay and carry on as I had in the past. Besides, look at the confusion into which the London party had fallen! I could only injure myself by plunging into that maelstrom. The Conference was going to be a fiasco anyway, and no one connected with it would come out with any enhancement of his reputation. Why get mixed up with it? I had everything to lose and nothing to gain by going. Why didn't I persuade F. D. R. to send somebody else?

I had great respect for the political judgment of both these men. I always respect hunches in a politician of experience. I told them that their doubts coincided with my own. I only wished I could get out of

[26] Among other things I told the press just what Bernie Baruch's function would be during my absence. Careful as I tried to be, I didn't reckon on Bernie's tremendous prestige throughout the country. Many newspapers placed upon the announcement that he would occupy my office the absurd interpretation that he was to be "Acting President" in the absence of Roosevelt and Hull. Baruch, dismayed by the blare of publicity which followed this misinterpretation, ducked out of my office on June 23rd and thereafter kept in touch with London and F. D. R. from the Carlton Hotel or from his own home in New York.

going. In fact, I'd put the question up to the President, in person, if he'd consent.

So, at once, I sent an inquiry to F. D. R. asking him if he would see me. Word came back that I should come ahead—proceeding to Nantucket by navy plane and there boarding a destroyer which would take me to the *Amberjack*. Art Mullen packed my things. At 3:00 A.M., Tuesday we left Washington. At 10.00 A.M., off Pollock light, I greeted F. D. R. on the *Amberjack*.

All the combined misgivings of Byrnes, McIntyre, and myself I described to him as I sat beside him on the *Amberjack* that sunny June morning. I asked to be excused from going. F. D. R. laughed at my fears. Nothing would do but that I must go.

I was matching hunches here. The politician whom I regarded as having superhunches was overruling McIntyre, Byrnes, and me. I yielded.

Then I reminded him that he had not yet answered the message that Sprague, Warburg, and Cox had sent on Sunday. He reached for a pencil and a small scratch pad and wrote out a cable. Far from consenting to endorse the principles the three men recommended, he stood on his judgment that the importance of a hard and fast mutual agreement on stabilization was being vastly exaggerated: our people were to remember that the United States held the cards in this particular game; our delegation was in a position to insist that the broad work of the Conference proceed without waiting on a temporary stabilization agreement.

In conversation then, when I asked for instructions, Roosevelt developed this idea. The way was still open for some sort of agreement to calm the gold-standard countries and "steady" the dollar, if that could be contrived without the shipment of gold from this country and without checking the magnificent advance of American prices which had followed our departure from gold in April.

I answered that there were those who believed that some part of the advance in prices was purely speculative. I myself was apprehensive about the rapidity of the rise. I felt that action could and should be taken which would temporarily slacken it. But I also felt, with him, that the sort of agreement which Cox, Sprague, and Warburg wanted would cause a chaotic decline. If we were ingenious, there was scope for action that would permit our recovery to proceed but, at the same time, check speculative excesses. Did that represent his beliefs?

It did, he answered.

And then he added the significant words: "You know, if nothing else can be worked out, I'd even consider stabilizing at a middle point of \$4.15, with a high and low of \$4.25 and \$4.05. I'm not crazy about it, but I think I'd go that far."

This didn't surprise me at the moment. It jibed with what I knew was in his mind. It became inexplicable only in the light of what happened eleven days later.

"I think Sprague and the others can probably work out something even more satisfactory than that," I said. "They'll probably be putting up proposals to you right along while I'm on the way over.

I took out of my pocket, at that point, a brief memorandum Swope had prepared the afternoon before and in which I concurred. It was, I explained, background material on stabilization. The President might find it helpful in replying to any propositions for a rigid and arbitrary stabilization.

F. D. R. took the memorandum. The whole transaction was over in a minute. I no more dreamed of its ironical consequences than de Maupassant's villager foresaw the consequences of picking up the piece of string.

Then, looking out over the sea, F. D. R. said, "The essential thing is that you impress on the delegation and the others that my primary international objective is to raise the world price level. Tell them about what our American recovery program is doing to raise prices, relieve debtors, and increase purchasing power. If the other nations will go along and work in our direction, as they said they would when they were in Washington, then we can cooperate. If they won't, then there's nothing to cooperate about. We can't be limited by their timidity. You know what Lippmann said a few days ago—something about international cooperation being a fine idea if it was cooperation in positive, forward measures but not if it was only to accomplish a negative stability.[27]

I replied that Lippmann was now in London. So was John Maynard Keynes, whose 1930 views, I knew, had greatly influenced F. D. R. in the past month.[28] Did F. D. R. think it would be well for me to con-

[27] The article to which Roosevelt referred had impressed him deeply. It appeared in the *New York Herald Tribune* on June 14th and the statement he paraphrased read: "International cooperation is an admirable ideal, but it should be a co-operation in powerful, concurrent and concerted measures, and not merely a cooperation which produces a negative and impotent stability."

[28] It is necessary to put an exact date upon the Keynes views in question, because Keynes has shifted since.

sult with them as soon as I got to London and perhaps put them in touch with Sprague and Warburg? That might be a good way of educating our people about his monetary objectives. He agreed.

Then I said that I'd like to have my status made clear and, remembering the unlovely episode of February 18th, I asked that F. D. R. not only write out and give me a statement describing it, but release it to the press.

Roosevelt took up his pencil again and wrote out the following:

> Asst. Secretary Moley is sailing tomorrow for London at the request of the President. He will act in a sense as a messenger or liaison officer on this short trip, giving the American delegates first hand information of the various developments, Congressional etc. in the country since the Delegation left and conveying the President's views of the effect of these developments on the original instructions given the Delegation before they sailed.
>
> Asst. Sec'y. Moley will stay in London only about a week and will then return to give the President full information of the Conference up to that time.

The significant point to note in this is that I was to act as a "liaison officer"—not as a part of the delegation. Now the term "liaison officer" is a technical term with whose meaning F. D. R., as one-time Assistant Secretary of the Navy, was perfectly familiar. It meant that on this mission he was my principal. I was acting for him. I was entitled to communicate directly with him. I was not subject to the discipline, if any, of the delegation to which I was being sent.

So we left it.

We turned, then, to somewhat lighter things. I said that I regretted that circumstances had forced me to fly up. Newspapers always had people "dashing" or "speeding" about, and such a flight as mine was bound to get more publicity than I enjoyed. "Oh, come now," F. D. R. said playfully, "I've half a mind to put you on the *Bernadou* [the destroyer which brought me from Nantucket], have the *Bernadou* meet the *Manhattan* tomorrow on her way out, and deposit you on her. Then you'd know what a big dose of publicity is. It would be lovely—to stop the *Manhattan* at sea for you."

I left Roosevelt after two hours of talk. When I returned to Nantucket, I learned that a strange accident had happened. I would be delayed a bit. It seemed that the stabilizer on the navy plane had been broken as we landed that morning at Nantucket. I'm not a superstitious man. If I had been, I would have regarded the broken-stabilizer incident as a wry portent.

When I got back to New York that evening, I reckoned that there were enough bad omens without including coincidences which suggested puns. Great black headlines told of "confusion" and "pessimism" in London, of the American delegation's preparations "to mark time" until my arrival, of Hull's being upset. Hull was actually quoted by the *New York Times'* distinguished Frederick T. Birchall as complaining, "Everything I do is misconstrued these days."

I sailed on Wednesday, June 21st.

6

What followed in the next days is, as such, of relatively slight historical importance. The story of the London Conference, even such bits of it as were publicly known, has properly faded into the filmy background of irrelevancy. The Conference failed, despite the honest efforts of many people to keep it going. The Conference, as a dream of world salvation, was in any case bound to dissolve into nothingness.

And yet there is historical reason for telling the story. For it throws a blaze of light upon one of the great figures of modern times. It reveals the character of Franklin Roosevelt in all its protean aspects. Properly understood, it provides the key to a score of policies that have profoundly affected America and the world in the past six years. To tell it with fastidious accuracy is to provide a broader understanding of one of the handful of statesmen who was causally important in this decade. That is why, if the story is to be told at all, it must be told without extenuation.

The more or less familiar version, as it appeared in dribs and drabs here and there, has it that I eagerly went to London to get publicity for myself and to do Secretary Hull an injury. In pursuit of these objectives I am supposed to have embarrassed and humiliated Hull deliberately. I am supposed to have endorsed a "stabilization agreement" which the President subsequently refused to accept. I am supposed to have made Hull bear the onus of announcing the President's refusal to the conferees. I am supposed, myself, to have been "repudiated" by the President. I am supposed to have played Hull and the delegation false by impugning their abilities to the President. And I am supposed to have left London with the Conference in a state of wreck, while Secretary Hull, alone, struggled futilely to keep it going.

This is the folklore. What are the facts? They follow in precise detail.

The first two or three days after my departure with Swope and

Mullen were a precious respite from the turmoil of the preceding weeks. What news we got was scanty, but it tended to be reassuring. We learned that the delegation had braced up, had decided to meet each morning to promote harmony, had urged the Conference to go ahead, even in the absence of any stabilization agreement, and had at last begun to act on its instructions by presenting proposals on long-time monetary policy, synchronized public expenditures, and so on for discussion.

But by Sunday the radios from Washington and London, while still fragmentary, had begun to grow disturbing. We could perceive vaguely that the delegation's spurt of energy and pragmatism had run its course. We learned that the stabilization negotiators had put another much more moderate proposition to limit the dollar's fluctuations to F. D. R., and that F. D. R. had turned it down. This had apparently undermined the delegation's new-found resolution. The result seemed to be complete paralysis so far as the delegation's attitude toward the Conference was concerned.

Our representatives were again expressing conflicting views to the newspapermen.[29] Partly because of what some of them were irresponsibly saying, and partly because the English, the French, and the rest of the gold-standard countries had worked themselves into a lather of despair over Roosevelt's continued refusal to stabilize and over the now violent fall of the dollar, the extraordinary idea that nothing could be decided until I arrived was gaining credence. There seemed to be rumors that I was coming with authority to peg the dollar—even that I was coming to displace Hull. The *New York Times* editorially said almost in so many words that the President was not telling the truth about the purposes of my trip.

> Few are so credulous as to be deceived by the official explanations of Professor Moley's trip to the London Economic Conference. It is gravely said that he is to furnish "reports" to President Roosevelt. As if the cables were not already crowded with such reports. It is added that Mr. Moley is also to be a kind of "liaison" officer at London. He will be one more of the grand coordinators working under the President. Yet everybody who has followed the dispatches knows that Secretary Hull and his fellow-delegates have been thrown into uncertainty and confusion by statements given

[29] On one day in the Conference Senator Couzens spoke against tariff reductions and, on the next, Representative McReynolds asserted that lower tariffs were the key to recovery. To complete the impression created by this episode, McReynolds denounced the Republican party, as though he were making a speech on the floor of the House.

> out at Washington. These have amounted to flat disavowals of what our representatives have said or proposed at the Conference. The result is that they and all the other members of it are now waiting for the appearance of the Professor *ex machina* to decide how much, or how little, is to be done.[30]

When the usually fair editorial page of the *Times* was publishing this sort of stuff, we could easily imagine what was appearing in the gossip columns.

Swope and I were horrified. We sat down to review our credentials and plan our course of action.

These were my instructions—verbal and otherwise:

(1) To convey to Hull and the delegation the need for the appearance of unity, at any rate, explaining that their obvious lack of discipline had attained the proportions of an international scandal.

(2) To convey the President's opinions on the significance and implications of his domestic program and its bearing upon the objectives of the Conference.

(3) To convey the President's desire to have the delegation induce the Conference to turn to long-range objectives. (The President conceived of the Conference not as a place where immediate and definitive decisions were to be made but as a study group out of which might come a crystallization of many points of view and many national aspirations. He had in mind developing through the Conference a new kind of international exchange. However strange this may seem, it was his attitude, and he wanted it described to the delegates.)

(4) To convey to the stabilization negotiators the limits to which the President was willing to go in making a temporary agreement.

(5) To bring back a candid report of the proceedings in London and an evaluation of the delegation's performance.

This was my official status:

(1) I was acting directly under the President's orders and as his agent. From the time that Roosevelt insisted that I accept the post of Assistant Secretary of State, in early February, it was understood by Secretary Hull that I enjoyed a direct and confidential relationship with the President, and that for the most part my work would

[30] This editorial, which appeared on June 22nd, was not radioed to me until three days later. It went on to discuss the "divided counsels" of the United States, the "fumbling and futility of our representatives at the Economic Conference," and to intimate that I had undertaken "to disown and virtually seek to humiliate the Secretary of State" by my radio address and article on the Conference prospects which, it inaccurately implied, had burst upon the public after Hull had made his opening speech to the Conference.

not be State Department work but whatever the President chose to entrust to me. This status had not been altered by word or hint.

(2) I had been throughout the spring and still was as much concerned with Treasury matters as with State Department affairs. I had maintained my confidential relationship with Will Woodin. All questions relating to stabilization fell within the jurisdiction of the Treasury—a fact not only recognized but publicly stated by Secretary Hull on July 3rd.

(3) As a liaison officer between the President and the delegation, I had no more responsibility to the delegation than it had to me. For the purposes of this mission Secretary Hull was in no sense my superior officer. In order to make perfectly clear what my relationship to the delegation was, it had been decided, with F. D. R.'s approval, that Swope, Mullen, and I should stay at our Embassy with Ambassador Bingham rather than at the hotel where the delegation was staying.

But when Herbert and I had reviewed all this methodically, we realized that, instructions or no instructions, official status or no official status, we had an exceedingly involved human situation to deal with.

Whatever Hull's share of the responsibility for the fix in which he now found himself, Roosevelt's share was infinitely greater. His half-encouragements and half-disavowals had left Hull and the rest of the world completely bewildered. Heartily as I disagreed with Hull's views, trying as I had found his dogmatic adherence to them, I could not help but feel that he had been treated pretty cavalierly. It was a pitiable Secretary of State who could cry out, "Everything I do is misconstrued these days." The collision of irreconcilable forces that produced his mortification had been wholly avoidable. That he himself had helped to precipitate the disaster made him no less pathetic.

I was sorry. I wanted to do everything I could, and as swiftly as I could, to restore his self-esteem and to deflate the fantastic rumors about myself.

Herbert and I thereupon drafted two statements—one to be made when the ship arrived at Cobh and another when we arrived at Plymouth—in which I ostentatiously subordinated myself, and said, in the most humble of terms, that I was merely a "messenger."[31]

The other move that we made was to radio to Ambassador Bingham in London to ask whether it would be possible to secure a plane to take us from Cobh to London. We had not decided to fly. But we

[31] These statements were radioed to F. D. R. for his approval and approved by him before release.

were turning over in our minds the thought that the sooner we could clear up the misapprehensions that were causing the French and the English to ignore Hull and prepare to flock to me the better it would be for Hull, for me, and for the Conference. A plane could speed things up more than twelve hours.

Bingham sent a reply. But his reply was not an answer to our simple request for information about the possibility of securing a plane. It told us that he had gone ahead and ordered a plane. And hard on its heels came press reports indicating that the news of what Bingham had done had already been made public, and that it was interpreted as confirming the very rumors we were determined to dispel if we could.

We immediately sent a radio to Bingham canceling the plane and assuming personal responsibility for any expenses which his over-eagerness to please had involved. It was too late. The plane, bearing a messenger from the Embassy, was already under way.

When we arrived at Cobh, I made the first of my self-deflating statements to the waiting newspapermen. The Embassy messenger, who had boarded the ship with them, then handed me a sealed envelope.

I withdrew and opened it. It was a letter from Secretary Hull—one of the most extraordinary letters I have ever read. It mentioned the grossly unfair newspaper reports and rumors that had heralded the view that I was to be virtually in charge of United States interests in London. It spoke of them as a handicap to the delegation, and implied the humiliation that it had been to him. A press statement from me, in these circumstances, might indicate the extent, if any, to which I was authorized by the President to "supervise and direct" the delegation.

Thus the plane which I did not use, and the fee for which Herbert and I personally paid and which I was excoriated in the American papers for having charged up to the government, served only to bring me this letter from Hull.

I was embarrassed. The despair the letter revealed was needlessly revealed, since only a fool or a sadist could have been unaware of it. I answered by radio as hearteningly as possible: the Secretary could be confident of my fullest cooperation in any way that I could extend it; I was certain he would find the statement already released at Cobh and another which would be released at Plymouth, both of which had been prepared before the receipt of his letter, reassuring.

We landed at Plymouth late Tuesday, June 27th, and there, to the waiting newspapermen, gave the second statement before boarding the train which was to take us to London. Once on the train, we were joined by a couple of American newspapermen whom we knew. Herbert and I listened to a recital of their impressions without comment. The most lucid reporter was George R. Holmes, who not only told us in detail of the indescribable confusion into which the Conference and our delegation had fallen but volunteered suggestions as to how we could meet the situation. Holmes knew Washington so well and his friendship with Michelson, Thurston, and others attached to our delegation was so close, that we were greatly relieved as we realized that his advice checked with the course we'd already determined upon so far as Hull was concerned. When we got to the Embassy around midnight, there to be greeted warmly by Bingham and his wife,[32] I'd already decided to call on Hull at the earliest possible moment the next morning and set him straight about my purposes.

At eight-thirty on Wednesday morning, the 28th, I was shaking Hull's hand in his rooms at Claridge's. I told him what my mission was and dismissed the idea, suggested in his letter, that I'd really been sent to "supervise and direct" the delegation. I told him how deeply I regretted the construction that had been put on my visit. I could not pretend to him that our views on international policy coincided. But that, I added, did not mean that I was any less desirous than he that the Conference should proceed smoothly. I asked for suggestions as to how I could best help. There was none forthcoming. But when I proposed that I give the day over to dispelling the misapprehensions of the delegation and the press, Hull's face had a look of unmistakable pleasure.

So that's what I did. That morning I met the delegation and announced I bore no mysterious message or authorization. Later I met the press, with Hull at my side, in a stuffy room in which it seemed that all the American and foreign correspondents in London were jammed. Hull introduced me cordially. I responded with equally cordial reference to him. I explained that I had nothing to add to my release at Plymouth and that I didn't intend to issue any further statements. But I'd answer questions, provided they fell within the scope of my mission. I was then bombarded with questions—most of them

[32] Both were, at the moment, extremely appreciative of the part which I had played, at Roosevelt's request, in ironing out the difficulties that had lain in the way of Bingham's confirmation by the Senate.

friendly enough—which I answered as well as I could. Only on debts and stabilization did I decline to comment.

I had the impression that I was really doing the job I'd set for myself. Birchall of the *New York Times* seemed to share this belief: his dispatch that day said that "of the day's incidents the conference debut of Professor Moley was the most interesting and provocative of the most comment, all favorable to the newcomer. . . . The Professor [left] the impression that he had emerged successfully from a rather trying ordeal." Other sophisticated newspapermen present also got the point. The report of a United Press man is relevant here: "Moley deflated himself," it read. "He did it completely, willingly, heartily. . . . [He] was innocent of the inflation of his own reputation. . . . The afternoon of his first day in London, he stood by the side of Hull . . . [and] made his act of deflation short and sharp and unmistakable . . . with the sure skill and efficiency of a great surgeon."

Hull made no attempt to conceal his appreciation. In token of it he drew me into his apartment and, for the first time in our strange association, did me the honor of speaking to me confidentially. The delegation, he told me, had been "disobedient and recalcitrant."

I assured him that he had the authority to discipline it. As head of the delegation he had every right to demand and insist upon conduct that would not impair the standing of the delegation as a whole. He pondered this for a moment in pleased silence.

Then he told me that he had no authority to deal with any question of importance in London and that he'd been compelled, whenever reference was made to these questions, to confess his lack of authority.

"No, no," I said. "You're letting these press stories get you down. It isn't a question of all or nothing. There's so much that can be done of a constructive nature here—perhaps not all that one could have hoped for, but still much that can bring you credit. The devising of a more efficient means of currency exchange, the devising of a more satisfactory international monetary standard, for instance."

After almost an hour of talk I left, happy that I'd done what I could to cheer him up.

That worry was for the moment, at any rate, laid to rest. Now I could get down to business.

The most pressing question seemed to involve the stabilization affair.

Roosevelt's rejection of the last of the stabilization proposals (put to him by our men while I was on the ocean) had left Warburg and Sprague at their wits' end and the gold-standard countries in a frenzy of panic. On the day that I landed at Plymouth, the pound had risen to $4.30; the guilder and franc were wobbling; throughout France, Italy, Belgium, Switzerland, and Holland there were rumors that gold would be forcibly abandoned and inflation resorted to; the dollar was at its greatest discount since our War between the States.

On the 28th, my first day in London, the pound reached a high of $4.43 and closed at $4.37½; the dollar was worth considerably less than eighty cents in gold; France and the gold-standard countries were groveling in the dust, howling for something, anything, that might save them from being pushed off gold.

England and France weren't talking about stabilization at $4.00 any more. They would have snapped at the kind of offer Roosevelt had suggested as a bluff on June 17th—an offer of unilateral action to keep the dollar from falling lower if the pound should go to $4.25. They would have fainted with relief had they known that Roosevelt had indicated to me on the *Amberjack* on June 20th that he'd be disposed to authorize stabilization with a high of $4.25 and a low of $4.05.

F. D. R.'s bargaining tactics had succeeded beyond his wildest imagining between June 17th and June 20th. The foreign nations now believed that he would not stabilize. They accepted this as a fact. They asked only that he make some gesture—some small gesture—that would in no way limit his freedom of action on the dollar and that would, nevertheless, tend to discourage the mad exchange speculation of the preceding three weeks.

The French, Dutch, Italians, and the other gold countries therefore drew up a short "declaration." On Wednesday they approached MacDonald and asked him to join with them in signing it. MacDonald indicated a general willingness to go along, provided the United States did too. Leith-Ross and Neville Chamberlain arranged to meet with a group of representatives of the gold countries at eleven o'clock on Thursday morning, the 29th. Sprague, Cox, and Warburg were scheduled to attend.

Of all this I learned late on Wednesday, the day of my arrival.

It was apparent that Thursday would be a critical day. As I reflected Wednesday night on just what it would involve, it seemed to me indispensable that Cox and Warburg be kept out of the impending negotiations. Cox, of course, had no leave to monkey with them at all. Warburg had received special permission from F. D. R. and, I knew, had worked doggedly to do his best during the preceding days. But messages signed by either Cox or Warburg would have to be shown to the entire delegation, and Hull himself had told me in our talks that confidential matters known to the delegation very soon became public property. I was not a member of the delegation. My messages, unlike those which Warburg and Cox signed with Sprague, would not have to be made available to all the delegates. Sprague, alone, as the special Treasury representative, might well handle communications back to Woodin and Acheson. But I had last-minute directions from F. D. R. on the subject of stabilization to impart. I had a direct means of communication, through the Embassy, not only to Woodin but, presumably, to F. D. R.—should that be necessary.

And so I sent a message to Hull early Thursday morning outlining these ideas and asking whether he did not think it would be wise to keep everyone connected with the delegation out of the negotiations over the proposed declaration and invest me with what responsibility he was able to. This last, he understood, was merely a gesture of courtesy. I was to act with Sprague on a matter within the jurisdiction of the Treasury because of my relationship to F. D. R. and Will Woodin. Hull's authorization was neither needed, nor, if given, valid. Still I wanted to ask for it for the same reasons I had spent two days publicly subordinating myself to him.

Hull's response was swift. When I arrived at Claridge's at 9:45 A.M. I found the delegation in meeting. The moment that I appeared, Hull announced that I was to join with Sprague in negotiations concerning what he called "temporary stabilization." To this move he was glad to give his formal consent. Cox and Warburg were to bring me up to date on the course of the negotiations and devote themselves thereafter exclusively to the business of the delegation. He added smilingly that while he himself, as a member of the delegation and as Secretary of State, had no authority to touch the negotiations into which I was stepping he could authorize me to call on anyone in the delegation or subject to its direction for assistance.

It was a warm answer to my question—more expressive than anything the Secretary had said the day before of his appreciation of my attempts to be friendly and helpful.

The meeting over, I went with Cox and Warburg to join Sprague and see, for the first time, a copy of the declaration of the gold countries.

I was amazed as I examined it. It was brief, simple, and wholly innocuous. It consisted of a rephrasing of one of the "instructions" given to our delegation by Roosevelt before the delegation sailed—a statement of policy that had been introduced into the Conference as a resolution on June 19th by Senator Pittman: this was a statement that gold would ultimately be reestablished as a measure of international exchange value, but that each nation reserved the right to decide when it would return to a gold standard and undertake stabilization.[33] The declaration also pledged the countries off gold to adopt such measures as they might deem most appropriate to limit exchange speculation and to ask their central banks to cooperate to that end.

The most fanatical inflationist could not have objected to this statement. Certainly Roosevelt—who had told me that if nothing better could be worked out he'd consider stabilizing between $4.25 and $4.05—would be overjoyed to learn that he had beaten the gold countries and England down to this. Still, it was not my job to suggest any such thing even to Cox and Warburg, much less to the foreign representatives.

Time was passing. Cox, Warburg, and Sprague reminded me that the scheduled meeting on the declaration would soon begin. Sprague and I ought to be starting out for it. But an instinctive caution, sharpened by months of risk, made me say that I preferred not to go into the meeting. Sprague might go, if he wished. I'd stay out and maintain my position of "liaison officer." Otherwise I was certain that the French would place an unwarranted interpretation upon the part I was playing.

The three were disappointed. Would I not be willing to see—wholly informally—just two or three of the conferees I already knew from the Washington conversations in April and May? I saw no impropriety in that. I'd be glad to see Leith-Ross of England, Jung of Italy, and, say, Rist of France, I said.

Leith-Ross, with his engaging canniness, the imperturbable and intelligent Jung, and Rist, quick and kindly, arrived after a few minutes. We had a brief and pleasant talk in which I explained that

[33] For a comparison of the texts, (1) of the fourth "instruction" given the delegation by Roosevelt, (2) of the Pittman Resolution, and (3) of the declaration proposed by the French and British on June 29th, see Appendix F.

I was acting merely as a conduit and indicated my willingness to *transmit for consideration* any suggestion their group might have. They understood perfectly. "You mean," said the blunt Leith-Ross, "you'll accept the declaration *ad referendum.*" "Precisely," I said. "I'll take it for transmission to the President—for *his* consideration. My transmission of it implies neither my advocacy nor my approval of it."

So the part I was to play was understood. It was never, from that moment on, in doubt in any foreign representative's mind but Georges Bonnet's (he was, at the time, Finance Minister and head of the French delegation), and MacDonald himself was to set Bonnet straight.[34] Its propriety was never brought into question in the United States except by newspapermen whom the clear distinction involved seemed to elude.

Leith-Ross, Rist, and Jung left for their meeting, and I returned to the Embassy to get the judgments of Keynes and Lippmann on the meaning and effect of the declaration.

Much to my surprise, directly after lunch, Leith-Ross appeared at the Embassy with Neville Chamberlain, Chancellor of the Exchequer.

That was my first meeting with Chamberlain. I was struck by the simple directness of the man, who was willing to waive all questions of precedence and come to confer with me, a minor official in my government. But he was a practical man. He told me that at the meeting, that morning, the British had toned down the innocuous declaration to a point where they felt sure that by no possible construction could it be held to impose even a moral inhibition on any steps the President might take to raise prices by monetary action. The declaration was completely harmless. But the representatives of the gold countries sincerely believed that it would end the panic of the Continental peoples which was now expressing itself in hoarding and in flight of gold. He had come to plead for the consideration and cooperation of the one man in the world, Roosevelt, who had it within his power to quiet the panic in the gold countries and turn the Conference itself to useful deliberations. He had come to plead not for his own government, whose immediate interests were not at stake, but for France, Holland, Switzerland, Italy, and the others.

This, apparently, was "appeasement"—a strategy for which Chamber-

[34] This was done on the basis of Sir Maurice Hankey's voluminous and authoritative notes. Hankey later told me that he read his notes to Bonnet and that Bonnet was compelled to acknowledge that I had accepted the declaration only *ad referendum.*

lain was later to become famous—appeasement, in this case, of Roosevelt.

I took the revised declaration he handed me then and read it carefully. Chamberlain was quite right. The declaration would commit Roosevelt to absolutely nothing except to ask the Federal Reserve to cooperate in limiting fluctuations due to speculation—a task simple enough since most of the big speculators in exchange were well known. *It did not mean stabilization.* Still, I suggested, informally, one or two minor changes of phraseology further devitalizing the limp document, so that it could not conceivably be interpreted as a promise, however vague, that the United States would forswear price raising by monetary action. Chamberlain assured me that the gold-country representatives would embody these few informal suggestions, and he did send me word the next day that the changes had been made.

Then he told me that MacDonald would like me to call on him at five o'clock. I telephoned Hull, informed him of everything that had happened since I'd left him that morning, and asked whether he had any objection to my accepting MacDonald's invitation.

There was none. And so, at two minutes of five on June 29th I walked up the staircase of 10 Downing Street, past the prints of all England's Prime Ministers, through the somber Cabinet room into the pleasant study that looks out over the Horse Guards Parade. MacDonald, who sat writing at a little desk near the windows, stood up and came forward to greet me. We sat down in large, comfortable chairs and began to talk.

Infinitely more emotional than Chamberlain, MacDonald described the European picture in more vivid terms than he. It was politically and socially indispensable that the governments of the gold countries have the simulacrum of general agreement on immediate currency objectives, he said. Their people's phobia on the subject of inflation was getting out of hand. These people had suffered the terrible consequences of uncontrolled inflation after the War or had seen their next-door neighbors suffer it. Fear of it, fear that the United States would push their currencies off gold and into inflation, was sweeping over Holland and Switzerland and France. The consequences of fear, unchecked, might even be revolution in those countries. The moment was critical. It would cost Roosevelt only a meaningless gesture to dispel the psychoses threatening Europe. Would I not tell him, in God's name, that acceptance of the declaration would not only save the Conference from possible wreck but repel the panic that held Europe in grip?

To this dramatic presentation I replied that I would gladly accept the declaration and transmit it to the President. I could not undertake to do more.

We left it that way, and I returned to the Embassy, where Sprague and Swope were waiting for me. Sprague sent off the declaration to Woodin, Baruch, and the President. I telephoned Acheson at the Treasury and Baruch in New York and asked them to meet, the next morning, at Woodin's house in New York, where he was lying ill. By then they would have the text of the declaration, presumably, and we could discuss it. So the President, just emerging from five days of fog in Lakeman Bay, could have the informed opinion of all his advisers on the subject before he made a decision. I arranged to call Woodin's house at 11:00 A.M. New York time (4:00 P.M. London time).

First thing next morning, Friday, the 30th, I brought Hull up to date again. He was pleased. At his request I went into the delegation meeting with him at nine-thirty and told those present, in a general way, what was up (without, of course, describing the terms of the declaration).

Then, impulsively perhaps, I suggested that when the President's approval was received—and knowing what F. D. R.'s state of mind had been when I left, I had not the slightest doubt that he would approve it—Hull himself meet the foreign representatives and tell them the news. I did this out of the most generous impulse in the world. I realized that, even discounting MacDonald's exaggerations, the situation in London was tense. Roosevelt's acceptance of the declaration would mark the end of two weeks of fears and alarms. It would be a moment of triumph. Whoever announced the news would receive the accolade of Europe and the United States. I wanted Hull, who had suffered so many disappointments and reverses, and who might still believe that he had suffered them because of my influence, to take the bows. Hull agreed.[35]

And now, Friday noon, it began to seem as though it would never

[35] It was to be one of the most bizarre pieces of irony that I've ever known that even this warm gesture would later be described by friends of the Secretary as an arrogant attempt to "convert him into a messenger." However, that was still in the future.

be four o'clock—time to speak to Woodin and the others. The hours of waiting went slowly, despite one or two distractions.

Couzens and Pittman lunched with us at the Embassy. During lunch I learned that Leith-Ross, Jung, Bonnet, and Bizet intended to call on me at three-thirty. I sent back word asking them not to come, since no answer on the declaration could conceivably come from the United States by then, and since Secretary Hull would, in any case, communicate the President's answer when it arrived. The four showed up anyhow—out of sheer anxiety, I imagine—on the pretext of wanting to show me the text of the declaration, as revised in accordance with my informal suggestions to Chamberlain and Leith-Ross the preceding afternoon, and also to show me the French translation of the declaration.

I found that, with characteristic subtlety, the French had twisted some phrases ever so slightly to make the declaration possibly capable of interpretation as stabilization. I went over the English version, compared it with the French, and insisted that the two be made to conform. They were—over Jung's cries that I was breaking his heart. I answered that he had a heart of gold, which was probably the reason it was breaking.

When they had left, I talked briefly to Couzens and Pittman, who'd been there when the four foreign representatives unexpectedly walked in, and whom I could not very well turn out. They both pledged themselves to secrecy about what they'd inadvertently heard—a pledge they scrupulously observed so far as I know. I now sent the President a copy of the declaration as finally revised.

Shortly after four o'clock Sprague and I called Woodin's house. Baruch, Acheson, and Harrison were seated at his bedside. I spoke for a minute or two to Woodin and Baruch and learned that, for some reason, they had not yet received the text of the declaration.[36] Still, they were prepared to consider its substance. I then put Sprague on the phone and he, as special Treasury adviser, described and discussed the declaration with the Secretary of the Treasury, the Under Secretary of the Treasury, the Governor of the New York Federal Reserve Bank, and Baruch, whom the President had chosen to "sit in" for me as his adviser.

In the course of this conversation there occurred one of the most

[36] The only explanation we were ever to find for this delay was the slowness of the coding and decoding process on both sides of the ocean. All messages of this kind, of course, were sent in code.

tragic moments in Woodin's long battle against his fatal illness. While the conversation was going on, with Baruch at the telephone relaying to Woodin what Sprague was telling him, Woodin lost consciousness. Baruch, Acheson, and Harrison feared that the end had come. They said nothing of this to Sprague. They just stopped talking. We thought the telephone connection was broken. Some minutes later the conversation was resumed by the others from a telephone outside Woodin's room.

It was to be the pleasure of certain newspapermen in London, who were informed that the length of this telephone call had brought the long-distance charges we incurred up approximately four hundred dollars, to announce that the call was so long because I had held the line open deliberately while I searched for certain documents. They never learned what had really happened. We didn't ourselves, until we returned to the United States. We only knew that, in behalf of Woodin as well as the others, Baruch gave us assurances that the acceptance of the declaration would be recommended to the President.

I called Hull immediately, informed him of this conversation, and added that it might be a good many hours before we had an answer from the President. F. D. R. was at Campobello, we'd learned, and Campobello was not connected by telephone with the mainland. That, plus the apparent delay in transmitting the text of the declaration even to New York, made it seem as though we would have a long wait. Hull spoke a bit fretfully of the meeting of foreign representatives that was scheduled for the evening. They would be disappointed at his failure to appear with the President's answer. I said that it wasn't to be helped. I would undertake to get in touch with the British and explain the circumstances. It would be most inadvisable, of course, for either of us to identify ourselves, by the appearance of overanxiety, with approval or advocacy of the declaration I'd transmitted. Hull agreed.

The suspense lay heavy on us all now. London and Europe were waiting on a President all but isolated on a little island off the Atlantic coast.

At eight o'clock in the evening (it was three o'clock in the afternoon in New York) Swope and I called Baruch, Acheson, and Woodin again. (Woodin had by now rallied from his earlier collapse.) They insisted upon knowing just what Herbert and I thought, personally, of the declaration. I explained that I'd accepted it only *ad referendum* and had not expressed my personal judgment of it to a living soul except Herbert. But since they insisted—and wholly unofficially—I was willing to say that by no stretch of the imagination, in my judgment, could it be construed as even a remote approach to stabilization. It could not possibly obligate us to ship gold. It would not check the steady rise of American prices in so far as that rise was based upon the sound revival of business. At most it would check only the ultra-speculative aspects of that rise. And that, Roosevelt had indicated to me on the *Amberjack*, he wished done. In brief, it would give the market the slight tap it needed now that prices had attained stratospheric heights; it would still leave Roosevelt free to do anything he wanted to do; it would be a better bargain than any Roosevelt had in mind when I last saw him, since it expressed no more than a detached, though sympathetic interest in the gold standard; and it would keep the Conference from breaking up as it threatened to do. I thought, I added, that there could be no doubt of Roosevelt's accepting it.

Baruch then answered that he, Woodin, Acheson, and Harrison heartily agreed. They had, at last, received the text Sprague had sent them and they had already sent a dispatch to Roosevelt urging that he accept the declaration for exactly the reasons I'd outlined. Baruch also told us that the dollar had risen slightly (the pound was $4.25 again) and that American stock and commodity prices were sagging a bit on the basis of rumors that a stabilization agreement had been reached. But, he added, that consideration will surely not weigh heavily with F. D. R. These rumors would naturally produce a speculative movement that would be corrected when the text of the declaration was made public. The conversation ended with the congratulations of Woodin, Acheson, and Baruch on what they called our "victory."

Now all of us—all Roosevelt's advisers on the subject—were definitively agreed that he should approve the declaration.

Shortly before nine o'clock we received a message that McIntyre would send us the President's answer from the mainland soon. For a happy couple of hours Herbert and I sat by the fireside in the Embassy talking contentedly.

But the hours continued to go by and there was still no word. So the torture of waiting really began. Sir Maurice Hankey came to the Embassy and sat waiting with us between eleven and one o'clock. I spoke to Hull two or three times during the evening.[37] He grew

[37] Incidentally, in one of those talks I explained how it had happened that Couzens and Pittman, who were at the Embassy for a purely social luncheon, had

increasingly worried by the delay as we talked. He began to remind me that he had not given me more than formal authorization to proceed on Thursday morning and had no real responsibility for what I had done since then. I, nervous myself by this time, had all I could do to be soothing. With the Secretary of State disclaiming responsibility for what I'd done, with the Secretary of the Treasury bedridden in New York, and with the President out of my telephonic reach and mysteriously silent still, I sat smoking cigarette after cigarette with Herbert until three or four o'clock Saturday morning.

Sleep was impossible. After a few hours of tossing, dressing again, and more waiting for the presidential message that was to have come "soon," I was called to the telephone. It was an encoding clerk in the offices of the American delegation. A message had just come through from Phillips! Phillips had learned by telephone (he did not say whether the President himself or a messenger had phoned from Eastport on the mainland) that the President would answer "as soon as possible" and that, meanwhile, we were to be warned to make no public comment.

This was ominous. The warning itself was strange. The fact that F. D. R. should communicate with me through Phillips rather than Woodin or Baruch was more inexplicable still. Was it possible that he had not received or had misunderstood the dispatch from Woodin and the others?

Now, extremely uneasy, I sent a cable directly to him referring to my conversation at eight o'clock, the night before, with Woodin, Baruch, and Acheson. I added that it was unlikely that the Conference would continue if he did not approve the declaration. This was the literal truth, as I saw it, and subsequent events were to prove the accuracy of that judgment.

Then I went to Claridge's. I met Hull on the staircase. He took me to his room and told me that "scads" of newspapermen (he did not name them) had just been telling him that the belief that I'd

---

been accidentally present when Leith-Ross, Jung, Bonnet, and Rist arrived, lest he feel the smallest affront over the incident.

I was particularly careful to do this because Couzens had been a thorn in Hull's flesh from the beginning. He had expressed to all comers in London his disagreement with Hull's policies and had threatened once or twice before my arrival to resign from the delegation. Hull had prevailed upon him to wait until I reached London, and then I had convinced him that his resignation would make still more acute the reports of confusion that had dogged the delegation since June 3rd. He had agreed, finally, to take a little vacation in Ireland or on the Continent instead, to avoid a public clash.

come to supersede him was still extant. Then, without pause, he went on to say that he had given up a seat in the Senate, which would have been practically a life job, to take the Secretaryship. This was followed by a review of the humiliations to which he had been subjected since March 4th.

I confess that my mind was more on the portentous message coming from the President than on the question whether Hull had made a prudent move in resigning from the Senate to become Secretary of State. I didn't, though, give my impatience any expression. I merely explained all over again that I had told him the truth about my mission and purposes on Wednesday and added that I had dealt with him as fairly as it was possible for one human being to deal with another.

That morning Michelson, the delegation's press officer, announced that Hull had had no knowledge of the negotiations on the declaration until five o'clock the day before. I expected as much, however.

Still the hours dragged on. At three o'clock Saturday afternoon Swope and I sat in the code room of the delegation. Practically everyone connected with the delegation was starting out for Cliveden to attend a garden party given by Lady Astor. Suddenly the coding clerk turned to us. The message from the President was coming through. I rushed out to find Hull. He was on his way out of the hotel. He received the news coldly. He would go to Cliveden anyhow, he said, and I could have his secretary bring him the message when it was ready.

So Herbert and I were alone with the coding clerk when the President's answer came.

Max Eastman says, "Humor is a kind of emotional chaos told about calmly and quietly in retrospect." But it is possible for the interval between the emotional chaos and the calmness of perspective to be very short, to be only a matter of seconds. Swope and I read the President's answer, looked at each other, and, I thank God, were able to laugh.

For the President's answer paraphrased and, in some passages, actually employed, the words of the memorandum Herbert had written and I had left with Roosevelt on the Amberjack *on June 20th. But that memorandum was an argument against rigid and arbitrary stabilization. And the declaration which I had transmitted to the President did not even suggest an approach to stabilization. The declaration was therefore rejected in terms that had no relation to what the declaration was about.*

The declaration indicated that the countries, in a general way, intended ultimately to return to gold, but that their hands were completely free as to when or how. The President, in his answer, made the extraordinary comment that the United States must remain free with reference to the stabilization of domestic prices in American money regardless of what foreign-exchange rates might be. This was incomprehensible to the experts who saw it.

To the passage in the declaration which provided that the governments off gold would ask their central banks to cooperate in limiting speculation, the President took exception on the ground that he did not know how governments could check speculation. That was too bad. It simply meant that he would have to learn (as, indeed, he did in the months that followed).

The President then went on to say—and here is one for the book—that so long as national budgets remained unbalanced currency would be unsound despite all efforts to stabilize. This was supposed to be a crack at France.

There was more, stating the case against a rigid stabilization which the declaration did not propose, but which the President, inexplicably, believed it did propose.

Our first thought, once we had collected ourselves, was that we must protect him at all costs. The message must be seen by as few people as possible. This was not Franklin D. Roosevelt, private citizen, saying that two plus two made ten. This was not even a man to whom we were both deeply devoted, and whom we wanted to save from the gibes of the informed. This was the President of the United States. And, as Bacon had said, "kings cannot err."

Because the President of the United States must not err publicly, if we could help it, we decided that his final suggestion—that the delegation issue a statement of his position—must be got round in some way.

We gave Hull's secretary a copy of the message and asked him to suggest to Hull that no comment about it be made beyond this: The President had rejected the declaration in its present form and a statement of the President's views would be given to the press by the Secretary of State on Monday. We also proposed that we get to work at once and prepare a statement justifying the President's rejection of the declaration.

That is what was done, to a degree. In an hour or so a terse, thirty-eight word report of the news was given out at Claridge's by Michelson, but not before the news had been served up at Cliveden—by whom I do not know—for the momentarily exclusive delectation of scores of distinguished guests. That polite company decided that the President's rejection constituted a repudiation of me. Was I not supposed to be the infallible index to Roosevelt's mind? Had I not urged him to accept the declaration? Had Roosevelt not refused to "endorse" me?

That kind of comment was blazoned in the newspapers of Saturday night, and for days, months, and years thereafter. But there was nothing I could do. In any case, there were more important things to ponder at the moment.

The American delegation was stunned. Hull himself—whatever his initial reaction—realized what the President's message meant to the future of the Conference. He was in no frame of mind to work on the difficult, the almost impossible, job of explaining Roosevelt's position without revealing the error of Roosevelt's message and without controverting views Roosevelt had recently expressed.

So, Saturday night, Herbert, Walter Lippmann, and I fell to work preparing the draft of such a document. The more we worked, the less we were able to understand how F. D. R. could have sent the message he did. We called Baruch to see if he could throw any light on what had happened. Baruch said that neither he nor Woodin nor Acheson could explain F. D. R.'s attitude. None of them had heard from him. Baruch added that F. D. R. was now aboard the cruiser *Indianapolis* en route to Washington with Louis Howe and Henry Morgenthau, Jr.

It was all that we needed to know. Now the picture began to make sense. Louis, who didn't know beans about monetary questions and who would naturally be concerned with the superficial public reaction to the sagging of stock and commodity prices on Friday; Morgenthau, whose rudimentary knowledge of monetary problems was largely provided by Professors George F. Warren and Frank A. Pearson (advocates of the absurd theory that changes in the price of gold would cause commodity prices to vary proportionately)—these had probably been F. D. R.'s advisers Friday night and Saturday. It was apparently the desire for some sort of commodity dollar that his answer bespoke.

Still, that was water over the dam. Herbert, Walter, and I worked until long after midnight and did achieve, finally, a rough draft on which Hull and the delegation agreed the next afternoon.[38] It was

[38] This draft was revised somewhat by Swope and Michelson Sunday morning. Several minor changes were also made in the delegation meeting.

conciliatory in tone. We hoped that it would soften the blow of the rejection and steady the reeling Conference.

For the Conference was breaking up.

The gold-country representatives had hastily assembled Saturday night and, though the soft-spoken Rist had emerged after two hours and intimated that they would not withdraw from the Conference, they were, in fact, prepared to quit if they were given no hope of cooperation in meeting their crisis.

More evidence—if more was needed—was a conversation that I had with MacDonald Sunday morning. At eight o'clock that morning of July 2nd MacDonald called and said, "This is the Prime Minister speaking. I am at Chequers. I am coming in at once to Downing Street. I must see you as early as possible. I will send Hankey around to get you." At ten o'clock Hankey guided me with great circumspection to the back door of 10 Downing Street. I was ushered upstairs to MacDonald's study and was not surprised to see that he was greatly agitated, for I'd realized as much from what he had said on the telephone. He frankly despaired for the fate of the Conference, he said. Could I tell him, in view of my knowledge of Roosevelt's methods, whether there was any hope that the President might accept some other kind of declaration that would satisfy the gold countries? I ignored, perforce, those of his remarks that related to my knowledge of Roosevelt's methods. I merely said that I was certain that Roosevelt did not want the Conference to crack up and, further, that I saw no reason why I couldn't transmit to him any other suggested agreements the nations devised.[39] Meanwhile, the statement of Roosevelt's position that Secretary Hull would make the next day would doubtless allay the excitement of the gold countries.

When I returned to the Embassy that Sunday morning, I found Elliott Thurston, the second press officer of the delegation, waiting. Thurston told me that Hull was even more upset than he had been late Saturday afternoon. In fact, Thurston said, Hull's realization of just what the President's message would do to the Conference was expressing itself in a kind of dirge of accusations against me. I ought to

[39] During that conversation I indicated to MacDonald my great concern lest my relations with Secretary Hull be clouded in any way by the fact that I had talked to him privately in this fashion. I asked him to make it clear that such contacts as I had had with him had been initiated entirely by him. He assured me that he would. He also added pointedly that he had had such difficulty in understanding what the wishes of the delegation were that he had sought me out to supplement the quite inadequate official means of communication between himself, as President of the Conference, and the United States delegation. To this I made no comment.

see him as soon as possible and get him to unburden himself to me. Thurston suggested that Mrs. Hull be present, too, so that her misapprehensions, which were many, might likewise be corrected. This last suggestion I vetoed. But I did see Hull before the delegation meeting Sunday afternoon.[40] I asked him to tell me in what way I had offended him. He failed to be specific. Then I said that it seemed to me that basically he felt I was trying to undermine his authority as Secretary of State. I made a long speech tracing our relations from the very beginning, describing why I had taken office in the Department of State, assuring him that I had no political ambitions at all, and so on and on. I seem to have convinced him, for the time being at any rate. After this talk there was no more unpleasantness in London.

The statement for his use was, to repeat, completed later that day. It was held for release on Monday morning.

But it was never to be made public. For by early Monday morning, July 3rd, a new chapter in this deplorable story had been written.

The President, steaming southward with Louis and Morgenthau on the *Indianapolis*, dispatched a message that reached London in the early-morning hours. It was the message that instantly became famous as "The Bombshell."

> I would regard it as a catastrophe amounting to a world tragedy [said the President] if the great conference of nations, called to bring about a more real and permanent financial stability and a greater prosperity to the masses of all nations, should, in advance of any serious effort to consider these broader problems, allow itself to be diverted by the proposal of a purely artificial and temporary experiment affecting the monetary exchange of a few nations only. Such action, such diversion, shows a singular lack of proportion and a failure to remember the larger purposes for which the Economic Conference originally was called together.
>
> I do not relish the thought that insistence on such action should be made an excuse for the continuance of the basic economic errors that underlie so much of the present world-wide depression.
>
> The world will not long be lulled by the specious fallacy of achieving a temporary and probably an artificial stability in foreign exchange on the part of a few large countries only.
>
> The sound internal economic system of a nation is a greater factor in its well-being than the price of its currency in changing terms of the currencies of other nations.
>
> It is for this reason that reduced cost of government, adequate government income, and ability to service government debts are all so important to ultimate stability. So, too, old fetishes of so-

[40] Key Pittman was present when I talked to Hull.

called international bankers are being replaced by efforts to plan national currencies with the objective of giving to those currencies a continuing purchasing power which does not greatly vary in terms of the commodities and need of modern civilization. Let me be frank in saying that the United States seeks the kind of dollar which a generation hence will have the same purchasing and debt-paying power as the dollar value we hope to attain in the near future. That objective means more to the good of other nations than a fixed ratio for a month or two in terms of the pound or franc.

Our broad purpose is the permanent stabilization of every nation's currency. Gold or gold and silver can well continue to be a metallic reserve behind currencies, but this is not the time to dissipate gold reserves. When the world works out concerted policies in the majority of nations to produce balanced budgets and living within their means, then we can properly discuss a better distribution of the world's gold and silver supply to act as a reserve base of national currencies.

Restoration of world trade is an important partner both in the means and in the result. Here also temporary exchange fixing is not the true answer. We must rather mitigate existing embargoes to make easier the exchange of products which one nation has and the other nation has not.

The Conference was called to better and perhaps to cure fundamental economic ills. It must not be diverted from that effort.

It was less the substance of this message that shocked us as we read it in Claridge's than its tone of belligerence.

What it said, in effect, was that the Conference, which had been called to discuss fundamental economic questions, had been diverted by the consideration of an immediate problem. That was true enough. What it was intended to do was to exhort the conferees to turn to long-time objectives, to see, for instance, whether they could not devise a formula whereby nations could maintain a stable internal price level at the same time that they adhered to an international monetary standard. That, too, was sound enough if one supposed, as I was willing to do, that human ingenuity might conceivably hit on such a formula.

But this scourging was to fall upon the backs of statesmen who, for no reason that they could see, had been denied the privilege of subscribing to Roosevelt's own views as embodied in the declaration.[41] It was to strike an adversary Roosevelt had already beaten. That was what would make its sting so sharp. Had he accepted the declaration on July 1st and then proceeded to lay down the law in this way on July

[41] See footnote, page 247.

3rd, the case would have been different. He was right in insisting that the Conference seek the ends he now described—provided he had not erred in rejecting the declaration two days before.

Parenthetically it should be said that, in the light of history, there are diverting touches in Roosevelt's "bombshell" message. For example, the passage that speaks of reduced costs of government as an element in the stability of currencies; the passage that speaks of Roosevelt's hope of attaining "in the near future" the kind of dollar that would have a fixed purchasing power; the passage that speaks of "the specious fallacy" of a probably "artificial stability in foreign exchange." There is not even need to inquire what Roosevelt and Morgenthau think of these passages today.

The cream of the jest was hardly apparent, though, on July 3, 1933.

The reading of "The Bombshell" completely demoralized Hull and all the rest of the delegation but Pittman. They were frank to say that they didn't know what it meant. They simply did not understand the references to the currency formula the President was suggesting. Warburg told me that he intended to resign because he neither felt that he could interpret the President's new objective—which seemed to be a currency based on commodity prices—nor believed that the President's ideas had crystallized sufficiently to enable the Conference to proceed.[42] The comments of the other delegation members, with the exception of Pittman's, indicated the same confusion and despair.

It was not possible to withhold this "bombshell" message. The President's tone left no doubt that he intended it to be given out as it stood. So it was. And, as Lindley puts it, Europe exploded with resentment and wrath. The Conference, in an uproar, refused to continue work. The gold countries determined on adjournment as their representa-

[42] Warburg did resign on July 6th, in a letter to Secretary Hull amplifying these views. "We are entering upon waters," he said, "for which I have no charts and in which I therefore feel myself an utterly incompetent pilot." (See Warburg's *The Money Muddle*. Alfred A. Knopf, Inc.; New York, 1934; p. 121.)

I have always felt that Warburg merited much more credit for his part in the preliminaries of the London Conference than has ever been given him. He came to Washington at his own expense, served without salary from March to May, and then went to London. There he served in the face of the most discouraging circumstances until all real hope of continuing the Conference was ended. That his views on monetary questions were at variance with the President's in July was the reason for his resignation; but, in fairness to him, it must be said that he made every effort to implement the President's purposes, so far as they were comprehensible to him. I am sure that the ultimate verdict of history will be on his side, although at the time I was much more willing than he to allow that the President's less orthodox views might possibly bear fruit.

tives asked sarcastically whether all knowledge of monetary questions was now located in the United States. The English and Continental papers in eight-column "streamers" shrieked their fury at the President's "preaching."[43]

Hull and the delegation were convinced that it was useless to go on. Late that ghastly day Hull went to work on a cable to the President describing the effect of "The Bombshell," saying that he felt the end of the Conference had been reached and asking for instructions.

That evening, at the Embassy, I tried to reach the President by telephone. I wanted to describe, myself, the desperate state of the Conference. I wanted to point out that the blame for adjournment at that moment would be laid on his doorstep. To spare him that and also, if possible, to further his apparently radically changed monetary plans, I had a measure to propose.

I felt that the only way to save the Conference would be to ask for a recess of from two to ten weeks. During that recess his ideas, which, it was clear, were wholly unlike the ideas he had held in May, could be put into specific form for consideration. Equally important, it would be possible to reorganize the delegation and its staff of experts. None of them was equipped to interpret what seemed to be in his mind except Pittman, who was familiar with novel currency ideas.[44]

Unfortunately I failed to reach the President. He was still on the *Indianapolis*. There was nothing to do, then, but to cable these sentiments, which I did. I knew that the delegation would hardly be pleased to have it set down in writing that Pittman was the only one of its members able intellectually and wholeheartedly to present the President's monetary ideas to the Conference. Still, I had been specifically

[43] Only Keynes, in an article, remarked that Roosevelt was "magnificently right"—on which I commented, "Magnificently left, Keynes means."

[44] Walter Lippmann, with whom I had not talked since Saturday night, reached this conclusion independently. In his dispatch to the *New York Herald Tribune*, published July 4th, he said: "Mr. Roosevelt cannot have understood how completely unequipped are his representatives here to deal with the kind of project he has in mind. For one thing, they do not know what is in his mind. For another, there is not among them a single man who understands monetary questions sufficiently to debate them. For another, they have been so frequently repudiated that they are demoralized. For another, they are divided among themselves. How can a delegation, which lacks authority, which lacks technical competence, which lacks unity, which lacks contact with the President, hope to undertake the kind of difficult negotiation for far-reaching reforms which the President desires? It cannot be done. Mr. Roosevelt's purposes may be excellent. He has completely failed to organize a diplomatic instrument to express them. If Mr. Roosevelt means what he says, he must send a new delegation to London which knows what he means and has power to act for him."

instructed by him on the *Amberjack* to give him an evaluation of the delegation's performance and now, if ever it was to be any use, was the time he must have it.

In order to protect the message as a confidential document, I indicated in the directions for its transmission that it was "Urgent, Confidential, Secret from Moley to the President Alone and Exclusively." Those were all the words to protect it that I found in the official handbook. I had no reason to believe that such a message would be pawed over by dozens of people. I had no reason to believe (knowing, as I did, the meaning of the term "liaison officer" and the absolutely confidential relationship to his principal a liaison officer enjoys) that an ambassador would make it possible for such parts of the message to be shown to members of the delegation as to suggest that I was commenting unfavorably on their general abilities rather than their understanding of the President's new monetary ideas.

This message was sent in the early-morning hours of Tuesday, July 4th. At eight o'clock MacDonald telephoned and asked me to come again to Downing Street.

I have rarely seen a man more distraught than he was that morning. He turned a grief-stricken face to me as I came in and he cried out, "This doesn't sound like the man I spent so many hours with in Washington. This sounds like a different man. I don't understand." He turned away and then he said, "A man told me this morning that it sounded like Lloyd George. And it does," he added bitterly. With a gesture of hopelessness, he went on to say that Roosevelt's action had wrecked the Conference. And then, with a curious kind of petulance, he began to speak of what the Conference meant to him. For years he had dreamed of such a Conference. Its successful outcome, he'd hoped, would be the crowning achievement of his long career. "The shadows," he said, were already "descending" around him.

Then came another change of mood. He grew angry. "Roosevelt cannot imagine what he has done to me—how hard it has been to stand between the frantic demands of the gold bloc, on the one side, and the reluctance of the United States, on the other. I give up now. I can do nothing. This thing is wearing me down. Only a day or two ago the King said, 'I will not have these people worrying my Prime Minister this way.' "

There was little for me to say. I did try to make it clear, however, that he must not take amiss the harshness of Roosevelt's language: I knew Roosevelt exceedingly well and he was, under certain circumstances, a man who did not do himself full justice because of his choice of language. Obviously, his feelings toward the objectives of the Conference and toward MacDonald himself were infinitely more sympathetic than his words had indicated.

It was no go. MacDonald refused to be comforted.

The anger and grief of all the foreign representatives became known to the delegation at ten o'clock that morning. Cox and Warburg, who had been designated by Hull to meet with them, reported that MacDonald had expressed himself in much the same terms that he had to me earlier in the morning. Colijn of Belgium announced that the subcommittees were refusing to go back to work. Chamberlain said it would be futile to hope for anything except to keep the merest shadow of the Conference alive. Colijn agreed that to continue the Conference would be a waste of time. Jung and Bonnet were for outright adjournment.

When Cox and Warburg had finished conveying this doleful news, there was a silence of two or three minutes. It was broken by Herbert, who spoke up and said that until a last, desperate effort had been made we should not give up. The part of wisdom would be to learn directly from the President what he wanted to do. Perhaps I could reach him now on the telephone. If he wanted to keep the Conference going, we must try to devise some means for doing it. Cox, Warburg, and several other delegates thought this would be utterly useless. Hull did not express an opinion. But he assented to the plan that I try to learn what the President wanted done by calling him.

Cox and Warburg were sent back to tell the Prime Minister that we were communicating with the President as soon as possible, and to ask the Prime Minister to take no action on adjourning the Conference until we were able to see what we could do. I tried unsuccessfully to reach the President. He was still on the boat.

So began the last anguished efforts to save the Conference, or rather to save Roosevelt from the onus of having wrecked what a month before he'd so enthusiastically hailed. Swope, Lippmann, Keynes, and I began to work on a restatement of the President's position in terms designed to draw together all the nations outside of the gold bloc. If the President opposed adjournment or recess, this would ease Conference tempers and prevent the gold countries from blaming Roosevelt for the Conference's ruin. The four of us talked over the problem. I gave the others every shred of knowledge that I could muster about the various economists—including Warren—who had probably influenced Roosevelt's thinking on the subject. We speculated on just what concessions to more moderate opinion his present state of mind would permit.

At 3:30 A.M. Wednesday morning, July 5th, Herbert began to copy on the typewriter our joint product. (Lippmann, Keynes, and I each tried to help with the typing process, but did so poorly that Herbert, in disgust, shooed us away and did the job himself.)

At 5:00 A.M. the call from Roosevelt finally came through. Lady Astor's guests on Saturday afternoon would have been bewildered to hear how it began. Roosevelt's greeting was breezy, warm, affectionate. And then, with the lightheartedness of a boy, he said that he had received my confidential cable of the preceding morning and appreciated my general size-up. Had the situation improved at all in the past twenty-four hours? I said that it had, to a degree. It would probably be possible to continue the Conference with a recess, if something were done to calm everyone down. If this was his desire, I had worked out a formula with Swope, Lippmann, and Keynes which he might be willing to accept, and which might do the trick. He quickly approved the plan. He wanted the Conference to continue. I was to send the text of the statement to him immediately.

Herbert and I sent it off and went to bed at six o'clock.

At nine-thirty we were again meeting with the delegation at Claridge's. Three cables had just come in from the President. One expressed his views on adjournment, the other dealt with the tariff, and the third with money. The delegation continued to be confused. Hull then called upon me, saying that I had something to offer for the consideration of the delegation. I replied that I wasn't at liberty to give the names of those who had worked on the draft, but that it constituted, in my judgment, an inoffensive statement of the President's views. It avoided the negative character of the "bombshell" dispatch and might bring into one camp, England, the Dominions, the Scandinavian countries, and the United States. The statement was then read.[45]

Secretary Hull spoke approvingly of our effort. The delegation members were enthusiastic.

At 4:00 P.M. that Wednesday the President called. He had the statement. He was prepared to accept it with certain minor changes—among which, with unconscious humor, was one designed to make a particular sentence "a little more polite." He wanted it understood that the Conference was not to adjourn: it was only to recess for a

[45] For text of this statement, see Appendix G.

sufficient time to let the experts of all the nations build up a program to implement this statement. There was no indication that he regretted having brought the Conference to this pass or that he appreciated our efforts to extricate him from that disagreeable position—even when Hull got on the phone and explained sadly that the Conference was in such a state the day before that it was "almost by accident" that we had prevented adjournment.

Still, with the first feeling approaching relief that we had had since Sunday night, Hull, Pittman, and I went to see MacDonald. Hull told him of our new statement and added cordially that I'd "directed" its preparation. I read it, then, at Hull's request. When I had finished, MacDonald blurted out, "Oh, Moley, tell me why this kind of message couldn't have been sent on Saturday. It would have saved the Conference. Maybe it will save it still. Will you give it to me now so I can present it to the others?"

We answered that there were still a few minor corrections to be made in it. But we agreed to release it at nine o'clock that evening.

Swope, meanwhile, had been directing the process of sounding out the representatives of the countries off gold, particularly the British Dominions. Their reaction was so favorable that we realized our plan would succeed. They would swing into line with us on this statement. That would not necessarily save the Conference, but it would make it impossible for the gold countries to force adjournment the next day and blame Roosevelt for it.

The statement—on the basis of which Hull made his moving plea, the next day, for the continuation of the Conference—was released at 9:00 P.M., as scheduled.[46] That moment marked my last direct connection with the Conference.

The next day, Thursday, the 6th, I said good-by to the delegation and talked with Hull at the Embassy. We were alone. I asked whether he was satisfied now about the good faith of what I had told him the morning of my arrival, Wednesday, and elaborated Sunday afternoon. He was, he said, completely satisfied. Then I asked him to give me any messages he might want to have taken to the President. He replied slowly, obviously choosing every word. Would I please ask the President not to change his policies again, because his sudden turns had

[46] President Roosevelt was to say of this in his *On Our Way*; *op. cit.;* p. 126: "Secretary Hull, with magnificent force, prevented the conference from final adjournment and made it possible, we all hope, for a renewal of its discussions in the broad field of international relationships."

been exceedingly embarrassing? Would I tell the President how difficult it had been to work with the delegation? Would I advise the President not to take up too many ideas all at once and not to give progressive Republicans too prominent a place in the administration, since they didn't seem capable of working with anybody? (This was a pointed reference to Couzens, which he then proceeded to elaborate.)

So we parted—Hull to go to the Conference meeting to make the fight on the lines drawn by the new statement, and I to sail home.

As I rode to Southampton, I had time to think about the mad eight days through which Herbert and I had been. It seemed to me that there was a bare chance that the Conference would go on. It would, at any rate, go on "twitching" for some days, as Warburg put it, before it rolled over and died.

It was fantastic, of course, that Roosevelt, who had let himself seem so eager, back in April and May, to have the Conference, should have put himself into the position of striking it down. He had made himself, first, when he agreed to let the Conference be held in June, the victim of his own enthusiasm. He had made himself on July 1st, when he rejected the harmless declaration on the grounds that it was a stabilization agreement, the victim of his own lack of knowledge. He had made himself on July 3rd, when he sent "The Bombshell," which he considered a way of scolding the Conference into a consideration of the problems he thought important, the victim of his own cleverness. He had thought that he, on the *Indianapolis*, understood the psychology of the conferees better than those who were in London. And statesmen cannot afford to be cocksure of their psychological insight.

As an independent person, and not as an agent trying to serve him, I certainly did not take the Conference's wreck to heart. At best I'd had no exaggerated hopes of what it might accomplish. It could be said that the United States had for once gone to an international conference without making ridiculous concessions. And I was gratified that the President's newly strengthened distrust of international "cooperation" even in its mildest form had been, at last, unmistakably proclaimed.

But as a man who had been sent, despite his reluctance, to do a specific job, as a man who had tried to serve Roosevelt faithfully, I could be neither indifferent nor pleased. Just for a moment there went through my mind the thought that Roosevelt must have known what the incidental effect of his rejection of July 1st would be. He, Hull, Woodin, Acheson, Baruch, Harrison, Swope, the foreign representatives, and a few painstaking newspapermen could know that no question of public endorsement or repudiation of me was involved in that rejection. But the rest of the world was thinking—and saying—that I had been kicked in the face and was now in the official doghouse. Roosevelt could not have helped but foresee that. Certainly Louis Howe must have. Suppose that Roosevelt hadn't, though. Suppose he had been surprised when it happened. Was it not possible for him to have set the newspapermen and the public right by a simple one-sentence statement of the fact when he returned to Washington? Or failing that, was it not possible for him to indicate to me over the telephone when he spoke to me some slight regret for the false impression that had grown up?

But this was a mawkish way of letting myself go—even to myself—I decided. It was the kind of self-pity I loathed in others. I must be as good as my word to Bernie Baruch. I had been expecting to be hurt for months. Now I was. So what?

Looking objectively at what Roosevelt had done, then, I reflected that the code that governs rulers in their relations with those who serve them has remained unchanged for centuries. It is known, but never officially promulgated—eternal and binding, but wholly implicit. The chief of a government does not move under the limitations of the normal amenities. He may regret it, but he proceeds on the basis of what is best for the state—kindliness to the contrary notwithstanding. Necessity and expediency loom large in such a code.

But while his latitude to hurt those who serve him is large, he himself is constrained by an iron yoke. He cannot fail, or he must, in all little things, be judged as he has judged others. He may do much in the interest of success. But he must succeed. Success is his warrant of freedom. But success is also his relentless, his inflexible judge.

What were Roosevelt's objectives? They seemed to be:

(1) To avoid shipping gold abroad.

(2) To avoid the drastic fall of prices in the United States.

(3) To have the Conference achieve a formula whereby nations could maintain a stable internal price level at the same time that they adhered to an international monetary standard.

(4) To devise, himself, "the kind of dollar which a generation hence" would have the same purchasing power "as the dollar value" he hoped to achieve "in the near future."

(5) To launch a sort of world crusade (hinted at in the "bombshell" message) for balanced national budgets.

We would see, I thought, as the docks of Southampton faded into the distance. We would see whether Roosevelt succeeded in attaining these five objectives.

We did see too.

(1) On the morning of Monday, July 17th, the President told me in the presence of Lew Douglas, "I've been thinking about the fact that the pound went as high as $4.84½ last week. I've just secretly ordered the Federal Reserve to export gold if it goes above $4.86." (To which I could not resist replying, "Then the only trouble seems to have been that I was two weeks too early.") On August 29th the President issued an order permitting the shipment of newly mined gold to foreign buyers.

(2) On July 19th prices collapsed violently. For two days thereafter stocks and commodities crashed downward. The time of reckoning and readjustment had come at last.

(3) On July 27th the Conference "recessed" after six weeks of accomplishing almost nothing.

(4) On October 22, 1933, the President announced that he was accepting the Warren theory. On January 15, 1934, he repudiated the Warren theory, which had proven an abysmal failure, and requested a stabilization fund of $2,000,000,000. On March 12, 1939, the Federal Reserve Board advised Congress, "Experience has shown . . . that prices cannot be controlled by changes in the amount and cost of money. . . . Cash and prices do not move together."

(5) The Roosevelt Administration is now operating on its seventh unbalanced budget.

Time was smiling over our shoulder.

CHAPTER VIII

LOST DIRECTIONS

THOSE strong ties of sympathy that nourish a personal relationship seldom snap between one second and the next. They twist and strain and fray so long before they crumble away that the moment of their final dissolution is anticlimax.

I think it was that way with Roosevelt and myself.

On Friday morning, July 14th, at nine o'clock I saw Roosevelt for the first time in twenty-four days. His breakfast tray had just been carried out, and he was sitting up in bed with the newspapers of Washington, Baltimore, and New York scattered on the counterpane and on the floor.

"Hello," I said.

"Hello there," he answered cheerfully. "Say, have you seen the papers for the days that you were gone? My statement certainly got a grand press over here!"

There was nothing to say to that, directly. It was too much part of what had happened in the days before. It was important only because at last I knew beyond the possibility of doubt that it would set the pattern of the days ahead.

No one listening or watching would have guessed that anything untoward had occurred. The talk that followed was quiet and friendly enough. I gave Roosevelt a report of my stay in London slowly, methodically, and with a frankness tempered only by a warning I'd written to myself at the head of my notes: "R. M.—don't seem to be offended by anything that happened." I made no secret of my belief that he should have accepted the declaration on July 1st. He did not question that or any other part of my recital. I doubt that anything anyone might have said to him that morning would have ruffled his egregious satisfaction and good humor. He made no comment about what had happened to me except to say it was too bad "we" couldn't have foreseen that I'd be greeted as the "savior" of the Conference.

And from this he went blithely on to a discussion of how the N.R.A. was being swamped with draft codes, how business was improving, what the next move on foreign debts should be, et cetera, et cetera.

I was to be taken back, it seemed—back into the "warm bed" from which I'd presumably been catapulted.

Louis was less subtle when we met that day. With the air of a man who felt he'd administered a resounding spanking to someone who badly needed it, he said, "Well, what happened to you over there? Did they take *you* into camp?"

I answered tartly, "If you'll consult the foreign representatives, I think you'll find them rather less convinced about my pliability than you seem to be."

Louis chortled and said, "Well, pliable or not, the declaration you sent would have been a moral obligation to stabilize."

"If that were true," I answered, "then the 'instructions' to our delegation and the proposal in the Pittman resolution, which F. D. R. approved, also placed us under a moral obligation. What about the repudiation of that?"

"Franklin hasn't done anything so popular as his rejection of the declaration since the bank crisis," was Louis' answer.

I knew it would serve no purpose to discuss the matter further with Louis. He had told me, by implication, what I wanted to know—or rather he had confirmed my sense of what the morning talk with Roosevelt meant.

A harsh reality had pierced the soft texture of personal relations. There were no regrets about the way that things had gone in London. No interest was manifested in setting to rights the general misconceptions that I had been "repudiated" and that I, rather than Roosevelt, was at odds with Hull. As I left the White House, that day, it was clear that I was expected to take up the many duties I had laid aside—to take them up humbly, to take them up gladly, because I had presumably been chastened by a series of events for which no one in authority had criticized me.

The only flaw in this neat scheme was its transparency.

I thought of resigning that night, and many times in the day or two that followed. But a sounder impulse made me wait.

To leave the administration then, precipitately, would involve explanations that were better unmade. And yet not to give them would be almost worse. To resign, directly after the mess in London, would suggest a "break" over policy. When domestic prices cracked, as it was obvious they must at any moment, my resignation would be embarrassing to the administration—would be a bit of ammunition added to the stores Roosevelt himself had manufactured for the administration's critics in the preceding month. The New Deal, which I'd helped create, compelled my loyalty now. I couldn't serve *it*, at the moment, by a refusal to continue serving its leader.

There was another and more selfish reason for going along quietly for a while. Having done my job through the "Hundred Days" and in London with hardly a thought of my own public relations, it was now necessary to consider them. The launching of the journalistic venture into which I planned to go required a favorable, friendly press. It wouldn't do to undertake it in the midst of rumors about what I'd done and what had been done to me in London.

The first of these ugly rumors was, of course, the "repudiation" story. Only the resumption of my familiar routine in Washington could help down that.

The second story, which hit me on the day of my return to Washington, I decided to quash directly. It came in the form of a dispatch from London stating that the bills for Swope's and my expenses there had been refused payment and that Hull was sending them back to Washington for consideration. Specifically mentioned were charges for the airplane sent to Cobh and for transatlantic telephone calls. Carefully unmentioned was the fact that the bills were being referred to Washington at my own request, made in London with the explanation that Herbert Swope and I wanted to go over the bills and hand them in with our checks for the airplane and personal telephone charges. The inference was that we'd attempted to saddle the government with frivolous charges and that Hull or Bingham was preventing this outrage.

It was clear that there'd been queer work either at the Embassy or at the delegation. Even Billy Phillips was shocked—apparently not so much by the fact that Herbert and I were being made the victims of a false impression as by the unprecedented discourtesy involved in giving any information about an envoy's expenses to the press. Phillips at once cabled Hull, asking how such a thing could have happened. The Secretary answered that the episode was unfortunate, but that he'd not succeeded in discovering how the misinformation had got out. He did not then state this publicly. Nor did Phillips. It was only after I gave an explanation to the press that a belated official statement was made.

And now came a whole flock of rumors as, with every boat from Europe, scattered members of the delegation and its staff drifted back, like Napoleon's army from Moscow.

After I left London, it appeared, the delegation had been shown a copy of my confidential cable to F. D. R., folded over so that only a paragraph was visible and so that its sense was wholly distorted. The story was that I had grossly insulted the entire delegation. I produced the complete text of the cable and handed it to the delegates who came to me and said they had seen a part of the message. They made it clear that the cable, seen as a whole, was an accurate statement of the facts—that no one in the delegation except Pittman was equipped to present the President's new ideas about money aggressively to the Conference either because they didn't understand them or because they didn't believe in them. But, meanwhile, the damage had been done. The story had been printed everywhere.

The legend grew. There were stories of wild roistering in the monastic quietude of the Embassy. There were stories of rudeness to the Secretary. There were stories that, on seeing my confidential cable to the President, Hull had cabled his resignation. There were stories that I'd planted spies within the delegation. There were stories that I'd betrayed official secrets to spies—French and Chinese, male and female—in the traditional dime-novel manner.

All were fabrications. None was worth answering. Most of them couldn't be answered without a plunge into those depths from which they sprang. And yet it was hard to resist.

There is nothing quite like the realization that such stories about one are going the rounds. "It is impossible," as H. G. Wells has said, "to challenge the assault, get it out into the open, separate truth from falsehood. It slinks from you, turns aside its face."

But it was even more unnerving to observe the pattern one's acquaintances followed at such a time. I have read somewhere that when one of a herd of animals is wounded the others come prodding at the wound with their horns until the victim falls. I don't know whether that is true. But it is certain that human beings behave that way. Not only men and women I scarcely knew, but "friends" would question me about the rumors—to see how I reacted, I suppose.

Three people were conspicuous for their abstention. Mary Harriman Rumsey, Vincent Astor, and Averell Harriman—the three people with whom I was to associate upon my resignation, the three people in the world who had the most right to be concerned about the stories—never mentioned them to me. It was as though the stories didn't exist. And when, in late July, I referred to them obliquely as a reason for deferring my resignation, these three, whom I hadn't even known six months before, urged me with the devotion and loyalty of lifelong friends to forget about the stories and let them announce the founding of our magazine.

I still thought, for their sakes and my own, that it was best to wait.

It was at this juncture that Louis (whom Roosevelt, at my request, had not told of my agreement with Mrs. Rumsey, Astor, and Harriman) popped up with one of his "ideas."

It has been characteristic of the New Deal to send officials far away from Washington on long expeditions when awkward situations present themselves. That technique was first tried out with me. It was later used in the case of Hugh Johnson—with no better success. Hugh was asked to go to Europe and investigate methods of recovery there in August, 1934. His answer was blunt and to the point. "Mr. President," he said, "of course there is nothing for me to do but resign immediately."[1]

Louis' scheme for me late in July, 1933, was more ingenious. It was, in fact, a product not only of his political acumen but of a romanticism induced by a lifetime of reading detective stories. Louis told me that he had been talking with Secretary Ickes about the administration of criminal justice in Hawaii: a certain *cause célèbre* a short time before had revealed pretty incompetent conditions there, the administration of justice on the island was difficult because of race mixtures, the system needed a thorough overhauling, no one in the United States had had as much experience in this particular field as I. Would I not, in short, go to Hawaii for three months?

I would not, I said.

Louis did not give up, however. In a few days he came through with another plan. This time, it was presented to me by the President. (I suppose it had become obvious that I wasn't going to permit Louis to feel that he had any responsibility for directing my services.) The President pointed out that a wave of kidnapping was sweeping the country. The Department of Justice was not wholly equipped to meet it.[2] It might be well to have someone outside the Department partici-

[1] *The Blue Eagle from Egg to Earth; op. cit.;* p. 387.

[2] Part of what was in Roosevelt's mind, I knew, was a doubt about the desirability of continuing J. Edgar Hoover in office—a doubt put there by Louis. When the administration had come into office in March, there were many rumors that Hoover was to be ousted in favor of a Democratic politician. I had vehemently defended the magnificent work of Hoover to the President and Louis. I like to think that

pate in a reconsideration of the Department's equipment and also to work out, with the Department, plans for legislation to be submitted to the next session of Congress. The Attorney General, with whom my relations were always excellent, would be happy to participate in this plan.

This was more practical from my point of view than Louis' first idea. In fact, the more I thought about it the better it seemed. In the field of criminal-law administration my reputation was established. No one could deny it. The news of such an assignment would serve to blanket the highly colored rumors out of London. It would turn the tide of publicity. It would give me a few weeks' breathing spell before I resigned.

I agreed, and on August 2nd the President announced the news. I would, he said, retain my status as Assistant Secretary of State and return to the Department of State when I had finished this special assignment.

This time I took occasion to protect every avenue of publicity, and Homer Cummings, William Stanley, Joseph Keenan, and Edgar Hoover, who were all heartily with me, helped. The press I got, except for a very few side shots to the effect that this assignment was an attempt to separate me from Secretary Hull, was astonishingly enthusiastic. I succeeded in preparing the way for a rational public reception of my long deferred resignation.

Despite all this, the hot, sticky month of August in Washington was pretty depressing. Hull returned, friendly enough in conversation with me, but obviously saddened and shaken by his London experience. A seemingly endless battle between the adherents of Professor Warren and those of us who were sure his ideas were unworkable began within the administration, and I had the sense of getting nowhere in my discussions on that subject with F. D. R. The word-of-mouth gossip about London persisted, together with the proddings of most of those to whom I talked.

Late in August I prepared my letter of resignation, setting the effective date at September 7th, so that I would round out six months in office. On Sunday, the 27th, I took the letter up to Hyde Park, where F. D. R. was staying. We agreed that I would continue my survey for the Department of Justice after I'd left the government and hand in my report sometime during the winter. We talked at

---

what I did in August, 1933, gave me the opportunity to strengthen Hoover still more and to work with him in the development of plans that proved to be successful.

length, then, of the plans Mrs. Rumsey, Astor, Harriman, and I had made. F. D. R. was enormously interested. At last he turned to his table, picked up a pencil, and began to prepare his answer to my letter.[3]

When he had finished, I said, "Now I have resigned. But I am not going to leave Washington voluntarily in this way without defending myself, if that is necessary, with regard to complaints about my conduct that Mr. Hull is rumored to have made to you. We've never discussed the London trip in its details. Not a word of dissatisfaction has come from the Secretary directly to me since his return. But there has been talk of threatened resignations cabled to you and the like. I have a right to ask whether he has made any specific complaint and, if so, to answer it here and now."

Roosevelt answered, "In all honesty, he hasn't. He did hand me an entire report on the Conference which is upstairs and which I haven't read. Suffice it to say that in our conversation he made no complaint except one. That was that one day in London you talked to the Prime Minister without asking his permission."

I recited the facts which I've given in detail in the preceding chapter. And then I said, "With reference to the truth of this, I don't ask you to accept my word. But I suppose you will have in mind the fact that, though I've served you in every conceivable kind of confidential capacity, you never had occasion to doubt what I've said. I would just as soon have things out in a three-cornered discussion with the Secretary."

"Of course, that isn't necessary," he said. "So far as I'm concerned the matter is closed."

And that's the final answer to the story that my resignation was demanded by Secretary Hull as the price for his failure to resign.

After a moment of thoughtful silence Roosevelt said, "Please stay here," picked up the telephone, and put a call through to Secretary Hull, who was in the Virginia mountains on a holiday. He told Hull that I was resigning to edit a magazine, and then suddenly, without warning, handed the phone over to me and asked me to speak to Hull. I did, elaborating what the President had said about my plans. The Secretary answered cordially, expressing his surprise and good wishes. He would issue a statement at once, he said.

And so he did. He had "had no information beforehand that Pro-

[3] For the text of my letter of resignation and the President's reply, see Appendix H.

fessor Moley contemplated resigning," he said. He had never at any time "offered the slightest suggestion to the President or to Mr. Moley relative to any present or future change of the official status of the latter as Assistant Secretary of State." He wished me "every success in [my] new field." He would "at all times gladly cooperate with [me] in every feasible way both in that field and in all possible joint efforts in support of the President."[4]

It was a statement which, in generosity and tact, was everything that could be asked. So far as I know, it was the literal truth.

I spent only a day or so of the week that remained of my official status in Washington. I cleared out my personal belongings and took to New York my two personal assistants who, I may say, left Washington for New York with profound relief and pleasure. They still work with me. The third member of my staff, K. C. Blackburn, was transferred to the White House to develop a clipping bureau under Louis Howe's direction and, subsequently, became head of the N.R.A. Division of Press Intelligence. The fourth, Arthur Mullen, Jr., stayed in the State Department for a while and then went into George Peek's office. The fifth, Mrs. Helen Cook, remained in the State Department.

When, on September 7th, at four o'clock, my job was finished and my assistants were suitably placed, I went into Secretary Hull's office to say good-by. We talked briefly about the situation then confronting him in Cuba. I said I hoped he would not question the sincerity of my wishes for his future good fortune. He replied in a similar vein. And so I passed through the long hallway and down the stairs, out into a world that looked brighter than it had for months.

2

The newspapers dutifully carried the story of the resignation as it was given them. Editorial comment ranged from praise of my service to an acidulous crack in the *New York Times* which likened me to Lucifer falling from heaven.

The day after the resignation was announced we called the newspapermen to Vincent Astor's office to describe the details of our plans, which had been so long in preparation. Perhaps it might have been

[4] Thus the words of Mr. Hull refute the subsequent statement of Mr. Farley (*Behind the Ballots*. Harcourt, Brace and Company; New York, 1938; p. 217) that there had been a "break" between myself and Hull and that "obviously the President was bound to defer to the latter . . . to prevent a Cabinet break."

wise to explain their history then, for it would have dissipated, once and for all, the myth of a forced resignation.

Early in March Mary Harriman Rumsey, a woman of fabulous energy and dynamic intelligence, came to my office and told me that she wished, with several others, to buy the *Washington Post.* If I would agree to retire from the government and assume the job of editor, she said, she would undertake to get together a group of people who were able and willing to buy it.

I thought it over for some weeks and, around mid-April, indicated that I was greatly interested. A day or so later Mrs. Rumsey arranged a meeting of her brother, Averell Harriman, whom I already knew, and Vincent Astor, whose acquaintance I'd made the day of the Zangara incident in Miami. Both Astor and Harriman were enthusiastic about Mary's plan. They offered to put up what we then thought would be the purchasing price of the *Post.*

A number of discussions followed. By the end of April we had reached a definite agreement.

Of all this, I kept Roosevelt constantly informed.

Mary Rumsey then brought into the group V. V. McNitt, a veteran newspaperman with whom she had been associated in a syndicate some time before. McNitt was the head of the McNaught Syndicate, and, curiously enough, I'd contracted with him, before I knew of his old association with Mrs. Rumsey, to write a weekly article for the newspapers. McNitt was designated to look into the status of the *Post,* to determine what the property was worth, and to offer a bid when the *Post* was auctioned off. Meanwhile, we decided, the contract to do the weekly pieces was all to the good. It would serve as a way of introducing me publicly in a new role and it would tide me over some sharp personal financial shoals until I actually stepped out of office.

I've referred earlier to the precarious state of my exchequer that spring and to the fact that my savings, outside of such insurance as I carried to protect my family, had largely been depleted between March, 1932, and March, 1933. Beginning in March, 1933, it was true that my modest salary as a professor had been supplemented by the salary of Assistant Secretary of State (less fifteen per cent under the Economy Act). But from that time on I was also maintaining two establishments—my own home and my temporary quarters in Washington—making a weekly train or plane trip to and from New York to teach and incurring the expenses incident to receiving, at breakfasts and dinners, men with whom there was no other time to confer in the

President's behalf. Altogether, my financial position was such that I was actually compelled to borrow money for the London trip from Art Mullen, Jr.

Several friends who knew of this state of affairs had suggested that if I wanted to continue in the public service I could count on them for loans which, in effect, would be sustaining gifts. One of them had told me that such contributions to the support of public men hadn't been unknown in the past, that no sinister suggestions were involved in his offer, that the only thing in which he was interested was serving Roosevelt by making it possible for me to stay in office. I was grateful, of course, for such generous assurances of confidence. But the subsidizing of public officials by private sources didn't jibe with my notions of the independence a public servant ought to maintain. In any case, that was no solution for a man determined to get out of public office.

In early May, while McNitt was looking into the *Washington Post* situation, Mrs. Rumsey, Astor, Harriman, and I decided that if we got the *Washington Post* we would establish, in connection with the daily, a weekly national magazine. There hadn't been for years a journal of the sort which we had in mind—primarily concerned with public affairs, independent in its political affiliations, presenting opinion as well as fact, liberal in outlook, and standing on its own financial feet. All deeply sympathetic with the objectives of the New Deal—objectives which we felt any enlightened American government, Democratic or Republican, must strive for—we decided upon the enterprise as a means of serving those objectives.

We failed to get the *Post*. After careful consideration of all the factors involved, we'd placed a limit of $500,000 on the bid McNitt was authorized to offer. A number of bidders appeared, two of whom, William Randolph Hearst and Eugene Meyer, put the bids beyond our limit. The property went to Meyer, finally. And early in June, before I left for London, we decided to go ahead with the weekly as soon as I got back.

Only my determination to stay in Washington until I could make an exit with reasonable grace caused us to modify our plans. But while I waited, the others went ahead with McNitt, so that on August 28th, when we spoke to the newspapermen, we were able to be very specific in describing what we intended to do.

The only sour note that greeted our announcement appeared in a Washington column, which had it that Vincent Astor, because of his friendship with Roosevelt, was building "a golden bridge" to remove a liability from the administration. But even this seemed funny to us. We'd learned a good deal in the preceding weeks about the cost of launching and promoting a publishing venture. The idea that anyone in his right mind would pay so fabulous a price for the simple act of removing me from public office seemed, at once, a flattering tribute to my influence and to the Astor-Harriman largesse.

It can be said now that when the first number of *Today* appeared in October, we were all appalled. Printed on rather grayish stock and hideously illustrated, it proclaimed the amateur, even to our parental eyes. We realized suddenly how very green we were, how much we had still to learn about the publishing business.

And so, for weeks and months we did our experimenting in the daylight of public view, learning our lessons not from experts in publishing (who told us that we weren't likely to get a circulation of over 25,000 on the basis of our publishing formula) but from bitter experience. Our first number ran about 100,000. After the curiosity sale declined, we ran through the winter at around 50,000. We improved our format and moved up, in the spring, close to 75,000. In the course of three years we reached a fairly stable circulation of around 100,000.

Ultimately we discovered that a modification of our formula, in order to incorporate in one periodical signed opinion, a compendium of the news, and an appraisal of the significance of the news, was desirable. To achieve that, we merged, early in 1937, with *Newsweek*, which was then a weekly digest of news. With a good deal of regret we dropped our title *Today*, which Arthur Brisbane had generously permitted us to use, and took the name of *Newsweek*. Then we enlisted the services of a superlative publisher, Malcolm Muir. After six years the success of which we dreamed began to be a reality.

All through the lean years the interest and enthusiasm of the magazine's backers never flagged. Mary Rumsey's death through a tragic accident, a year after we'd begun publication, was a blow to us all, for she had been indefatigable in her devotion to the magazine. But Astor and Harriman continued the uphill journey.

My job was never that of assembling the magazine. It was to write a signed piece every week. In the course of the six years that I've done that, neither Astor nor Harriman has ever, by the slightest suggestion of approval or disapproval, sought to temper or modify my expressions of opinion. What I have written or said or done has been my own business.

Such a relationship is precious beyond comprehension. Life and politics, with all their heartaches, disappointments, and disillusionments, have many compensating values, but none to offer for the loss of independence. I cannot do more than place this tribute in the record to these two men—descended of families which have so often been castigated as symbols of the destructive individualism of a bygone era in American life: I have yet to meet anywhere, in the world of education, politics, or in business, men with a stronger tradition of fair dealing, with a more profound respect for intellectual integrity, and with a more gallant faith in the right of each human being to his own opinion.

3

Just as I began to realize what a full-time job the magazine was going to be, I found the Washington routine reestablishing itself—easily, naturally—but with important differences.

The official trappings were gone. Roosevelt and I were American citizens, equal before the gods of democracy and equal before the law. What I gave of service, I gave to a common point of view—a shared belief in policies which, long before the gold-braid days, I'd helped formulate. There had never been any "boss" or "skipper" business between us. Now there never could be.

The books of mutual obligations were balanced, closed, and filed away. What I could do, I would. Friendship was there. I knew no way of reasoning that friendship depended upon unimpaired confidence, and certainly Roosevelt seemed completely innocent of any awareness that my confidence had been shaken. I knew how to help him think and how to make his thinking articulate. It was generally recognized by those who were close to him that I could insist upon his thinking a bit longer before the inevitable moment when his pragmatic oversoul summoned him to action. That, I told myself, was good for the country, for him, for me, for everyone who cared about those policies the New Deal represented.

And so when, before I had been out of office two weeks, I was asked to help him think over what he should say at the American Legion Convention in Chicago, I responded willingly. So, too, when I was asked to come to Washington on October 22nd. Over the telephone on the 21st I was told that the President had decided to adopt the Warren plan and announce it in a fireside chat the evening of the 22nd. Could I be at the White House the morning of the 22nd and help put the speech into shape? Clearly, I was not being summoned to argue. Roosevelt knew my views as of late June, July, and August. He had decided against them.

Ironic overtones were sounding somewhere in my consciousness as I walked into the White House study that Sunday morning and found, seated in a circle, George Warren, James Harvey Rogers, Henry Morgenthau, Jr., Dean Acheson (Woodin was still Secretary of the Treasury, but away), Henry Wallace, Henry Bruere of the Bowery Savings Bank, and one or two others.

F. D. R. began to dictate a statement of the Warren ideas. Rogers interrupted to argue against the drastic application of the theory that commodity prices went up and down automatically with the price of gold. The President waved him aside and went on dictating. Dean Acheson's eyes met mine. We both shrugged almost imperceptibly.

At one point in his dictation the President hesitated. He had just been saying that this step he was taking was not merely an offset to a temporary fall in prices but a move toward a managed currency. Now he obviously wanted to restate that idea more cogently—to put a snapper at the end of his paragraph. He said, "This—now let me see . . . This policy—no that won't do . . . This policy . . ." He looked hard at Warren. There was no response.

"This," I suggested quietly, "is a policy and not an expedient. Is that how it should go?"

"That's it!" he exclaimed, and the old ease came into our collaboration.

It seemed as if, after months, some mental log jam had broken.

When, with Henry Bruere, I put together the bits of dictation during the noon hour, Warren fluttered over the creation much as he might have watched a hatching experiment in the poultry laboratory at Cornell. He was clearly suspicious of me. But I was inexorably true to his thesis. It was put into such clear-cut language that the world could always know just what it was. I had no responsibility for it. The public didn't dream that the adviser who had "fallen" two months before was there. My conscience was clear. I had repeatedly argued against the scheme to F. D. R. I didn't think the Warren plan would work. On the other hand, I knew it would do the country no harm for just that reason. I was right. It didn't work, and it didn't hurt anything—except Warren.[5]

[5] One of the apocryphal stories told for decades on the Cornell campus about Warren had it that when a farmer told Warren about a herd of Holsteins that had

Thereafter, for two and a half years, there was scarcely a message or major speech in whose preparation I took no part. During that time I saw Roosevelt almost weekly in Washington—sometimes for part of a day, sometimes for two or three days at a stretch, occasionally staying at the White House, most often stopping at a hotel. The record of my trips for this purpose, beginning in December, 1933, is as follows:

For 1933—December 8th; December 15th; December 22nd and 23rd; December 29th-31st.

For 1934—January 2nd and 3rd; February 16th; February 26th and 27th; March 3rd; March 9th and 10th; March 16th and 17th; March 23rd and 24th; March 30th and 31st; April 13th and 14th; April 19th; April 25th; May 2nd; May 9th; May 21st-23rd; May 28th and 29th; June 6th and 7th; June 12th and 13th; June 15th and 16th; June 26th-29th; June 30th and July 1st; July 20th; July 27th; August 5th-12th (to meet the President at Devil's Lake, North Dakota); August 17th; August 29th; September 28th-October 1st; October 10th; October 17th; October 23rd and 24th; November 7th; November 13th; December 7th-9th; December 14th and 15th; December 19th; December 20th; December 23rd-25th; December 27th-31st.

For 1935—January 7th; January 11th and 12th; January 25th and 26th; January 28th and 29th; February 4th and 5th; February 7th-9th; February 17th and 18th; March 8th-10th; March 22nd and 23rd; March 29th-31st; April 13th; April 17th and 18th; April 20th and 21st; April 24th; April 26th-28th; May 4th and 5th; May 10th; May 13th; May 15th; May 17th; May 31st; June 3rd and 4th; June 7th; June 14th; June 17th; July 3rd; July 17th; August 11th and 12th; August 17th-19th; August 30th; September 24th and 25th; November 10th and 11th; November 17th and 18th; December 20th.

There were a good many other trips, scattered between, to Hyde Park whenever Roosevelt was there.

Needless to say, there was no reimbursement of any kind from the government or the Democratic National Committee for the expenses involved in these trips. The newspapers scarcely know of them. My name never appeared on the White House calendar. I never gave interviews. I came and went by the little back door to the Executive Offices, slipped into the Cabinet Room and thence through Missy Le Hand's

become prize stock after only twenty years of breeding, Warren whipped out pencil and paper and said it couldn't be done in less than three centuries. The farmer insisted that it had been done. Warren insisted that his figures proved it couldn't be done. Well, said the farmer, look at my herd. Warren checked his figures, and allowed that he might have been 272 years out of the way the first time.

office into the President's—a route unwatched by the reporters who spent their time around the White House. All this, at a time when some of the newspapermen who professed to purvey "inside stuff" about the Washington scene were referring to my "complete disappearance" from public life—one of them going so far as to remark pontifically, "There is nothing so dead in Washington as a resigned official."

Among the things that I was asked to do, in those years, there were a number of assignments like that of October 22nd. I'd be called in to put together ideas against which I had argued passionately. I was summoned, in such cases, as a technician at speech construction, just as I'd be called in if I were a plumber and a pipe needed fixing. That was worth doing so long as Roosevelt still respected frankness, still left the door open to disagreement. For every time I would be asked to put clarity into statements of which I thoroughly disapproved there would be two or three times when it was possible to modify or head off a step entirely. For all practical purposes, then, we were back where we had been during the campaign.

But soon there were other assignments—wholly divorced from the process of formulating policy in speeches.

Late in December, 1933, for instance, Roosevelt spoke to me of his intention to get securities-exchange legislation through the coming session. I reminded him of Sam Untermyer's bill, cast off as excess baggage in the final drive to wind up Congress during the "Hundred Days." But he would have none of Untermyer's bill. He suggested that I get someone else to prepare one. So, somewhat reluctantly, I called in Tom Corcoran and Ben Cohen.

Corcoran, I had first met in April, 1933, when Felix Frankfurter recommended him as an assistant. I had no need for his services then, planning, as I did, to get out of Washington. But I was favorably impressed by what Felix told me of Corcoran's record in the Harvard Law School, as secretary to Justice Holmes, and as one of the swarms of young lawyers in the R.F.C. Corcoran himself, on inspection, proved to be nimble-witted, well-informed, eager to work, and exuding that ambition that so often drives young men to solid achievement. Only a certain ineffable agreeableness, a way of saying "Sir" two or three times in the course of a five-minute conversation, a whispering deference, seemed exaggerated. But I had known enough cultivated Irish (including my own grandmother) to recognize the durable fiber underneath this cloyedness, the slyly superior eyes above the puckering nose and smiling mouth. There was no doubt that Corcoran had gifts which could be usefully employed and, as he assiduously kept alive his contact with me after I'd left Washington and, as I knew that he had become a warm friend of Cohen's since the days when Cohen and Landis had drafted the Securities Act, I asked him to call on me with Cohen.

Cohen had returned for a spell to New York and his lawyers' lawyer practice, after the passage of the Securities Act, only to be snapped back into the legal staff of the P.W.A. on the recommendation of Frankfurter and Corcoran. Corcoran had, by this time, achieved no small success in placing young Harvard Law School graduates, recommended by Felix, in strategic posts at the Labor and Interior Departments and the R.F.C. But of all his "kids," as he called them, Cohen alone had come to be recognized as his equal, his partner. Cohen's superior legal ability inspired a kind of worshipfulness in Corcoran. But Cohen's sensitiveness, his taste for the solitary, his intense and ingrown spirit, his indifference to his own comfort (not to say his pleasure) also seemed to appeal to some paternal instinct in Corcoran. It had become Corcoran's self-appointed task to watch over and care for this strange ascetic. Those who interpreted their association as that of "front" man and scholar missed its inner reality. It was a combination of a man who loved life, gloried in manipulating people, and of a man who feared life, despised compromise with reality.

These two men were in constant, almost daily, touch with Frankfurter. His function, so far as they were concerned, had come to be more inspirational than anything else. Felix was a patriarchal sorcerer to their apprentice, forever renewing their zeal for reform and their pride in fine workmanship. That their zeal and their pride would sweep them into political depths far beyond their mastery, as it did the apprentice in the medieval legend, he did not dream.

Nor, I must confess, did I, in January, 1934. But I did know what the kind of dogmatism with which they were imbued had made of the Securities Act the preceding April and May. That was why, after I asked Cohen and Corcoran to draft the Securities Exchange bill, I carefully described their abilities and limitations to the President. Cohen was a magnificent legal draftsman, I said. Corcoran might keep Senator Fletcher and Congressman Rayburn supplied with arguments when the fight over the bill began. But both would require watching, or their exuberance would get out of hand.

The President agreed and asked me to direct the fight for the Act. I did—by telephone from New York between trips to Washington.

With Rayburn I worked to make the Act more reasonable than its twin. It was, too, when we'd finished with it, although Richard Whitney, who led the onslaught of propaganda against it, shouted and pounded tables about its stringency. Together, F. D. R. and I planned the compromises that made the bill's final passage possible. Cohen and Corcoran, who had no contact with the White House then except through me, grumbled darkly about the "denaturing" of their bill. But they obeyed orders loyally enough, and there was no show of rebelliousness until they learned who were the members of the new Commission that was to administer it.

I had asked the President to talk over these appointments with me because, since the time I had assisted him in formulating his New York State parole system, I had seen so much good legislation for which he fought partly nullified by the appointment of poor administrators. At that very moment he was in process of frittering away his Communications Act in the same familiar way. It was clear that the Securities and Exchange Commission might be transformed into a purely perfunctory body if it fell under the influence of those interests it was supposed to supervise. Or, equally bad, it might fall under the domination of men who had no knowledge of the practical operation of the stock exchange.

The President listened to a recital of these facts good-naturedly and asked for a list of recommendations. This I laid before him early in June, 1934. It read as follows:

STOCK EXCHANGE COMMISSION MEMBERSHIP

MEMORANDUM

1. *Kennedy*	The best bet for Chairman because of executive ability, knowledge of habits and customs of business to be regulated and ability to moderate different points of view on Commission.
2. *Landis*	Better as member than as Chairman because he is essentially a representative of strict control and operates best when defending that position against opposition from contrary view.
3. *Mathews*	Familiar with operation of blue sky laws and with present Securities Act. He is a Republican from Wisconsin and failure to take him over would antagonize Republican Progressives in Wisconsin.
4. *Ben Cohen*	He is as able as Landis and more experienced.

He has participated to a greater extent than anyone else in the drafting of both Securities and Stock Exchange Acts. His personality would gain friends as people grew to know him. Enormously well thought of by Judge Mack, Frankfurter, etc.

5. *Paul Shields* — Expresses progressive ideas about regulation by law. Strongly recommended by Averell Harriman. Was associated with Dillon, Reed and probably would be strongly recommended by Clarence Dillon.

6. *Gordon Wasson* — A resident of New Jersey. Handled foreign securities for Guaranty Company. Has acted as liaison between Wall Street and Landis, Cohen and Corcoran, because his friendship with them was known downtown. Knows securities business and the act thoroughly, having helped in its drafting. Very well liked by Treasury and Commerce. Would certainly be recommended by the Guaranty and the Stock Exchange and therefore would be acceptable to Wall Street.

7. *Frank Shaughnessy* — Hiram Johnson would be an excellent judge of him. He is well thought of by Charles B. Henderson of the R.F.C. who knows him.

8. *Judge Healy* — Could be counted upon to be sound and liberal in his interpretation. However, he would be a better member of the Federal Trade Commission.

Party Affiliations:
Democrat—Kennedy, Landis, Cohen, Shaughnessy
Republican—Wasson, Mathews, Healy

Some days after I'd submitted this list, it developed that Ferdinand Pecora desired intensely to be Chairman of the new Commission. I added his name verbally to the list.

So the matter stood in mid-June, when the President told me he had practically decided to appoint Kennedy Chairman. Meanwhile, friends of Landis and Pecora had been waging a spectacular campaign in their behalf. Joe Kennedy, when he was mentioned in the newspapers, was often described as a Wall Street speculator whose appointment would shake the confidence of the public in the administration. The President began to waver somewhat.

He was particularly upset by a discussion he had with Roy Howard of the Scripps papers on June 30th. I had flown down to Washington that morning with Roy. We spent most of the trip discussing Kennedy. Roy was against him. I argued that it seemed to me exceedingly unwise to reject Kennedy simply because he had some professional experience in the field with which the legislation dealt. Finally, when I saw Roy couldn't be budged, I asked him to go to the President and present his point of view.

Roy saw the President. He left the White House to launch an editorial which, so far as I know, appeared in none of the Scripps-Howard papers except the late edition of the *Washington News*. It advised against the appointment of Kennedy.

That editorial I found lying on F. D. R.'s desk the evening of the 30th. Looking at it distastefully, he said, "Send for Kennedy. I'll get Baruch in." (Baruch happened to be at the White House.) I got Joe, who was at the Shoreham Hotel raging over the newspapers of the day.

The four of us sat down. The President pulled my memorandum out of the basket of papers on his desk. "Kennedy," he said, without looking at Joe, "is first on the list here. I propose to give him the five-year appointment and the Chairmanship."

Kennedy, who'd been deeply hurt by Roy Howard's editorial, rose to his feet and said, "Mr. President, I don't think you ought to do this. I think it will bring down injurious criticism."

At this point, knowing what was in F. D. R.'s mind as well as if he had put it in writing for me, I said, "Joe, I know darned well you want this job. But if anything in your career in business could injure the President, this is the time to spill it. Let's forget the general criticism that you've made money in Wall Street."

Kennedy reacted precisely as I thought he would. With a burst of profanity he defied anyone to question his devotion to the public interest or to point to a single shady act in his whole life. The President did not need to worry about that, he said. What was more, he would give his critics—and here again the profanity flowed freely—an administration of the S.E.C. that would be a credit to the country, the President, himself, and his family—clear down to the ninth child. (And in the job he made good on all he said that night.)

That ended the matter, and the President proceeded to the other names.

Landis was given the three-year appointment. Mathews, who, with Landis, had been administering the Securities Act at the Federal Trade Commission, was given the four-year appointment. The President passed over the next name on my list—a circumstance I've always regretted, because Cohen had earned appointment to the Commission: he, more than anyone else, had been responsible for the draftsmanship of the two Acts the Commission was to enforce. Healy, the President designated for the two-year term and Pecora's name was written in at the end of my list with the words "one year" after it.

These appointments were to be announced the next day, July 1st. On the 2nd the President was to leave for a long vacation trip to Hawaii. Knowing that both Landis and Pecora wanted to be Chairman of the S.E.C. and that, under the law, the Chairman was elected by other members of the Commission, I suggested that there might be some slip in getting Kennedy made Chairman unless the President made his wishes known. He agreed, laughingly, and scrawled in pencil a note addressed to Landis, Mathews, and Healy, a majority of the Commission, informing them of his desire.

It was significant that when I called Landis, told him of the President's wishes about Kennedy, and asked him to convey this information to his fellow appointees, Landis demurred. It was necessary for me to explain that I had a note from the President. Did he wish to see it? I asked. He did. Well, then, I said, he should see it. I was placing it in Joe Kennedy's hands. Joe would bring it to the first meeting of the Commission.

But infinitely more portentous than Landis' reaction to the news about the S.E.C. was Tom Corcoran's. When I told him who the President's appointees were, he exploded with indignation about Kennedy, winding up his tirade with the words, "Oh well, we've got four out of five anyhow."

"What do you mean by that?" I asked. "Aren't all five satisfactory appointees?"

"What I mean is that four are for us and one is for business," he replied.

I answered at length, and with some heat. I didn't regard the social order as being divided between business, on the one side, and some mythical "us" on the other. I had no class-struggle concept of the reforms that were going on in Washington, I said, and neither did the President. If Tom and his friends did, if as public servants they conceived of themselves as warriors in a battle against business, I should like to know it. Kennedy, as well as other members of the Commission, was appointed to work for the people of the United States—not to direct class struggles.

Tom looked like a misunderstood cherub. I'd got him wrong, he said. He was sorry. He couldn't begin to say how very, very, very sorry.

The apologies were so abject I decided I'd really flown off the handle. The incident faded from mind. It was not to be recalled for twelve months, for Tom could be discreet. Then, on a lovely late spring evening in New York, he remarked, "Fighting with a businessman is like fighting with a Polack. You can give no quarter."[6]

4

On August 7, 1934, Arthur Mullen, Sr., boarded the President's train at Devil's Lake, North Dakota. He described to F. D. R., Louis Howe, and me a critical political situation that existed in his state of Nebraska.

Congressman Edward R. Burke was running against Governor Charles Bryan for the nomination to the Senate. Bryan had the support of a strong political machine and, while Burke was popular, he was not at all certain of the nomination. Bryan represented a type of populistic radicalism with which the New Deal certainly had no sympathy. Burke, intelligently progressive, deserved whatever support the President felt he could give him. Wouldn't the President, Mullen asked, indicate a preference between the two candidates?

The President was noncommittal. Louis Howe was equally vague. Finally Mullen drew me aside and said, "If the President won't endorse Burke, will he, in some way, give expression to his approval of the definition of the New Deal Burke has made? It has been widely published in the West."

This seemed to me to be a good way to solve the problem. The statement was sound and eloquent, and I took it in to the President. He read it and exclaimed, "That's the best definition I have seen yet of the New Deal. I'll be glad to quote it in my Green Bay speech. If it helps Burke incidentally, so much the better. If it doesn't, I'll have endorsed a statement of my objectives that I'm proud of."

[6] As I look back at this remark, it seems to epitomize much that has been wrong with the procedure of the lawyer-minded New Dealers of the past six years. They see government operating successfully not through the process of consultation, compromise, and harmonious adjustment but rather through the litigious process. This implies that the art of government is a battle between the lawyers of the Lord and the lawyers of business. It assumes, wholly without justification, that businessmen are never concerned with the achievement of proper governmental regulation—that they aren't, even when they sincerely think they are. In the end, these assumptions cannot help but create, as they have created, class feeling of the most intense sort. And needlessly. For there is no reason why honorable and progressive businessmen should be made to feel that the government is not *their* government too.

Burke's definition—which ended with the words, "The New Deal . . . seeks to cement our society, rich and poor, manual worker and brain worker, into a voluntary brotherhood of freemen, standing together, striving together for the common good of all!"—became the peroration of the President's Green Bay speech. Burke got the Democratic nomination to the Senate.

In the years since, I have grown to know Senator Burke well. We were together on one occasion in 1937, speaking against the President's Court plan to an audience in New York. After the meeting I asked Burke when he began to feel that the President was abandoning that definition of policy on which we'd all agreed in August, 1934. Without a moment's hesitation Burke answered, "June, 1935—ten months later." Burke's recollection checked almost exactly with mine. By mid-June, 1935, I, too, became aware of a change in Roosevelt—a change so radical I couldn't help but face it.

The story of that change is, to me, the important portion of this narrative.

Change is relative, and can only be measured in terms of a fixed starting point. Wednesday, June 6, 1934, will do as well as any. On that day I sat with F. D. R. in his office and surveyed what he had accomplished since his inauguration. We were laying out not only a series of speeches to be made on his vacation trip to the West Indies, Panama, Hawaii, Oregon, Bonneville Dam, Glacier National Park, Fort Peck Dam, and Green Bay but two addresses to be made before he left Washington. The first was a message to Congress for delivery on June 8th. The second was a fireside chat scheduled for June 27th or 28th.

His was a record, we decided, with which he might well be pleased. In less than a year and a half he had all but completed the New Deal's legislative program. The only major addition that remained was a social-security program. When that had been worked out by the experts and translated into law, at the next session of Congress, the New Deal's legal framework would be complete. He was about to embark upon a stage of constructive revision, of administrative improvement and consolidation.

The speeches that we prepared were written in that mood.

The keynote of the message of June 8th was the simple statement: "Our task . . . does not require the creation of new and strange values. It is rather the finding of the way once more to known, but to some degree forgotten, ideals and values. . . . Among our objectives I place the security of the men, women and children of the Nation first."

The fireside chat of June 28th disclaimed innovation for the sake of innovation, emphasized unity, "harmony," "orderly, peaceful progress."

The speech at Green Bay on August 9th again stressed cooperation. "The processes we follow in seeking social justice," said Roosevelt, "do not, in adding to general prosperity, take from one and give to another. In this modern world, the spreading out of opportunity ought not to consist of robbing Peter to pay Paul. In other words, we are concerned with more than mere subtraction and addition. We are concerned with multiplication also—multiplication of wealth through cooperative action, wealth in which we all can share."

Perhaps Roosevelt's tone that summer was determined by my influence. But I doubt it. There was not the smallest hint that he did not sincerely share the convictions I expressed to him and in my editorials. There were no reservations when we discussed the future. He agreed wholeheartedly that some of his reforms (particularly the N.R.A.) had been pushed through too swiftly for adequate consideration and that their administration needed overhauling. He recognized that extremists among his supporters might "gum up the cards" (those were his own words to me on July 1, 1934). He admitted that the conservative members of his party had followed him a long way out of the accustomed grooves of their thinking and that the very fact that they had been loyal to him—loyal in the sense that a disciplined party organization can be loyal—indicated the indispensability of party unity as a means of political achievement in the United States. He realized that his function henceforth was twofold: as party leader, to keep his political support unified and, as President, to bind up the real and imaginary wounds inflicted by his revolutionary reforms.

It was clear, that summer, that wholly aside from the precise merits of the case a great majority of businessmen felt that the harness of the New Deal was chafing the business animal in too many places to permit an increased volume of production and reemployment. I felt that a sympathetic effort ought to be made to readjust the tensions in order to eliminate these irritations—that this ought to be done even though many of the constrictions about which businessmen complained were purely imaginary. We were dealing with a question of psychology—which meant that we must recognize quietly and reasonably not only what was true but what businessmen thought was true. Measures of far-reaching importance had fundamentally altered, during the first year and a half of the administration, the ways in which business had to be conducted. Business habits of generations had to be changed overnight to meet the new rules. It was only fair to slow down the pace of reform while business caught its breath and acquainted itself with the new order of things. Every political instinct that I had pointed to the soundness of such a course. Late in July I described it in an editorial that I called "Some Notes on Confidence."

Soon after my return from the trip to Devil's Lake a man named Allie S. Freed presented himself at my office. We had met casually during the preceding winter in connection with the work of a movement to combat religious intolerance in which we were both interested. But we never discussed national politics until Freed, who had been interested by the "Notes on Confidence" piece in *Today*, came to see me in August.

Freed was a businessman. He had never been what is called a captain of industry. He wasn't a leader in national business organizations. But he did have a wide acquaintance among businessmen. He knew what they were thinking. The battles he had been through, the scars he had received, and the blows he had struck had given him a tough, practical grasp of realities. Moreover, he was a vehement Roosevelt supporter whose enthusiasm for the New Deal policies would have done credit to an Alben Barkley on the stump.

Freed told me that he had been trying futilely to explain to his anti-New Deal friends how unjust some of their complaints were, how truly conservative, in the best sense of that word, were the repairs on the economic machine the New Deal had made. Would I, he asked, come to a dinner to which he would invite some of his friends and explain to them the fundamental objectives of the New Deal and the legislation that had been passed in furtherance of these objectives? In the give-and-take of conversation I could clear up many of their misapprehensions and learn, at the same time, which of their criticisms seemed reasonable. Such a dinner—small, informal—would serve as a means of justifying the New Deal to businessmen. If I thought it useful, after the first dinner, he would like to have five or six more. If there were anyone I should like invited, such as Rex Tugwell, for instance, he would be delighted to have him come. In the main, his object was to let some of his business friends examine a few New Dealers carefully, to see whether the horns and hoofs they reputedly wore were discernible at short range.

I agreed to attend such a dinner, provided it was understood that my presence lent it not the slightest official sanction. I would not come as a representative of the President, wouldn't, in fact, even tell him of the dinner. I would come as a free agent—as the editor of a magazine that was slowly acquiring standing in the country[7] and as a known supporter of the President's policies.

So began what newspapers later called, although Freed generously sent out the invitations and paid the bills, "the Moley dinners."

The first took place late in August—on the 23rd, to be exact. I agreed to attend a few others, partly because the first went so well and partly because it seemed a useful, though limited way of counteracting the attempts of the newly formed American Liberty League to convince businessmen that they must "fight" the "radicalism" of the New Deal.[8]

Freed's dinners took place at intervals of three or four weeks through the autumn. Donald Richberg, Rex Tugwell, Dan Roper, and other officials came informally. In all, more than a hundred businessmen attended—among them men like John D. Biggers and Charles R. Hook, who have since been given places on the small list of White House business friends. These men talked freely—asking questions, unburdening themselves of their grievances. I answered, trying to present the Roosevelt point of view, to suggest ways in which their differences with the various governmental agencies might be conciliated, and, above all, to caution them against anything smacking of bitter-endism. It was, in general, a helpful interchange of viewpoints.

Eventually the news of these little affairs leaked out to the newspapers, which promptly interpreted them as an attempt by the President to "feel out" business. This was a fine piece of irony. For just about the time this report gained currency, I began to have difficulties in Washington on the subject—not from the President directly, it must be said (I'd told him privately of what I was doing, in September, and, while he hadn't encouraged it particularly, he said it could "do no harm"), but from all those around him.

A newspaper columnist close to the White House criticized the dinners as fascist and suggested that businessmen were conniving to put me forward as leader of a fascist movement.

Morgenthau, still smarting over the beating the Warren plan had taken, struck out with the remark, "Ah, hobnobbing with the big boys?" when we met at the White House.

[7] It was just about then that *Time* referred to *Today* as "the most widely quoted magazine in America."

[8] Curiously enough, the formation of that organization was announced by Jouett Shouse on the same day that Freed had his first dinner.

Harry Hopkins asked—and he wasn't being consciously funny—if I had been able to learn, from my "associates" in New York, whether it was true that every time the President made a speech the Morgan partners met, decided whether its effect was bullish or bearish, and telephoned their decision to the editors of the New York papers and the presidents of the big banks.

Tom Corcoran called in alarm from Washington. He understood what I was doing, he said. Why, one of Felix's best friends was the conservative Lord Eustace Percy! But his "kids," his hundred and fifty "kids" in Washington who looked upon me as a guide and mentor (which, of course, was nonsense), had all required explanations. And if it was so hard for *them* to understand what I was about, what must *others* be saying? In fact, he knew what others in Washington were saying, and it was pretty awful. He then rattled off a list of names and specific comments.

This net reaction was so fantastic that, out of sheer irritation, I almost joined a committee Freed organized later that autumn. I sympathized with the purpose of his "Committee for Economic Recovery," which was made up of a number of those who had attended his dinners and who believed in continuing, in an organized way, the promotion of business-government understanding. But calm reason suggested that I take no part in it. It was one thing to go as a man's guest to informal dinners, and quite another to direct or participate in the work of a committee.

Freed understood perfectly, and took pains to announce that I was not associated with his committee. We remained warm friends, and it made me very happy indeed to see that, long before his sudden death in 1938, he was accepted by official Washington and by the President and Mrs. Roosevelt as the genuinely able, public-spirited citizen I had always found him to be.

But awareness of the atmosphere in which Roosevelt was living that October of 1934 gave me a rough idea of what might conceivably happen in Washington to the policy of unity and "harmony."

And so, when I was asked to assist Roosevelt in the preparation of a speech to be delivered at the American Bankers Association's annual meeting, and was told, in passing, that Morgenthau and Hopkins would participate in the drafting of the speech, I knew in a general way what I'd be up against. The particulars, as they developed, were beyond imagining.

With Roosevelt's consent I brought in Frank C. Walker, then Executive Director of the National Emergency Council. Frank was sympathetic to the "harmony" program of June, July, and August, and agreed to help me do battle with Hopkins and Morgenthau. The four of us—Walker, Hopkins, Morgenthau, and I—sat down in the President's study on October 23rd, the day before the speech was to be delivered.

At once Hopkins and Morgenthau began what has come to be known in political jargon as the "needling" process—that is, the process of recounting information or suspicions in a way likely to irritate or vex a man with respect to others. For over an hour they regaled F. D. R. with stories of business antagonism to him. The President listened, his face stiffening. I broke in from time to time, of course, but without being able to deflect the torrent.

Finally, I managed to remind the President of the well-known fact that the American Bankers Association had expressed the desire to make the occasion of his speech a hatchet-burying ceremony. Francis M. Law, the outgoing president of the Association and a Texas Democrat, was scheduled to make a speech sympathetic to most of the administration's banking reforms. There was no reason why the President's message should not be equally conciliatory. Besides, it had been arranged, at the President's special request, that Jackson Reynolds, of the First National Bank of the City of New York, would introduce the President. I understood, I said, that Reynolds' speech was to be friendly. (I did not learn until long afterward that the President had already seen Reynolds' speech and, through a secretary, had sent Reynolds word that he thought it was "perfect.")

At this point Morgenthau shifted to the edge of his chair and announced, with a look of triumph, that he had a copy of the Reynolds' speech and that it was enough to make a man's blood boil. The copy was then handed to me, and I was asked to read it aloud.

Obviously, it was designed as a friendly greeting. But there were two passages to which Morgenthau and Hopkins took particular exception.

The first one was an allusion to a clash between Scipio and Hannibal in Africa, before which unsuccessful peace efforts were made and in which one army was destroyed and the other decimated. There was a good deal of confusion among those present as to whether the passage meant to suggest that Mr. Roosevelt was the brilliant Carthaginian or the victorious Roman. There was also, I regret to say, only the vaguest notion as to which won the battle of Zama. Still, the objection was made that this passage implied that, in meeting the bankers, the President, representing the government, was put on an equal plane with them.

The second passage referred to the fact that when the President was a student at the Columbia Law School Reynolds had been his teacher. I was about to ask Morgenthau whether he didn't perceive that the reference was intended as a humorous one when I noticed the expression on F. D. R.'s face. He had a baleful look. It was obvious that public reference to his law studies wasn't calculated to improve his good humor. Apparently he didn't regard them as among the most significant achievements of his career.

After heated discussion I prevailed on Morgenthau to try, tactfully, to get Reynolds to take these two references out of his speech. The President relaxed somewhat and agreed to make his own speech pleasant and conciliatory.

But Morgenthau had done a good job. F. D. R. began to dictate a draft that was more like a thistle than an olive branch. When he had gone on for an hour or so, it began to seem as though there would be nothing short of a Kilkenny fight the next night at the bankers' meeting. I cautioned him a dozen times without effect.

Sometime after midnight of the 23rd I gathered up the President's dictation and went back to my hotel, deeply discouraged over the prospect but determined to try again the next morning.

By 10:00 A.M. of the 24th I had put together a friendly speech. With the aid of Missy Le Hand, who has always had a way of banishing distrust and bitterness from the President's mind, and without the accompaniment of catcalls Morgenthau's and Hopkins' presence seemed to involve, I was able to persuade him of the merits of the new draft. The speech, as included in the President's published papers, is headed "The Time Is Ripe for an Alliance of All Forces Intent upon the Business of Recovery."

But to some of the bankers, on the 24th, the time must have seemed about as ripe as a green apple.

While the President was finally agreeing to sound the note of moderation, Morgenthau, over at the Treasury, was all but undoing my work. Angrily, Morgenthau summoned Jackson Reynolds to his office. When Reynolds arrived, he found Morgenthau sitting in state in his office, the central figure in a half circle of co-inquisitors and aides. There were Under Secretary Coolidge, General Counsel Oliphant, the Treasury public-relations director Mr. Gaston, and a stenographer with a poised pencil. Facing this formidable array was a vacant chair.

Reynolds was directed to be seated. Without any preliminaries Morgenthau announced that if Reynolds should deliver his speech as it then read he would be "mobbed"—"torn limb from limb." Morgenthau's remarks were hardly calculated to elicit a calm answer from a man of spirit. Reynolds rose, remarked that it would probably be best if he did not make his speech at all, and made for the door. Ultimately Morgenthau was forced to change the tone of his comment, and Reynolds agreed to delete the two references to which the President had come to object, the night before.

The newspapers of the country hailed the President's speech as a laudable gesture of cooperation with business. But the atmospheric conditions in which the speech was perfunctorily delivered approached the frigid. The President was scarcely pleasant either to his audience or to Reynolds.

These facts, and the hammering that had been needed to box in an even more spectacular demonstration of ill humor, placed a heavy damper on my hopes. The President was, for the most part, surrounded by men with a genius for arousing his antagonisms toward business. A good many intransigent businessmen seemed to have a comparable genius for playing directly into their hands. The chances that the policy of "harmony," of "alliance of all forces intent upon . . . recovery" would prevail seemed none too good.

There was another discouraging episode that autumn.

On August 28, 1934, Upton Sinclair, who at one time or another had run on the Socialist ticket in California for congressman, governor, and senator, won the Democratic nomination for governor. Sinclair had campaigned on his EPIC plan, a platform of pure economic fantasy, and had, among his supporters, a choice assortment of crackpots. Came the question whether the Democratic party should endorse him.

Sinclair came East, talked to Roosevelt at Hyde Park, and emerged happily. His mood suggested that the New Deal and his own EPIC plan were wholly consistent. He had a friendly talk with Jim Farley in New York. In Washington, after conferring with Ickes and others, he stated that he was pleased to be a Democrat. Hopkins expressed the hope that Sinclair would be elected. "He's on our side, isn't he?" asked Harry. Back again in California, Sinclair published in his *EPIC News* a letter from Jim Farley urging Democrats to give their support to the full ticket, including Sinclair. (This was the letter Farley was to call, on October 26th, a stenographer's error, explaining that his signature was affixed to it with a rubber stamp.)

Greatly disturbed by this seeming endorsement, I pleaded with F. D. R. in September to dissociate his administration from Sinclair. He answered that Merriam, Sinclair's Republican opponent, was accepting the support of the Townsend-plan advocates and that the Townsend heresy was no smaller than the EPIC heresy. "Besides," he said, "they tell me Sinclair's sure to be elected."

My reply was an editorial in *Today* which appeared on October 4th. It read, in part:

> Sinclair's production-for-use program . . . is the call for a blessed retreat—back beyond industrial civilization, back beyond the established national financial structure, back beyond the use of gold and silver and currency, back to barter, back to nature. . . . To want to see a scrambled hodge-podge of proposals, some sound and some absurd, tried out under the leadership of a man with no experience in practical administration, is to confess the failure of whatever has been done in centuries of slow development of political institutions in the United States and abroad. I, for one, cannot subscribe to defeatism of this kind.

This piece was widely publicized in California. Though I had carefully explained that it represented my independent views, it was interpreted, in some quarters, as an expression of a close friend of the administration. Sinclair answered furiously. I expected that the President would repudiate me at any moment.

That was the situation during the second week in October. The only thing I know of that changed it during the next twenty-one days was the piling up of evidence that Sinclair would be licked. Politicians may back a heresy. But they will not back a losing heresy, if they can help it. Sinclair, whose direct endorsement by Roosevelt had been avoided by inches, was repudiated via George Creel and Jim Farley.

It wasn't a particularly cheering performance any way it was considered. I was left with the hope, though by no means the conviction, that those who were close to Roosevelt would regain their sense of direction after the congressional elections in November.

5

Things did quiet down for some time after the elections.

By December, 1934, there was evidence that business was executing a slow and majestic upturn. Through that month Roosevelt worked with Hopkins over the details of a program for work relief which Harry had sold him—a program to supplant the dole and the jerry-built made-work of the preceding year and a half with planned and supervised projects.

In January Roosevelt asked Congress for $4,000,000,000, plus $880,000,000 from the previous year's unexpended balances, to pay for this program. But the request for this staggering sum was not disquieting, business-wise. For, both in his budget message and annual message of 1935, he made it plain that he wasn't committing himself to the policy of purposeless public spending and that he intended to bring the budget into balance as rapidly as possible.

Even more important, the tone of his messages early that winter was conciliatory and friendly.

I spent fifteen days at the White House working with him in December.[9] His goal, as he saw it then, was the ultimate absorption of the unemployed in private productive work. He agreed that this was impossible without the recovery of private enterprise. He had no quarrel with business, as such. Certainly he did not regard it as an enemy. He felt that with a suitable educational effort, and with some give-and-take on both sides, a considerable body of business opinion could be brought to accept the New Deal program. He admitted that his liberal administration had nothing to fear at that point, except its own excesses. We talked at length, one evening, about how the liberal movements of the past had overreached themselves, divided their support, attempted the impossible and gone down to defeat. Skillfully managed, a liberal movement might continue in power for years to come.

On January 4, 1935, he said to the country: "It is not empty optimism that moves me to a strong hope in the coming year. We can, if we will, make 1935 a genuine period of good feeling."

Yet the year 1935 was to prove a period of growing bitterness, of gradual insistence by the President upon the passage of such a gorge of indigestible measures that the New Deal itself was completely transformed.

This metamorphosis was the result of no single factor. True, it was always potentially implicit in Roosevelt's psychology. But its substantiation, its actual emergence from the cocoon of potentiality, was not inevitable. Except for the interaction of a half dozen circumstances between February and June, it might never have happened. These circumstances were:

[9] These were not fifteen consecutive days, because it was necessary for me to shuttle back and forth to New York.

(1) The continuation of intemperate attacks upon him.

(2) The continuation of the "needling" process by his own associates.

(3) The irritation that comes from overwork and overstrain, which led him to resent the somewhat greater independence of the new Congress.

(4) The immediately resultant fact that he began to get himself into positions from which it was difficult to retreat, to commit himself irrevocably to measures which, at first, he had accepted only tentatively.

(5) The series of adverse Supreme Court decisions during those months, culminating in the invalidation of the N.I.R.A., which convinced him that the Supreme Court majority was out to destroy what he had accomplished.

(6) The growing political strength of Huey Long.

It is necessary to elaborate.

Undeniably, there were a number of unjustifiable attacks upon Roosevelt, in meetings of various businessmen's associations that spring. This wasn't always the fault of the organization before which the inflammatory words were uttered. But it was Roosevelt's impulse always to blame the organization for having permitted violent critics of his policies to appear. Coupled with this was a growing petulance about newspaper criticism. More often than not, during those months, when I came into his bedroom, he would comment angrily about the papers he had read over his breakfast. This paper had said "something untrue," that paper was being "consistently unfair," another paper was being "run by a publisher who exploits his men."

Finally, and particularly provoking, was a silly practice that flourished in many business quarters—the practice of passing around stories about the President or his family that were intended to be funny and were always derogatory. Almost all Presidents have been the butts of asinine jokes,[10] but it's hard to remember a more vicious crop of them than that spring produced.

Inevitably, some of these stories found their way to Roosevelt. Much

[10] I'm reminded of an incident that took place in 1938 when, accidentally, I happened to meet Herbert Hoover traveling to New York from California. We were sitting in a dining car together when the steward, who was not only an entrepreneur of food but of gossip, stopped by the table. "Do you think," he said to me, "that Mr. Hoover would like to hear the latest story about Mr. Roosevelt?" Hoover then gave expression to one of the most brilliant pieces of unconscious humor that I have ever heard. Glowering at the menu, he rumbled, "I don't like stories about Presidents." So vehemently was this said that the would-be storyteller beat a precipitate retreat.

more important, personal accounts of criticisms of his policies were brought to him, as a matter of course, by some of his associates.

I'm quite certain that this latter wasn't part of a deliberate effort to incense him. It came about naturally. Morgenthau, for instance, was essentially a suspicious man, and his normal tendency to worry about things was at its height while he was in process of learning the intricacies of the Treasury job. Hopkins had the typical social worker's distrust of businessmen. It seems almost incredible that these two men would become, three and a half years later, the outstanding administration proponents of business appeasement. But there is nothing that was not creditable about their evolution. Morgenthau in the Treasury underwent, perforce, a first-rate schooling in economics. Hopkins got to know a few businessmen socially and to learn that they did not spend their time weaving crowns of thorns for the poor. Unfortunately, by the time Hopkins and Morgenthau had reached this stage of development, they had helped create certain inexorcisable demons in Roosevelt's cosmos.

But the "needlers" were by no means the only irritants. There were others—men, such as Harold Ickes, who had been in the political minority so long before 1933 that they were slow to recapture the dignity and confidence the public expects of those who are parts of the ruling group. These men, used to the practices of political guerrilla warfare, accustomed to sudden sallies and hasty retreats, found it hard to sit calmly in the seats of power and smile at attacks in outlying provinces. This was the explanation for their extreme sensitiveness, their unnecessary and undignified replies to small-fry criticism, their continuous stirring up of the President by these replies.

Imagine, if you can, the effect of all this upon a President who was finding Congress a good deal talkier and balkier than its predecessor. There were two clear reasons why F. D. R.'s wishes carried less weight with the 74th Congress than with the 73rd: most of the patronage had been given out, and the administration itself, rather than Congress alone, had to face an election in 1936. But as the days passed, in April and May, the President thought of these things less and less. It was easier, for reasons that will appear, to think that waves of reactionary propaganda were sweeping over the national legislature.

Early in January, 1935, F. D. R. told me of his legislative plans. They weren't at all formidable. He wanted social-security legislation, a modest holding-company act, a work-relief program, a merchant-marine act, a revised N.I.R.A., and one or two odds and ends. That was all.

What actually happened that spring was this:

(1) To prepare the social-security act, the President had set up a Cabinet Committee. This Committee then established a research organization and asked a considerable number of citizens, including myself, to serve as an advisory committee. The advisory committee considered every aspect of the problem with care and made a series of recommendations to the Cabinet Committee, which promptly threw out many of them. The bill that was finally sent to Congress was so largely the result of an attempt to compromise irreconcilable views that frank observers recognized it for the mess it was. The two responsible committees of Congress naturally began to overhaul it. Net result—a long and agonizing fight between its administration sponsors and Congress.[11]

(2) Late in February it developed that three distinct holding-company proposals had been prepared for the President's consideration—one by Corcoran and Cohen after conference with me, one by Walter M. W. Splawn of the I.C.C. at Sam Rayburn's request (F. D. R. had, of course, suggested that Rayburn think about such legislation), and one by Herman Oliphant and Robert H. Jackson of Morgenthau's Department. These were progressively drastic—the last absolutely destroying holding companies. Frankfurter, Cohen, Corcoran, and I all urged that the President accept the moderate Cohen-Corcoran draft, but he inclined toward the stiffer proposals. In the end Cohen and Corcoran agreed to sharpen their pencils. The result was the "death-sentence" provision which neither they nor the President really expected to get through Congress, but which they intended to use for trading purposes. But in the course of the desperate struggle over the bill (in the Senate an attempt to remove the "death sentence" was defeated by only one vote) the President, Corcoran, and Cohen managed to sell themselves all they originally asked for. The two young men were in and out of the White House, day after day, night after night, reporting the progress of their campaign to "put the heat on" reluctant senators. Between them they generated enough indignation over the opposition to the bill to become the victims of their own strategy. The

[11] One of the reasons for the overhauling of the bill was, of course, the fact that Court decisions, that spring, had thrown doubts on its constitutionality. Quite clearly, the legislation should have been delayed for another year. The Act, as finally passed, had gross defects—like the reserve fund, which the administration was to refuse to recognize until March, 1939.

fight became a fight for all or nothing. *Aut Caesar aut nullus* was the mood of late spring.

(3) Nothing was done, that spring, to devise more than halfway plans to reconstruct the N.I.R.A. The President merely suggested slight revisions and asked Congress for an extension of the N.I.R.A., which expired in June. This throwing-up of the presidential hands was the signal for a long, acrimonious wrangle before the Finance Committee of the Senate.

(4) Senator Wagner's Labor-Relations bill, which the President had no intention of supporting in January, developed unforeseen strength in Congress. As spring came on, the President faced the necessity of deciding whether he would accept it. By early June, partly because he needed the influence and votes of Wagner on so many pieces of legislation and partly because of the invalidation of the N.I.R.A., he flung his arms open and suddenly embraced the Wagner bill—whose palpable one-sidedness could have been eliminated then and there.

(5) Meanwhile the Guffey Bituminous Coal bill, sponsored by John L. Lewis, came along. In May the President wisely refused to commit himself to it. On June 1st the United Mine Workers officials sent out strike orders. On June 4th, after the invalidation of the N.I.R.A., Roosevelt pressed for the enactment of the bill. On July 6th in an effort to avert a walkout of the U.M.W., he urged the House subcommittee considering the bill not to permit doubts as to its constitutionality, "however reasonable, to block the suggested legislation."

What happened, in short, was that Roosevelt dumped into Congress' lap three major puzzles centering in the proposed security bill, the proposed N.I.R.A. extension, and the proposed holding-company bill; that he grew impatient with the long debate over them; and that, either to buttress his position or for trading purposes, he then let himself be committed to other pieces of legislation he originally had no idea of demanding.

It was clear by early June, 1935, that he had bitten off far more than he could chew. But he was now in no mood to drop anything. His stubbornness was thoroughly aroused. The more sullen Congress grew over his "must" lists, the more positive he became of his rectitude. The ardor of his advocacy began to turn inward, feeding upon its own flame, enlarging and intensifying with every hint of opposition, every breath of criticism.

Still the situation might not have become explosive, but for Huey Long and the Supreme Court.

In the early spring of 1935 the Democratic leaders began to get an acute attack of jitters about the apparently growing political strength of the Kingfish. It is probable that they overestimated both the shrewdness and the political future of the blatant, picturesque, arm-flailing Louisiana dictator to the same extent that smug Easterners who dismissed him as a mountebank underestimated them. Certainly those in Washington who called his "Share-the-Wealth" movement "the greatest threat to Franklin Roosevelt and his New Deal" had lost all perspective.

Hugh Johnson's fierce radio attack on Huey in March, 1935, did nothing to dispel the Washington delusion. Huey answered the General in kind. The General answered Huey's answer. Huey answered the General again. Father Coughlin got mixed up in the vituperative exchange. The prosecution of the income-tax charges against Huey's Louisiana associates began to be called a "political persecution" of Huey—which I doubt that it was. But there could be no debate over the meaning of the delivery of Louisiana patronage to Long's political opponents.

By late March the Kingfish was threatening to campaign in states other than Louisiana for "Share-the-Wealth" candidates. By April the Democratic high command not only expected him to defeat Senator Joseph T. Robinson of Arkansas and Senator Pat Harrison of Mississippi, two of the party's elder statesmen, in 1936, but was chewing its mustaches over statistics purporting to show that he could make himself political master of the whole, vast Lower Mississippi Valley—perhaps even of great hunks of the West. Who knew where Huey, who was promising his followers a "guaranteed" income of $2,500 a year, would end?

F. D. R. began to doubt whether Huey's followers could be weaned away by logical argument. Perhaps it would be necessary to woo some of Long's support by making a counteroffer. One evening in midspring F. D. R. actually used the phrase "steal Long's thunder" in conversation with me and two other friends of his.

In the midst of all this the Supreme Court began to deliver one blow after another to the New Deal. On January 7th section 9 (c) of the N.I.R.A. was declared unconstitutional. On May 6th the Railroad Retirement Act was overthrown. On May 27th the President's removal of Commissioner Humphrey from the Federal Trade Commission was severely chastised, the Frazier-Lemke amendments to the Bankruptcy Act were declared unconstitutional, and, in the famous Schechter case, the code-making provisions of the N.I.R.A. were invalidated.

This series of reverses convinced F. D. R. that the Court majority was the implacable enemy of all change, that unless its basic philosophy was overhauled all that he had done would be undone.

A fairly just deduction was that the Supreme Court decision in the Schechter case delivered Roosevelt from one of the most desperate administrative muddles he ever confronted and gave him the opportunity to start over, in this field, with a fairly clean slate. Unfortunately, once the slate had been cleaned, Roosevelt seemed unable to make up his mind what to write on it.

Some queer stories have been told about what happened in the White House between the 27th of May, when the Schechter decision was handed down, and the 31st of May, when the "horse-and-buggy" statement was made in press conference. I didn't arrive in Washington until the morning of the 31st. But I talked to F. D. R. over the telephone several times during the preceding three days and was given, on the 31st, a fairly detailed account by both Hugh Johnson and Felix Frankfurter (who happened to be at the White House for one of the brief visits he made there two or three times a year).

Johnson's and Felix's stories differed sharply in import. Johnson maintained that Felix dissuaded the President from accepting his recommendations and persuaded the President to make the "horse-and-buggy" statement. Felix insisted that no one was more amazed than he by the President's statement. So far as I was ever able to piece the story together, what happened was this:

As soon as the N.I.R.A. was declared unconstitutional, Hugh Johnson developed the theory that there might be reenacted a law whose validity would be assured by the fact that it followed certain hints in the Hughes opinion in the Schechter case. He took this idea to the White House. Donald Richberg also had a plan for new legislation. I, over the telephone, took the position that I didn't see how an effective measure to achieve the permanent objectives of the N.I.R.A. could be constructed in the light of the Court's obiter dicta on the interstate-commerce clause. I argued for a constitutional amendment, enlarging Congress' powers to regulate industry. Frankfurter strongly opposed my idea of a constitutional amendment. He also opposed the Johnson and Richberg plans.

There's no doubt that Frankfurter, a Brandeis devotee, had a deep antipathy to both the A.A.A. and the N.I.R.A. He, as well as most of

Photo by Acme Newspictures, Inc.

"We . . . have every reason to keep our sense of humor and our sense of proportion . . ."

A typical campaign scene in 1932. Mr. Roosevelt addressing a meeting at Louisville, Kentucky, October 22nd. Left to right, Mr. Roosevelt, Governor Ruby Laffoon, Senator Barkley, and Mr. Moley. (See Chapter II)

Star Staff Photo

Arrival of President-elect Roosevelt in Washington, November 22nd, 1932, to confer with President Hoover on the foreign debts.

Left to right, Gus Gennerich, Mr. Roosevelt's bodyguard, Mr. Roosevelt, Mr. Garner, Mr. Moley, Mr. Farley and Col. Howe. (See page 72)

Photo by Pictures, Inc.

". . . like a schoolteacher urging a mother to make her naughty child do his homework."

Secretary of the Treasury Ogden L. Mills leaving Roosevelt's apartment at the Hotel Mayflower, Washington, D. C., November 23rd, 1932, the day after the conference on foreign debts at the White House attended by President Hoover, President-elect Roosevelt, Secretary Mills and Mr. Moley. (See page 78)

En route to Washington, January 19th, 1933, to confer further with President Hoover and members of the outgoing administration on foreign debts and the Economic Conference.

Left to right, Admiral Grayson, Norman Davis, Mr. Moley, Rex Tugwell, Will Woodin and Mr. Roosevelt. (See page 97)

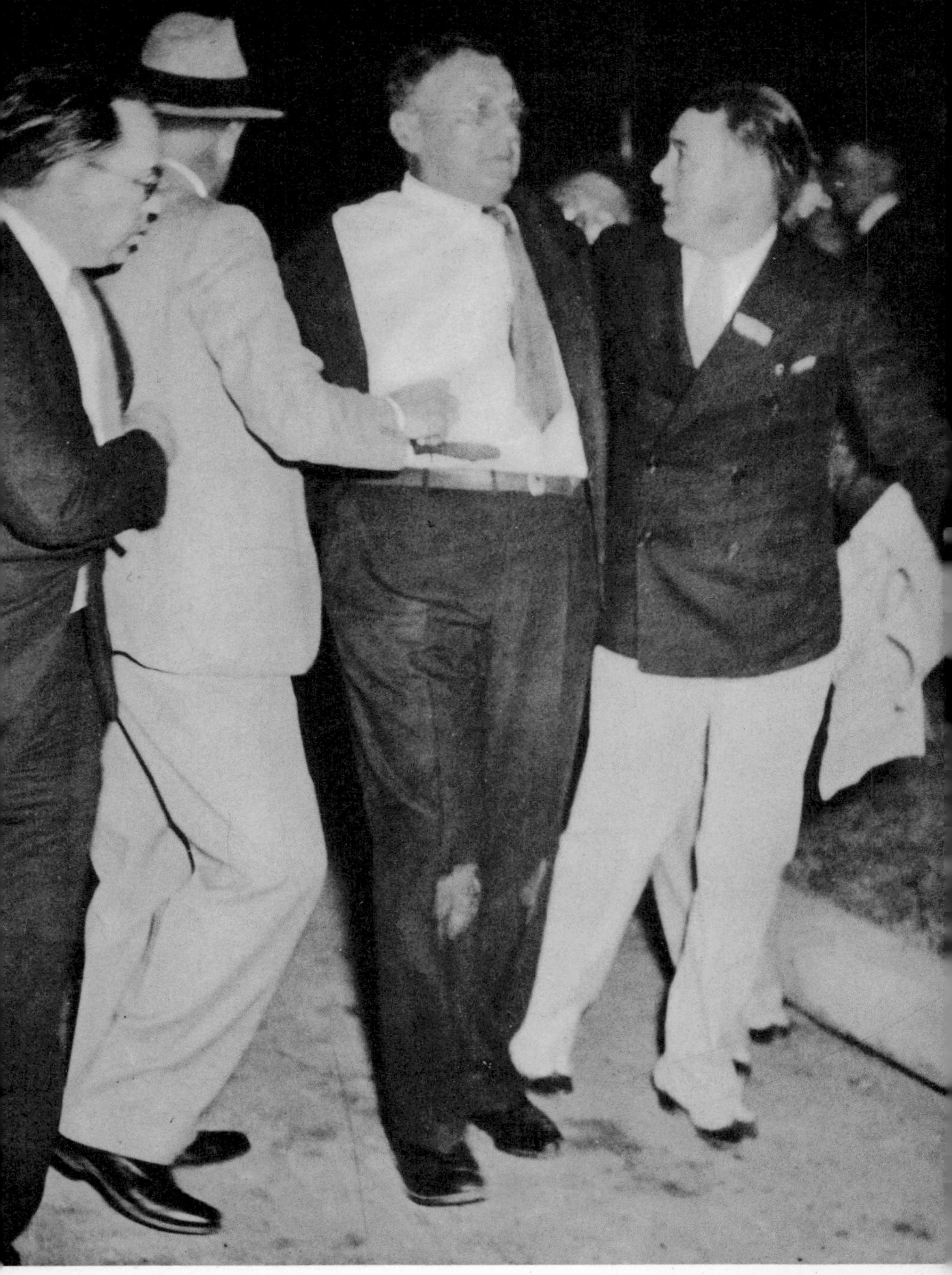

". . . how dangerous it was to subject a public figure to such risks."

Mayor Cermak of Chicago, mortally wounded at Miami, February 15th, 1933, after Zangara's attempted assassination of Roosevelt. (See page 138)

Photo by Wide World, Inc.

". . . past the deathwatch of reporters and photographers who were to snap pictures of the same group of us . . . bowed under the same weariness, for a week of nights."

One of the late impromptu meetings with the press during the bank crisis. Secretary Woodin at left. (See page 148)

© Sport & Genera, London

'n London at the time of the meeting of the ill-starred Economic Conference, June, 1933.

Herbert Bayard Swope and Raymond Moley. (See Chapter VII)

". . . that fight will go on."

President Roosevelt accepting the nomination at Philadelphia, Pennsylvania, June 27, 1936. (See page 348)

his young disciples in Washington, opposed the loosening up of the antitrust laws involved in the N.I.R.A. principle. As avowed enemies of bigness in business, viewing government's role as that of policeman, rather than coordinator, they looked upon N.I.R.A.'s invalidation with no little satisfaction. Frankfurter's advice to F. D. R. seems to have been to let things drift along.

F. D. R. leaned by conviction to that school of thought that looked upon the development of self-government in industry under government aegis as desirable and inevitable. But he seems, surprisingly, to have been taken aback by the conflict between the Johnson-Richberg views and the Frankfurter views. His vital mistake was an attempt to avoid a clear-cut choice between them, an attempt to reconcile them.

For hours on end he apparently pumped out of Felix the technical information about the Schechter decision and earlier Court decisions that he was to pass on to the newspapermen in his press conference. Then, without a word to Felix about his intentions, he went into the press conference on the 31st and held forth on the Court's "horse-and-buggy" interpretation of interstate commerce. But he gave the newspapermen and the public no idea of what he intended to do about the Court or the N.I.R.A. He simply thumbed his nose at the Court—thereby incensing still further those who already opposed him and leaving his supporters in utter confusion as to the next step he would take.

The confusion redoubled as the passing days brought still no indication that the President had decided how to proceed. Hugh stamped around Washington hurling imprecations against Felix. Felix dismissed Hugh's anger with a smile and began to urge F. D. R. to press for the immediate enactment of legislation to provide minimum labor standards in all industries producing materials for the government. I went down to the Capitol, got Vice President Garner, Jimmy Byrnes, and Bob La Follette together and found that they favored, as I did, frankly putting a constitutional amendment through Congress and sending it to the states.[12] At first, the President showed a flicker of enthusiasm for the idea of constitutional amendment. But, in the end, it dwindled,

[12] I felt very much encouraged by this meeting, and Byrnes and I, on the strength of our conviction, proceeded to put ourselves on record. I wrote an editorial in *Today* on June 8, 1935, strongly advocating a constitutional amendment. (I have never written a piece that created as much comment as this. A good half of the comment was adverse.) Byrnes went South and made a speech at Charleston, the ancient home of states' rights, in support of the idea.

and nothing seemed to come directly of all the talk about the Court decision.

Indirectly, though, its effect was startling.

The "horse-and-buggy" interview had provoked a storm of denunciation more violent than any other during Roosevelt's administration—denunciation that went on day after day through early June. It was, apparently, the last straw. Roosevelt was now both aggrieved and befuddled. Wasn't Congress resisting his requests for action? Hadn't the Court thrown itself athwart the path of progress? Weren't his advisers divided on the question of how he should meet the Schechter decision? Had he not saved, in 1933, the very businessmen, the very newspaper publishers who were now assailing his "radicalism"? As he looked back on it all, he was, like Clive, amazed at his own moderation. Yet he was being asked to accept defeat at the hands of "reaction" at the same moment that he was being bedeviled by the extremism, by the "Share-the-Wealth"-ism of Huey Long.

It was at that point that the two impulses—the impulse to strike back at his critics and the impulse to "steal Long's thunder"—flowed together and crystallized. He remembered something—a scheme that had come from the Treasury back in February—a scheme, it suddenly dawned on him, that might have been devised for the very purposes he had in mind.

This was a combination of tax measures that had been described in a draft message prepared for his use. He had read the message to me one night in February, and I had argued against it as a whole and in detail. Particularly had I opposed it as an attempt to put over dubious social reforms in the guise of tax legislation. It was one thing, I said, to reform the tax system—which certainly needed overhauling—and another to try to stand the industrial and financial system on its head under that pretext. F. D. R. had finally tossed the draft message aside.[13]

Now, in early June, he changed his mind. Whether he asked the Treasury for a more elaborate version of the February draft, or whether

[13] Roosevelt had already indicated, in his January budget message, that he did not "consider it advisable at this time to propose any new or additional taxes for the fiscal year 1936." . . . In his magnificent bonus-bill veto of May 22, 1935, he stressed, as he had done in the budget message, that the whole of the deficit proposed in the budget was to be applied for the "single-minded, definite purpose" of providing work relief for the unemployed. He did not propose, he said, in giving his reasons for vetoing the bonus bill, to let the budget be unbalanced by Congress' failure "to provide additional taxes for an additional expenditure" of the magnitude involved in the bill. The inference, then, as late as May 22nd, was that he stood on his budget message.

the Treasury volunteered it, I do not know. I only know that by mid-June he had in his possession a somewhat enlarged but substantively identical draft sent him by the Treasury. This, as well as its predecessor, was largely the work of Henry Morgenthau's counsel, Herman Oliphant.

Four years later Secretary Morgenthau's connection with the scheme would be described thus:

> Of the New Deal's two big tax plans, the highly political "soak-the-rich" bill of 1935 was substituted for a more orthodox Treasury program twenty-four hours before it went to Congress. At the last moment . . . unbeknownst to Morgenthau, one of his subordinates was called to the White House and worked all night drafting a new bill at the President's direction. Morgenthau had to like it or lump it the next day. As for the undistributed profits levy, that was invented in January, 1936, while Morgenthau was away at Sea Island, Georgia, recovering from one of the attacks of overstrain to which he is liable. Before he left, Oliphant and Dr. Jacob Viner, a Treasury economist, had merely discussed a surplus-profits tax in the most general terms. While he was away Mrs. Morgenthau, who is a careful guardian of her husband's health, would not let him talk on the telephone. Meanwhile Oliphant, an evangelistic trust-buster, got the notion that an undistributed-profits tax would prevent the growth of monopoly. He sold the tax to the President, whose approach to taxation problems is what sociologists call "anecdotal." Once again, when Morgenthau returned from Sea Island, he had to like it or lump it. He didn't like it much.[14]

This is my favorite bit of New Deal folklore. Of course it does not explain that the Treasury's "more orthodox" tax program of February, 1935, did not differ substantially from the program which Morgenthau presumably had to "like or lump" in June, 1935. It does not explain how a man with the administrative conscience of Morgenthau could have been ignorant of the tax program his Department sent to the White House in February, 1935. It does not explain how, if he was ignorant of it, he could have failed to discover it in the four months between February and June. It does not explain that Secretary Morgenthau gave no indication of a like-or-lump-it attitude in June and that, on the contrary, he greatly resented the few modifications that Frankfurter and I were able to persuade the President to make. It does not explain that before Secretary Morgenthau went to Sea Island he had had at least seven months, if not eleven months, to declare his opposi-

[14] From "Henny Penny," by Joseph Alsop and Robert Kintner, *The Saturday Evening Post*, April 1, 1939, Vol. 211, No. 40.

tion to the corporate surplus tax that was presumably sold to the President "unbeknownst" to him. It does not explain why, if Secretary Morgenthau really disapproved the surplus tax in particular and the "soak-the-rich" plan in general, he did not reprimand Mr. Oliphant, dissociate himself from Mr. Oliphant's proposals, or resign in protest himself.

But that's neither here nor there. The important fact is that on a June night in 1935 the President showed Felix Frankfurter and myself a draft message from the Treasury recommending the taxation of "unwieldy and unnecessary corporate surpluses," a heavy inheritance and gift tax, a sharp increase in surtaxes on incomes above $50,000, and a graduated corporation-income tax. The proposal as a whole was declared a revision of the existing tax system because it operated "to the unfair advantage of the few" and because "social unrest and a deepening sense of unfairness" required a "wider distribution of wealth."

This was the "soak-the-rich" scheme—designed to embarrass and annoy a few wealthy individuals, win the support of the "Share-the-Wealth" adherents, and "discourage" bigness in business.

To say that I was appalled by the satisfaction with which F. D. R. informed me that he intended to send this message to Congress (he added blithely, "Pat Harrison's going to be so surprised he'll have kittens on the spot") is to fall over backwards with restraint.

I tried to convince him that the proposals ran counter to the New Deal's most elementary objectives. As to the corporate-surplus tax, specifically, I reminded him that the idea had been rattling around in the dustbins of the Treasury for more than twenty years;[15] that Charles Roberts, a friend of Basil and John O'Connor, had attempted to sell it to him before his nomination in 1932; that I had asked Adolf Berle to look into the proposal then; that, on the basis of Adolf's researches, I had recommended that he leave the proposal strictly alone; that I had been able to demonstrate to him then that the proposal was unsound.

The New Deal, I went on to say, had been sold to the public in 1932 and 1934 as a means of achieving security and stability. This tax the Treasury proposed—a tax presumably designed to encourage small corporations and discourage large ones—would do precisely the opposite. It would:

(1) Accentuate booms and deepen depressions. It was obvious that if

[15] The scheme was not "invented in January, 1936," as Alsop and Kintner suggest.

corporations dispersed larger dividends in good years and had nothing left with which to pay dividends or employ labor in bad times the swings of the business cycle would be exaggerated.

(2) Make the workman's job more precarious. It was common practice to use slack seasons of the year to manufacture goods for future sale, financing the operation out of surplus. A business without a surplus could do this only with borrowed money—a procedure too expensive to be practical in competition with rivals whose interest costs were zero.

(3) Intensify the fluctuations of stock and bond prices, thus affecting the collateral behind loans, impairing the foundations of banks and insurance companies, and giving increased opportunities to the speculator.

(4) Put a heavy handicap on the process of rebuilding credit, preventing enterprises which had been losing money for years and depleting their reserves to the point where they'd been compelled to borrow heavily from accumulating a hump of fat in anticipation of the next hard winter.

(5) Give the larger corporations of the country an advantage over their smaller competitors in proportion to the size of their existing surpluses, and make it necessary for the smaller fellow henceforth always to borrow in emergencies.

(6) Check new business enterprises which must run in the red for a few years before they turned the corner. It would be a hardy investor indeed who would venture his money in an enterprise that had no opportunity to acquire the very essentials of permanent corporate health.

Finally, I pleaded, surpluses were the life-insurance policies of business firms. Neither Congress nor any administrative agency could fairly determine how much insurance any one corporation needed. That differed with the nature of the business and with the condition of the corporation. Companies in a business which is notoriously of the "feast or famine" type, like the steel industry, needed to lay aside large surpluses in good years to tide them over lean years. Others, conspicuously in the chemical industry, had to be ready for the obsolescence of plant or process that research so often brought upon them with lightning suddenness. In short, any law which imposed the same limitations upon corporate thrift for all corporations was bound to work great injustices and to wreck many enterprises.

The argument offered by the Treasury in support of this tax plan was that wealthy stockholders were avoiding the surtax by leaving earnings to accumulate, in sums beyond any possible needs of their businesses. But the fact that a wise and prudent principle might be abused was no reason for destroying the principle. There was already a provision in the Revenue Act of 1934 designed to reach this kind of evasion. Accumulation of gains or profits "beyond the reasonable needs of the business" was prima-facie evidence of a purpose to avoid surtax—so read the law—and some corporations had already been penalized under it. These were flagrant cases. Better let a comparative few get away with evasions which were on the border line of good business judgment than to undertake to destroy all possibility of prudent corporate thrift.

The best I could do was to persuade Roosevelt to narrow the range of the graduated corporate-income tax he insisted upon recommending and to dissuade him from asking for more than a study of the surplus-tax proposal. For the rest, he was adamant. The sense of regaining the whip hand gave him the first buoyant, cheerful moment he had known for weeks. He airily dismissed most of our objections.

The message was sent to Congress on June 19th.

It was on that day the split in the Democratic party began.

The message stunned the Congressional leaders. Those, like Pat Harrison, who felt that party loyalty compelled them to support it, bled inwardly. Many, cut to the quick by the peremptory tone of the message, said bitterly they'd "go down the line" this time, but that they'd be damned if they ever would again under like circumstances. Others announced in the cloakrooms that, party loyalty or no party loyalty, they were going to turn the scheme inside out and show of what it was made.

The Treasury chiefs were summoned. Acrimonious questioning in the House Ways and Means Committee revealed publicly that the proposals had originated in the Treasury, that no careful study of them had been made there, and that such data as the Treasury adduced to support them were utterly inadequate.

An uproarious drive to override most of the President's tax recommendations got under way in the House. Businessmen wailed that the President must be pursuing a private vendetta against his old friends of Groton and Harvard, that dangerous communists were scuttling in and out of his presence like messenger boys in a broker's office (ante 1929). Hot-headed administration subordinates talked of the need for "clipping business' wings." The President expressed amazement that capitalists did not understand that he was their savior, the only bulwark between them and revolution. The battle-to-the-death spirit was unmistakable.

I began to wonder whether Roosevelt had begun to see his program as an end in itself, rather than as a means to an end; whether he wasn't beginning to feel that the proof of a measure's merit was the extent to which it offended the business community; whether he wasn't substituting, for the attempt to coordinate the economic life of the nation, a program of *divide et impera*; whether the search for the Holy Grail of a just national economy wasn't being transformed into a strafing expedition.

So far as I could see, large sections of the American public were getting sick and tired of the rumpus in Washington.

> The man in the street [I wrote at that time] believes in a new deal—this New Deal, in fact. He does not believe that all the evils that vexed him will be exorcised by the magic of law. But he believes that things are better than they were and that some particularly "raw deals" of the Golden Decade cannot be repeated. He knows that the President has tried gallantly to give him a better break and he appreciates the extent to which the President has succeeded. But he does not believe that businessmen are all devils, and that unless crippled they will rise and smite him again. He is not concerned with abundance in the future. He wants a chance to enjoy the little additional abundance that he has now. Above all, he wants to get away from the strain of listening to so many people saying so many fierce things so many hours of the day. For the time being, he has heard enough about saving the world. . . .
>
> The public is developing a terrific thirst for a long, cool swig of political quiescence. The danger to liberalism at such a moment is that a reactionary party will offer it a long, cool but narcotic swig of "normalcy." The Democrats can, if they will, meet the situation gracefully by the simple process of offering a quiet interlude for adjustment, education and the taking of stock.
>
> This is the best way for Democrats to save the precious gains they have made. They must realize that such a policy is not reaction, but rather the assurance of continued progress. They must recognize that every social crusade, from Cromwell to Wilson, has sooner or later come face to face with the stubborn refusal of human nature to rise too high or stay high too long.
>
> "To every thing there is a season, and a time to every purpose under the heaven."[16]

[16] *Today,* July 13, 1935, Vol. 4, No. 12.

The rest of the Preacher's injunction kept running through my head:

"A time to break down, and a time to build up. . . .

"A time to cast away stones, and a time to gather stones together. . . .

"A time to rend, and a time to sew." . . .

But the President was of a different mind.

Toward the end of July I decided to go away for ten days or two weeks—out of reach of Washington and Hyde Park—to think things through.

CHAPTER IX

"*NUNC DIMITTIS*"

I RETURNED to a Washington more tumultuous than it had been when I left.

The tax program was being torn to shreds.

Senator Black was pursuing, in those hot, dog-star days, an investigation of the utilities' lobbying against the holding-company bill, and pursuing it with a fanaticism not surprising in a one-time Klan member. In his frenzy to uncover improper lobbying by certain utilities—and there was plenty of it—Black struck at the innocent as well as the guilty. Opposition to the bill became, *ipso facto,* an indication of bad faith. A dragnet for telegrams was thrown out. The subservient Communications Commission tossed private and wholly irrelevant messages into the maw of the Black inquisition.

Meanwhile the lobbying proclivities of Tom Corcoran, which Rayburn and I had kept under strict control the year before, had been given the open throttle. Old hands at executive lobbying, like Roper and Jesse Jones, had been shoved aside. They were compromisers, Tom was convinced, and this was a truceless war. The holding-company bill, as written for trading purposes, had become gospel, which it was treason, if not sacrilege, to question. When the House committee headed by Rayburn reported out the bill with a modified "death sentence," Corcoran had had the effrontery to suggest that Sam was weak and shaky.[1]

"Disloyalty" was suspected everywhere by the White House. On the other hand, the ruthless exertion of pressure to win votes was suspected in Congress. Representative Ralph O. Brewster had risen in the House and charged: "Thomas G. Corcoran Esq. . . . came to me . . . and

[1] When I heard of this charge, on my return, I took the occasion to make a vehement defense of Rayburn to the President. I don't know what effect I had. I don't believe it helped much to clear Rayburn of the suspicion that his orthodoxy was impaired, because as much as ten months later I heard comments in the White House to the effect that Rayburn wouldn't fight hard in an emergency.

stated . . . with what he termed 'brutal frankness,' that if I should vote against the death sentence . . . he would find it necessary to stop construction on the Passamaquoddy Dam in my district!" This charge, Corcoran denied.

Hot, tired, nervous, angry, Congress allowed half a dozen bills to get stymied in committee or conference by the first two weeks in August. Never in Washington's history had so much major legislation piled up at the last moment. The President fumed. But he was forced, finally, to compromise the holding-company fight.[2]

The log jam broke. Less than a week later Congress wound up its affairs and went home.

Roughly speaking, it had given the President seventy-five per cent of what he had asked for. He got a nine and one-half months' extension of a greatly enfeebled N.I.R.A.; a modified social-security program; a $4,880,000,000 work-relief appropriation; the Guffey Coal Bill; far-reaching amendments to the Federal Reserve Act; the Wagner Labor Relations Act; legislation regulating air, railroad, bus, and truck transportation; a revised Railroad Pensions Act; and miscellaneous odds and ends of legislation.

He did not get a Ship Subsidies bill, the Walsh Government Contract bill, the Pure Food and Drug bill, United States adherence to the World Court, or the almost unqualified holding-company "death sentence."

The inheritance-tax increase in his "Share-the-Wealth" program had been thrown out completely. The "principle" of his "soak-the-rich" plan had passed, the President said. But if it was the establishment of the "principle" of the graduated-corporation tax he'd sought, it was dearly bought. It had inflicted wounds on the party that would fester and corrupt. It had thrown the business community into paroxysms of fright. It had alienated thousands of Roosevelt sympathizers.

I, for one, couldn't help but think that Roosevelt was approaching a test, the crucial test of his statesmanship. Under stress he had permitted his sensitiveness to criticism to get out of hand, his impulses to find immediate expression in action. More than Congress, it was he

[2] It was Felix Frankfurter who persuaded him that he must yield. Instead of limiting a utility-holding-company system to one integrated system with not more than one subsidiary between the holding-company and the operating-company, Roosevelt agreed to permit a utility-holding-company to control more than one integrated system if all the systems were in the same geographic region and if the additional systems were too small, economically, to stand alone. I was at the White House the day that Felix brought the President around. It was suggestive of the President's attitude that he twitted Felix that day by calling him "John W. Davis."

who had been taken in by the technique of asking for two loaves when only one was expected. For somewhere, in those months, he'd lost the ability to distinguish between positions taken for tactical purposes and positions taken for principle's sake. They were all alike, all imperative, by virtue of his having taken them. Opposition had sufficed to transform bluff into indispensable precept.

But now that the angry struggle with Congress was over, would the intensity and fervor it had engendered in him persist? Would partial defeat leave him embittered; partial success, intolerant? Could calm and perspective be restored? If they could not, he would ultimately drive his administration to disaster. Everything hung in the balance. And not the smallest item in that balance, for me, was that faith in Roosevelt's political intuition to which I still clung.

Hundreds of miles away Roy Howard, a generally devoted Roosevelt adherent, must have traveled along part of the same dreary mental road as I, during the first weeks of August. For on the day that Congress adjourned, the 26th, he dispatched a letter to the President that read:

> . . . any experienced reporter will tell you that throughout the country many businessmen who once gave you sincere support are now not merely hostile, they are frightened. Many of these men, whose patriotism and sense of public service will compare with that of any men in political life, have become convinced and sincerely believe:
>
> That you fathered a tax bill that aims at revenge rather than revenue—revenge on business. . . .
>
> That there can be no real recovery until the fears of business have been allayed through the granting of a breathing spell to industry, and a recess from further experimentation until the country can recover its losses.
>
> I know that you have repeatedly stated your position on sections of the Nation's problems, but as an editor I know also the necessity for repetition and reiteration. There is need to undo the damage that has been done by misinterpreters of the New Deal.

It was a plea for a recognition of the pitfalls Roosevelt faced, a plea for a "breathing spell." And I had a feeling of immense relief when I was asked to prepare notes for the President's answer to Roy. Roosevelt was thoroughly aware of my doubts about the wisdom of his course during the hectic summer. The fact that he turned to me again, at this moment, could only mean that he wanted to answer Roy reassuringly.[3]

[3] Roy transmitted his letter to the President, with the message that if the President would answer it publicly he would be willing to change any detail of its

On Sunday, September 1st, I drove up to Hyde Park, and there, in the quiet of his spacious library, found F. D. R. in a mood more tranquil, generous, indulgent, than he had been for eight months. There was, to be sure, a touch of the swaggering when he teased me about my fears over the storm and fury of the summer. And when we spoke of the passage about taxation in Roy's letter, it was even possible to discern some of the summer's peremptoriness in his voice. But there was no mistaking his wish to be conciliatory. He not only took my notes but added a few gracious phrases of his own.

> I appreciate the tone and purpose of your letter [he wrote Roy], and fairness impels me to note with no little sympathy and understanding the facts which you record. . . . This Administration came into power pledged to a very considerable legislative program. It found the condition of the country such as to require drastic and far-reaching action. Duty and necessity required us to move on a broad front for more than two years. It seemed to the Congress and to me better to achieve these objectives as expeditiously as possible in order that not only business but the public generally might know those modifications in the conditions and rules of economic enterprise which were involved in our program. This basic program, however, has now reached substantial completion and the "breathing spell" of which you speak is here—very decidedly so.

This was the famous "breathing-spell" exchange, which was handed to the newspapers a few days later. The public reaction to it was so quick, so enthusiastic, that F. D. R. himself was astonished. Thousands of telegrams and letters of approval came pouring in. Fifty representative stock issues hit the best level since September, 1931—and not wholly by coincidence. Roosevelt's popularity, as shown by the Gallup poll, rose precipitately from the all-time low of 50.5 to which it had sunk on September 1, 1935.

The President was enchanted. When I visited him again in mid-September at Hyde Park to help plan the speeches he would make on his vacation trip across the continent, he said, with his old winsome enthusiasm, that he wanted to strike the note of peace and unity and harmony again.

All the speeches he made on that trip, between September 26th and October 24th, 1935, can be summarized in his own words at San Diego on October 2nd.

---

phrasing that the President wished—but not the tone of the letter. I made one or two minor changes in the text of Roy's letter to which Roy wholeheartedly agreed.

"Several centuries ago," he said, "the greatest writer in history described the two most menacing clouds that hang over human government and human society as 'malice domestic and fierce foreign war.'[4] We are not rid of these dangers but we can summon our intelligence to meet them.

"Never was there more genuine reason for Americans to face down these two causes of fear. 'Malice domestic' from time to time will come to you in the shape of those who would raise false issues, pervert facts, preach the gospel of hate, and minimize the importance of public action to secure human rights or spiritual ideals. There are those today who would sow these seeds, but your answer to them is in the possession of the plain facts of our present condition.

"The second cloud—'foreign war'—is more real—a more potent danger at this moment to the future of civilization. . . .[5]

". . . despite what happens in continents overseas, the United States of America shall and must remain—as long ago the Father of our Country prayed that it might remain—unentangled and free. . . .

"We not only earnestly desire peace, but we are moved by a stern determination to avoid those perils that will endanger our peace with the world."

Here were the twin objectives of the New Deal restated—the application of intelligence and good will to the solution of our domestic problems, and the avoidance of foreign entanglements. No one could have asked for more. Roosevelt seemed to be coming through the most difficult moment of his career as the master and not the creature of his own impulses. It seemed, somehow, as though there might exist in him a deep, inner stability that even I, who knew him so well, had failed to perceive through the variations of his conduct.

But by now I was too accustomed to sudden reversals to risk the anguish of another disillusionment. I kept my fingers crossed—and waited.

[4] This reference sent the literati to their Shakespeares, and elicited no small amount of good-natured chaffing. It was, I regret to say, a garbled one, and I was responsible for the garbling. Somehow or other, the phrase "Malice domestic, foreign levy"—levy meaning armed force—from Act 3, Scene 2 of *Macbeth* got mixed up in my mind with the phrase, "Domestic fury and fierce civil strife," from Act 3, Scene 1 of *Julius Caesar*. It was a boner. But I was always sorry Shakespeare hadn't said "malice domestic and fierce foreign war," because it would have been the perfect allusion for F. D. R.

[5] This reference was to the invasion of Ethiopia Italy was engaged in launching and to the threat of general European war Italy's moves precipitated.

So the only real surprise was the swiftness with which he veered again.

The foreign policy reproclaimed at San Diego on October 2nd was abandoned on October 30th.

The domestic policy announced in the reply to Roy Howard's letter, and reaffirmed at San Diego, died with the new year.

2

I don't doubt for a minute that Roosevelt sincerely believed that the statement on foreign affairs made at San Diego was spun of the same thread as his statement about trade with Italy twenty-eight days later. The man who could suppose that his tariff stand, during the campaign, was a "compromise" was surely capable of satisfying himself about his consistency on this point. Perhaps it was the very strength of Roosevelt's sincerity that left him so irritated with those whose minds were less flexible than his. Perhaps it was an impertinence to confront such conviction with inconvenient facts.

Yet it couldn't be helped.

"If you conceal the truth of those things from him which concern his justice or his honour," Bacon had said, "you are as dangerous a traitor to his state, as he that riseth in arms against him."

I had another obligation just as binding. A hundred thousand *Today* readers were planking down their money every week on the assumption that they were getting honest merchandise. I couldn't run out on my part of the contract. I made no pretensions to infallibility in my expressions of opinion. I might be a fool—and sometimes was.[6] But I couldn't be a knave. I couldn't sell adulterated goods. I had to write and publish what I thought was true. And this is how it seemed to me:

When the actual invasion of Ethiopia began, early in October, France and England moved, through the League of Nations, to apply sanctions. Needless to say, all the American internationalists itched to have us join "in collective action to prevent war"; *i.e.,* to cut off Italy's supplies. Acting under the Neutrality Act, Roosevelt, quite properly, prohibited the shipment of arms to both combatants, Italy and Ethiopia. But things were not permitted to rest there. On October 26th Secretary Hull expressed "sympathetic interest" with "the individual

[6] With respect to Roosevelt's silver policy, for example, I was completely taken in by the specious arguments of the silver senators—a mistake I deeply regret.

or concerted efforts of other nations to preserve peace or to localize or shorten the duration of war." On October 30th Roosevelt and Hull issued statements tantamount to a request that American trade with Italy cease.

Now the cutting off of trade with a nation, whether or not it is called a "sanction," is a hostile act. By no possible turn of phrase can it be considered a neutral act. And only in the curiously inverted doctrine of the League adherents (who think in terms of wars to stop wars) is it viewed as a war preventive. It was perfectly clear that we were drifting toward a policy of covert intervention.

The danger of such a course seemed doubly vivid to me in the light of what I knew about those who were advising Roosevelt on foreign affairs. I could not forget that it was in Billy Phillips' house in Washington that Colonel House met with the British Ambassador in 1914 and 1915 to discuss—no one knows how exactly—the American government's attitude toward the War.[7] I had seen the peace-loving Secretary of State in May, 1933, let Norman Davis commit the United States to as great a degree of "coöperation" with the League powers as could be imagined, short of actual adherence to the League.[8] I knew that the influence of Kellogg and Stimson still lived among the Department's subordinates; that they thought and talked of "aggressors," of "enforcing peace" by non-recognition (as in the case of Japan's conquest of Manchuria), by discriminatory measures against "treaty violators," and by abstention from "any action tending to defeat the collective efforts" of European nations to "restore peace." I knew, finally, how strong were Roosevelt's impulses.

So, as our policy became less and less neutral,[9] I said, in my editorials, just where I thought we were heading and just why I thought we were running smack into what F. D. R. had called at San Diego "those perils that will endanger our peace with the world."

There was a whole series of editorials on this subject through late October and November. And, sandwiched somewhere between, was a critical comment on the reciprocal-tariff treaty with Canada the State Department had just negotiated. I had written critically of the tariff

[7] Walter Millis, *Road to War*. Houghton, Mifflin Company; Boston, 1935; p. 223.

[8] See footnote, page 164.

[9] On November 15th, just before the League sanctions were to come into operation, it was announced in Washington that the shipment of oil, copper, and other commodities to the belligerents would be disapproved, and traders with Italy were warned that they were violating American policy--a contradiction of both the letter and spirit of the Neutrality Act passed by Congress the preceding summer.

policy several times before. This particular piece referred to a public statement by George Peek (who was even then being slowly forced out of the administration because of his disagreement with the Hull tariff policies). It went on to deplore the "furtive" character of the negotiations for reciprocal treaties. It pointed out that "not only was the Canadian treaty consummated without knowledge on the part of the people at large, but its details were kept secret even from persons high in the Administration for days after the treaty had been agreed upon. This secrecy," it said, "is one of the most unhappy aspects of our reciprocal treaty policy as it is now being administered . . . [and hardly fits well] with the liberal protestations of an Administration devoted to the masses of the people."[10]

Curiously enough, it was of this piece that Roosevelt decided to make an issue by doing something that was almost unheard of in our relations. He wrote me a letter.

The contents were decidedly tart. He had not read my "full article," he explained. But he had read portions of it quoted by the Associated Press, and I was wrong "about the 'furtive character' of the negotiations for reciprocal treaties." "Do not get into your head" that such and such is true, he said at one point. "You see how silly George Peek's argument is," he said at another juncture.[11]

It was the first time Roosevelt had taken this tone about anything I had said publicly, although I'd written in much the same vein on the reciprocal-tariff policy before. Clearly, he wouldn't have taken issue with the tariff piece unless he'd been piqued by what I'd been saying about his foreign policy generally. Such indirection was characteristic.

Yet, so far as I was concerned, there was nothing to be gained by beating around the bush. I decided to answer not only what he had written but what I knew he was thinking.

My reply, written on Thanksgiving Day, I give here in full because it's as good an illustration as any of my way of expressing myself to Roosevelt.

November 30, 1935.

The President,
Warm Springs, Georgia.
Dear Governor:

I was delighted to have your frank and earnest note of November 23rd. It gives me the opportunity to speak with equal freedom

[10] *Today,* November 23, 1935, Vol. 5, No. 5.

[11] It appears that he also wrote a letter—a very sharp letter—to George Peek at that time. The letter to me was dated November 23, 1935.

of matters which I have hesitated to discuss with you and so I shall ask your indulgence for what is going to be, I know, a rather lengthy outpouring. I ask leave to tell you, in this letter, just as I should like to if I were sitting with you, all of the thoughts your note has stirred in my mind.

The issues raised in your letter are of transcendent importance, not only to the country and your party but to your own future. I am concerned with these issues on that level, and not on the basis of personal feeling toward members of your State Department. Instead of these differences arising from the events of 1933, it is more truthful to say that those events arose from these differences of opinion which long antedated that time. I found in the State Department under Stimson, even before my official service began there, an atmosphere foreign, it seemed to me, to the vital spirit which characterized the campaign of 1932. That atmosphere has not changed since Stimson's departure. It closed around me and I had not served in office a month before I knew that it would be intolerable. I escaped with my convictions. Those who were in opposition to what it seemed to me were the interests of progressive thought in this country remained.

They remain.

But, as they labor in the shaping of policies that I deeply and earnestly believe to be dangerous, I have left to me the right to criticize, to oppose, and, if possible, to convince you, too, of the existence of the danger.

Now I want to speak to you specifically of the Canadian treaty. I have consistently advocated a general reciprocal agreement with Canada in many private conversations with you and with the Secretary of State before my resignation, in printed articles and in a speech made in Canada after I resigned. I say this to call attention to the record of my belief that we should seek more trade with Canada. Incidentally, I did not, in the editorial about which you wrote to me, discuss the wisdom of a trade agreement with Canada or the specific provisions of the agreement just concluded.

When the existing law on reciprocal trading was before Congress I published a carefully phrased editorial dated March 24, 1934, favoring the bill but indicating my belief that (1) to attempt to carry out the reciprocal-tariff policy while we adhered to the most-favored-nation principle[12] would lead to serious conse-

[12] Adherence to the most-favored-nation principle binds a nation to grant to a second nation, in certain stipulated matters, the same terms as are then, or may be thereafter, granted to any other nations. Some clauses in treaties, embodying this principle, are "reciprocal," requiring that concessions between the signatory states be at all times equal. Others are "imperative" or "unconditional," offering no compensating privileges in return. For years before 1933 our State Department had adhered to the unconditional most-favored-nation principle—even to the point, as Ernest Lindley has remarked, of once asking Brazil to remove the tariff preference which it accorded American automobiles.

quences, and (2) that, in making the treaties, a forum should be provided for discussion "under conditions that conserve the public interest." I have since held firmly to these two beliefs and in the face of that fact I should have been a dishonest journalist had I not spoken my mind once again, even in the face of a popular treaty with Canada.

What troubles me with respect to the present Canadian treaty is the fact that the quotas allowed are "global" and that hence, according to the experts, a certain proportion of the articles admitted will not come from Canada at all but from nations from whom we receive absolutely no *quid pro quo* on this deal. To that extent, the treaty is not a trade; it is a gift—at the expense of American producers.

But, as you say, the danger that we will be flooded with imports is avoided by the use of the quota. In other words, economic and political disaster is avoided by the use of the very device which Secretary Hull denounces. If such circuitous calculations must be followed to avoid the effects of adherence to the most-favored-nation principle, why not achieve our ends directly by eliminating the most-favored-nation concessions entirely and by making bilateral agreements in which we give and receive definite and specific concessions in trade limited by quotas?

Why bother at all to maintain the fiction of most-favored-nation treatment, if fiction it is, and then attempt (not altogether successfully) to avert the consequences of such action by the quota device?

The answer is that those in whom you have vested the authority to administer the reciprocal-tariff policy want to achieve a general downward revision of tariffs without congressional intervention—an end which will most certainly injure your administration and split your following. And I might add, in this connection, that it is this intent, this fixed purpose to lower tariffs on the part of those entrusted with the administration of the Reciprocal Tariff Act that makes so dangerous the indirect, roundabout method now being followed. If the Act were administered by men of another view, by a Key Pittman, or by a Bob La Follette, one might be less fearful: under the present circumstances, apprehension is understandable.

My education on the tariff question goes back a long time, but the conclusions to which it impelled me really crystallized during your preconvention campaign. You will remember that the reciprocal-treaty idea was set forth by you in your St. Paul speech. The position you took in that speech was not only an astute one, politically, but a sound one, from the point of view of economics.

The tariff plank in the Democratic platform was written subsequently without reference to your expressed views. It was so ambiguous that, despite every effort on my part to comprehend it, it remains to this day wholly meaningless to me. I believe that this was your own reaction to it also and that this was the reason why you quite properly carried into the campaign your own tariff policy.

May I add that it seemed perfectly clear to me at the time that the policy you advocated during the campaign could not be carried out if we adhered to the most-favored-nation principle, and that I took it for granted that we would abandon it.

In this connection, you will remember the communications received from Secretary Hull (then Senator) via Mr. Taussig, during the campaign, and the discussion of his suggestions by you, Senators Pittman and Walsh, and myself. Your Sioux City speech, which rejected the idea of any general tariff reduction, was the result.

When I served in the Department of State, I found opinion there unchanged with respect to general tariff reduction and adherence to the most-favored-nation principle, and, despite earnest consideration on my part, the arguments in support of this position seemed to me to be completely unconvincing. In fact, in May, 1933, I wrote a syndicated article (which you read in advance of publication) expressing my conviction that the London Conference could do little on tariff except to effect an exchange of views.

You will recall the fact, I know, that the general-reduction-by-ten-per-cent idea was introduced into the Conference and promptly withdrawn. You will recall further the speech of the Secretary of State addressed to the Conference advocating a general lowering of tariff barriers which you and Billy Phillips very considerably amended.

As to the element of secrecy in the consummation of treaties such as the one we have just made with Canada, I must stick to my guns. I made it clear in the editorial to which you refer that I was aware of the "hearings" that are granted, although the Associated Press dispatch which you saw did not.

But, in my opinion, the hearings now granted do not permit sufficiently detailed exploration of the specific points contemplated in reciprocal treaties. To say that if such hearings were granted some of those injured would make outcries so loud as to defeat the treaty is not an adequate answer to the objection that interested parties are not given sufficient chance to present their arguments.

The present method does not ultimately prevent the outcries, in any case. They only come after the event, rather than before, and then they are the more deadly to you politically because those who emit them can howl that they have not only been injured but that they have had no chance to defend themselves—a charge which always gets public sympathy.

I am not convinced, moreover, that a treaty would be defeated if a fair public hearing were given after initialing and before final executive action. At that point there might be introduced into the proceedings the admirable device embodied in Senator Norris' bill vetoed by Hoover and endorsed by you in your Sioux City speech in 1932, thus:

"Another feature of the bill . . . contemplated the appointment of a public counsel, who should be heard on all applications for changes in rates before the commission on the one hand for increases sought by producers, often greedy, or for decreases asked by importers, equally often actuated by purely selfish motives, or by others seeking such reductions. I hope some such change may be speedily enacted. It will have my cordial approval."

And now since you have made it possible for me to explain my views on this tariff matter I shall take the opportunity to speak of a much more serious question about which I have even graver apprehensions—neutrality. Here the issue is drawn in much the same pattern—conviction on my part that you hold views with which a vast majority of the country agrees, but with respect to which those through whom you are acting are intent upon making a quite different national policy prevail. I have given a great deal of thought to this of late and, while I have occasionally spoken to you of my uneasiness, I have not outlined the circumstances that cause it.

There are, of course, two extreme views with respect to our foreign policy, the one advocating utter isolation, the other, complete entanglement. If I were to describe your following realistically, I should say that, on the whole, your most loyal followers lean toward the first point of view. The first ballot at the convention in 1932 was a fair indication of the type of men who were supporting you, and the subsequent enlistment into their ranks of the western progressives reinforced this element of your support. Surely such internationalist advocates as the *Baltimore Sun* and the *New York Times* could not be counted as sympathetic supporters. Your domestic policies have accentuated this cleavage—a fact which has warmed my heart and enlisted my enthusiasm.

I realize, however, that you should not take an extreme position and hold dogmatically to it. In this instance, the task is to retain national independence of action but to move so far toward internationalism as is safe and expedient. To do this, however, compels the painstaking pursuit of a hazardous course of action. The success of such an operation requires fine instruments and accurate information. Otherwise disaster may result to the nation and to your own loyal following.

Now it requires little demonstration to show that the instruments you are using—that is, the men in whom the delicate execution of the job of preserving neutrality is vested—are, almost without exception, of that school of thought that believes that participation in international coercive movements can save us from war. They are of that mistaken group that guided Wilson along the road, first, to war and, beyond that, to bitter disillusion. I say "mistaken" because it was their advice in 1915, 1916, and 1917 which induced us to enter the war "to end war" and to "save democracy" and subsequent events have shown them to be wrong. Apparently they are still firmly in the saddle, some of them in person, some of them through protégés (*i.e.,* as Bingham, of House), others, career men trained under the old dispensation—all of them the intellectual brethren of the naïve Lansing with one foot at Broad and Wall and the other at Geneva. They tell us now, in one form or another, that we can stop wars by engaging in wars to stop wars. These are the men designated to effectuate your decisions and to provide you with the information necessary to guide you on a dark and dangerous road. (And no one knows better than you, I am sure, how settled are the policies of the State Department and how they differ from your own progressive principles.)

This apprehension concerning your international advisers explains why Congress acted as it did last summer when it rejected Section I of the McReynolds Resolution.

The issue was not new to Congress. In March, 1933, John Bassett Moore had written a letter, read in the hearings of the House Committee on Foreign Affairs, exposing the irreconcilability of a discriminatory embargo with law, common sense, or peace. J. B. Moore sent a copy of that letter to me.

Despite this warning and despite an obviously overwhelming opposition in the Congress, the State Department urged upon you the advocacy of a contrary course this August. Those who spoke for the Department failed to point out to you that a discriminatory arms embargo is a denial of neutrality, that to commit an act of war in the name of peace is a clear reversion to the notion of wars to end war. And, while there are those who believe in this principle, I venture to suggest that an overwhelming proportion of the country agrees with Congress that it is a notion which is self-contradictory.

It is true, as the Department argued, that the President may, by maladroitness, involve us in war. But the great power of the President does not in itself justify asking that he be invested with a complete and unreviewable determination as to which of two foreign belligerents is "right" or "wrong." Yet one of the very top layer of your advisers on foreign relations (not the Secretary) said *in writing* that he wanted this power for the President because *in an international crisis Congress might not act and thus sacrifice our vital interests*. This is a strange doctrine indeed!

The Pittman Resolution was passed in spite of these representations and under it you very properly recognized a state of war between Italy and Ethiopia, pronounced the embargo, and uttered the corollary warning. This was excellent.

But following that, a series of pronouncements came from members of the administration which have confused and alarmed me. Perhaps I can best express my feeling by quoting an editorial that I am publishing this week (issue of December 7th):

"Under our form of government, Congress determines what national policies shall be and expresses its decisions in the laws it makes. The members of the executive branch of the government have the duty of enforcing these laws. That is the meaning of their oath of office.

"When a neutrality resolution came up for consideration in Congress last summer, the executive branch of the government asked for discretionary power in imposing discriminatory restrictions and embargoes on American commerce in case of a foreign war. It asked, in effect, to be allowed to choose between nations engaged in foreign war upon the basis of a moral judgment as to the right and wrong of the quarrel. Congress refused this request and announced a policy of strict impartiality in all relations with reference to warring nations.

"That imposed upon the Department of State the obligation of leaning over backward in carrying out a policy which its duty but not its conviction commanded.

"How is the Administration carrying out the neutrality resolution of Congress? Let us look at its record, not legalistically, but realistically.

"In Europe the opinion apparently prevails that economic sanctions on the part of the League designed to coerce Italy will be ineffective unless the United States 'cooperates.' Europe does not care a rap (and let us not forget this for a single moment) what name we choose to call our participation in sanctions or what explanations we make as to the reasons for our policy. The thing that Europe cares about is the *effect* of our decisions.

"The early acts of the government of the United States in carrying out the neutrality resolution of Congress were correct and sound and raised no issues in Europe. But with the growing disposition on the part of our government to restrict the export of oil, scrap iron, copper, cotton, and other articles not included in the statutory embargo on arms, ammunition, and implements of war (and this despite the fact that Senator Pittman, Chairman of the Senate Committee on Foreign Relations, gave, on the floor of the Senate last August 21st, a definition of the term 'implements of war' which did not include such articles), the tension in Europe has become acute. It has become apparent that the coercing nations of Europe will move against Italy with respect to such items as these only if the United States takes the lead. More ironic still, it is not certain that they will all participate even if the United

States does take the lead. This has definitely made us a determinant factor in the general effort to coerce Italy. The members of the League recognize this situation. Italy must certainly recognize our course of action for what it is—the beginning of an almost inevitable logical sequence of acts which, if carried out, would most certainly end in downright hostility to Italy and which would violate the letter and spirit of the neutrality resolution.

"That we have already as a government passed moral judgment on the issue between the sanctionist powers and Italy seems to me to be obvious. The note sent by the Department of State to the League of Nations on October 26th, while it does not name Italy, nevertheless stamps Italy as a wrongdoer, using instead of the term 'League of Nations,' the alter ego of the League Covenant, the Kellogg Pact.

"Anyone who knows the subtleties of diplomatic language knows that when we, as a nation, look with 'sympathetic interest' upon the 'concerted efforts of other nations' to coerce Italy, which we euphemistically call an attempt 'to preserve peace or to localize and shorten the duration of war,' we obviously favor such action. There is no use quibbling about language. The meaning is clear.

"To express 'sympathetic interest' and then to stop with the expression is, of course, one thing; but to give utterance to this expression and then to follow it up with actions that have the effect of implementing 'sympathetic interest' definitely puts us into a position of taking sides in the present European situation. It is a departure from the letter and spirit of neutrality. I cannot say with too much seriousness that taking sides in this fashion will almost automatically make us a party to the wider war that might easily develop out of the present small war."

When in the pursuit of my duty as a journalist I find it necessary to disagree with my friends, it hurts. Nothing so hurts as to disagree with you. All I can do in such an instance is to be terribly sure that I am right and as nearly as possible consistent with myself. On these two subjects of the tariff and neutrality I feel that assurance. I am glad of only one thing, that they constitute a small—however important—minority of the public policies which you profess.

When I must disagree with any of them I share a feeling that the V. P. [Vice President] expressed to me on one occasion last winter. He said, "I love this man in the White House because he is for so many things that I have always hoped for and believed in. And when he does things that I don't believe in, I love him enough to tell him the truth."

Ever with sincere regard and affection,

To these unequivocal sentiments there was no direct, personal answer. Indeed, there didn't have to be. For on December 8th the news that England and France were agreeing to the dismemberment of Ethiopia burst upon the President, the State Department, and the American public. The hand of *Realpolitik* showed through the glove of international "cooperation." Every newspaper reader in the country could see that we had been gulled again by European diplomacy. The President was forced to withdraw the unneutral demands he and the State Department had made on American traders.

After this, an answer was scarcely possible.

Except that Roosevelt mentioned the receipt of my letter on the telephone, the next time he asked me to prepare some notes for a speech, the incident was never referred to. We went on as though it hadn't occurred.

But obviously it was a landmark—a mournful landmark. The thing I had feared was happening.

3

When I next saw Roosevelt—on December 20, 1935—he announced that he wanted "a fighting speech" for his annual message.

"Whom are you going to fight? And for what?" I asked.

He smiled leniently, and then explained at great length.

I gathered that there wasn't anything sweeping in the way of new legislation he wanted. But he was concerned about keeping his left-wing supporters satisfied. What was more, he wanted the speech to be a kind of prelude to the presidential campaign, a "keynote" speech. And "keynoting," as Ed Lowry has pointed out, "implies the ability to . . . give the impression of passionately and torrentially moving onward and upward while warily standing still."[13]

I seriously questioned that strategy. His progressive supporters had nowhere else to go if they decided to leave his camp, I said. Besides, he could persuade all but a scattering of them of what was the literal truth: that government is the art of adjustment; that, after the New Deal's bold, resolute advances, statesmanship compelled a halt for the perfection of method, the reorganization of administrative machinery, and the improvement of personnel that remained the New Deal's greatest needs. While it was true that many men in business and finance were opposed to much of his program, they could, with time and effort, be persuaded to take a more sympathetic and cooperative attitude. Business was improving—in no small degree because of his

[13] Edward G. Lowry, *Washington Close-Ups; op. cit.;* p. 12.

"breathing-spell" assurances. In our economy business flourished only when men were disposed to take risks. A threat of renewed uncertainty, of further undefined changes, would darken the prospect for production and reemployment. And for what—if it was meaningless? I could see the point of stirring things up only if he had some great objective which could not otherwise be gained, if, for example, he wanted to "fight" for a constitutional amendment. But I couldn't see any justification in provoking a fight for fighting's sake.

The President insisted that his moderate supporters couldn't fail to understand his strategy. He was determined about what he wanted.

He got it. I was the technician again. His "fighting speech" excoriated "entrenched greed," "our resplendent economic autocracy," those who sought "the restoration of their selfish power," those who would " 'gang up' against the people's liberties." It was passionate, stirring. As he came to the peroration and spoke the words, "I cannot better end this message on the 'State of the Union' . . ." a spontaneous guffaw went up from the Republican ranks on the floor of the House. A congressman turned to a colleague, "Message, hell! It's a campaign speech!" he cried. And it was.

Clear-eyed progressives were bitterly disappointed by its lack of substance. Bob La Follette, for instance, told me of his deep regret that it had contained no constructive recommendations.[14] Businessmen—including tens of thousands who did not want "power for themselves, enslavement for the public"—winced.

But the speech gave the country as a whole a thrilling sensation. Delivered at a new pitch of emotional intensity, its invective; its cries of defiance ("Let them no longer hide their dissent in a cowardly cloak of generality"); its oversimplified appeals ("Shall we say to the farmer, 'The prices for your products are in part restored. Now go and hoe your own row?' "); its talk of "great crises," of "unceasing warfare," of "new instrumentalities of public power" which, "in the hands of political puppets of an economic autocracy . . . would provide

[14] Radical opinion may be gauged by the following comments on the speech:

From *The New Republic* of January 15, 1936: ". . . in the long run he cannot hope to hold the masses of the people by expressions of sympathy which, no matter how brilliantly or movingly expressed, give hardly an inkling of what, after nearly three years of office, he proposes to do for them."

From *The Nation* of January 15, 1936: "He doffed the robes of a statesman and became in a trice pure politico . . . as he went on to convert what was supposed to be a thoughtful discussion of the nation's ills and ways of treating them into a political diatribe."

shackles for the liberties of the people"—all this caught, held, and swayed most of its listeners.

Infinitely more serious, it seemed to have caught, held, and swayed its speaker.

I was not unfamiliar with the practice of politics. But never until the moment that I heard Roosevelt deliver that speech on the night of January 3, 1936, did I realize the extent to which verbal excesses can intoxicate not only those who hear them but those who speak them. I had helped prepare the intoxicating brew of epithets and *défis*, and I alternately excused and loathed myself for doing it.

The next day I decided that, technician or no technician, I couldn't square things with myself. There was such a thing as paying too high a price for the privilege of service. So far as my participation was concerned, the incident would never be repeated.

4

But how to insure that decision?

It was obvious that there were only two ways. Roosevelt himself might be persuaded to drop the strategy of which the January 3rd diatribe was the first expression. Failing that, I must get out.

To face these alternatives realistically wasn't to expect the worst. It was merely to be prepared for the worst. Because Roosevelt had successively reversed the "harmony" policy of 1934 and the "breathing-spell" policy of late 1935 was no reason to assume that he wouldn't reverse the fighting-for-fighting's-sake policy of January 3, 1936. Quite possibly he might end up by pitching his campaign on a wholly different level. I must try again and again and again, if need be, to help bring that about. But at the same time I must prepare the way for a quiet, orderly departure. You put fire exits in a theater not because you are certain that there will be a fire but because you must recognize there may be a fire.

The story of the next five months is the story of these twin processes —of the attempt to induce Roosevelt to abandon the strategy of January 3rd, and of the preparations against possible failure.

When I next saw Roosevelt, I tried, for hours, to get him to clarify his objectives. Did he want to revert to the policy of unity and peace and harmony? Or, if not, if he felt that he must wage a militant campaign, would he fight for a constitutional amendment—the only honest way of letting the voters indicate whether they were willing to give the federal government greater power over industry and agriculture? Or, if he had decided to abandon his efforts to achieve something like self-government in industry because of the Supreme Court's adverse decisions, did he intend to embrace the anti-big-business, Brandeis idea?

That night I noted down in my journal:

> There was no clearcut decision as to whether there should be a frank repudiation of business support. A purely defensive campaign seemed to be in his mind. . . . I indicated today that my editorial duties were becoming more pressing, and that it would be necessary for me to cut to a minimum my active participation in the preparation of material for his use.

I tried again—and with no particular success—on February 17th. I gathered from Roosevelt's answers nothing more than that, while he'd like to make constitutional amendment an issue in his campaign, he doubted that the public could be convinced of the need for amendment. Then the talk became a discussion of what he should say at Temple University, Philadelphia, where he was scheduled to speak on February 22nd.

I asked, meaningfully, that day, that the speech contain no name calling. His eyes danced as he agreed. It was another of those bewildering changes of mood.

We talked then, casually, of Tom Corcoran. Late in September, when Tom seemed to have recovered from the hysteria of the holding-company fight, I had begun to let him assist me by gathering preliminary information for the President's use. Once or twice I had even brought him with me to the White House when Roosevelt and I had made plans for speeches and, with Roosevelt's knowledge, had let him try his hand at speech drafting.

Now, on February 17th, I pointed out that, while Tom was still no great shakes as a stylist, he had picked up a deal of what he needed to know by watching what had happened to his drafts. He had learned quickly. He showed promise of being able to absorb much more. This wasn't to suggest that his judgments on policy were sound, or that he didn't have to be watched for efforts to grind the Wilson-Brandeis little-business ax. But when that had been said, the fact remained that he could be exceedingly useful. Certainly he could relieve me of much of the time-consuming and enervating job of collaborating on speech drafting.

That seemed like a good idea, the President said urbanely.

Five days later, at Temple University, he made the peaceable speech on which we'd worked.

Ten days after that, on March 3rd, I read in the newspapers that he'd asked Congress for a corporate-surplus tax.[15]

I had lost the capacity for astonishment—even over the fact that he'd finally embraced the fantastic scheme out of which he'd been talked twice before. I could only be profoundly grateful that he'd seen what I was driving at, in our last two conversations, and had spared me the painful business of refusing to assist in the preparation of that message.

There was a curious little telephone conversation about it the next day. It would have been meaningless to the eavesdropper. Neither of us had the slightest doubt about its import.

What did I think of his message on taxes? Roosevelt asked.

Quite frankly, I said, I couldn't understand why he had taken such a step.[16]

"Well," he retorted cheerfully, "you're a good receiver, but you're no financier."

The reference was to my experience, the preceding year, as receiver of the Hotel St. Regis in New York. I had a momentary urge to answer that as receiver I had balanced my budget. I restrained myself.

Our talk went on amiably and trivially. Would I, he asked, be coming down before he left Washington on the 19th for a fishing trip?

I doubted whether that would be possible, I said. But we'd surely keep in touch over the telephone.

And so I welcomed the news from Steve Early, a few days later, that Stanley High had placed his services at the disposal of the President. I didn't know High, but I knew that he'd been, at one time or another, member of the Methodist Mission to China, correspondent of the *Christian Science Monitor*, lecturer on international affairs, and radio speaker on a program called "Religion in the News." High was then

[15] This request was made in a supplemental budget message. The federal government needed new revenues to replace the processing taxes thrown out by the Supreme Court's A.A.A. decision in January, 1936. That, of course, scarcely justified the recommendation of an essentially unsound method of attempting to raise such revenues.

[16] It was to appear that a good many members of Congress couldn't, either. The proposal was vastly watered down before it passed, in 1936. Even so, the measure operated as I'd predicted to Roosevelt the previous June. In the spring of 1938 Congress left only a stump of the corporate-surplus tax in the Revenue Bill of 1938, which became law without Roosevelt's signature. In 1939 even this small stump was rooted out by Congress.

perfecting plans for a "Good Neighbor League," an organization which was to rally Roosevelt support during the campaign, and Steve, who knew of my desire to unload, had introduced him into the Roosevelt circle.

I held no brief for Corcoran as against High. High was an experienced writer and speaker, but scarcely an economist. Corcoran knew vastly more about what was going on in Washington, but had a lawyer's incapacity for cogent and incisive writing. Either or both, I hoped, would prove to be satisfactory replacements. Possibly they would make a good team. My one concern was to inch out of my responsibilities without a fuss. The sooner someone was found who could take over, the easier I would be. I couldn't have been more pleased that the shift was being permitted to take place calmly, quietly, and undramatically.

In March and April we talked on the telephone several times, Roosevelt and I, about this or that step he was taking. The talk was so friendly, suggestions were asked for and received in such good part, the critical editorials I'd been writing on his tax policy were passed over so completely, that I took heart. If, as seemed increasingly probable, the kind of campaign in which I couldn't honestly participate was waged, I could leave without breaking through any walls. The way was being cleared.

On April 23rd I was asked to come to the White House to lend a hand with the speech Roosevelt was scheduled to make on the 25th, in New York. I was told that the President's speech in Baltimore, on the 13th, was considered "a flop." Such candor was engaging. I said that of course I'd come, though I did have a speech of my own to deliver in New York on the night of the 24th. I'd finish up my own speech and fly down. About all I could do, on such short notice, was to talk things over with the President and High.

When I got to Washington, I was able to make very little out of our talk. The President was thinking of a speech describing his economic objectives. But it developed that he'd not cleared up the indecision that preceded and followed his "horse-and-buggy" interview, and nothing that I could say—even my attempts to recall the fact that we'd been over this same ground numberless times—seemed to dissipate his irresolution. He was still obviously trying to reconcile the idea of industrial self-rule under government supervision with the big-business-is-bad-business philosophy. I did my best to caution against any such attempt. I urged that he avoid talk of economics until he'd come to a fundamental decision. Late on the 24th I left some general suggestions for the substance of the speech with High, whom I'd found exceedingly likable.

The speech turned out, unfortunately, not to be fish, flesh, or fowl. And included in it was one of the most infelicitous passages Roosevelt ever uttered. "Reduction of costs of manufacture does not mean more purchasing power and more goods consumed," said he. "It means just the opposite."

It's important to note that in the officially published papers of the President this statement has been made to read: "Reduction of costs of manufacture *by cutting wages or lengthening hours* does not mean more goods consumed. It means the exact opposite"[17] (italics mine). But as the statement was delivered, it was an absurdity. Needless to say, it provided the opposition press with a field day.

It also served as the starting point for one of the most unhappy conversations I've ever had in my life.

I'd been asked on the 24th to spend the first week-end in May sailing on the yacht *Potomac,* with the President and some Scottish friends of the Roosevelt family. On Sunday afternoon, May 3rd, Roosevelt and I found ourselves sitting alone on deck. I remarked that his statement about costs and purchasing power had been taken out of its context by those who criticized it. Other sentences in his speech had made it clear that he merely intended to reject the reduction of costs as a cure-all. Obviously he approved reducing costs of manufacturing by new machinery, new techniques, and greater efficiency of employees. Certainly he hadn't meant to imply that such reductions in costs caused a decline of purchasing power.

Whereupon Roosevelt replied, "There are two schools of thought on that subject, you know. One's right and one's wrong."

I had no chance to ask what this bewildering comment meant because he then went on to say angrily that he didn't care what the newspapers said. The speech was a hit. And he didn't mean just with the crowd in New York. The telegrams that had come in from the country would show me that it was one of the most completely successful speeches he had ever delivered.

That I didn't doubt, I explained. It simply seemed to me that a truer statement of his objectives would be that he was aiming for a reasonably stable price level, ultimately; that, meanwhile, he believed,

[17] *The Public Papers and Addresses of Franklin D. Roosevelt; op. cit.;* Vol. 5, p. 181.

some specific prices ought to come down and some go up. That was what he had been saying, at any rate. It was toward that goal, so far as I could see, that his administration had been working.

Any such selective process, he snapped, would involve a planned economy. And we couldn't have that in this country.

"But isn't planning—in the sense of intelligent attempts to insure stability of production and employment—just what you *do* want?" I asked. "Isn't that why you've encouraged reasonable businessmen . . ." I got no further. The phrase "reasonable businessmen" seemed to release a storm of pent-up resentment.

He had talked to a great many businessmen, he said. In fact, he'd talked to more businessmen than any other President. And they were generally very stupid. The trouble with them—and that applied even to so-called liberal businessmen—was that they had no "moral indignation" about the sins of other businessmen. "Did they," he cried, "denounce Charles E. Mitchell or Harry Sinclair? They did not!"

That went for the newspapers too. Not a single editorial, it appeared, had ever attacked Mitchell or Sinclair or Edward L. Doheny. And why? Why, indeed, except that the newspapers also lacked "moral indignation." All were, from time to time, guilty of falsifying news.

I doubted the wisdom of his taking them all on and fighting them, I said.

They were destroying themselves, he assured me. Their readers were losing faith in them. "That man over there," he said, pointing to a farmhouse on the shore, "has got into the nabit of saying, 'Well, that's only a newspaper story.' " For his part, he was not at all concerned. Nothing would help him more than to have it known that the newspapers were all against him. As for bankers and businessmen, he could wholeheartedly say that he welcomed their hatred. Every time they made an attack upon him, he gained votes.

I broke in then. It was one thing to welcome hatred and another to provoke it needlessly. Newspapers performed an elementary service in our democratic system. They were especially needed in periods like the one through which we were passing—when the opposition party was practically comatose and there was an almost complete lack of debate within the ranks of the party in power. As for business, it could scarcely be considered a parasitic growth on our civilization. It was part of it—in sickness and in health. Since this was true, since both newspapers and business were inseverable parts of our system, how could it serve the welfare of the country to attempt to discredit them?

Nobody objected to fair, constructive discussion and debate, was the answer. It was destructive, unjust criticism, an excess of debate, we were discussing. Only yesterday, it appeared, the President's Scottish friend had told him that the trouble with the then Tory Government was that there was too much discussion in the Cabinet.

But the only alternative to discussion within the government and the evolution, through discussion, of the proposals for which the political party takes responsibility was a dictatorship, I said.

"No," said Roosevelt. "It is leadership."

Could it be that he was referring to the kind of leadership Gladstone used to exercise? I asked.

Things had changed since Gladstone's day, the President informed me.

Things may have changed, but not that principle, I countered. The principle of consistent discussion, consistent criticism, provided the only check on irresponsible government. I, for one, would never concede that it ought to go. I intended to go right on criticizing publicly those of his policies with which I didn't agree.

He had no intention of suggesting that I shouldn't, Roosevelt said. Then he took up the "moral-indignation" theme again.

Mightn't "moral indignation" be a little anemic within the administration? I asked. Where was the administration's "moral indignation" when Senator Black ruthlessly invaded the privacy of citizens in his utility-lobbying investigation of the preceding summer?

For that, the President explained, there was ample precedent. Judge Seabury had "got the goods" on Sheriff Tom Farley in 1931 by going to the New York banks and demanding Farley's bank accounts. As a result, he, Roosevelt, had been able to lay down a new principle of public responsibility. And I was to consider what Senator Walsh had done to "get the goods" on those involved in the oil scandals. Walsh had subpoenaed all telegrams going into a certain town.

I said that, if Walsh knew what he was after, he ought to have subpoenaed certain telegrams specifically.

Ah! said Roosevelt. No doubt the telegrams were sent by and received by subordinates.

Then Walsh should have subpoenaed all telegrams sent and received by those subordinates, I insisted. I simply wanted to set in the record my opinion that it would have been better to let the guilty go free than to establish the principle of dragnet investigations. I did not believe that the end justified the means. I did not believe, as long as we were talking of "moral indignation," that the kettle of the newspapers was particularly blacker than the pot of the administration.

This nightmarish conversation went on and on in circles for some two hours. It left me with the harrowing intimation that Roosevelt was looking forward to nothing more than having the opposition of his "enemies"—the newspapers, the bankers, the businessmen—reelect him.

The chaotic violence of the summer of 1935 could be rationalized away. Then Roosevelt had been a man determined, at all costs, to drive through his program. Whatever one might think of its wisdom and of the methods used to get it through Congress, at least there had been a program. But when, in the calm that followed the storm, Roosevelt had said to Roy Howard that his program had reached "substantial completion," he had apparently spoken the literal truth.

Two courses were open to him now—the two between which I'd been imploring him to choose. He could proceed in fact, as well as in word, to perfect the institutions he had created, to improve personnel, to adjust the strained relationship between business and government, to encourage greater production by private enterprise. And, if that prosaic job seemed too tame for a man of his activism, he could undertake to champion a constitutional amendment.

In either of these courses I could follow him with enthusiasm. I had been pleading for a decision. But his compass had swayed back and forth. In the autumn when his foreign policy shifted so fast, in January when he delivered a "fighting" speech about nothing in particular, in January and February when I questioned him at length about what the issues should be and came away unenlightened, in March when he seized what he had twice rejected—the surplus tax—in April when his economic views swirled with inconsistency, the lack of decision was apparent. The conclusion was inescapable that he did not see that there was anywhere to go at all. He was a mariner more interested in the voyage than in the destination. I, in company with all his associates, was expected to go along for the ride.

Even that might have been tolerable, though barely tolerable.

But the conversation on the deck of the *Potomac* that afternoon of May 3rd was something else again. It precipitated heartbreaking questions. Could it be that, while Roosevelt's indefiniteness about his program from January through April had resulted from his disinclination to think things through, his indefiniteness was now calculated? Could it be that, knowing he was certain to be reelected, he had determined to present no clear-cut program to the electorate? Could it be that he was deliberately setting out to get a blank check from the American people—a mandate, not to the party, or a party platform, but to himself?

How else explain his willingness to continue denouncing business and the press? How else explain his use of the phrase "I welcome their hatred"? How else explain his indifference to the meaning and effect of such a policy? How else, finally, explain his portentous "No, it is leadership"?

Was he identifying the cause of progressivism with the maintenance of his own ascendancy? Had he actually grown to believe that his personality was an issue, a principle, in and by itself? Could he, on sober second thought, assert that he was the road and the chart and the compass—the way and the truth and the light? Had time and circumstance, the private adulation and public acclaim that went with the Presidency, the exercise of the unprecedented powers that had been granted him since March 4, 1933, and the partial victory of August, 1935, at last begun to endow him with a conviction of personal rectitude that would brook no dissent, suffer no challenge, recognize no truth but that which it proclaimed?

I had to know the answer to those questions.

Three years before, when I had resigned, we had written that we were joined on the basis of "our common ideals." If the answer to my questions was "Yes," the tie had been finally cut.

I would try again—desperately, this time—to persuade him to adopt a program in which he was *not* the issue. And if I failed again, then I had to do what I was prepared to do.

5

The stage couldn't have been more perfectly set when we next met, in the oval room of the White House, on an evening late in May.

For well over an hour I had no chance to focus our talk on the coming campaign. Still, long before we reached that question, I had learned what I'd come to find out.

It appeared that the President was, if anything, even more irritated with the press than he'd been when we'd last talked. He had struck out at several Washington commentators at the Gridiron Dinner and had excoriated the newspaper publishers, on another off-the-record occasion, for failing to live up to their duty to give the public unbiased news. Naturally, there had been back talk. By mid-May acidulous comments were being so freely exchanged that the row had become a matter of public knowledge. *Today,* among other journals, had described it. The article we carried, though written by two newspapermen highly sympathetic to the administration, warned that "the lucubrations of critical columnists—unpalatable as they are to the New Dealers—are part of the freedom of the press. . . . A dispassionate observer would go still further and say that . . . opposition . . . is a most wholesome influence."[18]

This article seemed to be very much in the President's mind when we began to talk. And second only to it were the newspaper accounts of two or three speeches I had made in the preceding weeks—speeches which referred to the growing misunderstanding between government and business and which discussed, frankly, the extent to which not only business but the administration was responsible for that ill will.

The President was distinctly annoyed. It appeared that the article in *Today* just went to prove how unfair the press could be. The article was entitled "Peeved at the Press." That, in itself, was unfair, the President said crossly, because he was definitely not peeved at the press. As to the newspaper accounts of my speeches, they, too, were written unfairly. They suggested that I had criticized him publicly.

I said that I'd be very glad to send him copies of the speeches in question. I hoped he would agree that they were fair. Certainly, they were honest. And they had, in point of fact, been critical of the corporate-surplus tax and several other policies. But that was nothing new—my discussion of public questions as I saw them.

Curiously enough, Roosevelt would not talk of the substance of my critical comments. He returned to the question of how the press had probably "misrepresented" what I'd said, and expatiated upon it at length.

I remarked quietly that it was impossible for me to regulate the way my speeches were reported. So far as I could see, the only way to prevent them from being occasionally reported in a biased fashion was not to speak at all.

Did I realize, I was asked, that when I made a speech or wrote an editorial I was quoted by the Republican press only because of the fact that I was formerly a member of his administration?

[18] *Today,* May 23, 1936, Vol. 6, No. 5.

It took a minute to answer that one as gently as I knew I must. After all, I had been critical of some of Roosevelt's policies. And so there was no reason to resent his criticism of me.

Quite possibly what he said was true, I replied. But that couldn't be helped. It seemed to me that there were two ways of serving with honor in public affairs. The first was service in office. There the essential virtue was loyalty to the "Chief." I had rendered that kind of service between March, 1932, and September, 1933—apparently to his complete satisfaction. But in the profession of journalism, which, since September, 1933, had commanded my first allegiance, the essential virtue was independence. And that I could not knowingly impair—no matter what the Republican papers or anyone else made of what I said.

Oh, well, said the President, considering the circulation of *Today*, it was of no importance to him what I said in it.

There could be no gentle answer to this. So I didn't try to devise one. I tried, instead, to bring the conversation around to issues. And without success. The talk wandered from the criticism of the press to the "violent attacks" of the Chamber of Commerce. Each "attack" helped him, Roosevelt repeated.

That was as might be. But was *all* criticism of his administration to be construed as "attack" upon him? I asked. Wasn't there a vital distinction? I, for instance, had been privately and publicly critical of the surplus tax sponsored by Oliphant. Did that mean that I was "attacking" the administration as a whole and that, hence, I had become an "enemy"?

"I am not interested in talking about the tax proposal," was the answer. "You can have any opinion you want on that. That's a detail." And then, impatiently, "You seem to be interested in personalities and details. I am not interested in personalities. It's not what you say or think about an individual in the administration or about a specific issue. There's one issue in this campaign. It's myself, and people must be either for me or against me."

That, really, was all I needed to know.

The rest—my futile effort to persuade him that he was describing a policy of negation, a policy that might win the battle but would certainly lose the war; my useless appeal for a campaign on issues of policy; his raising the question of my participation in the campaign and my answering that I could do no more than advise from time to time, as a friend—this was unimportant. It followed inexorably from his, "There's one issue in this campaign. It's myself, and people must be either for me or against me."

When I left the White House late that night, I had a complete picture of what the campaign would be.

I had failed.

Now my one thought, almost my prayer, was "Nunc dimittis"—"Now lettest thou thy servant depart in peace."

6

But for all my planning, all my building of emergency exits, even that was vouchsafed only grudgingly.

On June 7th Tom Corcoran came to New York to see me. He had come to inform me of the President's wish that I draft some plans for his second acceptance speech.

I was sorry, I told Tom. But I was convinced that I could be of little assistance to the President. Nothing I could prepare could possibly harmonize with his own approach to the campaign.

Tom was shocked. With no inconsiderable naïveté he reminded me that to work with the President as I had done was to secure an incalculable opportunity for influence. I was mad to pass up such a chance.

No doubt, I said. But it was a very special kind of madness. Some people called it "conscience." "You remember, Tom," I added, "that just about two years ago I gave you hell for talking in terms of a 'war' between government and business. I said that that wasn't the administration's policy. Well, it's turned out that it is. And I can't participate in that kind of campaign."

Tom urged that I "go along" anyhow. Surely I could slip into the President's utterances the note of moderation. "You write the music," Tom said. "He only sings it."

"Tom," I exploded, "I got you entree to the White House to serve Roosevelt's ideas, not yours. I've never, in my association with Roosevelt, insinuated anything into his speeches. He and I have argued endlessly over what the substance of a speech should be. But once he reached a decision, I've never slipped anything over on him. I can only plead with you to do the same. Remember, when you get to work on speeches, that you're a clerk, not a statesman."

Tom hastened to assure me that he'd spoken impulsively, that he'd picked the argument out of the air to move me to change my mind.

The talk went on hour after hour. It ended with a confession of stage fright by Tom. He was nervous. He would, since I was adamant, go ahead and try to get something written. But wouldn't I please, for *his* sake—since this was his first big job—dictate a few suggestions?

I did, and promised, finally, to look over his stuff before he submitted it to the White House.

Two weeks later the President himself telephoned to ask that I come to the White House on Wednesday, June 24th, "to lend a hand." This was the moment I'd tried to avoid. I thought he knew that Tom was at work, and that I'd promised to look over what Tom produced, I answered. "Yes," said the President, he knew all about it. But would I come on the 24th? It was a challenge—a direct, personal challenge. It could not be ducked without raising the false and irrelevant issue of friendship. I agreed to come.

On June 22nd I ran down to Philadelphia, where the Democratic Convention was assembling. There, in a hotel room, I met Tom and examined his draft. It was some twelve thousand words long. Far more important, it was, for the most part, an elaborate, involved exposition of the Brandeis little-business philosophy. I began to understand the urgency with which I'd been summoned.

I went over the draft at length, redictating and tossing out great gobs of it. But it was obvious that a fresh start would have to be made.

The President, on the morning of the 24th, proved to be in one of his most gracious and captivating moods. "I want the speech to be only fifteen minutes long," he explained. "And it must rise to a very serious note."

I understood that he had seen Bernie Baruch the preceding Friday, I said. Baruch, as the President knew, was sailing for Europe this very day. But two or three days ago Bernie had told me that he thought the theme of the President's acceptance speech ought to be Serenity and Service. Doubtless he'd said as much to the President. But I wondered whether this suggested anything to the President.

My reference to Bernie's suggestion was, of course, intended as bait. But I certainly didn't expect the answer it drew.

The suggestion was splendid, the President said. In addition to it, though, he would like to bring in reference to Hope, Faith, and Charity—Charity being interpreted as Love—and, on this framework, stretch the exposition of his objectives.

"Wouldn't Liberty, Security, and Cooperation have more pertinence?" I asked dryly.

They could be brought in too, the President assured me.

I could hardly suppress a grin. The thought went through my mind that with Baruch's "Serenity and Service," Roosevelt's "Faith, Hope, and Charity" and my "Liberty, Security, and Cooperation," there would be enough evangelism to spread out thickly over several campaigns.

But that, seemingly, was all there was to go on, all there could be to go on, in the absence of any coherent political and economic program. The one meager source of comfort was that the speech was to be Sweetness, if not Light.

I left the White House with Corcoran, went to the Mayflower Hotel, and, by evening, had dictated several pages.

Corcoran and I returned, by invitation, for dinner with the President, Missy Le Hand, Stanley High, and Sam Rosenman. (Rosenman and High were keeping in touch with the Democratic chieftains at the convention for Roosevelt, somewhat as Rosenman had done at Albany in 1932.) In the course of that dinner there occurred an interchange which has been described to the public in various ways and which, in justice to everyone concerned, deserves to be placed in its proper perspective. Alsop and Kintner, for instance, have described it thus:

> When the meal hour neared . . . they gathered around the President in the small family dining room, and for a while everyone relaxed. Work was over, school was out, and under the benign presidential eye they gave rein to an attack of high spirits. Long before, Ray Moley had been charged with the dreadful duties of liaison officer between the New Deal and business, and particularly since his attack on the undistributed profits tax he had been much courted by big businessmen. In the course of the teasing High twitted Moley on his rich friends, and the table laughed.
>
> Moley was annoyed, but for a moment it seemed that the table's laughter would end the incident. Then the President took up the chaffing, and Moley, being touchy, answered with some heat. The President grew angry. Moley grew furious. While the others reddened with embarrassment and Miss Le Hand tried frantically to create a diversion, Moley and the President had a loud, bitter and heartfelt quarrel. Before it was finished words had been exchanged which could not be forgotten.[19]

I don't know who, of those present, provided the press with this story. It certainly didn't come from me, and surely the President never told it. It is misleading chiefly in so far as it suggests that the episode

[19] Joseph Alsop and Robert Kintner, *Men around the President;* op. cit.; p. 104.

was the occasion of a final "break" between us.[20] And I quote it only for the purpose of giving it the perspective the person who described it to the press obviously lacked.

As Governor and President, F. D. R. had never imposed any formal prohibition upon my lifelong habit of plain, even rough, talk. He enjoyed a like privilege in dealing with me. Such exchanges had not been common. But they had occurred. I was never his playmate, his jester, his billowy surcease from mental strain. God had not endowed me with qualities for such a role. I had been with him in tough moments—moments when nerves were taut and decisions had to be made. When hard words are exchanged under such circumstances, they are not indicative of personal crises. They are the necessary by-products of candid, straightforward dealing. They pass with the moment of strain. Adult, civilized men take them for what they are worth.

This particular exchange of asperities was no different from the rest. It had vanished by morning, like a June mist over a fish pond. We even bantered about it. When Roosevelt read over the rough notes I'd dictated the preceding afternoon, and came to the sentence, "Governments can err, Presidents do make mistakes." . . . he looked at me for a moment, read these words aloud, and laughed uproariously. There was a joking reference to what had happened the night before. Then we went on working over the draft.

Late that afternoon, Thursday, the 25th, the speech was finished. The President then gave Corcoran and me copies of the draft of the Democratic platform of 1936, which had already been dispatched to Philadelphia. This, Roosevelt told me, he'd composed in his study with his eyes on the ceiling. I saw, as I read it, that it was remarkable for more than its curious origin. Unlike most platforms, it was a literary achievement. It was also susceptible of more varying interpretations than most other things of its kind.

I noted, at dinner that evening with Corcoran and Cohen on the Shoreham terrace, that it seemed to commit the party to a constitutional amendment permitting Congress to exercise wider control over interstate commerce. It was as though I'd threatened to drop a bomb on their heads. They hastily reread the draft plank on the Constitution. Yes, indeed, they cried. The plank did propose "clarifying amendment"

[20] No words were exchanged "which could not be forgotten." Incidentally, too, Stanley High did not begin the discussion of my "rich friends," and I did not, as is suggested in *Men around the President*, join with Corcoran "in detesting High." There was not the slightest friction there. I have always liked and respected High.

if various problems could not "be effectively solved by legislation within the Constitution." That, they announced, was suicidal. They believed, as did all the group associated with Frankfurter, that there was no need for amendment. It was their theory that with the Court reconstituted, and with the proper amount of judicial legerdemain, anything the President wanted might be achieved without amendment.

It was amusing to witness their agitation. They bolted their dinners and then rushed off—Cohen to write a memorandum to the President urging certain changes in the plank on the Constitution (this memorandum Tom later took to the President) and Tom to make frantic attempts to get hold of Senator Barkley and Solicitor General Reed and urge *them* to change the plank.

Their efforts were immediately unavailing, of course. The plank stood as it had come from the President. So did the rest of the platform—except for one change made by the Democratic Committee on Resolutions. That change consisted of the splitting of a sentence which, in its original form, read: "We have begun and we shall continue the successful drive to rid our land of kidnapers, bandits and malefactors of great wealth." Enough members of the Resolutions Committee rebelled over this statement to create a first-class rumpus. And it was hardly edifying to see the leaders of the party spend hours over the telephone arguing about whether a period ought to separate the "malefactors of great wealth" from the kidnapers and bandits, at a moment when the country believed they were thoughtfully determining their course in the coming campaign.

In any case, the rebels won a victory of sorts. The sentiment, as it finally appeared, was phrased thus:

"We have begun and shall continue the successful drive to rid our land of kidnapers and bandits. We shall continue to use the power of government to end the activities of the malefactors of great wealth who defraud and exploit the people."

With this insignificant alteration the President's statement of party policy was enthusiastically accepted.

Friday morning, June 26th, the President turned again to his acceptance speech, which I'd over-optimistically thought, the preceding afternoon, was finished. He decided, cheerfully, that there was not enough "fire" in the speech. And so he revised it—eliminating a long passage on cooperation and inserting in its place a diatribe about "economic royalists," "new economic dynasties, thirsting for power," "economic tyranny," "the resolute enemy within our gates," the Revolution, the

Minute Men, et cetera. An examination of the text of this speech, as finally delivered, will show the almost ludicrous juxtaposition of these fulminations and the invocation to Faith, Hope, and Charity. It was Friday morning that this oratorical Gryphon emerged.

It left me wholly unmoved. It was as though Roosevelt and I had been adding up the same column of figures and come out with different answers. I had tried to add up the past five months—his January message to Congress, his determination not to meet specific economic issues, his insistence upon capitalizing the hatred of his "enemies," his seeming determination to campaign as a kind of St. George—and had put down a conclusion which did not fit them. Roosevelt's new draft was an accurate summation of it all. I couldn't help but recognize that patent fact.

I made no protest. I offered no further suggestion when he showed me the draft. I picked it up, went into the Cabinet room, and, with a red pencil, inserted a number of inconsequential stylistic changes, took it back to his desk, and explained that I'd like to get back to the convention. He said, "Of course you do." I said good-by, and so we left it.

On Sunday, the 28th, he called from Hyde Park. He was delighted with the triumphant reception of the speech Saturday night. He thanked me for my help, far too generously, and went out of his way to remark that there'd been particularly vigorous applause after certain passages in the speech to which I'd contributed. He had forgotten (whether by accident or design, I did not know) that the issue of principle between us had been none the less present for being unspoken, as we worked over the speech. He was the same man who had greeted me, after London, with the gay comment that he'd had a great press on his "bombshell" message.

I don't remember what I said. It could hardly have been very coherent. But it was friendly enough. I valued for what it was his gesture of calling.

It seemed to me inevitable, now, that Roosevelt would ultimately sweep his administration into extreme positions that would expose it to the devastating counterattack of reaction. But that was his choice and his risk. I'd done my best. Now I was in a position to leave his service permanently and happily.

Late in July, with Vincent Astor, I had a pleasant little social visit with the President at Hyde Park. I carefully spent August in California—out of reach, for all practical purposes.

Directly after my return, in September, I saw Frank Walker. He asked whether I wasn't intending to participate in the campaign. I explained, with great restraint, why I couldn't.

In a day or two I noted in the newspapers that Walker was at Hyde Park. That night I received an invitation to lunch with the President the following Sunday. I went. It was a completely pleasant occasion. I was asked for advice about the campaign—another friendly gesture—and I answered with the recommendation that Senator Joe O'Mahoney be taken on the Western campaign trip to help with the speeches.

Joe was taken.

After the election I sent Roosevelt a congratulatory telegram. Through Miss Le Hand, it was graciously answered.

And there the story of personal relations ends. There was no "break," no trouble, no recrimination, no bitterness, and, so far as I know, no diminution in personal warmth.

That this conclusion isn't what the gossips might desire doesn't concern me. Lives aren't lived according to the vagaries of romancers. They're lived according to an inward light, however feeble. And I believe both of us would have the end of our relations as it was.

CHAPTER X

SUMMER WITHOUT INCREASE

"THERE'S one issue in this campaign," Roosevelt had announced in May. "It's myself." . . .

That was the essence of the campaign of 1936.

It asked no "great and solemn referendum." It did not undertake to register a national decision or even a series of national decisions on future policies. It did not ask the voters to sanction a specific course of governmental action. It invited only an expression of faith in a man.

By dint of much wishful thinking a number of doubtful Democrats were able to persuade themselves that, after the election, Mr. Roosevelt would suddenly be transformed. The responsibilities of his second term, they argued, would impose on him a less "political," less opportunistic, more measured administration of his office and a more generous attitude toward those who sometimes disagreed with him.[1]

Yet it seemed to me that the effect of the campaign and the election would be the precise opposite. There was nothing in Roosevelt's career to indicate that success would make him more judicious. And the danger of his belief that he was the embodiment rather than the servant of progressivism was intensified a thousandfold by the nature of his appeal.

[1] Typical of such opinion was an editorial in the *New York Times* of October 1, 1936, which read, in part: ". . . we believe that Mr. Roosevelt is a keen enough judge of public opinion to make his second Administration more conservative than his first, in the sense that conservatism means consolidating ground already gained and perfecting measures hastily enacted. We believe this both because the tide of public opinion is now running with steadily increasing strength against hasty experimentation and because the President himself has moved definitely in this direction. . . . The position taken by *The Times* is in line with its traditional sympathy for the main purposes and the moving spirit of the Democratic party. We believe that in this case conservatives and radicals can compose their differences within that party, and that the result will be to dissipate, rather than enlarge, class antagonisms, sectional jealousies and factional disputes. Tolerance is an essential part of the American tradition and national unity our most deeply prized possession."

The campaign began quietly enough, with trips to various projects where the use to which federal money had been put could be skillfully dramatized. By October its theme appeared less delicately. It was nothing more or less than an attempt to identify Roosevelt's objectives with the objectives of as many other people as possible. The new, organized army of the unemployed, mobilized Northern negroes, conservative Republican farmers from the corn belt, the growing membership of the C.I.O., Norman Thomas' vanishing army of orthodox Socialists, Republican progressives and Farmer-Laborites, Share-the-Wealthers, single-taxers, Sinclairites, Townsendites, Coughlinites, the medicine men from a thousand campfires—all were invited to give their allegiance to the Democratic candidate. They were to follow him because each saw, or thought he saw, the moon of his desire floating in the beneficent sky of Roosevelt's humanitarian aspirations. A mystic bond of sympathy was being created between Roosevelt and his audiences.

The crowds—excited by the rush of band-wagon riders to the obviously winning side, the reclamation of such prominent dissenters as James Warburg and Hugh Johnson, the free flow of money into the coffers of the party, the irrepressible enthusiasm of the party chieftains—assembled in unheard-of numbers.

But vast audiences cannot be electrified by the repetition of vague promises. And it was impossible to be explicit about future plans because there were no future plans. Since the statesman had left the orator in possession of the field, only one course was possible. New and more thrilling flourishes were required as the October days passed. The bond that words had spun, words had to make incandescent. Roosevelt and his listeners had to be fused by a flow of sensations—by hope, fear, gratitude, hate.

The speeches through October became increasingly emotional. So did the audiences. So did the speaker. For he had succumbed completely to the heady spell he was creating. That became unmistakable on the night of October 31, 1936.

There could be no question, by that time, of how overwhelming his victory would be. His political opponents were at his feet. His battle was won. It was the moment when a referee stops the fight and mercifully announces a technical knockout. That referee should have been Roosevelt's instinct for moderation. Had it been operating, these words could not have been spoken:

"We had to struggle with the old enemies of peace—business and financial monopoly, speculation, reckless banking, class antagonism, sectionalism, war profiteering.

"They had begun to consider the Government of the United States as a mere appendage to their own affairs. We know now that Government by organized money is just as dangerous as Government by organized mob.

"Never before in all our history have these forces been so united against one candidate as they stand today. They are unanimous in their hate of me—and I welcome their hatred.

"I should like to have it said of my first Administration that in it the forces of selfishness and of lust for power met their match. I should like to have it said of my second Administration that in it these forces met their master."

Thoughtful citizens were stunned by the violence, the bombast, the naked demagoguery of these sentences. No one who has merely read them can half know the meaning conveyed by the cadences of the voice that uttered them.

Roosevelt was the master of a great deal that night. But he was subject to a master, too. He was the plaything of his own desire for effect.

The election, of course, settled nothing so far as future policy was concerned.

In October I said: "Hardly will the stroke of midnight pass on November 3rd, hardly will the results of the election be known, than the *danse macabre* of unsettled issues will begin."[2] But as the returns came in, it was possible to make a more exact prediction.

Roosevelt had been reelected by a huge aggregation of hopelessly incompatible elements. He was not going to be able to discover the least common denominator of the wishes of all the groups that supported him because there was no such thing. Their unity rested not in attachment to each other, or even to him, but in the belief that Roosevelt had promised to provide an abundant life in accordance with each of a score of contradictory specifications. Such a victory carried the seeds of its own defeat.

But Roosevelt could not be expected to see that. The size of his majority, in itself, would produce that overweening confidence that would blind him to the dangers of his situation. Now more than ever, he would be certain that he could reconcile the irreconcilable, certain of his infallibility.

Jim Farley, a man never given to self-deception, might and did know

[2] *Today*, October 31, 1936, Vol. 7, No. 2.

better. Privately, he was frank to express his fears. Publicly, at the very moment that wildly triumphant songs were being sung to the accompaniment of Tom Corcoran's accordion at Hyde Park, Farley sounded the one generous and reassuring note of election night. His "no reprisals" statement was suggested and prepared by Herbert Swope. But it was Farley's no less than Swope's. It reflected Jim's warmth, his good will, and his political realism.

Not surprisingly, Jim seemed to have a monopoly of these characteristics so far as the high command was concerned. The mood of men like Tom Corcoran was far more suggestive of what lay ahead.

Tom, whom I'd not seen since June, came to pay me a visit on November 13th. He had, I knew, carried a heavy burden for F. D. R. during the campaign. As chief speech collaborator (of that the speeches gave internal evidence), he'd been closer to the President than anyone else. Because of propinquity, he'd shared the exhilaration of the whirl around the country. I was exceedingly eager to see the effect of the experience on him.

We talked of a number of things, and the conversation was a strange demonstration.[3]

I raised, first, the question of constitutional amendment, which, despite the platform, had scarcely been mentioned since June. I regretted, I said, that the President had so sedulously avoided discussion of the constitutional issue.

Tom answered by referring to a book about the Supreme Court that came out about that time—a book which was simply a personal attack upon certain of the Supreme Court Justices. He spoke enthusiastically of it. We must, he explained, "ease out" some of the Justices.

I asked him how he proposed to do that.

He mentioned a possible pension law or an age limitation.

I remarked wryly that any age limitation on the Justices would force Mr. Justice Brandeis off the Court at once.

Tom countered with a complete *non sequitur*. The book we'd been talking about, he said, gave Brandeis "a clean bill of health."

"You'll have a time drafting a law embodying the specific likes and dislikes of this book's authors, won't you?" I asked.

Tom ignored that. After all, said he, "Van Devanter and Sutherland are the only ones we need to get at."

Had it occurred to Tom, I asked, that, whether or not the member-

[3] The conversation that follows is taken from my journal of that day—written immediately after Corcoran left my office.

ship of the Court was changed, the White House would have to honor the implied promise of a Court appointment that had been made to Joe Robinson?

Tom's answer was extraordinary. "I've learned a lot about politics from being down there," he said. "When a politician makes a promise he knows that he is not binding himself, and the man to whom he makes the promise knows it too. That is one of the things you've got to learn. There aren't any binding promises in politics. There isn't any binding law. You just know that the strongest side wins."

I suggested that society somehow runs along on the basis of people's faith in one another's commitments.

Tom said, "No, you must make your side win."

"How do you choose a side, as you call it, Tom?" I asked.

"You have a feeling in your viscera, perhaps," he told me.

Tom was clearly wandering about in a realm which is traditionally opened to first-year law students—a realm of iconoclastic sociological concepts designed to give the embryonic lawyer objectivity. But most young men usually go on to another stage of intellectual sophistication. They learn to evaluate such stimulating concepts in the light of what they learn of practical human relationships. Tom evidently hadn't. Or if he had, he'd forgotten, under stress, the nub of what he'd learned. At any rate, he apparently believed now that the ancient verities could be ignored with impunity by those who were momentarily strong. I felt, as he spoke, that I was witnessing a curious phenomenon. Tom had been, figuratively, stricken with a rare occupational ailment. He was falling to the ground from the sheer weight of the power and responsibility that he was carrying.

I turned the subject to the utilities. Tom assured me that the utilities were "licked." I asked whether that meant that the T.V.A. was going to try to take over the Commonwealth and Southern.

"You're damned right it will—and all the rest of them too," Tom said.

"You realize what that means?"

"Well, we're going to squeeze them for a couple of years, at any rate," Tom said.

I remarked that you don't do that kind of thing for "a couple of years." If you did it, it stayed done.

"Yes, I suppose so," was the answer. "It won't come fast, but twenty years from now the government will own and operate all the electrical utilities in the country."

This oracular pronouncement was delivered with such finality that I could only sit staring at him.

Tom broke the silence by asking me whether I knew when Tugwell was "getting out." I knew that Tom disagreed with Tugwell, and I was about to answer noncommittally, when Tom ran on and said:

"I've never seen anything like him for arrogance. He picked up the draft of a speech the Skipper was to make, laid it down in front of me, pointed to the word 'competition' and said, 'That ought to come out.' When I paid no attention to him he turned to the President and said, 'You know you don't believe that.' The President ignored him. Can you imagine the nerve? Well . . . we'll take care of him. Not that he doesn't serve a useful function. He is a sort of catfish to keep the herrings from getting sluggish when the fishermen take them back in tanks to port. But the Skipper shouldn't get the idea that he is an edible fish."

That seemed to dispose of Rex.

Tom proceeded to the question of administrative reorganization, suggesting that I write something about it. "Go after the Byrd Committee, Brownlow's bunch, and the rest," he counseled. "They're just going to make nice charts. You've got to build government agencies around men and not build up agencies and then try to find men to fill the jobs."

That gave me a fairly clear idea of Tom's notions about reorganization, I said. But I was interested to know what would happen to Jesse Jones (Jesse was Tom's boss at the R.F.C.), for instance, if Tom's notions prevailed.

"Well," he answered, "of course I think Jesse can do a useful job on the things he knows best—collecting loans. But most of the crowd down there thinks he will not go along."

"What crowd?" I asked. "And where won't he go?"

"The liberal crowd," Tom answered.

Then Tom offered me a little advice. The day of the printed word, he announced, was over. "You have no idea what a good thing it is for your soul to have to address yourself to a big radio audience. You've got to clarify your meaning, make things simple, reduce them to their ultimate essentials if you want to get them over to a big audience, because human beings in the mass are a hell of a lot stupider than you would ever think."

The conversation ended with my comment that it looked as if Tom would be staying on close to the White House for some time.

"I'm clearing out," Tom assured me. "Nobody made any promises to me and I didn't ask for any."

Of course he didn't clear out. Tom's ascendancy grew, over the years. What he said to me that day in November is significant in view of that ascendancy.

2

The Court Disapproves, Roosevelt called the 1935 volume of his collected papers, and the 1936 volume, *The People Approve.*

That no such appeal from the Court to the voters as these titles suggest was made in 1936 is a matter of record. Still these titles afford a significant clue to Roosevelt's psychology. No doubt his firm belief, or rather his firm will to believe, that the people of this country had given him a general cease-and-desist order to execute against all who challenged him led him to his greatest defeat.

The announcement of the plan to pack the Supreme Court caught wholly off guard a public and a Congress lulled by three months of exquisite calm. Roosevelt's pronouncements in the course of his good-will trip to South America would not have frightened the birds of St. Francis. His quiet message to Congress asked cooperation from the Supreme Court in a manner to which even the sternest constitutionalist could not object. His second inaugural speech was peaceable and statesmanlike. For the most part, the man-sobered-by-great-victory tableau was accepted without reserve. Only a few lynx-eyed observers pointed to the jokers in the Reorganization message of January 12, 1937. Only a few people who knew the President very well indeed wondered, privately, just how and when the quiet would be shattered this time.

The stunning answer came on February 5th.

The President's bare attempt to pack the Court was not at all concealed by his arguments that the Court needed enlargement because it was inefficient, because age was related to inefficiency, and because age and conservatism went hand in hand. It was recognized at once for what it was—a plan to provide in advance for Supreme Court approval of whatever legislative reforms Roosevelt happened to espouse, a plan to enable Roosevelt to control the Court.

As such, a number of citizens, like myself, were compelled to fight it with all the resources at our command, although we felt no less strongly than the President that the majority of the Court had arbitrarily held too narrow a view of the powers the Constitution confers upon Congress. In editorials, speeches, and in testimony given to the Senate Judiciary Committee, I opposed it as a palpable makeshift that would remove only temporarily the evil it was designed to remedy, as an impairment of those democratic institutions and traditions that make progressive evolution possible, as a fundamental change which the citizens *alone* had the right to authorize.[4] My opposition was open, wholehearted, complete, despite a suggestion from Tom Corcoran that I'd better not stick my neck out, because my "side" was going to lose anyhow.

There's no need to review the complicated and fascinating history of the six months' battle over Court packing.[5] As everyone knows, it ended well, and will doubtless insure the people of the United States against any similar presidential attempt so long as our democratic republic lasts. It's relevant here chiefly as the overt expression of the mood I had feared and resisted for over a year.

The story is supposed to have begun some months before the election of 1936, when Roosevelt directed his Attorney General, Homer S. Cummings, to assemble all possible plans for getting around the obstacle represented by the Supreme Court majority. Cummings' researches were discussed by the two men before the President's departure for South America on November 17, 1936,[6] and the President took with him a sheaf of plans for dealing with the problem.

Thereafter the story is less easy to follow. According to one theory, Cummings and his assistants devised the final scheme the President adopted on his return, and Corcoran and Cohen remained completely ignorant of what was up. According to another theory, Corcoran and Cohen had planted the seeds of the scheme in the President's mind some nine or ten months before. (The basis for this belief is Senator Wheeler's allegation that as far back as the spring of 1936 Corcoran urged him to launch a drive for Court packing and proposed to write

[4] See Appendix I for the statement opposing the Court-packing plan which I made to the Senate Judiciary Committee on March 23, 1937.

[5] The best history of the fight is *The 168 Days*, by Joseph Alsop and Turner Catledge (Doubleday, Doran & Company, Inc.; New York, 1938). The authors not only watched the public record unfold day by day but had access to much "inside" material through friends in Congress and in the administration. They were misled and are in error at certain points, but, with one exception—the exoneration of Cohen and Corcoran from any connection with the Court plan's origin—those errors are trivial.

[6] A by-product of these researches seems to have been a bulky volume which appeared early in 1937 under the authorship of Homer Cummings and an assistant, Carl McFarland—*Federal Justice*. The Macmillan Company; New York.

a speech for him advocating it.) And in the years since the defeat of the plan the principals on both sides have made extensive private efforts to shove the blame for the plan on one another's doorsteps.

The responsibility lies somewhere between. Both Corcoran and Cohen unquestionably knew, in November, 1936, that action to curb the Court would be taken. Possibly because of their undisguised intellectual disdain for Cummings, Roosevelt preferred to keep his discussions of the subject with Cummings secret from them—much as a youngster hides himself from his more serious-minded brother when he wants to read French novels. It had, in any case, always been Roosevelt's way to carry on discussions with various sets of advisers, each of which was kept in the dark about the others' activities. Still, by December, it is certain that Corcoran and Cohen had learned that Court packing was one of the plans under consideration by the President, and had begun preparing a memorandum in which there was no protest against Court packing that was not counterbalanced by some argument in its favor.

Sometime before the end of December a critical decision was made by Roosevelt and Cummings—the decision to dress up a Court-packing scheme as a general reorganization of the federal judiciary, and slip it through as such. This strangely transparent plan of presentation was not solely a Cummings' adaptation of a recommendation made in 1913 by the then Attorney General James Clark McReynolds.[7] It was also the derivative of a suggestion received in a letter from a friend of the President who lived far from Washington. But unquestionably, in finally deciding on the scheme, the President was swayed by the consideration that the plan could partly be traced back to his archenemy on the Court—McReynolds. Such a straining for incidental effects which appeal to his sense of humor or drama was to appear over and over again in Roosevelt's career thereafter. It is clear the President was carried away by his intense desire to be astute. And it was a tangled web he wove in the name of cleverness—a web that ultimately closed around him.

But if Corcoran and Cohen took no part in the decision about how the plan was to be presented, the fact remains that they nevertheless share the responsibility for the President's adoption of the plan. For they had urged upon him, over a period of months, a course of action that made inevitable his adoption of some such scheme.

[7] It should be noted that McReynolds specifically exempted the Supreme Court from his recommendations in 1913.

Following up where Frankfurter had left off in late May, 1935, Corcoran and Cohen had persistently assured the President that it was not necessary for him to seek to amend the Constitution in order to secure validation for the legislation he wanted. Before and after their attempt, in June, 1936, to change the plank on the Constitution, they had told the President over and over again that the trouble was with the Court, and not the Constitution. Against all efforts to prevail upon Roosevelt to present the issue fairly and squarely to the voters by asking them to pass on an amendment expanding the power of Congress, these men had fought with the most intense certitude. According to them, it was necessary only to get new Justices to read new economic predilections into the Constitution.

In diverting Roosevelt from a straightforward approach to his problem they simply succeeded better than they intended. In focusing his attention upon clever methods of achieving his ends through legalistic indirection, they merely forgot the psychology of the man with whom they were dealing. The oversight was vital. The methods they advocated could not have been better calculated to lead Roosevelt to the proposal of February 5, 1937.[8]

Whether or not Roosevelt realized that the plan he championed that day was an assault upon a fundamental principle in American government is another question. Certainly Corcoran, to whom he unfolded the complete plan days before he chose to announce it to the congressional leaders, was appalled only by its indirection. Neither Corcoran nor Cummings objected to it as the violation of a constitutional tradition as binding as a written provision of the Constitution. Roosevelt, himself, familiar though he was with the superficies of American history, had never evidenced, in the years of my association with him, any appreciation of the basic philosophic distinctions in the history of American political thought. The simple principle that democracy exists only in so far as its objectives are attained in terms of its own institutions—this is not necessarily known to the connoisseur of historical anecdotes.

But even if it had been, how much of an obstacle would it have been

[8] This is not to suggest that I believe that Frankfurter, despite his continued intimacy with Roosevelt after May, 1935, or his exceedingly close relationship with Cohen and Corcoran, was immediately connected with the Court-packing plan. Certainly Frankfurter had no advance notice of the plan. Frankfurter's previous record on the subject of enlarging the Court and his scrupulous silence during the entire Court fight suggest his horror over such an ill-disguised effort to influence the Court's opinions. His respect for the Court as an institution is indicated by the fact that to be a member of the Court was his fondest dream.

to a man who believed himself the personification of the will of the majority? Passionately convinced, as Roosevelt was, of the essential purity and rectitude of his intentions, how could he have been expected to remember the injunction in the *Federalist*: "Until the people have, by some solemn and authoritative act, annulled or changed the established form, it is binding upon themselves collectively, as well as individually; and no presumption, or even knowledge, of their sentiments can warrant their representatives in a departure from it." Completely assured, as he was, that he himself embodied the desire for progressivism—that he was progressivism—how could he have been expected to consult those men, many of them immediately within reach at the other end of Pennsylvania Avenue, who might have refreshed his memory?

And so came the second tactical blunder in the proceeding—the failure to take counsel with the congressional leaders on the assumption that they would not dare to oppose his wishes. The election had so far erased the picture of the reception of the "soak-the-rich" program in the summer of 1935 that the Court plan was thrown before Congress with even more imperious abruptness.

On the morning of February 5th Roosevelt presented the congressional leaders with his bill, read a few snatches from his message to them and the Cabinet, and rushed out of the meeting into a press conference. That was all. There was no discussion, no request for advice. He was not asking them: he was telling them. The mechanical processes of preparing these documents for transmission to Congress were all but completed. Exactly two hours later the message was being read to Congress. At no point did he seem to doubt that the tried and true leaders of his party would supinely do his bidding.

One of the most saddening facts in the history of this decade was the extent to which his supreme confidence was justified. Within an hour or two after the delivery of the Court message, before they could conceivably have read the bill thoughtfully, scores of senators and congressmen had endorsed the plan. Those endorsers included the Chairman of the Judiciary Committee of the Senate, who, less than two weeks before, had denounced Court packing as the "prelude to tyranny." It is probable that the accolade of approval Roosevelt received that day from those who placed undue weight upon personal devotion and party regularity made him proof against the ominous silence of those, like Hatton Sumners, who had decided to "cash in their chips."

They were not silent for long. Wheeler, Burke, Clark, Van Nuys,

Connally, King, and others roared that they would fight the scheme, although, through February and early March, the same argument was brought to bear against them that Corcoran had flung at me. "After they are all talked out, we will call the roll," Jim Farley crowed. "You will find we have plenty of votes."

When it became apparent that the opposition would not be deflected, that the ranks of the faithful included many who inwardly deplored the scheme, the President was asked to compromise. His private answer was a burst of scornful laughter. His public answer, delivered before thirteen hundred Democrats in the Mayflower on March 4th was a warning to the members of his party in Congress that ". . . we cannot afford . . . to run away from [the] fight on advice of defeatist lawyers."

"Defeatist" was the response made again and again that spring to all proposals of compromise that were put to Roosevelt, as the noble fight "of all those who truly believe in political and economic democracy" became a protracted process of political bludgeoning. What was euphemistically called "trench warfare" in behalf of the measure ranged from vague threats to last-minute offers of patronage by powerful subordinates. These things, plus the effects of a series of Supreme Court decisions boldly cutting the ground from under the plan's proponents, plus the growing evidence of public abhorrence for the plan, plus the feeling in the Senate that the President should have made it unmistakably clear if he intended to give Joe Robinson the Van Devanter vacancy on the Supreme Court—all were the ingredients of the most elaborate crow pie any American President had eaten for eighteen years.

On June 14th a majority of the Judiciary Committee of the Senate issued the magnificent report that will rank as one of the major state papers in the history of the country.

> We recommend the rejection of this bill as a needless, futile and utterly dangerous abandonment of constitutional principle [it concluded].
>
> It was presented to the Congress in a most intricate form and for reasons that obscured its real purpose.
>
> It would not banish age from the bench nor abolish divided decisions.
>
> It would not affect the power of any court to hold laws unconstitutional nor withdraw from any judge the authority to issue injunctions.

> It would not reduce the expense of litigation nor speed the decision of cases.
>
> It is a proposal without precedent or justification.
>
> It would subjugate the courts to the will of Congress and the President and thereby destroy the independence of the judiciary, the only certain shield of individual rights.
>
> It contains the germ of a system of centralized administration of law that would enable an executive so minded to send his judges into every judicial district in the land to sit in judgment on controversies between the government and the citizen.
>
> It points the way to the evasion of the Constitution and establishes the method whereby the people may be deprived of their right to pass upon all amendments of the fundamental law.
>
> It stands now before the country, acknowledged by its proponents as a plan to force judicial interpretation of the Constitution, a proposal that violates every sacred tradition of American democracy.
>
> Under the form of the Constitution it seeks to do that which is unconstitutional.
>
> Its ultimate operation would be to make this government one of men rather than one of law, and its practical operation would be to make the Constitution what the executive or legislative branches say it is—an interpretation to be changed with each change of administration.
>
> It is a measure which should be so emphatically rejected that its parallel will never again be presented to the free representatives of the free people of America.

On July 20th John Garner solemnly announced to the President that the plan was licked. The bill was officially buried on July 22, 1937.

Before that day every characteristic implicit in Roosevelt's development between May, 1935, and November, 1936, had reached its full flower. There was the snatching at a half-baked scheme which commended itself chiefly because of its disingenuousness. There was the essential carelessness of its preparation. There was the arbitrary secrecy before its launching. There was the indifference to the fact that it was an unjustifiable means to an end. There was the conviction that he epitomized the progressive will, that his New Deal represented the Ultima Thule of progressive reform. There was the assurance of unquestioned mastery. There was the incredibly stubborn refusal to yield when he still might have escaped absolute defeat. There was the ruthless way in which he lashed supporters, like Joe Robinson, insisting that they serve him beyond their power to serve with conviction or effectiveness. Finally, in defeat, there were the supreme confidence that "the people are with me" and the bitter determination to exterminate politically all who had committed the treason of disagreement.

The purge of 1938, unofficially announced in the early autumn of 1937, and attempted despite all warnings that there has never yet been a successful party bloodletting in this country,[9] was the direct product of that dogmatism—dogmatism that led all unwittingly to an attempt, more covert than the Court plan, to impair a fundamental constitutional principle.

James Madison and Alexander Hamilton had pointed out that "in order to lay a due foundation for that separate and distinct exercise of the different powers of government, which . . . is admitted on all hands to be essential to the preservation of liberty, it is evident that each department should have a will of its own." That is the philosophic explanation for Article 1, Section 1, of the Constitution, which vests the legislative power in Congress.

Over a century later Woodrow Wilson attempted to amend the Madison-Hamilton doctrine by suggesting that the President is "the national voice"—and, as such, presumably the true interpreter of the people's will—perhaps a truer interpreter than Congress itself.

Wilson's experience—which proved that the more a leader becomes obsessed with the idea that he speaks the people's will the less he is able to divine that will—was unfortunately lost on the White House cabal. In the late spring of 1938 they set up a test of the loyalty required in senators. Stated rhetorically, this test was "one hundred per cent for Roosevelt." Specifically, it meant that failure to support Roosevelt's Court packing marked a sitting senator for political annihilation.

This campaign the President felt obliged to disavow by implication. Yet the references to "yes-but" liberals in his stinging fireside speech of June 24, 1938, and the preparations that preceded his departure for a trip across the country, all suggested his wholehearted interest in the purge.

"Yes-but" members of Congress were to be given the cold shoulder as the President passed through the country. Their opponents were to

[9] Farley and most other old hands at the political game resisted the purge to the limit of their strength. Among others outside the inner circle, I, too, warned: "There will be no general destruction, no people's purge, of those who opposed Roosevelt on the Court scheme. In fact, there is every indication that independence on the Court issue has tended to strengthen rather than weaken the position of most Democratic senators. The tradition of senatorial independence is strong in this country, and few men who have already been successful at the polls have ever been defeated by the high command's withholding of census takers' jobs, federal appropriations, social favors, and public compliments.

"Attempted purges are not signs of strength; they are signs of weakness."

be encouraged. Two senators who were clearly invincible were to be ignored. Corcoran, Hopkins, and the other political "experts" who were directing the purge disdained the Venetian maxim that one should kiss the hand one cannot bite off. But the routing of the President's train through a state in the late night hours would do as well. The President was to split his personality and leave the chief magistrate of the nation to inhabit the White House like a ghost during the hot summer. The leader of the party was to take his sword from the wall and fare forth to smite the infidels.

But this bit of mysticism did not sit well with the country. Such a conception of dualism not only affronted the logic of the intelligent but strained the credulity of the ignorant. And so, largely because of the shrieks of public protest against presidential intervention in the primaries, what began as the conquering march of a Tamerlane turned out to be the good-will trip of an Edward VII. Still, the presidential lieutenants were none the less diligent. They labored on, enlarging the pit which Roosevelt himself had begun to dig in November, 1936. Their faith in Roosevelt was ultimately justified. The purge was resumed with renewed vigor and boldness when he returned to the Atlantic seaboard.

The denouement came on November 8, 1938. Only one victim marked for excision had fallen, and a Republican party which two years before had sustained the most humiliating defeat in its career staged a comeback of astounding proportions.

3

It was one of the most revealing aspects of the Court fight that at no time in its course did the President indicate, except in terms so general as to be meaningless, the kind of economic reform that his "reinvigorated" Court was supposed to approve. That he didn't because he had still not resolved the indecision which began with the N.I.R.A.'s invalidation in May, 1935, seemed a reasonable assumption. But it remained for the onset of the "recession" of 1937-38 to confirm it publicly. The crisis that set in during September, 1937, provided, in fact, the most spectacular demonstration of presidential irresolution since the days when Hoover had stood nonplused before some of the same ugly economic realities.

For seven long months Roosevelt blew hot and cold, delayed, temporized, played his subordinates against each other, alternately echoed and contradicted them, while business indices sagged, unemployment rose, and Washington officialdom fell into a rancorous, raucous, many-sided quarrel.

The action that circumstances finally wrung from Roosevelt in April, 1938, was not in the least the result of a final decision on fundamentals. It was a rationalization of make-shift measures into which he had been pushed by his very irresolution. And from that moment on, Roosevelt gave economic problems only such time as could be spared from purging and plunging the country into international power politics.

The crisis of indecision that became a matter of public knowledge in the autumn of 1937 cannot be understood except as an extension of what had gone before. I suppose it was significant that Roosevelt's formative years were coincidental with the growing ascendancy in American thought of William James' pragmatism. At any rate, in the realm of economics and politics, Roosevelt carried to its logical and perhaps tragic ultimate the philosophy of trial and error so joyously preached by James. I have never known a man so receptive to the new and unorthodox. During the critical years of 1932 and 1933 it was my most difficult job to see that he took the opportunity to examine skeptically the "plans" and devices that attracted his interest. Even so, the most extraordinary fragments of rejected ideas would remain in his mind to be played with, when time permitted, and, sometimes, as in the case of the "soak-the-rich" scheme, to be suddenly announced as settled policies.

This receptiveness to innovation was not in itself objectionable. On the contrary, it was this very quality in Roosevelt that made it possible for him to root out the economic shibboleths to which most of our best-advertised thinkers had stubbornly clung after 1929. It was this quality that made it possible for him to begin repairing, on a monumental scale, a system which a decade of abuse had left racked and broken.

The hitch came with Roosevelt's failure to follow through. Pragmatism requires the application of the test of utility or workableness or success. And by this Roosevelt refused to abide. He would launch an idea as an experiment, but, once it had been launched, he would not subject it to the pragmatic test. It became, in his mind, an expression of settled conviction, an indispensable element in a great, unified plan.

That Roosevelt could look back over the vast aggregation of policies adopted between March, 1933, and November, 1936, and see it as the result of a single, predetermined plan was a tribute to his imagination.

But not to his grasp of economics. One had only to review the heterogeneous origins of the policies he had embraced by the time of his reelection, the varying circumstances, impulses, beliefs that had produced them, to guess at their substantive conflict and contradiction.

Roosevelt's *monetary measures* began with an abandonment of gold compelled by the various exigencies of April, 1933. The rise in prices which immediately followed that move encouraged him to believe that he had touched a magic key that he could manipulate with mathematical precision. From that point it was only a short step to the acceptance of Dr. Warren's elixir for anemic prices—a formula based upon the theory that there was an absolute relationship between gold prices and commodity prices. The unacknowledged failure of this sovereign remedy prompted the devaluation of the dollar, on January 31, 1934, in accordance with traditional inflationist doctrine. This was followed, in May, by the President's adoption of a silver policy urged on him by Pittman and the other senators from the silver states who presented him with voluminous arguments intended to show that "doing something for silver" would send commodity prices up. The silver policy was partially an acquiescence in these arguments and partially an attempt to satisfy the senators from the silver states. Finally, there was the rejection of the joint international declaration on monetary policy in July, 1933—a rejection prompted by a complete misunderstanding of the declaration's meaning and by Roosevelt's belief that "the world will not long be lulled by the specious fallacy of achieving a temporary and probably an artificial stability in foreign exchange on the part of a few large countries only." This policy was reversed in September, 1936, when the Treasury completed a stabilization agreement with France and England, prompted by the wholly orthodox desire to prevent France's forced abandonment of gold from ushering in a wild currency warfare. Characterized as "the culmination of a three-and-a-half-year dream" by Secretary Morgenthau, this essentially "sound" and conservative financial agreement was, in fact, the abandonment of the three-and-a-half-year dream (the theme of the "bombshell" message) of relating to a new international monetary standard a currency managed to achieve a stable internal price level.

Roosevelt's *banking policies* were, in their early phases, largely adaptations of Senator Glass' conservative plans for consolidation of state and national bank systems—plans opposed by state bankers, farmers, and small-town businessmen who feared the concentration of credit in the East. The separation of investment and commercial banking had for years been advocated by students of American banking practices as a way to prevent the kind of abuse revealed by the senatorial investigation in 1933. The insurance of bank deposits, reluctantly accepted by Roosevelt in the spring of 1933, grew out of the experience of eight Western states and the insistence of Western and Southwestern senators that they would not accept the Banking bill of 1933 unless provision for the guarantee of deposits was included. The concentration of instruments of credit control in the hands of a Federal Reserve System subject to Treasury direction was championed by such men as Woodin and, later, Eccles, and largely opposed by men of the Glass persuasion.

Roosevelt's *lending policies* were essentially the extension of federal functions operative long before Hoover came into office and dramatized by Hoover through the creation of the R.F.C. Primarily, the objective of these policies was emergency or rescue work—to protect private equities by buttressing their shaky underpinning with the credit of the federal government, to scale down old debt, and to reduce interest charges.

Roosevelt's *tax policies* consisted, first, of no more than the time-honored beliefs that returning prosperity would produce increased revenue; second, that more drastic administration of existing tax laws would yield a considerably greater return than the Hoover regime was securing; and, third, that a thorough revision of our jerry-built, overlapping state and federal tax systems was needed. The first and last of these tenets were all but forgotten with the passing years. The "soak-the-rich" and corporate-surplus proposals represented a complete departure from the principles of taxation for revenue and reform *in* taxation. They signalized the adoption of a policy of reform *through* taxation, of taxation for reform. Being punitive in intent, an expression of Roosevelt's mood in June, 1935, they had little to do with the more conventional theories about a balanced budget to which Roosevelt made obeisance from October, 1932, through January, 1937.

Roosevelt's *spending policies* began with the practical realization that the finances of the states were inadequate to meet the relief burden in 1932. To the policy of spending for public works to stimulate the heavy industries, Roosevelt was won only reluctantly in 1933. This idea had been sponsored by men of such varying outlook as Tugwell, Hearst, Al Smith, Wagner, and La Follette. But it was Roosevelt himself who gradually subordinated spending for public works through the P.W.A. to spending for work relief, through the W.P.A., and who slowly came to regard spending for work relief as much as a needed economic stimulus as a relief measure. This ultimate confusion of purposes was largely the result of circumstances. The P.W.A., under Harold Ickes, had proved too slow and cautious in the release of money for great public works. Harry Hopkins, head of the Federal Emergency Relief Administration, originator of C.W.A.'s "made-work" program, and, finally, Administrator of the W.P.A., was not only closer to the President than Ickes, but got things done faster. It was almost inevitable, therefore, that the main stream of spending should shift from public works to work relief. But no doubt somewhere in the course of that shift a consideration of its political advantages gently obtruded itself. The end result, by 1937, was a rather apologetic justification for the Hopkins expenditures on the grounds that they were designed both to avoid the "narcotic" effects of a dole and to return dividends in economic recovery. Roosevelt had still to take the final step to the belief in spending for spending's sake.

Roosevelt's *social-security policies* were a form of preventive relief. But primarily they sprang from his desire to set up in this country some of those services for social amelioration already established for years in England, Germany, and the Scandinavian countries.

Roosevelt's policies in the field of *securities regulation and public-utility control* were, at first, essentially expressions of the desire to remove grave economic abuses. They included the broader application of conventional methods of public-utility control and the enlargement of the federal government's concern to include securities, the interstate transmission of electricity, the traffic in buses and trucks, and the telephone, telegraph, and radio. But at least one of these manifestations of the orthodox impulse to prevent exploitation of the public was transformed into an outright experiment in state socialism. Particularly, the T.V.A. became, because of the ardor of those who administered it, an adventure in government ownership and competition with private utilities rather than an embodiment of the traditional regulatory philosophy. Another of the group of measures in this field of regulatory controls—that involving transportation—took the form of an attempt to do precisely the opposite. Whereas the electrical-utility measures presumably stimulated competition, the transportation measures were designed to reduce it.

What Roosevelt's *tariff policies* contemplated, originally, was modified protectionism to safeguard his experiments in wage and price raising. What Roosevelt's tariff policies became, because of the patience, perseverance, and insistence of Secretary Hull, was modified free-tradism. The policy of reciprocal trade concessions generalized to all countries enjoying the benefit of the most-favored-nation clause has, in fact, been a policy of tariff reduction—a policy of which the editors of the London *Economist* could in truth say, by 1937:

> In this tariff-ridden world the sight of any nation deliberately seeking to lower its tariffs is both rare and refreshing. . . . It is fully possible, for example, that Great Britain has already gained more from the concessions given by the United States in her treaties with other countries than could be obtained in a direct Anglo-American treaty. British trade has gained in particular from the concessions on whisky in the Canadian agreement, on linen in the Belgian, on special steels in the Swedish and on lace and similar goods in the French agreement.[10]

Roosevelt's *N.I.R.A. and A.A.A.* were primarily intended as collective, cooperative efforts on the part of producers to achieve a systematic control of production. They were experiments—not in restriction, but in "planning." N.R.A., in which varying social and economic purposes existed side by side, was also intended to abolish child labor, assure minimum wages, and encourage the growth of organized labor by guaranteeing the right of collective bargaining. But essentially both measures sprang from a philosophy which encompassed realms unknown to those New Dealers who drew initial inspiration from Brandeis, and who would have limited Roosevelt to the remedying of abuse and the curtailment of "special privilege." They were based on the assumption that the nation was not suffering a hangover from a single speculative orgy in 1932, but that it had chronic dyspepsia of its economic system. And the further assumption was that if the A.A.A. and N.R.A. were not the solution of the nation's problems of unemployment, of wasteful competition, of glut followed by scarcity, then somehow, some way, the federal government, through cooperation with industrial and agricultural producers, would have to devise other national means of dealing with these problems.

If this aggregation of policies springing from circumstances, motives, purposes, and situations so various gave the observer the sense of a certain rugged grandeur, it arose chiefly from the wonder that one man could have been so flexible as to permit himself to believe so many things in so short a time. But to look upon these policies as the result of a unified plan was to believe that the accumulation of stuffed snakes,

[10] *The New Deal*, by The Editors of *The Economist* (London), by permission of and special arrangement with Alfred A. Knopf, Inc.; New York, 1937; p. 118.

baseball pictures, school flags, old tennis shoes, carpenter's tools, geometry books, and chemistry sets in a boy's bedroom could have been put there by an interior decorator.

Or, perhaps it would be more apt to say that the unfolding of the New Deal between 1932 and 1937 suggested the sounds that might be produced by an orchestra which started out with part of a score and which, after a time, began to improvise. It might all hang together if there were a clear understanding between the players and the conductor as to the sort of music they intended to produce. But nothing was more obvious than that some of the New Deal players believed that the theme was to be the funeral march of capitalism; others, a Wagnerian conflict between Good and Evil; and still others, the triumphant strains of the *Heldenleben*.

Yet what could be said of the conductor who emerged from such an experience and who announced that he and his orchestra had produced new and beautiful harmonies?

It was Roosevelt's insistence upon the essential unity of his policies that inevitably brought into question his understanding of economics. Except in terms of misunderstanding, there was no way to comprehend such phenomena as an attempt to rehabilitate the soft-coal business which proceeded without reference to simultaneous efforts to encourage the production of electricity through vast water-power projects. There was no other possible explanation for the slow blurring of the distinction between temporary and permanent economic policies, the retention of expedients designed to meet emergency problems, and the justification of such expedients on grounds quite unlike those which had warranted their initial employment. There was no other possible explanation for the two-and-a-half year indifference to the obstacles that thwarted a huge potential demand for additional houses and dammed up a potent force for stable economic recovery. So, too, there would be in 1939 no other possible explanation for the plea that the loss of dollar-devaluation powers would remove "the only check we have on . . . speculative operations" by the same President who, six years before, had announced that he knew of no way governments could check exchange speculation.

Underlying these and a host of other incongruities were two misapprehensions which were basic.

The first centered in a failure to understand what is called, for lack of a better term, business confidence.

Confidence consists, on the one side, of belief in the prospect of profits and, on the other, in the willingness to take risks, to venture money. In Harry Scherman's brilliant essay on economic life, *The Promises Men Live By,*[11] the term is, by implication, defined much as Gladstone defined credit. "Credit," Gladstone said, "is suspicion asleep." In that sense, confidence is the existence of that mutual faith and good will which encourage enterprises to expand and take risks, which encourage individual savings to flow into investments. And in an age of increasing governmental interposition in industrial operations and in the processes of capital accumulation and investment, the maintenance of confidence presupposes both a general understanding of the direction in which legislative and administrative changes tend and a general belief in government's sympathetic desire to encourage the development of those investment opportunities whose successful exploitation is a *sine qua non* for a rising standard of living.

This, Roosevelt refused to recognize. In fact, the term "confidence" became, as time went on, the most irritating of all symbols to him. He had the habit of repelling the suggestion that he was impairing confidence by answering that he was restoring the confidence the public had lost in business leadership. No one could deny that, to a degree, this was true. The shortsightedness, selfishness, and downright dishonesty of some business leaders had seriously damaged confidence. Roosevelt's assurances that he intended to cleanse and rehabilitate our economic system did act as a restorative.

But beyond that, what had been done? For one thing, the confusion of the administration's utility, shipping, railroad, and housing policies had discouraged the small individual investor. For another, the administration's taxes on corporate surpluses and capital gains, suggesting, as they did, the belief that a recovery based upon capital investment is unsound, discouraged the expansion of producers' capital equipment. For another, the administration's occasional suggestions that perhaps there was no hope for the reemployment of people except by a share-the-work program struck at a basic assumption in the enterpriser's philosophy. For another, the administration's failure to see the narrow margin of profit on which business success rests—a failure expressed in an emphasis upon prices while the effects of increases in operating costs were overlooked—laid a heavy hand upon business prospects. For another, the calling of names in political speeches and the vague, veiled threats of punitive action all tore the

[11] Random House; New York, 1938.

fragile texture of credit and confidence upon which the very existence of business depends.

The eternal problem of language obtruded itself at this point. To the businessman words have fairly exact descriptive meanings. The blithe announcement by a New Deal subordinate that perhaps we have a productive capacity in excess of our capacity to consume and that perhaps new fields for the employment of capital and labor no longer exist will terrify the businessman. To the politician, such an extravagant use of language is important only in terms of its appeal to the prejudices and preconceptions of a swirling, changeable, indeterminate audience. To the businessman two and two make four; to the politician two and two make four only if the public can be made to believe it. If the public decides to add it up to three, the politician adjusts his adding machine. In the businessman's literal cosmos, green results from mixing yellow and blue. The politician is concerned with the light in which the mixture is to be seen, the condition of the eyes of those who look.

Mutual misunderstanding and mutual ill will were, of course, unavoidable in the circumstances, and the ultimate result was a wholly needless contraction of business—a contraction whose essential nature was so little understood that it was denounced in high governmental quarters as a "strike of capital" and explained as a deliberate attempt by business to "sabotage" recovery.

The second basic fault in the congeries of the administration's economic policies sprang from Roosevelt's refusal to make a choice between the philosophy of Concentration and Control and the philosophy of Enforced Atomization.

It was easy to see that the early New Deal, with its emphasis on agricultural and industrial planning, was dominated by the theory of Concentration and Control—by the beliefs that competition is justified only in so far as it promotes social progress and efficiency; that government should encourage concerted action where that best serves the public and competition where that best serves the public; that business must, under strict supervision, be permitted to grow into units large enough to insure to the consumer the benefits of mass production; that organized labor must likewise be permitted to grow in size but, like business, be held to strict accountability; that government must cooperate with both business and labor to insure the stable and continuous operation of the machinery of production and distribution.

But with the invalidation of the N.I.R.A., there was a shift in emphasis. And this shift took not the form of a complete repudiation of Concentration and Control, but of an endless wavering between it and the philosophy advocated by those Brandeis adherents, like Corcoran, who preached the "curse of bigness," the need for breaking up great corporations on the ground that their growth was the result of the desire for financial control rather than increased efficiency, the desirability of "atomizing" business in order to achieve a completely flexible competitive system which would work without much intervention by government.

This wavering appeared in the tax bill of 1935, which was definitely intended to discriminate against corporate bigness.

It appeared in Roosevelt's championship of the Wagner Labor Relations Act, which, in the large, was an attempt to foster collective forms of action.

It appeared in the meetings held by Major Berry, the Coordinator of Industrial Cooperation, in December, 1935—meetings intended to devise some sort of substitute for N.I.R.A.

It appeared, to me at least, from January through April, 1936, in conversation with Roosevelt.

It appeared in June, 1936, when, despite their common origin, the platform of 1936 favored Concentration and Control and the President's acceptance speech advocated Enforced Atomization.

Roosevelt obviously clung to the belief that he could *blend* the two philosophies by persuasion and skillful compromise, though the evidence proving that he could merely *mix* them piled up through 1936 and the first half of 1937. And since, in this world, bitterness and distrust are as likely to arise from bewilderment as from inborn propensities, the indecision which had begun in May, 1935, in no small part contributed to the business collapse of 1937.

So the stage was set when the depression struck in September, 1937. And so began the noisy pulling and hauling in Washington between the advocates of budget balancing, the advocates of spending, the believers that the price fixing of monopolies had caused the contraction of business, and the believers that the uncertainty and confusion of administration policy had made impossible those long-term business plans which sustain employment and consumer purchasing power.

The reaction was a steadily deepening indecision.

In November, 1937, the President approved a speech by Secretary Morgenthau intended to reassure business because it committed the administration to stringent budget balancing.

In December, 1937, and January, 1938, the President acquiesced in a campaign launched by Corcoran, Cohen, Ickes, Hopkins, and Robert H. Jackson for the purpose of blaming the depression upon business. Jackson and Ickes at once began an oratorical "trust-busting" offensive—a series of bitter speeches, replete with references to "corporate earls," "corporate tentacles," and "aristocratic anarchy"—planned and partly prepared, according to Alsop and Kintner,[12] by the young lawyers and economists Corcoran had welded into what he called his "well-integrated group" and into what Hugh Johnson characterized as "the janissariat."

On January 3, 1938, Roosevelt spoke, in one breath, of great corporations created "for the sake of securities profits, financial control, the suppression of competition and the ambition for power over others" and, in the next breath, announced, "We ask business and finance . . . to join their government in the enactment of legislation where the ending of abuses and the steady functioning of our economic system calls for government assistance."

On January 4th Roosevelt suggested that he would like to see businessmen and industrialists draw up chairs to a table with government representatives and work out a scheme to adjust production schedules to coincide with demand.

On January 8th the President denounced the "autocratic controls over the industry and finances of the country."

Through February and March the battle over policy, the effort to force a presidential decision dragged.

Governor Eccles of the Federal Reserve Board pleaded for pump priming and the removal of legislative and administrative constrictions—especially in the fields of labor and housing—that were blocking the normal course of business. Secretary Morgenthau harped on the need for a balanced budget. Jesse Jones of the R.F.C. campaigned for the repeal of the corporate-surplus tax. Donald Richberg urged a resumption of cooperative efforts to plan production. S.E.C. Commissioner John W. Hanes appealed for gestures reassuring to business. The Corcoran-Cohen-Hopkins-Ickes brigade, armed with memoranda provided by Leon Henderson, economic adviser to the W.P.A., and by others of the "well-integrated group," planked day in and day out for a combined spending and antimonopoly campaign.

There were passionate arguments between many of these advisers, secret meetings in homes and offices to patch up alliances, dashes to

[12] *Men around the President; op. cit.;* pp. 134-137.

Warm Springs where the President was vacationing late in March, importunate telephone calls, desperate and extravagant pleas for action.

It was April, with all business indices plummeting, before Roosevelt agreed, at last, to ask Congress for an investigation of monopolies and for a $3,012,000,000 spending program.

This move was hailed by the "well-integrated group" as the earnest of Roosevelt's complete conversion to their point of view.

In the sense that they had sold to him, together with the emergency program for spending, an elaborate philosophic rationalization of the inevitable, they had won a real victory. The rationalization, of which the most vociferous evangel was David Cushman Coyle, insisted that expenditures which returned dividends only in social benefit or esthetic pleasure were no less "assets" than those which paid dividends in taxable capacity, that a mounting deficit stimulated recovery. Corcoran's susceptibility to this strange and jumbled doctrine seemed to trace back to Brandeis' beliefs, expressed to me in detail in 1933, that private capital investment was virtually at an end because business could no longer find enough attractive opportunities for investment and that government must fill the void thus created. Roosevelt unquestionably embraced the doctrine as a handy way to justify a continuing budget unbalance for which he had excoriated Hoover during the campaign of 1932 and against which he had repeatedly pledged himself, up to January, 1937. But, aside from the reasons for the doctrine's adoption, it became, once adopted, a kind of pansophy—a scheme of universal wisdom. Embellishments appeared. Money must be "shoveled out," Corcoran remarked in private conversation.[13] Roosevelt put it differently. In his budget message of 1939, he said that an indispensable factor in prosperity was government "investment" great enough to lift the national income to a point which would make tax receipts cover the new level of expenditure.

So far, the "conversion" was absolute.

But the claim that Roosevelt was won over to a policy of "antibigness" in April, 1938, did not stand up. True, the President, in a fiery message, prepared with the assistance of Corcoran, Cohen, Jackson, and others of the "well-integrated group," denounced monopoly. Yet he went no further than to ask for a thorough congressional study

[13] Amos Pinchot reports that Corcoran announced that money should be scattered from airplanes.

of "the concentration of economic power in American industry"—a study which was to go on for a year or two.

This request for a study was, certainly, the final expression of Roosevelt's personal indecision about what policy his administration ought to follow in its relations with business. The creation of the "monopoly" committee, or rather the Temporary National Economic Committee, merely relieved Roosevelt, for the moment, from the nagging of subordinates who, whatever the differences in their own economic philosophies, recognized that an administration which was of two minds on this all-important question would contradict itself into disaster.

It merely put off the adoption of a guiding economic philosophy.

It merely freed Roosevelt's mind for matters which, so far as he was concerned, transcended these in importance and interest.

4

But those who charge that Roosevelt threw himself into foreign affairs in 1938 because of a calculated desire to swing the attention of the country away from the unsolved economic problems at home do not know their man.

There was nothing of conscious cynicism in Roosevelt's psychology. He had none of that hard, bright realism that made it possible for a Clemenceau to talk of permanent peace, in 1919, while he privately admitted that the Treaty of Versailles was a way of hamstringing France's enemies before the next war. In this sense Roosevelt was never an actor, creating illusions for others which he did not share himself. On the contrary, he had an almost Wilsonian need for justifying himself to himself, for assuring himself that there was always a "good" reason for his acts. The intuitive pranks of his mind, the deep-rooted principles, the variations occasioned by circumstances, and the steps toward long-time objectives—all had to be explained in the same terms. Roosevelt was no cold-blooded moral opportunist. In fact, he felt so intensely the need to do right that he had to believe he did right. He was incapable of sustaining a planned duplicity. His exoterics almost automatically became his esoterics.

In this case the shift was the more easily made because the play of forces in Europe had so long been described in moral terms by our internationalists. There was no need to see in preoccupation with foreign affairs a new political vehicle, if one could visualize it as a crusade to provide for the common defense of international laws and principles. Besides, for nearly twenty years our internationalists had assured us that neutrality was not only impossible, but "immoral."

Day in and day out such doctrine as this had been preached by those who advocated our participation in collective efforts to "enforce" peace:

> Neutrality is the negation of law and order. Neutrality is a denial of the principle of collective responsibility upon which any system of international law must rest. Neutrality is contrary to the fundamental conceptions of law which have prevailed between man and man in every civilized State and prevailed between State and State in the United States. . . . I cannot see that we have any international law in this world if we are going to have neutrality. . . . Neutrality must go as a legal conception.[14]

Roosevelt himself, as a League advocate in the early 'twenties, had subscribed to the theory of a collective world order to maintain peace through force, if necessary. In fact, if one overlooked such inconvenient items as his rejection of that part of the internationalist doctrine which related to the debts, his blasting of the London Economic Conference and his announcement in October, 1935, that "despite what happens in continents overseas, the United States shall and must remain . . . unentangled," it might fairly be said that his foreign policy had been characterized, from the beginning, by a slowly deepening and strengthening internationalism.

In January, 1933, he had—for reasons of personal sentiment, he said—supported the Hoover-Stimson Manchurian policy, which rested on a formula of nonrecognition of political changes wrought in violation of existing treaties.

He had appointed a Secretary of State with an active desire to marshal public opinion on the side of "treaty keeping."

He had permitted Norman Davis, in May, 1933, to commit the United States to "refrain from any action tending to defeat" a collec-

[14] Professor Charles G. Fenwick, *Proceedings of the American Society of International Law,* 1933 and 1936.

This and a number of similar pronouncements are cited in the extraordinarily illuminating book of Edwin Borchard and William Potter Lage, *Neutrality for the United States* (Yale University Press; New Haven, 1937; p. 251). For six years I've frequently sought, and always received, the intelligent advice of Professor Borchard on foreign affairs. My indebtedness to him and to my old teacher John Bassett Moore is immense. In these days of confusion no one has expressed the true interest of the United States with more clarity than these two men.

tive effort by other nations against "a state [which] has been guilty of a breach of peace in violation of its international obligations."

He had, three times between 1935 and 1938, authorized his State Department to ask Congress for the right to discriminate between nations engaged in a foreign war upon the basis of a moral judgment as to the right or wrong of the quarrel.

He had gone beyond the terms of the Neutrality Act in October and November, 1935, to discourage shipments of raw materials to Italy.

He had allowed his State Department to include, in a number of the reciprocal-trade agreements, a provision enabling the contracting parties "in exceptional circumstances" to embargo materials "needed in war."[15]

And finally he had failed to invoke the Neutrality Act in the autumn of 1937 on the ground that its enforcement would hurt China more than Japan.

So much was largely a policy of scolding, protest, and ineffectual gesture. Added up, it amounted to more or less cautious adherence to the doctrines of the devotees of collective security.

It assumed that there had been set up a new world order, based upon such agreements as the Kellogg-Briand Pact and the Versailles, Locarno, and Nine Power treaties. It disregarded the injustices of the Versailles Treaty. It viewed the Locarno Pact not as an attempt to preserve the *status quo* but as a mutual guarantee against "aggression." It left out of consideration the fact that the Kellogg-Briand Pact, including those reservations which are part of it, is a renunciation of war in the abstract, coupled with the most definite sanction of specific wars that has ever been promulgated. It forgot that the Nine Power Treaty was based on a condition contrary to fact; that China had not been a state for many decades, but merely a geographical name; that China had no territorial or administrative integrity; that its sovereignty had been impaired by many powers, including the United States. It assumed that a sticking out of tongues at nations attempting to revise such treaties by force or the threat of force would prevent the use of force.

Clearly, it had never occurred to Roosevelt or Secretary Hull to raise the question why treaties were being broken throughout the world—to forego a wringing of hands over the breaking of treaties and

[15] This clause, as Professor Edwin Borchard has pointed out, "embodies the authority for sanctions, an authorization not to be found in the enabling Reciprocal Tariff Act of June, 1934." *Neutrality for the United States; op. cit.;* p. 331.

to inquire why treaties were so brittle. American foreign policy up to October, 1937, was like nothing so much as a penology that considers only the apprehension and punishment of criminals without a thought of what makes people criminals.

As might have been expected, our continuous harping on the sanctity of treaties which established existing world boundaries actually seemed to strengthen the German and Italian governments at home. It made it possible for them to tell their people that the United States was allied with those determined that there should be no readjustment. We laid ourselves open to the charge of wishing for peace less than we wished for the guarantee and maintenance of the so-called peace treaties. In a realistic world, by evading facts and talking about a strict enforcement of the letter of the law, we were dissipating not only our energies but our influence.

Still, unfortunate as these forays into internationalism had been, they were a long step removed from the policy foreshadowed in Roosevelt's "quarantine" speech at Chicago on October 5, 1937. It was one thing to scold, lecture, and make diplomatic faces, and another to take a position of active leadership in mobilizing a concert of powers to prevent the repudiation of what force had achieved two decades before. And yet those intimates who had heard Roosevelt yearning, in the spring of 1935, "to do something" about Germany could not be surprised by the open invitation (Prime Minister Chamberlain hailed it as a "clarion call") to the "peace-loving nations" to join with the United States in "a concerted effort to uphold laws and principles." When such magnificent precedents, such elaborate formulas of morality could be adduced to justify Roosevelt's eternal impulse "to do something" about the afflictions to which humanity is exposed, what else could be expected?

And so the transition from viewing-with-sorrow-and-alarm to doing-something-about-it had already been made in October, 1937. By January, 1938, a policy of active, though unacknowledged, "cooperation" with England to oppose "those violations of treaties and those ignorings of humane instincts which today are creating a state of international . . . instability from which there is no escape through mere isolation or neutrality"[16] was under way.

After Munich, Roosevelt at once summoned home our ambassador to Berlin. There were consultations with Ambassadors Phillips, Kennedy, and Bullitt. The consensus seems to have been agreement that

[16] President Roosevelt's address at Chicago, October 5, 1937.

the time had come to do "something practical," to stop Germany, Italy, and Japan and to assist England and France. That "something" was to be a revision of the Neutrality Act to permit France and England to buy guns and munitions in this country. And the reason for that frankly and designedly unneutral step, it presently appeared, was no longer the "lawlessness" of the axis powers so much as it was the belief that only by throwing our weight on the side of England and France could we protect our own interests.

Ambassadors Bullitt and Kennedy then went off to Florida. When they had spent some weeks there, it was suddenly discovered that they were in possession of burning secrets which must be communicated to the House and Senate Military Affairs Committees. There followed a magnificently publicized dash back to Washington, intended to convey the idea that a world calamity was in the offing, and, on January 10, 1939, the imparting of information presumably so sensational that it could not be made public.

Observers recognized in these dramatic maneuverings signs of a State Department campaign to "educate" the American public to the need for a "stronger" foreign policy.

The drive apparently started four days after the incorporation of Austria into the Reich, on March 17, 1938, when Secretary Hull spoke of "collaboration" along "parallel lines" to prevent the spread of "the contagious scourge of treaty breaking and armed violence." It had been carried on through the device of speeches and statements by administration subordinates during the spring and summer. In the autumn it seems to have been given impetus with the mysterious spread of fear-provoking stories out of Washington. There had been rumors that (1) the Japanese would seize the Dutch possessions in the East Indies; (2) the Germans would conquer England, seize the English Navy, sail it over to our shores, and attack us; (3) the Germans would put pressure on Denmark and secure air bases in Greenland, Iceland, and the Faeroes Islands; (4) they would also put pressure on Portugal and establish German bases in the Azores and Cape Verde Islands; (5) they would also induce Belgium and Holland to let them establish colonies on the west coast of Africa and in the Far East, and these colonies would provide threats to the Western Hemisphere; (6) they would also join with the Italians in militarizing the South American states against us; (7) they would also, as the result of some sort of deal with the British, be permitted to build a base at Newfoundland or Labrador. The President himself had helped the "educational" campaign along with the announcement, in his annual message of January 4, 1939, that "there are many ways short of war, but stronger and more effective than mere words, of bringing home to aggressor governments the aggregate sentiments of our own people."

But now, after January 10th, and the ambassadors' reports on conditions in Europe, a new argument gained currency. One variant of it was the statement that the preservation of the British sea power was essential to our national future. Another had been phrased by the Marquess of Lothian, recently appointed British Ambassador to the United States, months before. "The British Commonwealth," it ran, "is the United States' outer ring of security. . . . If it disappears or is smashed by the Fascist states, so that Gibraltar, the Suez, Singapore, Capetown, and the Falkland Islands fall into the hands of Germany, Italy, or Japan, then, as the British Empire disintegrates, the military powers would crowd around the United States."[17]

To still a third variant, it was charged, the President gave expression late in January, after the fateful crash of a new bomber designed for the United States Army drew the veil from an airplane deal with the French that mysteriously began in the Treasury, moved from there to the White House and from there to the War and Navy Departments, with the State Department apparently looking on inactively while Ambassador Bullitt acted as master of ceremonies.

When the lid blew off this transaction, the President, instead of giving out the facts to the public, called in the Senate Military Affairs Committee, clamped a gag on them, addressed them for an hour and a half, and then sent them packing. He must have known that to talk to a considerable number of members of Congress under such circumstances was to invite not only leaks but the most unhealthy speculation. At any rate, stories of a fantastic foreign policy emerged. The President was alleged to have said that America's frontier was on the Rhine.

This story was heatedly denied by the President on February 3rd. "Some boob" among the senators had "thought that one up," Roosevelt exploded, and the newspapers had embroidered it into "a deliberate lie."

But the facts were still not made public, though even so staunch a supporter of the President as Senator Logan of Kentucky said that he remembered "something being said about our frontier being in France." Instead, a vague four-point statement of American policy was given the press—a statement which left the Senate, the newspapers, and

[17] Lothian, in a press interview, July, 1938.

the country cold because it did not explain the bungled plane deal, it did not make clear what American interests were so endangered that the facts must remain a secret, and it certainly did not convince reasonable people that the administration was not up to its neck in the game of power politics.[18]

Since that day the evidence has all pointed to our active and tireless participation in the game, on the twin theories that our interposition on the side of England and France might prevent a war and that, if it did not, we could give aid and comfort to England and France without involving ourselves in military warfare. Thus the introduction of the Pittman "Peace Act" as a substitute for the neutrality legislation on our books.[19] Thus the President's message of April 14th to Hitler and Mussolini, asking for a pledge of ten years of peace in return for a conference to achieve "progressive relief from the crushing burden of armament" and to open up "avenues of international trade to the end that every nation of the earth may be enabled . . . to possess assurance of obtaining the materials and products of peaceful economic life." It was obvious that this message was sent with the clear realization that its chances of favorable reception by Hitler and

[18] This statement read:

"No. 1: We are against any entangling alliances, obviously.

"No. 2: We are in favor of the maintenance of world trade for everybody—all nations—including ourselves.

"No. 3: We are in complete sympathy with any and every effort made to reduce or limit armaments.

"No. 4: As a nation—as American people—we are sympathetic with the peaceful maintenance of political, economic, and social independence of all nations in the world."

[19] The Act of 1937 imposed a ban on the export of arms, ammunition, and implements of war to belligerents, provided the President has declared that a war exists, and prohibited credits and loans to belligerents. It also gave the President discretion to prohibit American ships from carrying to belligerents such materials as cotton, copper, oil, and iron (essential commodities in the waging of modern warfare) and provided that title to such materials had to pass to a foreign government, corporation, or national before the goods left the United States. The Pittman proposal was designed to win the support of the Senate isolationists, by certain ingenious concessions. It would have compelled the President to recognize the existence of a state of war (whether war was declared or undeclared)—thus removing one element of presidential discretion. It would have compelled the President to require that such materials as cotton, copper, and the rest be paid for in cash and to prohibit their shipment in American vessels—thus removing a second important element of presidential discretion. But it would also have removed the mandatory prohibition on the shipment of arms and munitions to belligerents—a provision admittedly intended to give those nations which have control of the seas (England, France, and their allies) an advantage over Germany. This was not an incidental by-product of the "neutrality" law's revision. It was its purpose.

Mussolini were nil. It seems to have been designed largely for American consumption. As such, it was of a piece with Roosevelt's "I'll be back in the fall if we don't have a war" statement[20] and his Pan-American speech, with its denunciation of "Huns" and "Vandals."[21]

However well-intentioned this policy of building up support for our unneutral intervention in the affairs of Europe by arousing the fears and prejudices of the American people may be, the fact remains that it is a dangerous business. Hysteria rules by no half measures. When you touch off the powder of terror, you get not illumination but a blinding explosion. When you have awakened the animosities of a people, you have created the foreign policy that will carry you into war whether you will it or no.

The American people have been told that they must help the democracies because two or more forms of government cannot coexist in the world, because the world must become either all democratic or all totalitarian. This, of course, is a fallacy. Should we act on it, entering a war in the belief that we were engaging in a holy war to "save democracy," we would find ourselves embarked on wars as hopeless and as bootless as the religious wars of three or four hundred years ago. We should have to learn—as we learned that different religions could coexist within a state under the principle of toleration—that different political ideologies can live side by side.

In point of fact, there has been no scintilla of evidence that Britain and France are at all concerned with the defense of abstract democracy or with a desire to bring all nations to the democratic form of government. The alliances with Turkey and the overtures to Rumania and Soviet Russia and Italy prove otherwise. War has threatened not because of the internal horrors produced by Hitler's intolerance but because of a struggle over the boundary lines of Europe. Only our bellicose patriots forget the distinction. They tell us that, regardless of the *Realpolitik* of all European diplomacy, we must join the "democratic front" against Germany because of her fiendish brutalities to religious, political, and social minorities.

There is no question but that Hitler has created in the minds of all the decent people in this country a feeling of horror and revulsion. But, however strongly we may feel on this subject, a practical consideration enters. Will war against a government because it is intolerant to its own people help those the government persecutes? Or will it result

[20] April 9, 1939; Warm Springs, Georgia.
[21] April 14, 1939.

in an intensification of their persecution and an immediate destruction everywhere of human lives and other precious human values which will be irreplaceable? Will it, for instance, strengthen democratic government in the United States? Or will war bring upon us here a centralized control of life and speech and press and property so absolute that we lose in the United States the very values for which we fight abroad?

If we participate in another general war, we shall certainly be compelled to "stand by the President." Free criticism will be restricted. Beginning with the communications industries, our industries will be nationalized one by one. Wages and hours will be fixed. Profits will be conscripted. The gamble we are asked to take is that, after it is all over, the iron hand of government will be withdrawn from our liberties and our property.

The promise implicit in all Roosevelt's moves—the promise in which he assuredly believes with all his heart—is that we can prevent or shorten war by active intervention in European affairs and still keep out of war ourselves. Unfortunately, it is a promise no living human being can guarantee. You cannot frankly give to one side in a quarrel what you withhold from the other side without courting, first, reprisals and, ultimately, hostilities. There is no such thing as a little unneutrality. When a nation declares and implements its hostile sentiments toward one side in a conflict, the chances that it can persuade that side of its disinterestedness are pretty slim. It is on this hairline margin of safety that we are now operating.

There is little reason to believe that our intervention in Europe to date, for all its lofty motives, has succeeded in doing any more than (1) to wangle the United States into a position where Prime Minister Chamberlain can and does act as though the British might be willing to cooperate with us in our war with Germany, and (2) to throw the United States athwart those belated forces for appeasement whose earlier appearance would have made the growth of fascism impossible in the first place. Any peace enforced now, while the fundamental problem of the distribution of populations, raw materials, and markets still remains unsettled, cannot last. It is futile to inveigh against the symptoms of that disease—the armies, treaty breakings, and "unprovoked aggressions"—while the causes of the disease remain untreated.

To the extent that we have caviled over the process of rectifying the evils of the Treaty of Versailles and encouraged the British and French to abandon appeasement because of reliance upon our active support, we have contributed toward war in the illusion that we were serving the ends of peace. Like poor Romeo, who "thought all for the best" when he threw himself between Tybalt and Mercutio, we have merely heightened the tragedy.

We have weakened our capacity to do our job in this hemisphere—which is to protect the integrity of the nations from the North Pole to Cape Horn and build up a genuine community of interests there.

We have destroyed our ability to act, as Wilson implored in his neutrality plea of August 18, 1914, as "the one people ready to play a part of impartial mediation and speak the counsels of peace and accommodation, not as a partisan, but as a friend."

We have lost the opportunity to show ourselves "in this time of peculiar trial, a nation fit beyond others to exhibit the fine poise of undisturbed judgment, the dignity of self-control, the efficiency of dispassionate action; a nation that neither sits in judgment upon others nor is disturbed in her own counsels and which keeps herself fit and free to do what is honest and disinterested and truly serviceable for the peace of the world. . . ."[22]

And whether we meant to, or not, we have neglected our unsolved problems at home.

5

If, in the course of this categorizing, the emphasis has been always on change, that is because change is as much the central fact of Roosevelt as it is of a kaleidoscope: the bits of brightly colored glass remain the same, but, with every shift, the brilliant and complex pattern falls into new arrangements.

Yet, like most analogies, this, too, is inexact. One cannot imagine a kaleidoscope, however superb, coming to believe it is the glorious rose window of Chartres. And perhaps, after all, that is the change more essential than any.

To say this, is not to lose the sense of Roosevelt as a living, lovable person. The magnificent physique, the bold, handsome features, the fabulous energy, the radiant vitality—these staples are not unimportant because they have become less important. If they were, both Roosevelt and his influence upon our times would remain incomprehensible.

[22] Wilson's Address to the People of the United States appealing for American neutrality. New York *Times*. August 19, 1914.

One day back in February, 1933, two strange individuals presented themselves at Warm Springs and demanded an interview with the President-elect. They represented a "movement" for the amelioration of society, they told McIntyre, and they were eager to have Roosevelt avail himself of the opportunity to support it. So much was routine. But then they announced wildly that they were "Reds," that their "movement" was holding a meeting in a neighboring city in Georgia in a day or two, and that they weren't sure that they could prevent their people from "marching" on Warm Springs if they brought back the news that Roosevelt had refused to endorse their plans. If the marchers started, heaven only knew what eruptions might result, the two strangers said.

McIntyre was alarmed. He called me over from the inn and asked me to talk to them. I was to tell him not what I thought of their ideas but how I thought they could best be bundled off. Did I think the Department of Justice should be called?

It developed that the visitors were trying to sell a magic-money scheme. They argued for it with enough incidental threat to make me understand McIntyre's concern. My efforts to ease them out of the town with assurances that I'd bring their plan to Roosevelt's attention failed. They stubbornly held out for an immediate hearing from Roosevelt.

Finally, Mac and I put the question how to dispose of them to Roosevelt. To our amazement, he suggested that they be brought in. We protested. He insisted. We gave in. McIntyre warned me darkly to stay near while they were talking with Roosevelt. Meanwhile, he would see that adequate Secret Service reserves were on hand.

The two disturbing visitors met a smiling customer on the little balcony at the back of the Warm Springs cottage. Roosevelt invited them to tell him all about their ideas, and they fell to at once. After a time, when violence failed to develop, I wandered away. Much to my surprise, when I returned a half hour later, I found that papers had been drawn out and that the two reformers *and* Roosevelt were covering them with penciled calculations. The visitors and Roosevelt were fascinated by one another. They talked, and he talked. The discussion went on and on. Meanwhile, I reflected, banking legislation of the greatest importance was before Congress, the economic system of the country was cracking under the greatest strain in a generation, the agricultural program was stymied, and a Cabinet was being selected.

There were a thousand things of importance to claim the attention of the man who was about to become President of the United States.

Suffice it to say that after two solid hours of this the "Reds" went away feeling, as their subsequent correspondence showed, that they'd convinced the President-elect of the soundness of their scheme but that, if they hadn't, he was a wonderful man anyhow. And Roosevelt, himself, gave every evidence of feeling that he'd had an absorbingly interesting, informative, and not at all extraordinary experience.

The hero of this adventure would be no stranger to the Roosevelt of today. There is the same physical courage, the same friendliness, the same susceptibility to the new and untried.

An observer of Roosevelt gets the sense that he has the completely integrated nervous system of a great athlete. There is never any taking or asking of odds. In fact, Roosevelt's indifference to physical danger is a source of distress to those whose business it is to guard him. It was McIntyre who gave this anxiety classic expression one day at Hyde Park, when he'd learned that Roosevelt had gone off for a drive without telling the newspapermen. "Good grief," he scolded. And then, with completely unconscious humor, "Think, if something happened to him. Some accident, or something. Why, all these newspapermen would lose their jobs!"

The Presidency is inevitably an extrahazardous occupation. Of the thirty-two men who have held that post, three have been murdered and two others have been shot at. But the vast gap between the customary resignation of most men in the face of such danger and Roosevelt's sheer indifference to it is attested by the joy and zest with which he goes his way. Sports writers speak of those who "can take it," and those who "can't take it." Roosevelt can.

Another kind of courage—the courage of a man like the elder La Follette, who, time and again, gambled his political career on a matter of intense conviction—is characteristic too. Roosevelt has taken such chances again and again. Almost always they have been successful. It is no disparagement of him and no prejudging of his response to adversity to suggest that he has not had to "take it," as old La Follette did, in the sense of fighting desperately for a political cause that he knew to be hopeless, standing up and slugging in the face of a political defeat apparent even to him. The defeats that he has suffered in the past two or three years provide no clue. He has been able to rationalize to his own satisfaction both his Supreme Court defeat and the defeat of the purge. If unwillingness to admit defeat, if getting one's "Dutch" up and holding one's ground constitute the ability to "take it," then Roosevelt has that too.

But these qualities also go by other names. And perhaps it is Roosevelt's refusal to recognize the possibility of defeat that makes him awkward as a defensive fighter in the field of politics. He doesn't know how to "bicycle," how to gain time and strength by yielding ground. His impulsiveness rules out caution and strategic retreat. He firmly believes that the only defense is offense—a stirring aphorism, but hardly a précis of statecraft.

Machiavelli seems to have covered the ground more serviceably:

> A man is not often found [the old reporter said] sufficiently circumspect to know how to accommodate himself to the change [of times and affairs], both because he cannot deviate from that to which nature inclines him and also because, having always prospered by acting in one way, he cannot be persuaded that it is well to leave it. . . . Pope Julius the Second went to work impetuously in all his affairs, and found the times and circumstances conformed so well to that line of action that he always met with success. . . . But if circumstances had arisen which required him to go cautiously, his ruin would have followed, because he would never have deviated from those ways to which nature inclined him.

On the other hand, among those ways "to which nature inclines" Roosevelt, is one of the most precious assets a public man could have —a seemingly unaffected warmth and cordiality. There was nothing that wasn't spontaneous about the reception he gave the two zealots at Warm Springs. It transcended self-interest or formal courtesy. Roosevelt is interested in people. He wants people to like him. And the combination is almost irresistible.

Few of those malformations that are usually the aftermath of the kind of hothouse boyhood Roosevelt spent are discernible in his personal relations with others. Critics have suggested that, during his youth, his personal contacts with that vast area that lay outside the circle of his selected associates were marked by unmistakable gingerliness. But I surmise that his attitude was never either snobbish or patronizing. If it was anything like that tentativeness that characterized so many of his contacts in recent years, it probably sprang from a sense of unfamiliarity, a faint envy of experiences and interests he hadn't shared.

I imagine that this is what prevented him from ever enjoying a genuine camaraderie with Al Smith, Robert Wagner, Jimmy Walker, and others with a Tammany background. Somehow, in the depths of consciousness, there fluttered a hint of the alien—not in them, but in him. In his dealings with Lewis, Green and horny-handed congressional brethren the same uneasiness is apparent. He calls them "John" and "Bill"; but there is always the suggestion of some inner watchfulness, some subtle incompleteness that makes intimacy impossible. These men may be his allies. But they can never be his friends.

Roosevelt's contacts with those whose upbringing was like his own suggest the surer touch, although he can hardly disguise a little pooh-poohing of the abler of them and an ostentatious contempt for those who disregard what he calls their social "opportunities and obligations."

In one of the plausible passages of that effusion about Roosevelt in which Emil Ludwig sounds like the Widow of Windsor writing of her beloved Albert, Ludwig says Roosevelt "much prefers to take a holiday on a yacht with millionaire friends, which does not prevent him from laughing in their faces and taking sixty to eighty per cent of their incomes away through new taxes a week later. He does not hate them, he only wants to shear them."[23] This is a paraphrase of something everyone who knows Roosevelt has heard him say over and over. It is the expression of a characteristic need for apology that a deeply philosophical radical among the Brahmins would not feel, in the circumstances. But even more so is the unadulterated seriousness with which Roosevelt will explain to an old friend of the family that he has saved her from Revolution—that, but for him, her well-coifed head would have been among the first to roll into the basket. Possibly the remark is true. But the argument is either gratuitous or futile. One finds one's self wondering why, if Roosevelt thinks this sort of kindergarten persuasion is needed, he should value the good opinion of its object enough to bother arguing at all. A plebeian Andrew Jackson did not care what the Van Rensselaers thought of him. An aristocratic Thomas Jefferson had too much certitude to spend his time justifying himself even to a Timothy Dwight. Only a Teddy Roosevelt felt the need to explain, to convert his old associates—and violently, at that.

But close to T. R. as Franklin Roosevelt is, in this respect, he has never been able to maintain long relationships with men whose minds are strong and assertive. It would be impossible to imagine him preserving an intimacy with men like Hay, Root, and Henry Adams. The independence and positiveness of such men would discomfort him. In the disagreement of, say, a Bronson Cutting, he sees a kind of danger-

[23] *Roosevelt,* by Emil Ludwig. Copyright, 1938, by Viking Press, New York; p. 330.

ous malevolence that he would never think of imputing to an Alben Barkley. It is this shortcoming that leaves him so tragically, at the end of his second term, with no man among his close associates to whom he can point as a likely successor.

There is another curious aspect of Roosevelt's need for amiable, pleasant relationships. He hates to hurt people, if he must be exposed to a view of their suffering. The gnarled Louis Howe, who had no such inhibitions, was used constantly to deliver unpleasant messages. On occasion, he was even obliged to fire officials for the President. I don't think I shall ever forget Roosevelt's anguish as he once braced himself to ask for the resignation of one of the most inept appointees of his early administration. Word came to him that the man was waiting outside. Roosevelt sat with his chin cupped in his hand, rehearsing speeches under his breath. He played with the pencils and ash trays on his desk. He smoked. He fidgeted. At last, he shook his head despairingly. He turned to me. I shook my head just as hopelessly. There was nothing I could do to help. The one and only time I had ever tried to fire a man, I'd been saved only because the firee, after listening to me muttering indirections for a half hour, came over to me, clapped his hand on my shoulder, and said pityingly, "Look here. You want to fire me, don't you? Well, I'm fired." Roosevelt sent for Louis. It was Louis who did the job.

Unavoidably, this intense distaste for making people suffer in his presence has been a source of trouble. Dozens of misfits, which he recognizes as such, are kept in Washington because he cannot bring himself to rid his administration of them. Blunders (like that in the St. Paul tariff speech of 1932, for which I consider myself responsible) go unreproved. Visitors leave his office thinking that he has agreed with them simply because his extreme desire to be agreeable makes it impossible for him to say a clear-cut "No." Perhaps, in the long run, fewer friends would have been lost by bluntness than by the misunderstandings that arose from engaging ambiguity.

Something of the same thing might be said of that deeper sensitiveness to the afflictions and deprivations of people in the mass, people to whom life has not offered the enjoyments he has known. This is not assumed. The politician in Roosevelt knows that the people along the railroad track to whom he waves have votes. But he waves to them chiefly because he likes them. He speaks of the "underprivileged third" because from the bottom of his heart he wants them to be as happy as he is. He is outraged by hunger and unemployment, as though they were personal affronts in a world he is certain he can make far better, totally other, than it has been. He wants to protect the Weak against the Strong, against the few villainous and predatory Strong.

This militant tenderness has given his administration a reputation as a golden age for social workers. And no cynical talk about relief in politics can tarnish that reputation. It is firmly based in the fact that there can be credited to his sympathy and interest enormous advances in many fields of experimental social welfare, that it has always been easy for men and women interested in such questions to get to him, that none of the weariness that made Mark Hanna say "What's the sense in increasing the supply of damn fools?" has ever dampened his ardor and his generous concern.

More than anything else, Roosevelt's warm-heartedness came, in middle life, to focus his attention upon the pressing economic and social problems of our time. Yet to say this is not to say, "Better the occasional faults of a government that lives in a spirit of charity than the consistent omissions of a government frozen in the ice of its own indifference,"[24] because these are not the sole alternatives.

The trouble seems to be that, as Santayana has remarked of William James, "Love is very penetrating, but it penetrates to possibilities rather than to facts."[25] The bonhomie, the romantic sympathy that made Roosevelt spend two hours exploring an absurd money scheme in Warm Springs on the chance that some new economic revelation might have come knocking at his door, was a fault as well as a virtue. In so far as Roosevelt's desire to make life better in the world has led him to challenge old theories and experiment with new ideas, it is indispensable in a progressive leader. But when that open-mindedness is not checked at every point by a critical and disciplined intelligence, it becomes something akin to gullibility. The mere will to transform the ugliness and abuse that exists becomes a faith in economic and social miracles.

In the last analysis, a pragmatic approach to public problems is nothing more than an enlargement of the realm of unsettled questions. It is a willingness to submit fairly well-established axioms to periodic reexamination. But it does not free those who practice it from the

[24] Roosevelt's acceptance of the renomination for the Presidency, Philadelphia, June 27, 1936.

[25] *Character and Opinion in the United States,* by George Santayana. Charles Scribner's Sons; New York, 1920; p. 94.

need for logic and judgment. Belief that we are perpetually on the verge of discovery is not in itself virtuous. Nor is it discovery. Belief is important, certainly. But—to dip once more into the wisdom of Santayana—"believe rationally, holding what seems certain for certain, what seems probable for probable, what seems desirable for desirable and what seems false for false. . . . What is good . . . is a clear head, aware of its resources, not a fuddled optimism, calling up spirits from the vasty deep."[26]

There is a broad streak of the Colonel Sellers in Franklin Roosevelt. New schemes, neat paper formulas for solving this or that problem invariably intrigue him.

It seems to be generally believed that Roosevelt's drift down the stream of capricious experimentation can be explained by the death of Louis Howe. As a matter of fact, Howe was as much the lover of experiments as Roosevelt. Fortunately, though, the two men rarely got the itch to carry out the same experiment at the same time. So the relationship actually was a rough corrective.

But there is no reason to suppose that Louis' restraining influence wouldn't have suffered the same diminution as that of Roosevelt's other close advisers. For, more and more, belief has become the impulse to act immediately. To perceive a wrong is "good." To deplore that wrong is also "good." Therefore "to do something" about it is "good." Not to act is to be untrue to the insight that made the wrong apparent in the first place. To wait and study and reflect is, as Hamlet called it,

> Bestial oblivion, or some craven scruple
> Of thinking too precisely on the event,
> A thought which, quartered, hath but one part wisdom
> And ever three parts coward.

Roosevelt, too, cannot live and say " 'This thing's to do.' " It must be done. War must be stopped. People must be fed and clothed and employed. And to hem and haw over the method by which these ends are being sought, even to wonder whether we know enough to get very far, is "bestial oblivion"—or, in the modern world, "reaction."

So far as Roosevelt is concerned, skepticism indicates itself only in reverse. Among his favorite words are the words "definite," "definitely," and "practical." Those who have assisted him with state papers have probably eliminated hundreds, perhaps thousands, of "definite"s and

[26] *Character and Opinion in the United States; op. cit.;* pp. 87 and 90.

"definitely"s and "practical"s from his dictation. Without attributing too much importance to this quirk, I seriously believe that the repetition of the word "definite" is intended as a reassurance to himself as well as to the public. Some inner voice murmurs that it is not possible always to be definite in our social and economic prognoses. To this Roosevelt answers by verbal table pounding. He very "definitely" thinks that such and such must be done: so-and-so is not a theory worth trying, but a "practical" way of doing it.

This necessity for assertion does not differ in the slightest from T. R.'s. Experts in natural history, in literature, in economics, in jurisprudence, and in the scientific aspects of politics were forever quarreling with T. R.'s violently assertive statements of fact about their specialties. But a calm appraisal of Teddy indicates that his voracious mind had reached out after an enormous quantity of scientific, literary, and historical learning. The picture of Teddy which Thomas Beer has drawn—of Teddy regaling a group of his friends with judgments on Goya, Flaubert, Dickens, and Jung, and discussions of Louis the Fat or the number of men at arms seasick in the fleet of Medina Sidonia—this could never be mistaken for one of Franklin Roosevelt.[27] F. D. R.'s interests have always been more circumscribed. His moments of relaxation are given over exclusively to simpler pleasures—to the stamp album, to the Currier and Ives naval prints, to a movie or to good-humored horseplay.

Perhaps the most perfect sense of the quality of his humor is conveyed by Ernest Lindley's description of part of a St. Valentine's Day at the Executive Mansion in Albany. The Governor is reading and signing letters.

> In the adjoining dining-room, behind drawn curtains, one gathers that the table is being prepared for a dinner for the Governor's office staff. Louis Howe, the diabolic impresario of such occasions, has been busy all afternoon with cardboard and scissors and paints making a fancifully humorous centerpiece and valentines peculiarly appropriate to each guest. Occasionally a shriek of laughter comes through the curtain. One overhears a voice in the hall reporting that Howe's masterpiece is an excruciatingly funny valentine for the Governor. Roosevelt looks up for an instant, smiles knowingly. . . . Mrs. Roosevelt slips in, hands him a piece of paper with a head pasted on it and whispers that he will have to draw the valentine for Howe. He puts aside his correspondence for a second, swiftly sketches an absurd picture of a man in a long nightgown, holding a candle, and puts on a nightcap for a finish-

[27] *Hanna*, by Thomas Beer. Alfred A. Knopf, Inc.; New York, 1929; p. 241.

ing touch. He puts some caption beneath it which makes them both burst into laughter. Mrs. Roosevelt exits and he returns to his work again. He is finished in a few minutes and ready to go up-stairs to dress for dinner. Just then another visitor arrives, a department head of sober demeanor.

"Come along and talk to me up-stairs," says the Governor. They start down the hall, conversing very seriously. At the entrance to the dining-room, Roosevelt turns away for an instant, draws back the curtains, shouts triumphantly, "I've seen it." Shrieks and moans from within are his reply. He turns back to his visitor and, continuing their conversation, they enter the elevator.[28]

In one form or another this scene repeats itself endlessly in the Roosevelt entourage. And no one ever enjoys it the less for its repetition.

Despite this abundant and lusty humor, no trace of it illumines for Roosevelt the incongruity between word and fact. But then, perhaps it never can, in the political mind. Essentially the politician is dealing with illusions and images, like Plato's people in a cave, who see only the distorted shadows which the firelight throws on the wall. It is the art of the politician to create imagery. He is concerned so much of the time with the effect of his words upon his hearers that he tends to forget their exact meaning. Words are for him the brush of the artist, the chisel of the sculptor, not the sensitive film of the photographer. And because he must reckon less with what is true than with what people will believe is true, his mind comes to impose upon itself an interpretation of facts favorable to his purposes.

So Roosevelt will tell of verbal passages-at-arms with people—little anecdotes that invariably end in victory for him and discomfiture for his adversary. "Yesterday," he will say, mentioning the name of a well-known official of an oil company, "I was told that I ought to conciliate business." Ensues a long description of the conversation which finally ends in Roosevelt's saying, "You deal in barrels of oil. I deal in votes. I know nothing about selling oil. You know nothing of winning votes." Whereupon the oil man is quoted as flinging down his sword with the words, "I never thought of that."

Now if the listener happens to know the oil man in question, he has a fairly good idea that the oil man could not possibly have overlooked the fact that he has been selling oil for many years and that Roosevelt's business is getting votes. And if the listener knows Roose-

[28] *Franklin D. Roosevelt,* by Ernest K. Lindley. Copyright, 1931; used by permission of the publishers, The Bobbs-Merrill Company; p. 340.

velt, he knows that there was no deliberate intention of recounting the conversation inaccurately. The anecdote is simply a way of saying that businessmen persistently misunderstand him. The addition of the oil man's confession of ignorance at the end is merely an embellishment, a bit of artistic license, as it were, to round out the story.[29]

So, too, with such statements as this, to Ludwig, explaining how the nomination for the vice-presidency had come to him in San Francisco, "Suddenly I heard my name being called. I did not believe it at first. Then my friends called me over. The whole thing lasted ten minutes. They chose me because my name had become known during the war."[30] It is possible that Ludwig did not report accurately what Roosevelt said. But probably he did, for the remark is not unlike dozens of others Roosevelt has made. Some things he says because he wants so intensely to believe them. It is nicer to believe that he was nominated for the vice-presidency in 1920 because his "name had become known during the war" than it is to accept the general opinion that the Democratic leaders wanted to use on their ticket a name which T. R. had made a household word.

Roosevelt would like so much to convince the members of the Senate Military Affairs Committee that he knows the risk his foreign policy involves because he has himself endured all the horrors of war that he tells them he had as much experience on the actual fighting front in France as anybody.

This is not serious, politically, except in so far as it misleads Roosevelt himself. The quality is known and discounted by those who are associated with him. But it has, on occasion, thrown his own political judgment out of kilter. It explains his insistence that "the people are with me" throughout the Court fight, despite all evidence that they were not. It explains the angry dismissal of a poll of the American Institute of Public Opinion, which indicated that the public disapproved a measure he wanted to see passed, with the announcement that the state of public opinion would be different after he had discussed the problem with the people. The distinctions between things as they are and things as they may be or might be or ought to be sometimes grow blurred. Possibly this is what Huey Long meant when he said to me, "Roosevelt ain't smart." Whatever may have been

[29] Until recently these "straw-man interviews" were reserved for private *racontage*. Now, perhaps illustrative of growing self-confidence, Roosevelt relates them in speeches.

[30] *Roosevelt; op. cit.;* p. 80.

Huey's public inaccuracies and exaggerations, he never deceived himself.

Yet all these qualities I knew, or guessed at, by March 4, 1933. The one factor of which I never dreamed was the intensifying and exhilarating effect of power upon such a temperament.

For Roosevelt in 1932 was not immodest. He listened patiently to advice. No one respected more than he the right of others to their own opinions. No one seemed less likely to be overwhelmed by the illusion of his own rectitude. He was the batter who had no expectation of making a hit every time he came up to bat, not Judge Landis. I could not have conceived of him in the role of a Napoleon taunting Caulaincourt, his onetime Ambassador to Russia, for warnings against the Russian adventure, with the words, "The Tsar Alexander has made a Russian out of Caulaincourt," and, on a particularly mild autumn day, "So this is the terrible Russian winter that Monsieur de Caulaincourt frightens the children with."

What seemed likely to distinguish him was his moderation, his smiling indifference to extravagant criticism, his instinctive response to the nuances of public opinion, his desire to persuade and to win over people, his tentative and undogmatic approach to public problems, his complete freedom from that sense of personal destiny that makes rulers confuse their own triumph with the exaltation of principle.

I would not have believed that Roosevelt would succumb to the unlovely habits of "telling, not asking," of brusquely brushing aside well-meant tenders of information and advice, of asserting things in a way calculated to suggest that to assert them was *ipso facto* to guarantee their wisdom and veracity. Nor did I foresee the growth of that irritable certitude that led Roosevelt to ascribe self-interest or cowardice or subtle corruption or stupidity to people who questioned the rightness of his impulses to action.

I could not imagine that the quality of refusing to admit defeat would become the incapacity to admit error except in the vaguest of generalities.

I could not imagine Roosevelt's envisaging himself as the beneficiary of a vote based upon the challenge that he was the issue, that people must either be friends of the friendless, and hence "for him," or enemies of the friendless, and hence "against him."

I could not imagine that a growing identification of self with the will of the people would lead him on to an attempted impairment of those very institutions and methods which have made progressive evolution possible in this country.

But then, I did not reckon with what seemed, in a United States which cried out for action and assertion, perhaps the most irrelevant political axiom wise men through the ages had ever devised. I had not yet learned that no temperament, however fluid, is immune to the vitrifying effect of power, that the uses of power "like a mould, take in all temperaments and turn out the same prototypes."[31] The failing is that of all men, not of one man.

Power itself has ways of closing the windows of a President's mind to fresh, invigorating currents of opinion from the outside. The most important of these ways is the subtle flattery with which the succession of those who see the President day after day treat him. Nine out of ten of those who see a President want something of him, and, because they do, they are likely to tell him something pleasant, something to cozen his good will. They are likely to agree with him, rather than disagree with him. If a man is told he is right by people day after day, he will, unless he has extraordinary defenses, ultimately believe he can never be wrong.

Until the very end of my association with Roosevelt, I hoped that his quality of pragmatism would keep some of the windows of his mind open. I finally found that he was not only being shut in by the usual process of flattery but that he himself was slamming shut windows. He developed a very special method of reassuring himself of his own preconceptions after hearing an unwelcome bit of advice. This consisted of telling Visitor B that he had just heard so-and-so from Visitor A and that A was "scared" about something, or that A didn't know what he was talking about. Usually B would agree with the President. But whether or not he did, if he was a man of spirit he decided that he, for one, wouldn't put himself into the position of being made ridiculous to Visitor C. So he would withhold all disagreement by way of self-protection. And so was another window closed.

Ultimately, of course, a man closed off, by one means or another, from free opinion and advice, suffers a kind of mental autointoxication. He lives in a world of ideas generated only by himself, a world of make-believe, a world like Prospero's island, where his magic can create things in the image of his own desires—an insubstantial pageant of unanimity.

[31] Ralph Roeder, *Catherine de' Medici and the Lost Revolution*. Copyright, 1937. Published by the Viking Press, Inc., New York; p. 196.

That is why the problem of restraining power has always been the central problem of government—the problem that will never be settled in an absolute sense so long as there are men in the world. The traditions that have grown up around the Constitution—the tradition of the right of the Supreme Court to review acts of Congress, the tradition that prohibits tampering with the independence of either the legislative or the judicial arms of the government, the tradition that no President shall serve more than eight years—all spring from the bitter teaching of experience that power is dangerous. It grows by what it feeds upon, dulling the perceptions, clouding the vision, imprisoning its victim, however well-intentioned he may be, in that chill isolation of a self-created aura of intellectual infallibility which is the negation of the democratic principle.

Possibly no one who has not seen its insidious attack upon a living and very dear person can feel its tragedy.

6

Time makes its own inexorable estimates, and they cannot be prejudged. But it would be dishonest for me not to end this seven years' story on a note of deep regret.

The great surge toward orderly and progressive economic reform that gained impetus during the sixty years following the War between the States has had few parallels in modern times, except perhaps the movements for political reform in England and the sweep of republicanism on the Continent after the Napoleonic wars. Like those movements, progressivism in the United States grew out of the efforts of thousands of disassociated, dissimilar individuals and groups. There were reform administrations in cities and states. There were scores of local legislative experiments. There were numberless political preachers. There were teachers and books that gave a new cast to people's thinking about economic questions. By the onset of the depression millions of Americans realized that economic civilization, as we had known it, was not and need not be an eventual absolute. Millions wanted to see it made more equitable, more efficient, more productive.

It was Roosevelt's special fortune that he became President when, in economic calamity, progressivism at last won the adherence of a majority of our people. In that sense he was handed a torch that had been carried by others for generations. He was the trustee of a magnificent tradition. That he was able to go so far in so short a time was in large part the result of the accumulated force of what had been so long denied fulfillment.

Roosevelt's administration has achieved much. It has outlawed many abuses. It has readjusted some of our lopsided economic relationships. It has established firmly in the nation's consciousness the principle of economic interdependence. There will remain, after Roosevelt has left office, a vastly changed philosophy of business enterprise, an improvement in the methods of social-welfare activities. Many of the New Deal measures, even those that have failed, have had an important educational value, for they have shown what will not work. These gains are incontestable.

But it is difficult to reconcile them with what they have cost. It is not alone that immense treasure has been spent for economic rehabilitation that has not materialized, that, after seven years, investment remains dormant, enterprise is chilled, the farmers' problem has not yet been solved, unemployment is colossal. It is that thousands of devoted men and women, who felt, as sincerely as Roosevelt, that we must redefine the aims of democratic government in terms of modern needs, have been alienated. They asked only that the repair work done upon the structure of policy follow a consistent pattern of architecture. They pointed out only that unskillful combinations of Gothic, Byzantine, and Le Corbusier defy the law of gravity, and invite ultimate collapse.

These men and women have been told that they are "yes-but" liberals, that they are "copperheads," that they must subscribe to either all or nothing. Their position on such perversions of progressive doctrine as the Court-packing plan has been made a test of personal loyalty. Often the fact of their employment as the managers of businesses has automatically subjected them to the suspicion of self-interest. Their enthusiasm and their energies have been lost. They have been told, in these latter days, that their collaboration is no longer wanted.

Even the submerged third, whose interests the President has so persistently championed, have been thoughtlessly injured. Extravagant promises have raised expectations far beyond any reasonable hope of realization. Disillusionment must ultimately be the bitter harvest of such planting.

But perhaps the most serious injury that has been done the cause of orderly progress has been the impairment of the nation's unity by the repeated suggestion that benefits can come to one group only at the expense of others. Progressivism depends upon cooperation, not upon conflict. It looks to the creation of an increasingly large number of shared values, not to the establishment of "an economy of maintenance" which can do no more than redistribute the wealth that already exists.

Roosevelt has never condemned businessmen or newspaper publishers as a whole. He has always qualified his denunciations with reference to the "small, bad" minority in those groups. But the fact that he has limited himself to denunciation of the "small, bad" minority in these specific groups and ignored the "small, bad" minority in all other groups has been just as effective in developing class antagonism as a general denunciation. An administration that leaves more rather than less consciousness of class has done the country a disservice.

Progressivism has always thrived upon the attacks of its enemies. It remains to be seen whether it can survive the mistakes of its friends.

A golden moment has passed—a moment for the demonstration that a liberal movement can preserve its unity and direction by restraint. True, the moment will come again, because faith in progressivism is a hardy growth. But precious time has been squandered for illusions. True, political action, regardless of party labels, will never again be what it was before. But the conviction that progressivism is no more than a vague and muddled impulse to do good, will make the next effort so much the harder.

"The harvest is past, the summer is ended, and we are not saved." Vastly important reforms still remain to be achieved. Yet, the essential institutional integrity of this country remains uninjured. Our Constitution has shown, in the face of ill-considered attacks, a vitality hitherto undreamed of. Our economic system has suffered no basic injury, although its activity has been unnecessarily repressed. Fortunately, not only are our natural resources greater than ever but our understanding of them is greater.

Our future can be what we choose to make it, if we can implement the power of government with a measure of fine thinking as well as of generous impulse.

APPENDIX A

TEXT OF BROADCAST TO THE NATION BY GOVERNOR FRANKLIN D. ROOSEVELT FROM POUGHKEEPSIE, NEW YORK, NIGHT OF NOVEMBER 7, 1932

For twenty-two years it has been my custom to end every political campaign with my friends and neighbors of all political parties here in Dutchess County. I began my public service here many years ago.

I have learned much of what I know of human life and of political affairs in country and in city from you, my friends. I have held to the belief and I still hold it firmly that you, whom I know so well, represent in a great degree the ideals, the hopes, the standards and the problems of all Americans. This year I continue my custom, although science and circumstance have widened the circle of my neighbors. In earlier years I talked to you alone, then to the whole state. Now the entire country is within earshot, and my travels and contacts have made many Americans everywhere, I hope, my friends and neighbors.

These many weeks of the campaign have been crowded with action, motion, change. They have been marked by a thousand impressions. The bare facts do not tell the story.

I have traveled many miles; it doesn't matter exactly how many. I have visited many states; the number isn't significant. I have spoken many times; my hearers will be kind and not tell just how many. And I have seen millions and millions of people.

Statistics, numbers, percentages applied to human things like these take from—they certainly do not add to—their strong vital importance. The impressions count, the vivid flashes tell us of the essential unity of things. Some of them I shall never forget—the great crowd under the lights before the Capitol at Jefferson City, the patient attention of the Kansans under the hot sun at Topeka, the long day through Wyoming, with the strong, direct kindness of the people who came, some of them, hundreds of miles to bid me welcome; the men and women who made a great city in the valley of Salt Lake, the stricken but dauntless miners of Butte, the world consciousness of Seattle, the citizens of Portland who sustained me with keen understanding through a long technical discussion of public utilities.

A thousand such impressions crowd my memory. Farmers again

from the California valleys gathered under the sun at Sacramento, the welcome of San Francisco, that magnificent city where the old East meets the new West; Los Angeles, the miracle of a city built—as history measures time—in a moment.

I shall never forget the sunset at McCook, Nebraska, and the strong progressive farmers. Sioux City and Milwaukee, and Chicago and Detroit, Pikesburg and Indianapolis, and Springfield and Louisville. And then my neighbors in my Southern home in Georgia. The children in wheel-chairs at Warm Springs, all so happy in a great hope; and north to New England at Portland and Boston and Providence and Hartford.

Each of these memories and many others have their individual significance to me. If I can catch them all together and give them vitality and meaning and life, I shall have fulfilled the purpose of my travels. These people, all of them, these neighbors of each and every state have made one thing clear: they have expressed some hope in the future, confidence that things will be better. I set out to learn, more than to teach. All of you, East and West and North and South, have helped me.

And you have graciously helped me, too. You may not universally have agreed with me, but you have universally been kind and friendly to me. The great understanding and tolerance of America came out to meet me everywhere; for all this you have my heartfelt gratitude.

Out of this unity that I have seen we may build the strongest strand to lift ourselves out of this depression.

If all of this multitude of my friends and neighbors give expression tomorrow to your united confidence in the invigorating tonic of a change, I may in some modest way bring this unity of purpose to practical fulfillment.

A man comes to wisdom in many years of public life. He knows well that when the light of favor shines upon him, it comes not, of necessity, that he himself is important. Favor comes because for a brief moment in the great space of human change and progress some general human purpose finds in him a satisfactory embodiment.

To be the means through which the ideal and hopes of the American people may find a greater realization calls for the best in any man; I seek to be only the humble emblem of this restoration.

If that be your verdict, my friends of America and my next-door neighbors of Dutchess County, and that be the confident purpose behind your verdict, I shall in the humility that suits such a great confidence seek to meet this great expectation of yours. With your help and your patience and your generous good will we can mend the torn fabric of our common life.

On this very eve of the exercise of the greatest right of the American electorate, I bid you good night. And I add to that, God bless you all.

APPENDIX B

QUESTIONS TAKEN BY FRANKLIN D. ROOSEVELT TO CONFERENCE WITH PRESIDENT HOOVER, NOVEMBER 22, 1932

Can the December 15th payments be discussed separately from the whole question at the present time?

Was there any discussion of failure of Great Britain to include the debt payments of December 15th in its budget estimate?

Can debt matters (in view of the negotiations thus far) be separately discussed with each debtor, or must all debtors be treated alike?

If December 15th payments can be separately discussed, can the problem of transfer be divorced from the question of forgiveness or moratorium?

And can these questions be separately discussed with each country in each case?

What specific results do you consider could be expected to flow from a "period of tranquillity" suggested in the British note?

Would this "tranquillity" be greater if the December 15th payments were not made?

How much is the private debt of foreigners to United States nationals?

How much does that require to be transferred annually in payment? Specifications:

1. For service charges: interest and sinking fund.
2. How much is in default and is interest being regularly received on the rest?
3. How much is being placed in escrow abroad for the account of American bondholders?

Why, in your judgment, did the debtor nations not avail themselves of the 90-day clause in the debt arrangements?

What are the gold holdings of our chief debtors?

How does this compare with one year ago?

How much gold has each of them withdrawn from the United States which might have been left here to meet December 15th payments?

What change has there been in the debtor countries in the last 18 months?

Is their position with relation to the United States worse than it was 18 months ago?

You have suggested a reconstitution of the debt funding commission. What is it that you expect this commission will do?

A. Will it re-examine capacity to pay: in relation to (a) the relative situations of U. S. and other countries in 1923-26 and 1932, (b) the relative abilities of various debtors?
B. Will it examine the desirability of readjusting interest rates? If so, on what principle?
C. Will it re-examine the value of the debt? (Our relation to our creditors is the same as their relation to us.)
D. Would the commission be guided by the rate of interest at which conversion can be accomplished in the United States? or in the debtor countries?

Why a debt *commission* at all?

Has any promise been made to European governments that debts will be re-examined because of the conclusion of agreements among European nations to forego reparations payments? (The Lausanne agreement.)

What arrangements were made with Premier Laval?

Does the present move to re-examine the debts represent, in any sense, a fulfillment of informal agreements made with MacDonald and Laval?

What is the position of the Federal Reserve Board in regard to the debt situation?

Has the Federal Reserve Board any understanding with the Administration with regard to a debt policy?

What relation, in the view of the Administration, does the debt question hold to:

A. The objectives of the disarmament conference.
B. The negotiations regarding the Manchurian situation.
C. The coming world economic conference.

Has the Administration:

A. Conveyed any view to the foreign Governments with respect to the foregoing?
B. Given *any instructions* to any of its representatives with regard to the foregoing?
C. Has any member of the disarmament commission asked your views as to the foregoing? And what did you reply?
D. Given any *other* intimation as to the foregoing?
E. Does the Administration have knowledge of any conversations of responsible individuals affecting the situation?

APPENDIX C

TEXT OF STATEMENT FOLLOWING CONFERENCE BETWEEN PRESIDENT HOOVER AND PRESIDENT-ELECT ROOSEVELT, JANUARY 20, 1933

The conference between the President and the President-elect this morning was attended by Secretaries Stimson and Mills and Messrs. Norman Davis and Moley. The discussions were devoted mainly to a canvass of the foreign situation and the following statement covering the procedure to be followed was agreed upon:

The British Government has asked for a discussion of the debts. The incoming administration will be glad to receive their representative early in March for this purpose. It is, of course, necessary to discuss at the same time the world economic problems in which the United States and Great Britain are mutually interested, and, therefore, that representatives should also be sent to discuss ways and means for improving the world situation.

It was settled that these arrangements will be taken up by the Secretary of State with the British Government.

APPENDIX D

TEXT OF SYNDICATED ARTICLE BY RAYMOND MOLEY: "LOOKING FORWARD TO THE WORLD ECONOMIC CONFERENCE"

The World Economic and Monetary Conference which begins this month in London, was conceived and partially planned at Lausanne a year ago. Its objective is to decide upon the measures to solve certain economic and financial questions "which are responsible for, and may prolong, the present world crisis."

The plan of calling to Washington, individually, representatives of various countries to discuss such questions in a preliminary way before the conference was President Roosevelt's, however. These individual conferences between the representatives of the United States and of a score of nations served a most useful purpose. They provided the opportunity for a kind of exploratory review of the topics which will be discussed at the conference itself. This has probably saved many weeks of preparatory discussion at London. But even more important, it has brought about a pleasant acquaintance among the representatives of the participating powers which cannot help but promote agreements, wherever agreements are possible.

It would serve no useful purpose, however, to lead people to feel that the world is going to be transfigured by the conference. To raise expectations too high is to drive ourselves to almost certain defeat.

The problems most difficult of solution will be related to trade, the barriers against trade and the readjustment of these barriers. Tariffs and other restrictive devices are deeply rooted in the policies of the various countries and are closely integrated parts of their economic life. All of the nations, including our own, have been moving toward self-support for a long time. Industrial and agricultural life has developed in that direction with remarkable rapidity of late. Manufacturing has grown in even such remotely industrial countries as China and India. American capital and industry, by the establishment of factories abroad, have themselves gone far toward the acceleration of this tendency. The inexorable laws of cheaper production and reduced costs of transportation help. Thus a combination of forces is arrayed against extensive attacks upon trade barriers. Moderate results must be anticipated. The groundwork can be laid for many bilateral agreements and a more enlightened point of view. But we shall not have a vast new commerce on the seven seas, even after a successful economic conference.

To admit this is not to embrace "isolation." No one can anticipate such an objective in an age of growing intellectual and cultural interdependence.

It is not too much to expect that vastly improved relationships will be established as a result of the conference, not only between the central bank of each country and the government of that country but among the central banks themselves, as a world group. Progress should be made in the removal of exchange restrictions. A much more general agreement will probably be reached as to the sort of an international monetary standard or common yardstick toward which we should work, and the United States has every reason to believe that something will be done to improve the price of silver. Finally, it is possible that progress will be made in bringing about the proper employment of monetary means to increase economic activity and improve prices generally in the various countries, somewhat along the lines of the effort in which the United States is now engaged.

Certainly we shall know, by the end of the conference, whether the best interest of the United States will be to follow a policy of intranational economy. If that be the direction toward which we must work, we shall be able to proceed toward it without further delay.

One thing ought to be clearly kept in mind to avoid not only misunderstanding as to the purposes of the conference, but to forestall disappointment in its results. Too many people are likely to think that because the depression is world-wide its causes rest solely upon international conditions or that the solution for this world-wide depression is solely through international remedies. This erroneous impression is based upon the notion that we suffer from a depression in one country only because other countries are depressed. The fact is that a good many of the economic ills of each country are domestic. They did not drift across the borders from other countries. They are predominantly internal, not external. Much of the remedy, then, must be what the nations do within themselves.

In the face of this realization, however, it is well to remember that the meeting at London is to be not only an international conference but a conference of nations. This suggests a great value to be captured which has been almost entirely overlooked by commentators on the subject.

Enlightened leaders of many nations come and live together for many weeks. These men are likely to be those who have had much to do with domestic policy as well. They find that a large part of recovery has to do with the domestic policy of each individual country. They compare notes, match experience and gather for the sake of their own country's policy, the best of a varied assortment of the experiences of other countries.

I remarked this to Professor Rist, who shared with Herriot the leadership of the French delegation here, and tried to prevail upon him to extend his stay a few days to give the leaders of the Congress and the Administration the benefit of his advice on our domestic program, particularly as it is related to public works and reemployment. In these domestic problems he has made a distinct contribution to French recovery.

This illustrates what we can learn from practical methods abroad. We do not need their political theories, but we do need their technical advice. Much can be gained for us and for all other nations by such an exchange of ideas at London this summer.

If we can picture the conference in advance not as a scene for the performance of miracles, not as a glorified market place, but as a means for the friendly exchange of ideas, for the development of a common understanding of universal difficulties and for the final solution of many, although not all, of international problems of exchange and trade, we should look forward to it with genuine and justified optimism.

APPENDIX E

TEXT OF RADIO BROADCAST BY RAYMOND MOLEY ON PROSPECTS OF WORLD ECONOMIC AND MONETARY CONFERENCE MAY 20, 1933

The World Economic and Monetary Conference which begins next month in London, is the result of the historic conference at Lausanne a year ago. Toward the close of that Conference in July of last year, a resolution was adopted suggesting that the general program of the London Conference should be divided into two parts—financial and economic. Among the financial questions were monetary and credit policy; exchange polices; the level of prices; and the movement of capital. Among economic questions, the Lausanne resolution suggested the general subject of improved conditions of produce and trade interchange, with particular attention to tariff policy; prohibition and restrictions of imports and exports; quotas and other barriers to trade; and producers' agreements.

In preparing for the Conference, the nations created what was known as an Agenda Committee, charged with the duty of exploring the field in a preliminary way and of setting up a program for the consideration of the Conference. The work of this Committee can not in any restricted sense bind the Conference itself and insofar as the Agenda Committee expressed opinions, these can not be binding on the Conference. It did, however, set up a fairly satisfactory list of topics to guide the Conference and make some helpful suggestions with regard to the consideration of each.

It may be interesting in view of the importance of the Agenda in planning the course of action for the Conference, to describe its essential outlines. It begins with a discussion of the conditions under which a successful restoration of a free gold standard may be considered. No positive and dogmatic conditions are laid down with regard to this. This following statement indicates the care with which the Agenda Committee handled this subject: "The time when it will be possible for a particular country to return to the gold standard and the exchange parity at which such a return can safely be made will necessarily depend upon the conditions in that country as well as those abroad and these questions can only be determined by the proper authorities in each country separately."

It should be noted that this was said by a Committee meeting some months before the United States left the gold standard. It was no doubt an expression which met with the full approval of the representatives of countries that were then off the gold standard, and presumably, represented the particular conditions to be faced by a country in such a status. No doubt the consideration and thorough exploration of this question will be one of the most useful discussions of the Conference.

The Agenda, moreover, suggests the importance of a joint consideration of currency policy to be followed prior to such a general restoration. It invites an examination of various practical questions related to the functioning of the gold standard, such as the relation between political authority and central banks, a question now under discussion here in the United States. The problem of monetary reserves is also involved. The Agenda suggests the lowering of cover ratios and other methods of economizing gold, and, finally, in this connection, the cooperation of central banks and credit policy.

One of the very important questions to be considered will be the status of silver in world economic policy. Not only the United States, but many other nations have a deep concern in this question, which will probably be centered around various methods of raising the price of silver. In preliminary discussions, foreign governments have expressed themselves as sympathetic to this general point of view. As is pointed out by sound advocates of silver, it is not a question of remonetizing silver so much as the enhancement in the price of silver in order that Oriental and South American countries may again be able to purchase American goods.

A major section of the Agenda deals with the level of prices. It points out that the tremendous fall in the price level makes the position of debtors exceedingly disquieting and unpleasant. This general situation produces a world-wide distress. Moreover, decline in prices has not proceeded at the same pace for all classes of commodities. This has caused very serious confusion in international adjustments. Here again, the majority of the representatives of the various nations participating in the conferences in Washington in the past month have favored constructive action to increase the price level.

A further section of the Agenda is entitled, "The Resumption of the Movement of Capital." This covers not only the question of existing indebtedness, but suggests the possibility of new and safer methods of international lending. Probably the most perplexing and difficult part of the Conference will have to do with the restrictions on international trade. The report of the Agenda Committee very strongly points out the innumerable methods now used by nations to establish trade advantages, including not only tariffs, but exchange restrictions, clearing agreements, measures relating to the obligation to affix marks of origin on imported goods, quotas, prohibitions and many others. It points out the various methods of dealing with these restrictions, the difficulties and advantages in the case of each. Practical measures with respect to this subject will no doubt be presented for consideration.

The Agenda suggests economic agreements with respect to specific articles like wheat, and, also, various metals. Finally, the Agenda suggests some consideration of shipping and of ship subsidies.

The American delegates on the Agenda Committee were especially enjoined not to permit the introduction of the subject of the debts owed to the United States by foreign governments into the list of topics to be discussed at the Conference. This wise prohibition represented not only the point of view of the Hoover Administration, but of the present one as well. It was the firm conviction of President Roosevelt, expressed even before his inauguration, that the subject of these debts should not be considered in connection with general economic matters of mutual interest, although they might be discussed concurrently. His contention has been that the various matters involved in the Conference, can, most of them, be adjusted to the mutual advantage and satisfaction of the various parties concerned and, except in unusual cases, the settlement of one need not be based upon the settlement of another. It is, for example, exceedingly difficult to measure the relative values of a trade concession, let us say, against an agreement to stabilize currency. Any general process of trading results in an international market place rather than in an economic conference looking to the general rehabilitation of the world on a sounder and more enlightened basis.

Somewhat in the spirit of this position is the contention of the present Administration that the debts are not a matter to be traded against other matters, but are essentially questions to be determined in consultation with the countries concerned. The further point is that the debtor countries can not be recognized collectively in the consideration of the debts and that each one separately and distinctly should be heard at any time that it wishes to present suggestions or requests.

It was clear very early in this present year that much of the success of the Conference would depend upon the extent to which the participating governments understood each others' problems and points of view, before the Conference should assemble. Therefore, President Roosevelt invited to Washington individually representatives of various countries to discuss the considerations involved in the Economic Conference. This invitation resulted in individual discussions between representatives of the United States and a score of nations. Some of the nations, notably England, France, Italy, Germany and China, sent special representatives, accompanied by expert delegations. Others delegated their accredited representatives in this country to carry on these conversations. In these conferences there were reviewed the various topics in the Agenda of the Conference, and the points of view of the various governments were mutually and sympathetically reviewed. These preliminary conversations were not intended to be definitive. Agreements were not sought, but rather mutual understanding was sought.

One thought has come to the foreground of my own mind as I have met and talked with these various representatives. It is the thought that the people of the world, as well as their own rulers, have so suffered during these years of the depression that there is everywhere a feeling of nervousness, not to say fear, in the face of the problems which are involved in recovery. It is not bitter-end chauvinism nor cold and calculated selfishness that makes the way to universal agreement so difficult. It is fear and uncertainty.

The disposition of all these delegates to lend a willing hand to general recovery was unmistakable. The communiqués of good will and hope issued by President Roosevelt and the various leaders during these conferences were not mere formal expressions of international piety, but bespoke a concerted desire to be helpful. No one who came into intimate contact with these representatives could fail to discern their sincerity.

But they were, nearly all of them, just as we have been, afraid. They had all experienced the heart-breaking burdens attendant upon participation in the governing of nations which were, for many economic reasons, deeply depressed. If the nations have taken measures to protect themselves even to the extent of shutting out contacts with others, it is largely due to this psychology. To become resentful in the face of these matters is to make them still worse.

This deep fear of the nations of the world is the most serious problem which must be met at the World Economic Conference. That it can be partially dissipated by the initial meetings can be confidently expected. But it must be remembered that each delegate in London will have come from a nation over which the icy atmosphere of economic fear has prevailed. The delegates may, as individuals, join in a common spirit of give and take, but their conclusions will always be modified by what their parliamentary bodies will be willing to approve. This means, for one thing, that the thought of what reaction they will meet when they return home will act as a restraint upon what they are able to accomplish at the Conference itself. And it means, in addition, that they will be actuated by a personal pride in achieving as much as they can—in other words, in achieving a diplomatic victory for themselves. This suggests a competitiveness among the delegations which will reflect and intensify the larger competitiveness among the nations they represent.

One of the great problems of the Conference will be to reduce to a minimum this spirit of competitiveness. It can be done in part by mutual understanding and in part by a limitation of the efforts to those suggestions that provide the opportunity for a genuine meeting of minds. In other words, the Conference will best serve the hopes and expectations of the world if it does not attempt the unattainable. That this will be true no one can doubt after a calm review of the views of the practical men sent here by the foreign nations to discuss their problems with us.

There are, however, some problems for which solutions will probably be found. The first of these relates to the immediate monetary policy of the various governments. No doubt the establishment of better relationships between the central bank in each country and the government of that country, together with a closer cooperation between all central banks, would help recovery. This is primarily a matter for the action of the central banks, but it might well be supplemented by an agreement among governments to synchronize policies of internal public expenditures with the aim of increasing internal trade and employment. Of course the details of such policies of public expenditures and other action will necessarily be left to the governments themselves; but there is a great value to be derived from coordinating these policies by international understandings.

At the present time, specifically, the United States is in the act of working out its own internal policy of public expenditure. That is in part the import of the message sent by President Roosevelt to the Congress last Wednesday. Part of the philosophy behind this measure is that the government is seeking to counteract the element of uncertainty in our economic life which makes individuals unwilling to engage in normal business activity. It is necessary to repeat, however, that determination of such policies must in the final analysis be left to each government. But the coming Conference should provide the theatre for a better mutual understanding of the policies of the participating governments.

The second problem with regard to monetary matters relates to exchange. It is generally agreed that out of the Conference there must come progress in the removal of exchange restrictions. These restrictions exist because of top heavy debt structures but action with regard to this is not, however, primarily a government problem. These debts are for the most part private debts. But it is possible for governments to guide their nationals toward the finding of a solution.

Turning from the financial questions to the second class of problems, economic matters, we find questions much more difficult of solution. All of the nations, including our own, have in the past years erected tariffs and other barriers against trade, designed to secure for themselves a favorable balance of payments. The erection of such barriers has often gone hand in hand with various exchange operations. The process by which this has happened is long and intricate and need not be gone into here. But the fact is that in the past ten years each nation has been moving in the direction of setting up a self-contained economic life within its own borders. Thus it will be difficult to make extensive attacks upon trade barriers, however much this may be desired.

This points to a fact which should be made very plain. It should not be expected that the Conference itself is going to be able to lay out a plan for a series of international measures which will bring about the alleviation of economic difficulties all over the world. It is a popular fallacy that the depression has acted like a kind of disease which has swept over one nation after another by the process of contagion. It was argued by a number of distinguished Republicans in the last campaign that our own depression came as a result of a bank failure in Austria. The fact is that there are many depressions in many countries which did not come upon them at the same time and which have not affected them in the same way. It is overwhelmingly clear that a good part of the ills of each country is domestic. The action of an international conference which attempted to bring about cures for these difficulties solely by concerted international measures would necessarily result in failure. In large part the cures for our difficulties lie within ourselves. Each nation must set its own house in order and a meeting of representatives of all of the nations is useful in large part only to coordinate in some measure these national activities. Beyond this there are relatively few remedies which might be called international remedies.

The failure of international conferences arises from two mistakes. The first is that the general public is led to expect altogether too much from such international action. They are led to expect the unattainable. The other mistake is that the mutual enthusiasm of those participating in conferences leads them to attempt more than can reasonably be expected in the way of accomplishment. The clear understanding of these possibilities of danger must be had in approaching this Conference. It is very important that such mistakes be avoided. With clear understanding of the nature of the Conference and its objectives, the people of the United States can place the advantages that they may expect from it in the proper relation to their general view of their own economic recovery. Above all, they must recognize that world trade is, after all, only a small percentage of the entire trade of the United States. This means that our domestic policy is of paramount importance. We must recognize, all of us, that common sense dictates that we build the basis of our prosperity here and direct all of our efforts to the end that our national welfare and prosperity may lead us away from the distress into which the depression plunged us. But wise international cooperation can help distinctly and permanently.

APPENDIX F

1. TEXT OF THE FOURTH "INSTRUCTION" GIVEN THE AMERICAN DELEGATION TO THE WORLD ECONOMIC AND MONETARY CONFERENCE

WHEREAS, confusion now exists in the field of international exchange, and

WHEREAS, it is essential to world recovery that an international monetary standard should be re-established,

NOW THEREFORE, BE IT RESOLVED, that all the nations participating in this Conference agree

(a) That it is in the interests of all concerned that stability in the international monetary field be attained as quickly as practicable;

(b) That gold should be re-established as the international measure of exchange values;

(c) That the use of gold should be confined to its employment as cover for circulation and as a medium of settling international balances of payment. This means that gold, either in coin or bullion, will be withdrawn from circulation;

(d) That in order to improve the workings of a future gold standard a uniform legal minimum gold cover for the currencies of the various countries which shall adopt the gold standard shall be established, and that this legal minimum reserve shall be lower than the average of the present reserve requirements;

(e) That the Central Banks of the various nations be requested to meet at once in order to consider the adoption of such a uniform minimum reserve ratio and that a metal cover ratio of 25% be recommended for their consideration,

AND FURTHER,

WHEREAS, silver constitutes an important medium of both international and domestic exchange for a large proportion of the world's population, and

WHEREAS, the value of this purchasing medium has been impaired by governmental action in the past, and

WHEREAS, it is necessary that the confidence of the East should be restored in its purchasing medium, which can only be done if the price of silver is restored to equilibrium with commodity price levels,

NOW THEREFORE, BE IT RESOLVED that

(a) An agreement be sought between the chief silver producing countries and those countries which are large holders or users of silver to limit arbitrary sales upon the world market;

(b) That all nations agree to prevent further debasement of their subsidiary silver coinages;

(c) That all the nations agree to remonetize their subsidiary coinages up to a fineness of at least 800 when, as and if consistent with their respective national budget problems; and

(d) That it be recommended to the Central Banks that they agree that 80 per cent of their metal cover shall be in gold and 20 per cent shall be optionally in gold or in silver, provided that silver is obtainable at or below a price to be agreed upon as corresponding to the general commodity price level; and that the governments agree to modify their respective laws to this effect.

2. *RESOLUTION SUBMITTED BY SENATOR PITTMAN OF THE U. S. A. DELEGATION—LONDON, JUNE 19, 1933*

WHEREAS, confusion now exists in the field of international exchange, and

WHEREAS, it is essential to world recovery that an international monetary standard should be re-established,

NOW THEREFORE, BE IT RESOLVED that all the nations participating in this Conference agree

(a) That it is in the interests of all concerned that stability in the international monetary field be attained as quickly as practicable;

(b) That gold should be re-established as the international measure of exchange values;

(c) That the use of gold should be confined to its employment as cover for circulation and as a medium of settling international balances of payment. This means that gold, either in coin or bullion, will be withdrawn from circulation;

(d) That in order to improve the workings of a future gold standard a uniform legal minimum gold cover for the currencies of the various countries which shall adopt the gold standard shall be established, and that this legal minimum reserve shall be lower than the average of the present reserve requirements;

(e) That the Central Banks of the various nations be requested to meet at once in order to consider the adoption of such a uniform minimum reserve ratio and that a metal cover of 25% be recommended for their consideration,

AND FURTHER,

WHEREAS, silver constitutes an important medium of both international and domestic exchange for a large proportion of the world's population, and

Whereas, the value of this purchasing medium has been impaired by governmental action in the past, and

Whereas, it is necessary that the confidence of the East should be restored in its purchasing medium, which can only be done if the price of silver is restored to equilibrium with commodity price levels,

Now therefore, be it resolved that

(a) An agreement be sought between the chief silver producing countries and those countries which are large holders or users of silver to limit arbitrary sales upon the world market;

(b) That all nations agree to prevent further debasement of their subsidiary silver coinages;

(c) That all the nations agree to remonetize their subsidiary coinages up to a fineness of at least 800 when, as and if consistent with their respective national budget problems; and

(d) That it be recommended to the Central Banks that they agree that 80% of their metal cover shall be in gold and 20% shall be optionally in gold or in silver, provided that silver is obtainable at or below a price to be agreed upon as corresponding to the general commodity price level; and that the governments agree to modify their respective laws to this effect.

3. PARAPHRASE OF THE "DECLARATION" PROPOSED BY THE FRENCH AND BRITISH ON JUNE 29, 1933

It is agreed that stability in the international monetary field be achieved as quickly as practicable, and the common interest of all concerned is recognized.

It is agreed that reestablishment of gold as a measure of international exchange value should be accomplished but the time at which each of the countries off gold could undertake stabilization and the parity at which each of the countries off gold could undertake stabilization must be determined by the respective governments.

It is reasserted by governments, the currencies of which are on the gold standard, that it is their intent to maintain the free working of that standard at current gold parities and in conformity to their respective monetary laws. They believe that maintenance of the gold standard by their respective countries is in the interest of world recovery.

Governments subscribing to this declaration whose currencies are not on the gold standard take note of the above declaration and recognize its importance without in any way prejudicing their own future ratios to gold, and reiterate that the ultimate objective of their currency policy is to bring back an international standard based on gold under proper conditions.

Each government whose currency is not on the gold standard agrees to adopt such measures as it may deem most appropriate to limit exchange speculations, and other signatory governments undertake co-operation to the same end.

Each of the governments signatory hereto agrees to ask its central bank to work together with the central banks of other governments which sign this declaration in limiting exchange speculation and, at the proper time, re-establishing an international gold standard.

Signatures for gold countries Signatures for countries off gold

APPENDIX G

TEXT OF STATEMENT PREPARED FOR PRESIDENT ROOSEVELT BY HERBERT SWOPE, WALTER LIPPMANN, JOHN MAYNARD KEYNES AND RAYMOND MOLEY, NIGHT OF JULY 4, 1933

In my communication to you of July 2, I endeavored to make clear that I saw no utility at the present time in temporary stabilization between the currencies of countries whose needs and policies are not necessarily the same. Such stabilization would be artificial and unreal and might hamper individual countries in realizing policies essential to their domestic problems. I urged the Conference to move to consideration of its fundamental task of facilitating policies by the different nations directed, not to temporary expedients, but to mitigating and, if possible, remedying the harassing evils of the present economic situation. In the hope that I may be of some help to the Conference, to whose success and friendly cooperation I continue to attach the greatest importance, it may be useful that I should develop this thought somewhat more fully.

In saying that the value of the dollar has not fallen so far as I should like to see it fall, I naturally intended its value in terms of American commodities, which alone matters to us in remedying our maladjustments. The revaluation of the dollar in terms of American commodities is an end from which the Government and the people of the United States cannot be diverted. I wish to make this perfectly clear: we are interested in American commodity prices. What is to be the value of the dollar in terms of foreign currencies is not and cannot be our immediate or our ultimate concern. The exchange value of the dollar will depend upon the success of other nations in raising the prices of their own commodities in terms of their national monies, and cannot be determined in advance of our knowledge of such facts.

I seek no competitive exchange depreciation going beyond actual and anticipated price movements. I have no intention of encouraging American domestic price levels to rise beyond the point required by the American debt structure and American costs. And I have every intention and ample resources to prevent an inordinate and uneconomic rise of prices. There is nothing in my policy inimical to the interests of any other country, but I cannot allow the American government to be embarrassed in the attainment of economic ends absolutely required for the economic health of our country.

If other countries represented at the Conference desire a rise of prices in the same or in a different degree according to the special circumstances of each, I suggest that it is the task of the Conference to consider ways and means of putting into circulation the additional purchasing power by which alone their object can be attained. I see no necessity for uniformity. But no progress can be made until the different needs of the different countries have been elucidated and determined. If there are countries where prices and costs are already in equilibrium, I do not regard it as the task of the Conference, as it certainly is not the purpose of the American government, to persuade or compel them to pursue policies contrary to their own conception of their own interests.

But if it should emerge from the discussion that there is a group of countries whose requirements are broadly the same as those of the United States and if those countries were to make it clear that they were prepared to take appropriate measures for an effective movement in this direction, I should welcome informal arrangements between the Central banks of these countries and the Federal Reserve System of the United States for the avoidance of meaningless and harmful exchange fluctuation which did not correspond to price policies, though such arrangements should be, in my judgment, of a day-to-day character and without embarrassing commitments of either side.

There is also to be considered the policies appropriate to the period after the existent maladjustments in the price structure have been remedied. It is not sufficient to escape from the present evils. It is our duty to consider together how to avoid their recurrence in future. The first task is to restore prices to a level at which industry and above all agriculture can function profitably and efficiently. The second task is to preserve the stability of this adjustment once achieved. The part which gold and silver should play as reserve monies after price adjustment has been secured would seem a further subject suitable for consideration by the Conference. I would link with this the problems of exchanges and of commercial and tariff policies, with a view to the avoidance of unbalanced debtor and creditor positions between nations which have been so fruitful a cause of the present evils. It would be chimerical to hope that much progress can be made in diminishing the excessive hindrances to profitable international exchange during the period before prices have been adjusted, when each country is endeavoring by any means at its disposal to protect what seems a perilous domestic situation. But it is not too soon to consider the general lines of a code which should attain the mutual advantages of legitimate international trading, when the special causes which have led to widespread action of an injudicious and mutually injurious character have passed away.

I conceive, therefore, that the great problems which justified the assembling of the nations are as present today and as deserving of exploration as was the case a few weeks ago; and I find it difficult to conceive that the view which it has been my obvious duty to take on the minor issue of temporary stabilization which was not before the Conference and has not figured on its agenda can in any way diminish the advisability of such discussions.

APPENDIX H

RAYMOND MOLEY'S LETTER OF RESIGNATION AS ASSISTANT SECRETARY OF STATE, AND THE PRESIDENT'S REPLY, BOTH DATED AUGUST 27, 1933

Dear Mr. President:

For months I have given long and considered thought to the two happy and pleasant alternatives of either remaining in an official capacity in your administration or of discontinuing my official status to resume my professional interests in writing and teaching. The development of the idea of a national weekly which has now been consummated by Mr. Astor and his associates has provided for me the answer. I have decided that in joining in this new venture I can not only serve you best, but also my own inclinations and interests.

The regret that I should otherwise experience at severing my official tie with your administration is absent on account of the fact that this new work permits me not only to further the ideals common to us both, but to continue to enjoy the friendly association with you that has marked the many months, both before and since your inauguration.

As you well know, my participation in national politics these past two years has arisen from two motives, the one, my friendship for you together with the deep conviction with which I have shared your political views, and the other, my personal dedication as a life work to the writing and teaching of politics and government. This new venture enables me to fulfill both of these purposes in a way that no official or business office would permit.

My service as an official in the Government was professedly temporary. It has continued through the preliminaries of your administration and now reaches a convenient time for its termination. I therefore offer you my resignation as Assistant Secretary of State to take effect, if convenient to you, September 7. As I do so I pledge you my active and continued support of the ideals to which you have given such a hopeful and auspicious realization. I have with many thousands of others found renewed belief in turning the power of government to the alleviation of human burdens and of ordering for the better the economic life of the Nation. We have believed and you have justified us in our belief.

I regard this present opportunity to edit a national weekly as opening the door to a most important means of furthering these ideals.

Friendship for you as a great warrior and chief and a deep sharing of political ideals are precious. These remain and give me encouragement and hope as I undertake this new task.

Faithfully yours,
RAYMOND MOLEY

Dear Raymond:

It is with a sense of deep personal regret that I accept your resignation as Assistant Secretary of State.

I need not tell you that I appreciate and shall always remember your participation during these two years in the development of policies based on our common ideals. You have rendered a very definite service to your country: and your departure from an official position to undertake an editorship will give you opportunity to carry on the task in an equally wide field.

The ending of our official relations will in no way terminate our close personal association. I shall count on seeing you often and in the meantime I send you every good wish and my affectionate regards.

Faithfully yours,
FRANKLIN D. ROOSEVELT

APPENDIX I

STATEMENT OF RAYMOND MOLEY BEFORE THE SENATE COMMITTEE OF THE JUDICIARY, MARCH 23, 1937

Mr. Chairman, Members of the Judiciary Committee:

In presenting the reasons for my opposition to the proposal of the President to provide for new appointments to the Supreme Court, I should like to pass over the original arguments advanced for this plan—the idea that the Court is inefficient, the notion that age is related to efficiency and even the contention that age and conservatism inevitably go hand in hand. These preliminary, and, it seems to me, somewhat irrelevant arguments, have now been brushed aside by the logic of facts, and, happily, the sponsors of the plan themselves seem to have abandoned them.

Debate is now on quite a different basis. It is frankly admitted that the real purpose of the plan is to secure within the letter, though, I submit, not within the spirit of the Constitution, a Court that will lift the cloud of doubt from a number of New Deal measures now in process of preliminary adjudication and to provide in advance for favorable action by the Supreme Court upon a number of measures not yet formulated. The main premise of this argument is that the Court may be expected to strike down these now inchoate legislative proposals when they finally come before it, on the basis of the same economic and political theories on which the majority has acted in the immediate past. It is to this argument, it seems to me, that those of us who oppose this measure may well address our attention.

In stating their case, the proponents of the President's plan have embraced a series of economic and political ideals with which all but the most hardened reactionary must agree. They have then proceeded to the conclusion that their way is the only way to the achievement of those ideals. In so doing, they denounce all other means of reform and condemn those who quarrel with their means as being opposed to their ends.

I, for one, deny the validity of this assumption. I deny further that failure to agree with this specific plan necessarily implies a disposition to defend those judgments of the Supreme Court which, we all agree, have been the proximate cause of the whole issue. I believe that curative measures have flowed in abundance from Mr. Roosevelt's leadership; that more national laws are needed to supplement them; that three successive elections have shown that Americans believe in the soundness of his objectives; that our Constitution was not intended to impose rigid limitations upon progressive legislation in the public interest; that the Supreme Court should use every effort to make the Constitution a living charter; that the present Court as a whole has held too narrow a view of Congressional power; that its interpretation of the Constitution has often been determined by its own economic predilections; and that "we must find a way to take an appeal from the Supreme Court to the Constitution itself."

It is not necessary to take up the time which this Committee has so courteously allotted to me by a lengthy recital of what I have had to say publicly with reference to the various decisions of the Court during the past two years. And so I ask leave to file with the Committee copies of my published statements referring to the Court during that period. My reason for this will be apparent in a moment. In submitting them, however, I should like, by brief reference to some of them, to emphasize the fact that no one has been more outspoken than I have been in criticizing the Court for its arbitrary refusal to find a way to modify the law and to preserve its continuity and unity so far as possible in a period of striking, almost unparalleled social and economic change.

Neither the Attorney General, nor his Assistant, Mr. Robert Jackson, nor the learned law deans who have spoken to you advocating the President's proposal have protested publicly with more force and regularity than I have against the abuse and misuse of judicial power by some members of the Court. I wish to refer briefly to the record on this point.

Three weeks before the decision in the Schechter case, in commenting on the five-to-four decision declaring the Railroad Retirement Act unconstitutional, I said: "Judicial supremacy which curbs arbitrary action may be the bulwark of liberty. But judicial supremacy which arrogates to itself arbitrary power and usurps the right to determine legislative policy is tyranny."

Early the following year, in commenting on the decision in the Hoosac Mills case, I said: "Whether the AAA decision is an abuse of judicial power is a question which transcends every other one of the multitude of lesser practical questions which the decision precipitates . . . Gripped by the determination to constitute themselves the exclusive instrument 'for the preservation of our institutions,' and recklessly singling out as paramount among those institutions the ways of an economic society sanctioned by the economics of a century ago, a majority of the Court is prepared at all costs to mold the Constitution to its end."

Neither the Attorney General nor the learned law deans who support the President's proposal have been more outspoken in their warnings to the Court that if it persisted in this course, it would inevitably provoke reckless and arbitrary change.

As early as May 18, 1935, I said: "No democratic community such as ours can be expected to consent to the interposition, by the judiciary, of its own arbitrary judgments as to the ultimates of legislation in place of the judgments of the community's democratically elected representatives."

On December 14, 1935, I said: "If the majority of the Court should yield to the temptation of anticipating questions of constitutional law when the Court does not need to decide them, it would be borrowing trouble for itself and for the country. For if it so yields, the Court will bring to a head, prematurely, gigantic political issues which could be adjusted more painlessly outside of the Court."

A year and a half later, following the Minimum Wage decision, I said: "In human life extremes beget their opposites. During the past year there has been reason to fear that some exponents of the New Deal might provoke swift and bitter reaction by pushing reform too far. The Minimum Wage decision puts this fear in reverse. It encourages blind, intemperate change because it seems to interdict even the mildest reform."

The proposal which you are now considering seems to me to be a fulfillment of the direst of these prophecies.

Why, then, feeling as I did and still do, with reference to Mr. Roosevelt's humane objectives and the obstructionism of the Court, do I oppose his plan to "reinvigorate" the Court?

I view this proposal not so much with alarm as with a deep regret that, after a period of many years during which progressive ideas have been taking shape and have been moving toward the achievement of somewhat fundamental changes in our economic system, a proposal has been injected into the situation which is not only wholly inadequate to meet the present situation, but is so destructive of the institutional consistency of this republic that it may obstruct progressive development in the future as well.

A good many of us can remember the many years of battle during which great men labored heroically for the achievement of a more just and a more stable civilization in this country. I know from my own experience how the selfless efforts of these men inspired the youth of this country. They were brave men. They fought for progressive principles when the odds against them seemed insuperable. In cities, in states and in the nation they gave the best they had. Altgeld, Bryan, Henry George, La Follette, Tom Johnson, Pingree, Theodore Roosevelt, Woodrow Wilson, and, in a later day, some of those who are still happily with us—William Borah, Hiram Johnson, George Norris and Louis Brandeis—each in his way fought for the liberalization of our economic life.

Progressivism did not begin in 1932. But progressivism found in the immense majority of the past three elections an indication that a generation of education had finally resulted in a popular mandate to bring to realization the aspirations of more than twenty-five years. That mandate imposed a grave responsibility upon those who direct our government. And certainly implicit in that mandate was the assumption that reform should be achieved through the methods with which the predecessors of the New Deal had labored and fought.

The danger in taking a short-cut now, when the consummation of this progressive evolution is at hand, is that its entire consistency will be distorted or destroyed. And yet without reference to the institutional traditions under which it was possible for liberalism to make the immense progress it has made during the past generation, and without the common counsel of members of this Congress who have given so much of their lives to the progressive movement, a proposal has been made which imposes upon one man—the present Chief Executive—the almost sole responsibility of determining the final objectives of liberalism, and which divides not only a party, but a movement. It seizes the great enthusiasm and unity of a popular mandate and squanders it for the mirage of a solution, not a solution.

I am opposed to this plan because I do not believe it will achieve the job that is immediately before us. I am opposed to it because I believe that even if it did temporarily remove an obstacle to the evolution of progressive reform, it would, in the end, impair those institutional methods and traditions which make progressive evolution possible. I am opposed to this plan because I believe that there is a better way to achieve the immediate and the ultimate objective.

It seems to me that this proposal will not do the job for a number of reasons.

First, it is based upon emergency—or if you will, crisis-psychology. It is submitted as a make-shift, unsatisfactory panacea accompanied by apologies that a better solution is not possible. It is justified mainly on the basis of its alleged ease of attainment. But must we always have legislation for reform based upon the existence of a crisis? Must we always have emergency measures? Shall we never achieve that happy moment when sound and liberal counsel can consider not the immediate future but the longer future? It seems to me that a moment such as this, when economic life has risen to something like a normal level—and here I am merely repeating the statement of fact presented by the Administration in the past campaign—that this is the time for careful, reasoned planning. In a word, the time has come for the best of remedies and not the second best.

Second, this proposal does not offer a permanent solution. It does not prevent the recurrence of exactly the same evil it is designed to remedy. I believe in the purposes of this New Deal. But I am not for this New Deal alone. I am for future New Deals as well, unhampered by the dead hand of the past, even if that past be our resplendent present. I am not just against the dead hand represented by the majority of this Court. I am against all dead hands through which the past seeks to control the future. Our New Deal will be an Old Deal sometime. All of us who believe in the reforms of the past four years and who had some part in bringing about those reforms, will become old. Even the six justices that the President now wants to appoint will become old, and, as the President says, will wear glasses fitted to the needs of another generation. I do not want Presidents then to feel free to remake that Court again and again and again—as Presidents will, if we set this bad example. Nor do I want to fasten our present reforms upon future generations. I want a sound method followed which will be workable in the future, so that reforms that our children and our children's children want can be attained through flexible, orderly means. I do not want this generation to teach future generations to sacrifice means to ends.

Third, I believe that this proposal is inadequate because it will still leave the Congress without the specific powers it needs to regulate industry and agriculture in the public interest. In this connection I think it is important to note that wide gaps exist between the economic philosophies of many of those who have come before this body in advocacy of the Court proposal. Though it might seem that they do not differ as to the nature of the economic reform that this country needs, it is a well-known fact that some of them believe business should be kept little through vigorous opposition to the growing tendency toward centralization, and others maintain with equal conviction that business must inevitably grow large and that governmental efforts toward control must themselves become large, more centralized and more Federal. The first group do not want the NRA in any event. The second group are favorable to the purpose behind it.

We really cannot know exactly what kind of economic reform is in store for us until, after the Court has been revamped, economic proposals are brought down from the generality in which the exponents of this plan have left them to the hard ground of Congressional debate and action.

It seems to me that sound statesmanship would dictate that the kind of reform that the new Court is expected enthusiastically to approve should be determined in advance. Perhaps we may assume that these reforms will tend toward a greater Federal control of economic life and toward a lessened responsibility on the part of the states. That is only an assumption. But if it should prove to be true, then, I believe, even a "reinvigorated" Court would not validate these reforms under the Constitution as it now stands. And if it should prove to be untrue, then, at long last, a number of supporters of the Court plan will realize what they do not realize now: that in accepting generalizations as to a "modern outlook" or "socially-minded judges," they will have bought a pig in a poke.

Finally, I have grave doubts as to whether the present proposal will completely fulfill the requirement of haste which seems to be one of the major arguments of its proponents. This proposal cannot conceivably be approved for some months. There must then be reckoned the time required for the selection of the judges and the approval of the Senate. Perhaps I am carrying coals to Newcastle when I remind a Senate Committee that this is not always expeditiously performed. That will take us, it seems to me, to the end of this session of the 75th Congress. The second session of this Congress will undoubtedly devote itself to a consideration of those economic measures that the new Court is expected to approve and, in view of the wide difference of opinion that I have already mentioned as to the general nature of economic reform, it may be assumed that a considerable part of that session will be so required. Then there will come the process of litigation. It therefore seems to me that it is a fair inference that the present so-called crisis cannot possibly be met and definitively liquidated until the beginning of 1939. This does not suggest, in the matter of speed, a great advantage over an alternative method by which the Administration might put its great prestige and power behind an amendment or several amendments. But to the question of amendment I shall return presently. I am simply suggesting that it is strange to present in the name of a crisis a proposal which cannot finally achieve fruition short of a year or two.

Leaving, now, the question of whether this proposal can actually do the immediate job its proponents say it can, let us look at another even more important aspect of the situation.

Assume for the moment, that the proposal will relieve a temporary situation—that the cloud can be raised from legislation whose constitutionality is now in doubt, and that future legislation according to the specifications of the President and Congress can be assured of favorable consideration at the hands of the Court. What will be the cost of this temporary relief? I think it is within the realm of reason to assume that we may buy such temporary relief at too high a price.

"Our difficulty with the Court today," said the President, "rises not from the Court as an institution but from the human beings within it." Let us suppose that it is entirely accurate to say that our trouble rises from the human beings within the Court. How would the President remedy the defect? By the selection of other human beings to sit on the Court reading their personal economic predilections into the law. And, presumably, when their predilections become "outmoded," newer men will be found to read newer new definitions of liberty into the law—certainly a strange way to achieve "a government of law, not men," to quote the President again. It seems to me that a great British Prime Minister once stated in a sentence the objection to all proposals based on such a fallacy as this, when he said: "Individualities may form communities, but it is institutions alone that can create a nation."

We who "honestly believe" in the purposes of the President but oppose his reorganization of the Court, cannot help but see in his course the perpetuation of a basic wrong. Does the President mean that we shall have no more amendments to the Constitution? Does he mean that in the future there will be change to meet the changing times only through interpretation? Does he mean that the Constitution must always be what the judges say it is? Is our constitutional destiny, from generation to generation, to be vested in a long succession of reinvigorated Courts? These are the clear inferences to be drawn from his statement that "Even if an amendment were passed . . . its meaning would depend upon the kind of justices who would be sitting on the Supreme Court bench." And if we accept these inferences, then we are indeed abandoning the idea of "a government of law, not men," of a written Constitution outlawing personal government, protecting minority rights and defining the limits of governmental power.

But I should like to pursue this point further. If I read correctly the testimony presented here by two of the learned exponents of this plan, Assistant Attorney General Jackson and Professor Corwin, it means that they are grieved by the cloud which now rests upon much of the New Deal legislation. This is a strange position indeed. Stated concretely, it means that they are grieved by the fact that citizens are exercising their constitutional right to bring litigation before the Courts with reference to enactments of Congress. I am simple enough to believe that all legislation under such a system as we have is properly subject to adjudication by the Courts. Are we to designate that as a "cloud"? I can well realize that the task of the legal officers of the government would be greatly lightened if they could be assured of the sunshine of certainty. But the task of clothing the law in certainty is, as lawyers know, a long and difficult one. Even in those branches of the common law over which Dean William Draper Lewis has labored so intelligently through the American Law Institute, we have only some measure of clarity—not certainty. Even in a civilization dominated by the American Law Institute there would still be room for courts. To say that the existence of litigation enshrouds the law in a cloud is to raise serious questions about our whole tradition of jurisprudence. A lusty blow by Babe Ruth which drives the ball over the fence must, in fairness, rest under a temporary cloud until the umpire has decided whether it is within the foul line. It seems to me that any plan which raises serious questions about this fundamental of jurisprudence is deserving of careful scrutiny lest its very implications dissipate the fundamental rights of the citizen to a fair hearing by impartial judges.

Up to this time I have said very little about the fundamental and basic principle underlying our entire governmental system—the division of power between the Executive, Legislative and Judicial branches of government. It is true that circumstance and the frailties of men have at times in the course of our history thrown out of nice balance the actual authority of these three branches. There have been periods, such as that immediately following the War between the States, when Congress seemed to be supreme. There were other times, in the midst of great crises, when Presidential authority rose to dizzy heights. But a deliberate attempt by one branch of the government to weaken another branch has very few parallels in our history. And none of them is creditable.

It seems to me that a weakening of the authority and prestige of the Court must inevitably follow the kind of reorganization which the present proposal contemplates. We have been frankly told by the proponents of the plan that men will be appointed because their appointment will lift the cloud of doubt from certain policies, defined and undefined. The peculiar nature of such appointments must expose the Court to a not too certain estimate of independence. A great judicial tradition is not preserved that way.

That way has always been open to the purposes of any dominant Executive and Congressional majority. But the very fact that it has not been employed, except in one or two cases of which we are not very proud, has established an inhibition upon the use of this method—an inhibition based upon custom and tradition. In other words, a custom has been established that fundamental changes should not be so attained—a custom of the Constitution, or a doctrine of political stare decisis, if you will, which is as binding upon public officials as a written provision of the Constitution itself. It is this custom of the Constitution which prevents Presidential electors from exercising independent judgment after election. It is this custom of the Constitution which wisely limits the Presidency to two terms. It is the custom of the British Constitution that the King shall give effect to the will of Parliament. All of these constitutional customs are insuperable obstacles in the way of hasty institutional change. They rest upon acceptance, and their violation is as indefensible as the violation of the express provisions of the instrument itself. The maintenance of the custom of the Constitution is essential to the preservation of a stable government under which people are able to plan their lives and direct their actions. It is true that the custom of the Constitution changes, but it changes slowly and its existence is an indispensable element in a democratic government.

What, after all, is the distinguishing feature of a democratic government? It is not the objectives of such a government alone. Justice for all in economic life, a fair division of the good things of life, education, health, better housing and security—these were objectives in the German Empire of Bismarck. They are objectives in nearly all of the Western World today. But it is the glory of the democracies of the world that the means to these ends involve that spiritual education of citizens gained only when the citizens participate in the attainment of these ends. It is the glory of democracies that they educate the citizen in the practice of self-government while they protect his political, religious and economic freedom.

Democracy continues to exist only insofar as objectives are attained in terms of its own institutions. We cannot hold democracy as a basic ideal and ignore the method of democracy in the attainment of that ideal. There may be coercion of a minority by a majority in a democracy, but that coercion must always be exercised within the terms of our own institutions, safeguarded, as they are, by the Constitution and its custom. The majority does rule; but it rules in terms of a covenant deliberately adopted and scrupulously maintained. Government by the consent of the people means not the unrestrained exercise of the will of the majority: it means that the agents of the people act only in the light of public consent secured through customary means.

And this does not imply that such consent may be secured by inference. As the *Federalist* points out: "Until the people have, by some solemn and authoritative act, annulled or changed the established form, it is binding upon themselves collectively, as well as individually; and no presumption, or even knowledge, of their sentiments, can warrant their representatives in a departure from it." This fundamental stricture of democratic government applies not only to infractions of the Constitution, but to impairment of the established tradition of an independent judiciary.

Now what are the indicated means by which popular consent should be secured? When the objective is outside the limits of the Constitution consent must be secured by the amending method prescribed in the Constitution. When the objective is within the letter of the Constitution but involves, nevertheless, a decision of basic importance, consent should be secured by the submission of the proposal, through a party platform, to the electorate.

That is a basic justification for the existence of political parties. They offer the means for the formulation of issues to be voted upon at elections. In England, in fact, public appeals to the electorate are precipitated whenever organic governmental change is proposed. And as late as 1934, that principle was recognized in this country in connection with the Social Security program. The President, in June, announced the program as an objective; candidates for office in the Democratic Party carried it to the electorate, and, after the election of that year, the measure was presented, debated in the Congress and adopted by it.

That is the only legitimate way for a democratic government to secure consent for basic change which falls within the letter of the Constitution. And that course has not been followed. In spite of ample evidence that basic changes were necessary, the party in power gave the public to believe in 1936 that, unless the objectives named could secure the approval of the Courts, "clarifying amendments" would be proposed.

We all know that needs and purposes change; methods tested and acquiesced in should remain. These methods were at hand when the necessity of which we now hear was evident, in fact when it was declared to be evident.

We will have to answer to our conscience and to future generations if we abandon that American method which, despite minor flaws, has proved to be the truest and best avenue to the achievement of desirable ends. That method, the American method, is to tell the public in an orderly fashion precisely what is necessary in the way of economic and social change, to seek to convince the people of its wisdom, and then to ask approval of the change. The ends which Mr. Roosevelt has so courageously made his own can be achieved within the grand mosaic of the American constitutional tradition. But to seek to achieve them through the destruction of the American tradition is to open the way to the death of the ideals that gave them birth.

And now, if I may, I should like to describe the reasons for my third main objection to the present proposal. I believe that there is a better way to achieve the objectives toward which the President is striving. That way is amendment.

I shall not tire you with a recital of the fact that, beginning more than two years ago, I have consistently pointed to the need for constitutional amendment. I am certain that this Committee is not especially interested in what I may have thought or said. And I have submitted the record of those expressions of a single and not very important citizen in the material which I handed to you earlier, merely to indicate that there were voices, however thin and ineffective, which reminded those in charge of our governmental destinies that amendment was needed. I have submitted them also to avoid the charge that so consistent a critic of the Court as I have been is inconsistent now.

We have been told that we who advocate amendment are misguided, first, because it is impossible to frame one agreeable to the various advocates of amendment; second, because it is virtually impossible to secure the passage of a Constitutional amendment; and third, because even if we got an amendment, the amendment would still mean only what the judges say it meant. I am not disposed to accept these objections without some argument.

In the first place, I know of no real attempt in the past year to bring about agreement among the Congressional leaders who favor amendment. I feel certain, however, that such an agreement is quite within the realm of probability now, being profoundly impressed by Senator Wheeler's assurances on this subject. I feel certain that liberals outside of official life would follow the leadership of Congress and the President in the support of amendment.

I should like to say, in this connection, that those Senators who favor amendment rather than the present proposal cannot be blamed if they differ on the subject of what amendment would be best. The one political force to which they look for unity has suddenly left them to their own devices.

If unity among liberals is desired, let there be an attempt to achieve agreement between the Administration and the liberal Congressional opponents of this plan on an amendment or a series of amendments, instead of an attempt to compel unity by contemptuous statements with reference to the company kept by liberals who oppose this plan. If unity among liberals is desired, let there be an effort to attain it reasonably, instead of an effort to force it.

But let us return, for a moment, to the second argument that is used against amendment at this time—the argument that amendment will take too long. The advocates of the President's plan cite the Child Labor Amendment as the horrible example. I am not impressed by this comparison. This amendment labors under a particular political handicap to which general Constitutional amendments would not be subject. Further there has been no united Party support for the Child Labor Amendment and, while leaders of the Party have expressed themselves favorably with respect to it, the Party itself, I believe, avoided definite commitment on the subject in its platform of 1936. If comparisons must be made, I think it is more appropriate to cite the success of the Party in putting through the amendment repealing prohibition. The energetic efforts of the Administration through its efficient organization afforded relief on this subject in a comparatively short time.

But we are offered direful pictures of the danger of a conspiracy on the part of enemies of progress which might permanently tie up the votes of thirteen states through pelf, plunder and propaganda. There are appropriate Committees in Congress with powers quite adequate to deal with unfair propaganda and the unfair use of funds. There are also the Department of Justice, the Communications Commission and other well established agencies of law enforcement capable of safeguarding the public against improper pressure and propaganda.

And this brings us to the third argument against amendment—the argument that even if amendment were obtained, the justices might twist and distort its meaning to thwart the will of the people. But that I have attempted to answer at several points in the course of these remarks and I do not think it is necessary to elaborate further my belief that it is a fallacious argument whose logical conclusion is that we must have no more change by amendment—but only by judicial interpretation.

I should like, in concluding, to stress once more a point which I have made in the course of this statement. The time is ripe for a basic and fundamental restatement of the law to make possible the attainment of the humane objectives of progressive thought. I deeply regret to see that golden moment pass. We have, as the President pointed out, a rendezvous with destiny. There are generations ahead whose welfare and aspirations and hopes can be realized if we, at this moment, avoid the easy path of expediency and spend our labors and our energy in facilitating the future evolution of our society and our nation on a democratic basis. The institutions of democracy grow and strengthen only through their use. When they are neglected in the interest of quick and easy material gains, atrophy sets in and death ultimately results. Let us make democracy work by working through the instruments of democracy.

INDEX

Set in Linotype Baskerville type
Format by A. W. Rushmore
Manufactured by The Haddon Craftsmen
Published by HARPER & BROTHERS
New York and London